CW00422079

ALSO BY B. F. SKINNER

The Behavior of Organisms: An Experimental Analysis

Walden Two

Science and Human Behavior

Verbal Behavior

Schedules of Reinforcement
(with Charles B. Ferster)

Cumulative Record

The Analysis of Behavior
(with James G. Holland)

The Technology of Teaching

Contingencies of Reinforcement: A Theoretical Analysis

Beyond Freedom and Dignity

About Behaviorism

Reflections on Behaviorism and Society

Enjoy Old Age
(with Margaret E. Vaughan)

A THREE-VOLUME AUTOBIOGRAPHY

Particulars of My Life
The Shaping of a Behaviorist
A Matter of Consequences

A Matter of Consequences

A
Matter
OF
Consequences

Part Three of an Autobiography

B. F. SKINNER

New York University Press
Washington Square, New York
1984

Copyright © 1983 by B. F. Skinner

Library of Congress Cataloging in Publication Data
Skinner, B. F. (Burrhus Frederic).
A matter of consequences.
Includes index.
1. Skinner, B. F. (Burrhus Frederic), 1904–
2. Psychologists—United States—Biography.
I. Title.
BF109.S55A32   1983   150.19'434'0924   [B]   83–47788
ISBN 0–8147–7845–3
ISBN 0–8147–7846–1 set

Manufactured in the United States of America

A Matter of Consequences

T WENTY YEARS AFTER ARRIVING at Harvard as a graduate student, I returned as Professor of Psychology. I had spent five of those years as a postdoctoral fellow at Harvard and the rest on the faculties of the University of Minnesota and Indiana University. In Minnesota I had married Yvonne (Eve) Blue, and in 1938 our daughter Julie was born. Later that year *The Behavior of Organisms* was published. During the war I taught pigeons to guide putative missiles, and in the Guggenheim year that followed I worked on my book on verbal behavior, built the "baby-tender" for our second daughter, Deborah, and wrote *Walden Two*. An invitation to give the William James Lectures brought me back to Harvard, and while there I was asked to join the department. *Walden Two* was published a few months before I returned to Cambridge.

Postwar shortages were still severe, and we were happy to rent a house at 8 Ellsworth Avenue, a few blocks from, but on the wrong side of, the Harvard Yard. I could have built something like it with the German stone blocks I had as a child. Its largest room was an entrance hall finished in dark oak (which the owner would not let us paint white), with a fireplace and plenty of room for the baby-grand piano. (The clavichord had a former sewing room to itself.) A dining room also in dark oak had plate rails on the walls. In the kitchen the sink was soapstone, and the gas water heater was to be turned off after each use on pain of explosion. In the basement a great pile of coal delivered through a window spread across the floor, and three or four times a day I put a few shovelfuls into the furnace. Someone had insulated the hot water pipes with old rags, scraps of which now hung down like stalactites, raining dust when touched. A few pieces of furniture discarded by former tenants had sucked moisture from the earthen floor and were warped into gently grotesque shapes. It could have been the setting for a Gothic novel.

MEMORIAL HALL, WHERE I WOULD HAVE my office and laboratory, was neo-Gothic—a cathedrallike structure of red brick with an unused portico on the west end, a roof of multicolored slates, and a gargoyled, patinaed clock tower visible from a great distance. The nave, originally a dining hall, was now used only for registration, examinations, and an occasional dance. Sanders Theater was in the apse, and the Boston Symphony still played a few concerts there each year for the Harvard community.

The basement had once been full of boilers, but the University had found other ways of heating its buildings, and during the war S. Smith Stevens had converted the east end into his Psychoacoustic Laboratory. The west end went to ROTC and a rifle range, but when the new Department of Social Relations crowded psychology out of Emerson Hall, Smitty Stevens and Edwin B. Newman spent a year of their lives supervising the conversion of the whole basement into useful quarters.

It was almost completely subterranean. I could descend to my laboratory on a sunny morning and emerge at five to find heavy rain or snow. The rooms were small and in some of them great unfinished stones at the tops of the walls made it all too clear that they were unexpandable. I had to plan my laboratory with an eye to the best use of space. At Indiana, instead of using four similar "boxes" as I had once done (let alone the twenty-four that Heron and I had built at Minnesota), I used a single apparatus for each experiment, working with two or more pigeons in tandem, and since I was now planning to study complex contingencies demanding a great deal of programming equipment, I decided to continue with single settings. But I turned to automation. A motor-driven turntable divided into six pie-shaped spaces, with a pigeon in each, exposed one pigeon at a time to an instrument panel for three or four hours, the experiment running around the clock without attention.

The department was much as I had found it the year before as William James Lecturer. Of my own teachers only E. G. Boring and J. G.

Beebe-Center remained, but Smitty Stevens and Eddie Newman, graduate students shortly after my time, and George Miller, much later, had stayed on. Smitty's wartime collection of talented colleagues in psychoacoustics—Walter Rosenblith, Robert Galambos, and J. R. Licklider—were still there, but would shortly move to academic appointments elsewhere. Fred Frick, one of Fred Keller's recent Ph.D.'s, had just joined the department.

We spent a good deal of time together. Garry Boring had been proud of his daily luncheon, which had drawn the department together in troubled times, and it was still in force. Coffee and sandwiches were laid out in a pantry, and we took customary places around a long table in the seminar room, with Eddie Newman as chairman at the head. We talked about almost everything, though seldom about psychology, and on all subjects Békésy, the Hungarian physicist whom Smitty had brought into the department, was the final authority.

Department business was conducted daily until I asked that it be saved for a single day of the week, so that an occasional absence would not be too costly. For there was another side to Garry's strategy. Many Harvard professors lunched at the Faculty Club, a lively place where people from different fields talked with each other and with distinguished visitors. (With the visitors, a conversation piece, if not the *pièce de résistance*, was the horse steak. It had been added to the menu during the war, when red meat was scarce, and there were protests when it was dropped afterwards.) Biology had a table at the Club, where I occasionally joined old friends, and there was a long table where one could find an aging aficionado like Samuel Eliot Morison. Garry's luncheon was cutting psychology off from that part of University life.

Departmental solidarity was furthered in other ways. Smitty had installed an old Coke machine and sales were heavy; profits were put aside for a Christmas party with harder liquor than Cokes. We sang Christmas carols (for which I played a parlor organ acquired years before for research in psychoacoustics, now blown by a vacuum cleaner), and the graduate students usually staged a play—a travesty of the faculty, with characters named Stanley Steamer, E. G. Roaring, E. B. Human, and now B. F. Skinneybox.

Eve and I made a small contribution to the *ésprit de corps* by organizing a group of playreaders, to which two wives of members of

5

the department, Kitty Miller and Louise Licklider, both interested in the theater, made notable contributions. We began with *Arsenic and Old Lace* in the large entrance hall at 8 Ellsworth Avenue, with George Miller in the role of Teddy, the emulator of Theodore Roosevelt, charging up and down the stairs as if they were San Juan Hill. When suitable living rooms proved to be scarce, we began to use the lecture hall in Memorial Hall, and the plays became even more a departmental function.

WHILE WE WERE IN CAMBRIDGE for the James Lectures, Julie had attended Shady Hill School and, well prepared by schools in the Midwest, had had a good term. We now registered both girls. Shady Hill teachers were well disposed, though underpaid, and most of the students came from the Harvard community or from a few affluent families. Eve drove the girls to and from school, a long way from Ellsworth Avenue, and when she brought them home she would occasionally bring a classmate who would stay for dinner to be driven home afterwards. Otherwise they would not have seen their friends out of school. A brief membership in the Skating Club did little to expand Julie's social life.

IN THEIR INTRODUCTORY COURSE at Columbia, Fred Keller and Nat Schoenfeld had found that a behaving organism, if only a white rat, was more instructive than a textbook about behavior, and I had found a pigeon equally useful in teaching a graduate course at Indiana. I chose the same scheme for my first course at Harvard, a small graduate seminar. The department had no pigeon equipment, but I showed my students how to convert cardboard cartons into living cages, as we had done on Project Pigeon, and to make experimental chambers of the same material, in each of which a hungry pigeon could peck a colored spot and the behavior could be reinforced with the aid of a manual food dispenser. The students "shaped behavior through successive approximation," reinforced on intermittent schedules, and brought behavior under the control of discriminative stimuli. One of them, William McGill, produced a rough "generalization gradient" by intermittently reinforcing pecks on a yellow triangle and noting how fast the pigeon then pecked triangles of other colors during extinction. George Heise recorded a gradient for the size of a spot on the key. When pecking a particular size of spot was reinforced, how fast would the pigeon peck other sizes? (My laboratory assistant, Sam McLaughlin, used the same method to test a pigeon's ability to tell the difference between the figures used on license plates. He built up a high rate of pecking the figure 6 and then, during extinction, replaced the 6 for short periods with other figures from o to 9. The pigeons pecked at rates which reflected what would be called, in the human case, "perceived differences between the figures." They agreed with human observers, except that they missed the similarity of 6 and 9, presumably because they had seen the figures only in one position.)

It was a kind of course within reach of the least affluent of departments, and one of my students, Katherine Safford, and I wrote a small manual, of which mimeographed copies were distributed—one as far away as Japan. I alerted Charles (Andy) Anderson, my editor at Macmillan, to a possible book, but Kathy was soon off to teach at Mount Holyoke, and we never finished a publishable manuscript.

ON OUR WAY EAST FROM INDIANA, I had stopped in Yellow Springs, Ohio, to talk about *Walden Two* with Arthur Morgan. He had run the Tennessee Valley Authority for many years and had published a study of Edward Bellamy, whose *Looking Backward* was the great economic utopia of the nineteenth century, and a paper on "The Fellowship Group as the Way to a New Society." He picked cherries from a tree near his house as we talked. "Of course the cherries are not worth the time it takes to pick them," he said. He dismissed my concern about the problems raised by a science of behavior; we would cope with them as the science developed, as the highway system had coped with the developing automobile.

Walden Two was selling fairly well, and throughout the summer a clipping bureau sent reviews. Macmillan ran a few advertisements, and that fall the trade editor in charge of the book, Donald Porter Gettes, took Eve and me to dinner in some of the most expensive restaurants in New York. (Gettes's expense account was, he said, the largest in the company; it was a burden of which the company soon relieved itself.) Eve had acquired a chic black hat, and we dined in style, usually with Mrs. Gettes and Andy Anderson. I had never known that a meal could cost so much. Nothing could have been farther from the dining rooms of Walden Two.

Horace Titus, the son of Helena Rubinstein, wrote that he had "enjoyed the book enormously" and had "so far bought five copies, which I am distributing judiciously." Had I considered making it into a play? Titus had not liked the rather cramped private rooms in Walden Two and suggested a stage setting by Frank Lloyd Wright, based on his Usonian House. Perhaps there should be a communist and a capitalist in the cast; a male capitalist and a female communist or vice versa would supply a love interest.

When an editorial in *Life* magazine contended that "if the community does not at least agree on the proposition that natural, moral law can be determined by a close study of human nature and all its manifestations, then we have no defense against . . . the 'monstrous state,'" I wrote to remind the editors that they had called *Walden Two* "a slander on some old notions of the good life" and "a triumph of mortmain or the dead hand, . . . not envisaged since the days of Sparta." Were they not now making my point—except that I would replace "a close study of human nature" with "a scientific study of the human environment?" No, they replied, that was just their point. "Any changes in man's makeup and social adjustment must come from within, and these changes cannot be forced on him from outside." But I was not talking about force.

Oliver Field, a political scientist I had known at Indiana, wrote that he was making a survey of utopian writings in other cultures. There was apparently only one utopian book in Arabic.

In Chinese culture I found a few pieces only. In Hinduism and Buddhism there seem to be none. Nor in these three cultures do there seem to be any evidences of utopian communities, nor in Arabic nations either. Others, as in France, had both utopian literature and experimental communities. Spain seems to have neither, and Germany seems devoid of serious attempts at either on a sizeable scale, which to me is surprising.

I particularly liked one point:

Cultures having no experimental communities nor utopian literature usually have a literature on the training of the king, or of the calif, or of the prince—trying, as it were, to obtain improvement through lifting the sights of the ruler.

I knew what Frazier, the protagonist of *Walden Two*, would say to that, and how he could use it to answer those critics who called the book totalitarian.

Horace Titus also said he would be glad to help establish a community along the lines of Walden Two. Other would-be members began to write. "I'm not acquainted with the difficulties, obstacles, and complexities of it," wrote a sixteen-year-old girl, "but why in heaven's name can't it start? Honestly, I'd spend my whole life at it and it would be worth it to find out WHY it didn't work if the project failed." Willard Van Orman Quine, possibly not quite so seriously, wrote, "Do get going; I expect, in spite of minor misgivings hereinafter noted, that I'd play Burris to your Frazier at the drop of a hat." The misgivings concerned alcohol and tobacco "until the needs dry up" and "not publishing the products of my leisure, in full onymity [a typical Quinian usage] in the outside world."

In Minnesota I had talked with a group led by James Brown, who later tried to set up a community in Indiana, then in California, and eventually in the Kitseookla region of British Columbia. And when I received a telegram reading: KINDLY REPLY COLLECT WHETHER OR NOT WALDEN TWO WAS WRITTEN SATIRICALLY. MATTER IN CONTROVERSY ON CONTROVERSIAL WASHINGTON CAMPUS. PREFER AUTHOR'S OPINION, I replied: WALDEN TWO BY NO MEANS SATIRICAL. FRAZIER'S VIEWS ESSENTIALLY MY OWN—MORE SO NOW THAN WHEN I WROTE.

When I gave a colloquium on verbal behavior at the Institute for Human Relations at Yale, I spent a night in a cooperative house organized by a graduate student, Arthur Gladstone. Gladstone was looking for a place to start a Walden Two, and I turned to Charles Curtis, the Boston lawyer whom I had known when he was a Senior Fellow. Charlie had many affluent friends and I thought one of them might have a bit of land, possibly near Walden One, which could become the site of a community. Charlie talked with Guy Murchie, who had run a summer camp, now closed, in a suburb of Boston, and the following summer Murchie invited Gladstone and his friends to live in it while planning further steps. They drew up a statement of purpose which I told them "should take its place beside the Preamble to the Constitution of the United States." Like Jefferson—or Frazier in *Walden Two*—they were not escaping from the world; they were trying to make it better.

THE PROVOST HAD AUTHORIZED the expenditure of about $10,000 to support my research during the first year. I could then have $5,000 a year for five years, but beyond that I would have to find funds elsewhere. Fortunately, I soon received support from an unexpected quarter. The December 1946 issue of the *Atlantic Monthly* carried an article called "Bats in the Bomb Bay" by Louis D. Ridenour, a physicist. He reported a wartime project in which thousands of bats were to be released over Tokyo, each carrying a timed incendiary bomb. They would take shelter under the eaves of buildings, and thousands of fires would break out all over the city. The project was abandoned because it could have been mistaken for biological warfare, with retaliation in kind. The editor promised an even more incredible story in the next issue, "in which even the strangest detail is stoutly supported by Dr. Ridenour. We asked him, for instance, if he could really back the statement that the man carrying on the pigeon project fed the birds marihuana to step up their rate of peck. . . ." Obviously the *Atlantic* was planning to publish an account of Project Pigeon, which was still classified. When I sent a wire to the editor asking if he had cleared the story with Washington, he replied that he had not and that, unfortunately, the issue was in press.

According to Ridenour, a man "who will be called Ramsay" believed that "the flight controls of a steerable bomb" could be hooked up with an animal to "give information on the line of sight between bomb and target." Further details were not exactly stoutly supported. Ramsay was said to have prepared his pigeons for many targets—"not just Tokyo pigeons, but Emperor's-palace pigeons and Mitsubishi-factory pigeons, battleship pigeons and destroyer pigeons, and pigeons trained to peck at aircraft carriers." He had induced them to peck rapidly by "doping" them with marijuana, but "often, before half the bomb's time of fall had elapsed, a pigeon full of hashish would quit pecking entirely, lean its head over on its shoulder, and abandon itself to its dreams. To allow for this possibility, Ramsay put in ten pigeons." By the time Ridenour lost contact with the project, "the technical problems seemed to be pretty well in hand." He could not say why the project was abandoned. "Maybe the aggregate of the operational problems loomed so large that the Air Force decided they'd rather wait for the atomic bomb, which you don't have to be very accurate with."

The *Atlantic* had not taken the project seriously, but early in 1948 Paul Fitts, a psychologist at the Aero Medical Laboratory at Wright Field in Dayton, Ohio, suggested making a study of it, and I told him I was sure that General Mills, Inc., which had supported the project, would be glad to cooperate. They had planned to publish a story in their house magazine, but had discovered that the project was still classified. At the annual meeting of the American Psychological Association that fall, Franklin V. Taylor, a psychologist at the Naval Research Laboratories in Washington, told me he wanted to bring the project to the attention of the General Missiles Division of the Navy's Bureau of Aeronautics. Could I give him any help? General Mills had a demonstration film in which a pigeon held a simulated missile on target for several minutes, and I asked them to send it on to Frank. They did so, but only after sending by mistake the film of a classified project involving balloons.

When Frank showed it to people at the Naval Research Laboratories, he reported "everything from interest to high enthusiasm." (I was told later that the new science of cybernetics, which Norbert Wiener had launched only a year or two before, made the idea particularly attractive. Our pigeons could supply "feedback.") The usual questions were asked: how accurate were the pigeons, how consistent was the force of their pecks, how far did they lag behind a target moving back and forth in a sine wave? The answers were evidently satisfactory, and a project was set up under the name ORCON (for "organic, or organismic, control").

I was asked to serve as a consultant, and a young colleague of Frank's, John Hill, came to Cambridge to learn more about pigeons. By November I was writing to Fred Keller that I looked forward to "practically unlimited funds for pure research as well as for the development of some of the applied aspects of the problem." We did, in fact, do some related work (on the pigeon's visual acuity, for example), but it was hard to conceal our reasons and classified projects were taboo at Harvard. (At one point Frank wanted to see a piece of the apparatus used in Project Pigeon which was still stored in Minnesota, and it was sent on to me. It lay around the laboratory for several days until two armed guards in an armored truck came to collect it. We hastily popped it into a carton, taped it securely, and handed it over with due ceremony.)

IN MY LAST YEAR IN INDIANA, I had been elected President of the Midwestern Psychological Association, and the following year I returned to give a Presidential Address. My title, "Are Theories of Learning Necessary?," owed something to James Thurber and E. B. White, whose *Is Sex Necessary?* carried the same wistful reference to a lost cause. There would be sex, with all its problems, and there would be theories of learning.

Psychologists turned to theories because their data were unsatisfactory. The behavior of a rat in a maze, for example, did not change in an orderly way, and only by averaging cases could one get a smooth curve. Hence, one turned to imagining smooth curves—showing supposed changes either in the nervous system or the mind. In an operant analysis the behavior of an individual showed a reasonable order, and theories were unnecessary. The answer to my title was No.

I soon found myself being called "antitheoretical." My listeners, and later my readers, forgot that I was talking only about theories which appealed to "events taking place somewhere else, at some other level of observation, described in different terms, and measured, if at all, in different dimensions," and that near the end of the address I had called for another kind of theory, "a formal representation of the data reduced to a minimum number of terms, yielding a greater generality than any assemblage of facts."

The best current examples of the theorists I was attacking were Clark L. Hull and Edward C. Tolman. Both spoke of "intervening" variables—states of the organism said to explain observed relations between stimuli and responses. Hull's were neurological, Tolman's hypothetical or cognitive. Tolman was in the audience, and after the lecture, as I was talking with a few people, he came up, whispered, "You son of a gun!" and walked away.

*　　*　　*

SMITTY'S LABORATORY WAS still supported by the Office of Naval Research, and I sponged on its facilities for a year or two. Rufus Grason and Steven Stadler in the Electronics Shop solved some of my problems. I had been programming reinforcements at irregular intervals ("aperiodic reinforcement," I was then calling it) with a commercial phonograph disk made of aluminum covered with plastic, on which small bits of plastic were cut away so that, as the disk slowly turned, an arm occasionally made contact with the aluminum and closed a circuit. The Electronics Shop made a much more flexible timer using punched holes in a moving tape.

I had brought some equipment from Indiana—a cumulative recorder resembling one of our improvisations on Project Pigeon, in which a pen on a taut string was pulled across a moving strip of paper by a ratchet, and a food dispenser giving a pigeon access to a revolving dish of grain for a few seconds at a time. I began to use the snap leads that Norman Guttman had learned about during the war. As I wrote to Burt Wolin, a student at Indiana,

> *my new apparatus has surpassed all expectations. Each relay is mounted on a panel which clips into place, and which carries a functional wiring diagram in the shape of studs to which leads can be snapped. I can throw together an apparatus of complexity comparable with my old matching apparatus in an hour or two. . . .*

I had also brought a notebook containing more than thirty plans for experiments. Some were left over from Project Pigeon; others had been conceived during my Guggenheim Fellowship and put aside under pressure of administration at Indiana.

One of my old experiments needed to be repeated. A spot of light moved across a screen and food was dispensed when it reached the edge; a hungry pigeon began to peck the spot as if driving it across the screen. As I wrote in a note, it seemed as if an innate repertoire of "moving things about" went into action when, through a kind of Pavlovian conditioning, the "movement of the spot became important." I built an apparatus in which the size and speed of the dot could be varied, and urged a graduate student, Ruth Page, to take on the project for her thesis. Unfortunately, it did not appeal to her and was never carried out.

I put Kathy Safford on another ethological project. Human vocal behavior was shaped by contingencies of reinforcement maintained by a verbal community, but cries of alarm, mating calls, and other vocal behavior in lower species were presumably due to natural selection. Could they also be conditioned as operants? Cooing was a convenient example, and I asked Kathy to watch a hungry pigeon and dispense a few grains of food whenever it cooed. A rather complex pattern emerged, with wing flapping and cooing, but it could have been an emotional response to the unpredictable delivery of food rather than an increase in frequency due to reinforcement. Certainly, the behavior could not be shaped as easily as turning the head or pecking a spot on the wall.

Douglas Anger, a student of Fred Keller's, had been at the second meeting of the Conference on the Experimental Analysis of Behavior at Indiana and had come on to Harvard for graduate work. He was interested in a more precise analysis of rate of responding and in what that meant for contingencies of reinforcement. He began to measure interresponse times—the intervals between successive responses—and to make reinforcement contingent on chosen values.

Paul Schiller, a young Hungarian psychologist at the Yerkes Laboratory of Primate Biology in Orange Park, Florida, had been watching monkeys and chimpanzees as they solved the kinds of problems discussed by Köhler in *The Mentality of Apes*. Where Köhler's apes seemed to reach solutions suddenly through insight, Schiller found that they acquired the behavior in stages which Köhler had missed. Some of the behavior also appeared to be innate; apes would put two sticks together to form a longer stick whether or not there was a banana to be raked in.

To familiarize himself with operant techniques, Schiller asked if he might spend some time in my laboratory. The Siamese fighting fish, *Betta splendens*, attacks its own image in a mirror, and Schiller wanted to compare that behavior with striking a nonreflecting surface reinforced as an operant. He came to Cambridge and soon had the necessary apparatus in working order. He used live Daphnia as reinforcers, and Ralph Gerbrands built a ring of small cups which tipped and dropped them into the tank one at a time. They fell into a beam of light and, responding phototropically, swam to the side of the tank, where the fish easily picked them off.

The experiment was never finished. In the late spring Schiller went skiing in Tuckerman Ravine, near North Conway, New Hampshire. He skied onto snow that had melted and refrozen, lost control, slid into the ravine, and was killed.

My undergraduate teaching at Minnesota had been generously reinforced. More than five percent of my sophomores had gone on to get Ph.D.'s in psychology. I had kept hands off the entrenched undergraduate courses at Indiana, but I hoped that Harvard would mean some introductory teaching again. Garry Boring still taught Psychology 1, using a text which he and two friends had written, and I could not touch that, but it was agreed that I could give a different course, Psychology 7, to be called "Human Behavior." It was described in the catalogue as "a critical review of theories of human behavior underlying current philosophies of government, education, religion, art, and therapy, and a general survey of relevant scientific knowledge, with emphasis on the practical prediction and control of behavior."

To Harvard and Radcliffe students that looked like a "gut" course, and by early January I was writing in some panic to Fred Keller: "According to preliminary estimates, I will be starting off with at least 200, and perhaps 300, students instead of the small, intimate group I expected. This means a frantic search for nonexistent Section Men and some long thoughts about the future." In the end 438 students signed up, and when the course was underway I reported that it was "a hell of a lot of work and I find myself doing nothing else but."

The students soon discovered that it was not a gut course, and I discovered that I was not making myself clear. There was no text. Halfway through the term I was able to get mimeographed copies of Keller and Schoenfeld's *Principles of Psychology*, but they covered a part of the course we had already finished. I began to hand out brief mimeographed summaries of my lectures.

With more than four hundred students and no informed readers, I saw no alternative to multiple-choice tests. I composed items from scratch (validation in the Minnesota style was out of the question) using a particularly confusing format. Each question was composed of five statements, of which the student was to find the one which differed from the other four as either acceptable or unacceptable. Here is a sample:

> The argument that human behavior differs in an essential way from the behavior of lower animals:
>
> (1) Begs a question which a science of behavior is concerned with answering.
>
> (2) Is as unsupported as the argument that there is no difference.
>
> (3) Is supported by the observed fact that human behavior is more complex and more varied than the behavior of other animals.
>
> (4) Supports the contention that facts about animal behavior cannot be extrapolated to explain human behavior.
>
> (5) Suggests that behavior is a function of the organism which differs in some important way from digestion, respiration, circulation, and endocrine functions.

I was asking my students to evaluate 225 sentences of that sort in one hour. Many who knew the material ran into trouble with the logic.

I marked and graded the papers "on the curve," and when I saw the class again, it was nearly in revolt. When I picked up the glass of water on the podium and pretended to examine it suspiciously, a few students—those, I am sure, who had got the better grades—understood and laughed. At the next meeting I handed out a mimeographed sheet:

A CONVERSATION BETWEEN ACHILLES '51
AND PROFESSOR TORTOISE

Achilles '51: Excuse me, professor, I thought you might want to know that some of us thought your hour exam was pretty tough.

Professor Tortoise: Tough? Nonsense! No examination is tough. The competition may be, but not the examination. In the long run you students set the pace.

A: But I only got 20 points out of 45! That's a C minus!

T: That's a C minus only because a lot of people got more than 20 points.

A: Yes, but aren't you making the whole thing awfully competitive?

T: The whole thing *is* awfully competitive. I'm only making the competition fair.

A: Couldn't you have put in a few easy questions, though—just to encourage us?

T: I'd have to leave out some of the hard ones. It would have skewed my curve.

A: Does that matter?

T: It does if you want A's and B's to go to the people who deserve them.

A: I suppose that's what I don't want. The trouble is, I can't be sure I know everything I ought to know about the course.

T: No one ever knows everything he ought to know about anything. Don't let that bother you.

A: But at least I ought to feel I'm *learning* something?

T: Exactly to the extent that I ought to feel I'm *teaching* something. . . . We've both learned something from your C minus.

A: Would you object to being called Professor Taught-us?

T: Not if you wouldn't mind being called a Kill-Ease.*

* Lewis Carroll, *What Achilles Said to the Tortoise*

In spite of the practical problems, I hammered out a course which, to my knowledge, was entirely new. Its principal themes had been conceived in discussions with my colleagues on Project Pigeon and with the Minnesota *philosophes* and had undergone gestation during my Guggenheim year. I touched on many of them in *Walden Two*. I made a central point at the Conference on Current Trends in Psychology at the University of Pittsburgh in 1947: There were many disciplines dealing with human behavior, but each had its own theory; we needed a single theory suitable for use whenever human behavior was discussed or whenever anything was to be done about it. Such a theory would come from an experimental analysis.

A precise explanation of human behavior was not to be expected for a long time, but we gained nothing by turning to explanatory fictions like the pseudo-physiology of taut nerves and brain fag or the mental life of the "inner man." The explanation would be found, not in our stars *nor in ourselves*, but in the world in which we lived—in the environment responsible for the natural selection of the species and for the shaping and maintenance of the behavior of the individual.

I gave my students rules for analyzing an instance of behavior.

Consider the example: "Wars begin in the minds of men" (UNESCO).
1. *Rephrase expressions referring to behavior*—in this example, "war."

Do we mean the actual behavior of dropping bombs, firing guns, etc.? Or the verbal act "I declare that a state of war exists?" Or a newspaper headline inciting to any of these?

2. *Rephrase references to factors important for the practical control of behavior.* UNESCO seems to be saying that to reduce the probability of war we must reduce some sort of mental inclination to go to war. A current project of UNESCO calls it "tension." Avoid this sort of double-talk. A man's "inclination" to go to war is simply the probability that he will go to war. To "change the minds of men" in this respect is to change their tendency to emit warlike acts. How to do this is not specified, but it is a distinct advance to get rid of the middle term "mind."

UNESCO might better have said that war is behavior and is to be controlled through techniques derived from a science of behavior. That doesn't solve the problem but it opens it to attack.

The latter half of the course dealt with social behavior and the organized agencies of government, religion, education, economics, and psychotherapy. In each field I identified (1) those who control, (2) those who are controlled, (3) the power making control possible, (4) the processes and techniques through which it is used, (5) the resulting effects on the controlled, (6) measures taken in countercontrol, and (7) the maximized entities or principles said to "justify" the agency.

I WAS PRETTY SURE of my position as a behaviorist, but I was not unwilling to expose myself to a very different discipline. Several funds were supporting an ecumenical movement by paying for the psychoanalysis of anthropologists, sociologists, and psychologists, and I took a necessary first step by applying to the Boston Psychoanalytic Society and Institute. I promised not to practice; I simply wanted to find out more about psychoanalysis. I was interviewed by three analysts, one of them Helene Deutsch, but an unusually large number of applicants were being considered (the government was paying for analyses under the GI Bill of Rights), and a year or so later I was asked to withdraw my application.

*   *   *

OUR COTTAGE ON MONHEGAN ISLAND, Maine, was pleasant and convenient. The girls had their own rooms, and cots for guests could be set up on the balcony behind a balustrade carved by Rockwell Kent. The island store delivered ice for the icebox and kerosene for lamps, water heater, and stove. The girls liked the little snails called periwinkles, which they collected on the unpolluted eastern side of the island. The shop was in constant use, and at least once a week we sent off to Sears Roebuck for tools and supplies. I had bought a steerable kite—surplus from the early days of the war, when kites were put up from the sterns of ships for target practice—and we made kites of our own design, though I never duplicated the pinwheel model I had made in the early thirties. One summer we built a beanbag concession for the library fair. Unfortunately, Eve was not interested in building things, and she quickly exhausted the small library.

I had gone to Monhegan twenty years earlier to escape (unsuccessfully) from an early-summer hay fever. Antihistamines were now helpful, and we bought the cottage in the belief that the problem had been solved. We were wrong. I took so much antihistamine that much of the time I staggered about the island half asleep. In the hope of spending allergy-free nights, I built a hood over my half of our bed. A stovepipe, purchased from Sears Roebuck, rose from the hood to the ceiling, went through the wall and down to the floor of the shop. Under a horizontal section at the bottom were two lanterns, and when they were lighted, warm air rose through the pipe and descended into the hood. One section of the pipe contained a mass of steel wool soaked in motor oil to pick up pollen. (I had not learned that fumes from motor oil were possibly carcinogenic nor had I provided for breathing if the lanterns happened to be blown out by a heavy wind, which could be felt in the well-ventilated shop.) The air I breathed smelled reassuringly of oil, but my symptoms were not alleviated.

JOY HAD GONE OUT OF my father's professional life. His text on Pennsylvania Workmen's Compensation Law was in its fourth edition, and he was a member of the State Bar Association's Committee on Statutory Law, but workmen's compensation was not exciting, nor were his services as consultant for a small coal company operated mainly for the sake of the officers' salaries. A judgeship had never come his way. It was not the profession he had entered with so much pride so long ago.

Nor had he really enjoyed it. His mother had given him aspirations which he struggled to meet, but he was never quite successful. As he rose in the world, he found himself ill prepared for each new step. Any assurance that he was successful was terribly important. Praise became almost unbearably reinforcing. He listened for it, glowed under it. He often praised himself, obliquely or openly, and my mother was always there to protest.

He made other mistakes and suffered from them. My grandfather Skinner had not been greatly bothered by his deafness. Too gentle, or perhaps too lazy, to force himself upon others, he appeared to listen as we carried on a conversation of which he caught no word. When he then brought up a topic we had just discussed, my mother would be the first to laugh, and my father must have remembered it when he in turn grew deaf. He once told me how he had sweated when he could not hear what a judge had said to him and did not dare ask him to repeat.

Mistakes grew more frequent as his contact with the world grew less reliable. He once told me he had given a talk at a church on "philanthrophy." I did not catch myself in time, and corrected him. He gave no sign, but he probably spent many miserable hours punishing himself for the mistake. It would be at times like these that, as my mother once told me, he would throw himself on his bed and cry, "I'm no good. I'm no good."

He retired with relief. The secretary who had come with him when he left the Hudson Coal Company more than twenty years earlier became critical in little ways and, eventually, when she told him that she had had another offer, he immediately said, "Take it." He and my mother left their hotel suite in Scranton and moved to a pleasant house in a suburb near the country club. They spent much of the winter in a hotel in Bradenton, Florida.

Like a great many other people, my father thought the world was going to the dogs. He had seen Roosevelt wasting money on shiftless people in the WPA, the war had not meant the end of communism, Truman had beaten Tom Dewey just when it looked as if the Republicans would again take over, and the national debt continued to mount. If it were not for the evidence in his own family, it would be hard to believe in progress. But as he drove his Packard to the country club and played golf with affluent friends, he could still tell himself that he had come a long way beyond his father and that I, a Harvard professor, had gone far beyond him. He once reviewed that happy story in a talk at the Kiwanis Club. America was still a land of opportunity; a man could move up if he only had gumption. But there were private doubts.

My father and mother came to Cambridge for Thanksgiving in 1949, and when I drove them back to the Commander Hotel that evening, I saw my father for the last time. He had suffered from what must have been angina, but his doctor had, perhaps wisely, assured him that the pain was due to digestive trouble. (He had been quite angry when another doctor suggested that there might be something wrong with his heart.) Early on the morning of New Year's Day, one of his Bradenton friends called to tell me that he was dead. I asked for my mother, and when she came on the phone she said, "It is all over." She and my father had stayed up to greet the New Year, and my father had made some particularly tender remarks. He had awakened in the morning in great pain, struggled to get out of bed, and collapsed.

There was a plane to Tampa that afternoon. It was before the day of the credit card, and the banks were closed, but I was able to borrow money for the ticket from Garry Boring, part of it in fifty one-dollar bills. A friend of my father's met me at the Tampa airport, and I joined my mother in the hotel. The next morning at breakfast as I started to say something, she interrupted me: "Now don't say anything bad about your father." I had not been going to do so. My father had been as good to me as he knew how to be. As a child I was punished only by disapproval, and I can remember only one instance in which it was my father who strongly disapproved. It was my mother who would say "Tut, tut" and warn me of what people would think. (She never stopped playing that role with me. In the late forties, I wrote to them at their new suburban address, but put "Scranton" on the envelope. Somehow it reached them, and my mother returned the envelope with "Wake up!" written across it.) I had grown away from my father intellectually and culturally, even during my high school years, and he had not tried to follow my professional career, but he never criticized what he knew of my way of life. On the contrary, he generously supported it. Because of my grandmother's silly pretensions, which he paid for so dearly with never-quite-fulfilled ambitions, Eve and I and the children lived for many years in much pleasanter circumstances than would otherwise have been possible.

There were the usual painful things to be done—my father's clothing and golf clubs to be disposed of and arrangements made for a funeral. My father had not wanted to be cremated, and I was consulted on preparing his body for viewing. Should his pince-nez be left off as if he were sleeping? Left on, I thought, since his body was fully clothed. But when the undertaker responded to something I said by beginning to change the shape of my father's mouth, I broke off the proceedings. When my mother asked me whether she should view the body or simply remember my father as she had last seen him, I made the wrong decision. She took one glance and quickly turned away.

A few friends came to a simple funeral, and I went to Scranton by train with my father's body. I saw it buried beside my brother's grave; on the other side there would be room for my mother's ashes. My grandfather and grandmother Skinner were buried in the same plot.

My mother moved back to the Jermyn Hotel. She still had a few friends in Scranton, and she volunteered as a Gray Lady in a hospital and performed other services. But the compelling task of her life had vanished. It was all too true that it was "all over." As a friend had said, "Grace Burrhus made quite a man of Will Skinner." Her work was now finished.

THE DIRE PREDICTIONS of what would happen to Debbie when she was no longer spending much of her time in "the box" were not confirmed. On the contrary, she was spared many of the usual troubles of childhood. At six she had never had a cold, and I could think of a reason why. In winter, in many parts of the country, babies in ordinary cribs breathe dry air nearly thirty degrees below body temperature, and the superficial layers of the nose, throat, and bronchi, evaporating moisture, must grow at a temperature still lower. This would not have been the case in the tropics, where the species originated, and the species may not have had time to adjust genetically to colder climates. (I had heard that babies who live for the first two or three years in the tropics and are then taken to temperate zones are also resistant to colds.)

I could not prove that babies raised in baby-tenders were healthier and happier until more of the devices were available. When I told Andy Anderson at Macmillan about my failure to find a manufacturer, he introduced me to William Thompson, of Thompson and Rittmaster, a firm of business and investment analysts. They drew up a rather elaborate presentation, including my article in the *Ladies' Home Journal* and articles from *Life* and the *New Yorker,* and approached a manufacturer of hospital equipment, the American Sterilizer Company in Erie, Pennsylvania. (Presumably a different company name would appear on the product.) A representative of the company came to New York and met an enthusiastic user of a homemade model, and the company looked into costs and the probable market. I went to Erie to see a full-scale model. When I went again with Thompson, we were invited to the president's house for cocktails and, unfamiliar with business practices, I assumed that my problem was solved. On the way to the station Thompson said he thought the president was saying goodbye, and so he was.

Two couples in the department made baby-tenders. Bob and Jeanette Galambos used theirs for less than a year, for reasons I never discovered, but Fred and Gerry Frick were enthusiastic devotees. I was still getting requests for plans and more were under construction than ever before (and I began to receive photographs of happy babies in their ideal worlds.) Since costs were rising, Thompson and I tried to find a company to make kits—of heaters, thermostats, and other small parts which parents could use in making their own, with plywood cut locally to save shipping costs, but by the spring of 1950 he was caught up in other matters and our association came to an end. And so, for a time, did my promotion of the baby-tender.

PSYCHOLOGY 7 POSED a problem. Garry Boring's introductory course, which he had taught for more than two decades, was losing students. New introductory courses in Social Relations were taking their toll, and a second course in the department was an added drain. The problem was solved by moving my course into the General Education program and calling it Natural Sciences 114.

It was a much more appropriate title. I had not given my students a general survey of psychology; I had taught a very different subject.

The new title also attracted students whose major interests were in the social sciences or humanities but who needed a sophomore-level Natural Science course, and they were just the students who needed to know more about a science of behavior.

There was a practical advantage. The department had not been able to give me any help in Psychology 7, but General Education, President James Bryant Conant's baby, was generously supported, and I hired a young psychologist, Kay Montgomery, as an assistant. The Keller and Schoenfeld *Principles* was available at the beginning of the term, and Kay suggested some outside reading that he thought would be helpful. We followed the plan of Psychology 7, with new material which had come to hand, and more extensive summaries of my lectures.

The enrollment was down. The course was now open to freshmen only with special permission, and I was drawing from much the same population as before. Moreover, there were rumors about my examinations. A smaller course meant that I could let my students see some behavior in the flesh. I did not have space or equipment for the Keller and Schoenfeld system, but I could use demonstrations. Fred thought I should let my section people run them in order to bring them as close to the students as possible, but I decided to work them into my lectures.

No matter how much one has read about a behavioral process, it is always a surprise to see it at first hand. With a few grains of food I could quickly "shape" behavior in a hungry pigeon. I could get it to turn around by reinforcing any small movement in the right direction and then waiting for larger ones. By shaping left and right turns separately and putting them together, I could get the pigeon to pace a figure 8. When I withheld reinforcement, the behavior disappeared in "extinction," and I could then use the sound of an empty food magazine as a "conditioned reinforcer" to bring it back. As E. R. Hilgard once wrote to me, in such a demonstration you can actually "see learning take place."

In another demonstration, the pigeon pecked a "key"—a translucent disk, the color of which could be changed. If pecking was reinforced when the key was red but not when it was green, the pigeon soon responded at different rates; it had "formed a discrimination" between red and green. In another demonstration, pecking one of four panels bearing the words *Yellow, Blue, Red,* and *Green* was reinforced when it described the color of the light on the ceiling of the apparatus. The pigeon appeared to be reading the words and "using them to name the colors." Another pigeon played a tune on a six-key "piano." One of my section people, Ogden Lindsley, built an apparatus in which a rat, appropriately named Samson, pulled down a lever to lift a weight. The force required was gradually increased until by bracing itself against the screen wall the rat was lifting several times its own weight.

Natural Sciences 114 was far more "social" than some of the courses in Social Relations, and I responded to the rivalry between the two departments by demonstrating two "synthetic social relations." As an example of competition, two pigeons played a kind of Ping-Pong. A small table with rails along the side was slightly canted so that a ball would roll toward one end or the other. The pigeons pecked it back and forth until one of them failed to return it. As it fell off the table, it operated a food dispenser at the other end, reinforcing the successful shot.

The other synthetic social relation, cooperation, was more interesting. Two pigeons were separated by a pane of glass. On the wall along one edge of the glass were three pairs of buttons, each pigeon having access to one button in each pair. The birds received food when they pecked a pair simultaneously, but only one pair paid off at any one time. It was necessary for one pigeon, acting as leader, to move from button to button until the right one was found and for the other, as follower, to peck the corresponding button at the same moment.

The pigeons were first taught to explore their buttons separately, and when they first worked together, exact simultaneity was not required, but the final performance was so precise that, viewed from one side, the glass plate seemed to be a mirror showing one pigeon and its reflection. It was hard to see which was the leader and which the follower, but either one could be made a conspicuous follower by making it less hungry. The coordination was extraordinary. The pigeons ate, of course, at the same time, but they also began to go to their drinking glasses at the same time.

When I used the demonstration in a colloquium in the Department of Biology, someone asked me to change sides, and when I did so the pigeons immediately turned a hundred and eighty degrees around, tails toward the buttons, and, although there were no buttons to be pecked, began to move their heads up and down in unison. Cooperation and competition were not traits of character; the behavior to which the words referred was traceable to, and capable of being constructed by arranging, special contingencies of reinforcement.

The Harvard *Crimson* picked up the demonstrations, and then the Boston papers and the news services, and eventually Arthur Godfrey on the radio, and news programs on the infant television. The *New York Times* and the *Christian Science Monitor* reported them. Metro-Goldwyn-Mayer asked whether they could borrow any film we might have. When *Life* magazine came to get pictures, the Electronics Shop arranged a stroboscopic light under which the camera showed a trail of immobile balls stretching across the table. I myself had found it hard to play Ping-Pong in stroboscopic light, but the pigeons played successfully. The stroboscopic photograph published in *Life* misled the caption writer, who said that the pigeons were pecking at a flying Ping-Pong ball.

Unfortunately, the stories emphasized the performances rather than the contingencies responsible for them, which were, of course, the point of the demonstrations, and I began to emerge in the role of an animal trainer—in particular, as the man who taught pigeons to play Ping-Pong.

GRADUATE STUDENTS WERE BEGINNING to work in the pigeon laboratory, and as the number grew we began to hold meetings on Friday afternoons to review each other's research. We called ourselves the "Pigeon Staff." Cumulative records were spread out on the table in the seminar room, appropriate parts held flat by the cans of beer which also contributed to the spirit of the occasion.

ALTHOUGH MY COURSE WAS CALLED "Human Behavior," the students were soon calling it "Pigeons," and for good reason. I talked about people with principles derived from pigeons. Of course, people were more complex, but science began with simple facts and moved on as soon as it had dealt with them successfully. There were advantages in beginning with pigeons. They were pretty much alike genetically, and we could give them fairly similar individual histories. We could study their behavior in well-controlled environments for long periods of time. None of this was possible with people. If it eventually appeared that some kinds of human behavior remained unexplained, we should have to study them in their own right.

My treatment of human behavior was largely an interpretation, not a report of experimental data. Interpretation was a common scientific practice, but scientific methodologists had paid little attention to it. I chose examples of behavioral processes from history and literature:

Superstition: Give a hungry pigeon food every twenty seconds, and it will develop a superstitious ritual. The food reinforces whatever the pigeon is doing at the time, even though there is no "real" connection. A second instance is then more likely to occur, and the behavior may become so strong that further "reinforcements" are almost inevitable. According to Lecky (*History of European Morals*), "Roman soldiers believed that by beating drums and cymbals they could cause the moon's disk to regain its brightness after an eclipse," but did they do so because of the belief or because of the contingencies? The fact was that when they beat the drums, the moon was restored. One soldier might not beat, but others were presumably beating elsewhere to explain the return of the moon.

Pavlovian conditioning (aversive): In a play by Lope de Vega, a monk is punished by being forced to eat off the floor with the cats, who steal the choicest morsels. On a dark night, he takes the cats out in a sack. He coughs and then beats the sack. He continues to do so until the cats moan and yelp whenever he coughs. Thereafter, when eating off the floor, he has only to cough and the cats run away.

Pavlovian conditioning (positive and negative): In *Rameau's Nephew*, Diderot's hero tells of a tax collector, Bouret, whose dog takes the fancy of the Keeper of the Seals, whom Bouret wishes to please. He would like to give the Keeper the dog, but it is frightened by his uniform. Bouret borrows a spare uniform from the Keeper's valet and has a mask made resembling the Keeper. He puts on the robe and mask, calls the dog, pats him, and gives him a choice morsel. Then he throws off robe and mask and, appearing as himself, whips the dog. "Less than three days of this make the dog flee Bouret the Tax Collector and run to Bouret the Keeper of the Seals."

Punishment as a deterrent: Rudyard Kipling is said to have missed the Poet Laureateship because he wrote the bawdy poem "The Bastard King of England." Were later poets more cautious? Franz Cumont's advancement to a professorship at the University of Ghent was impeded by his analysis of the Mysteries of Mythra (with its pagan rite of "eating the god"), which offended the Catholic party in Belgium by the suggestion it conveyed of a similarity to the Mass. Would other scholars subsequently be more careful?

Stimulus generalization (Pavlovian): Turgenev cites the adage, "A scalded dog fears *cold* water."

Stimulus generalization (operant): According to Dodds (*The Greeks and the Irrational*), a wealthy and cultivated gentleman in Normandy, rejected by a lady, ran a needle through the forehead of her photograph.

Response generalization (operant): In a *New Yorker* cartoon, a woman stands in front of an old-style elevator, above which a pointer on a dial indicates the floor the elevator is on. She is using her umbrella to turn the pointer back.

IN THE *American Psychologist* of June 1949, Fred and Nat described their introductory course in psychology—the "new deal" Fred had told me about four years earlier. The Committee on Instruction at Columbia had approved the proposal "after lengthy discussion," and 120 students (twice the number expected) had enrolled. Each student had his own lever box and rat and conducted experiments ranging from conditioning and extinction through discrimination, punishment, and avoidance, to "an experimental prototype of 'masochism.'" The following year, enrollment rose to 180—all that space and equipment permitted.

Gerald Wendt, who had taken his degree under R. S. Woodworth at Columbia and was now at the University of Rochester, wrote to the editor: "I recognize that the Columbia system is enthusiastically received by the students," he said, "but all cults have that advantage, which rests on the fact, well known to students of propaganda, that simplification introduced into confusion has high acceptance value. . . . Systems have their function when eagerly developed by individuals, but their administrative imposition on a college can be only harmful in the end."

Because Wendt identified the cult as "Skinnerism," I drafted a reply. I agreed that my name appeared too often in Fred's and Nat's mimeographed text (I had told them so), but Wendt was overlooking the extraordinary achievement of bringing students into direct contact with behavior under controlled conditions. "I cannot see that the use of a method or an apparatus suggests a 'cult.' We might with equal justification refer to Roentgenology or electroencephalography as a cult."

I read the letter to the Pigeon Staff, and no one liked it. I sent it to Fred, and he also thought I should not submit it. He said Wendt had shown him an earlier version and had asked what he thought of it. "I said 'Fine,' " Fred wrote. "I patted him on the shoulder and sent him along." I did not submit the letter. A year later Fred wrote, "Of course, our colleagues will continue to find fault with us, but we are having a wonderful time and I wonder what *they* are giving their kids that is so much better—chronaxie, Phi, 'schools of psychology,' level of aspiration, the Zondi test, electroencephalography? Hey, nonny, nonny!"

More constructive things were being published. In a summer conference on learning theories held at Dartmouth College in 1950, William S. Verplanck, who had rescued me from most of the burden of the chairmanship at Indiana, gave a sophisticated analysis of my position.

In "Are Theories of Learning Necessary?" I reproduced an extinction curve recorded four years after conditioning. (The pigeon had been salvaged from Project Pigeon, but I was not allowed to say so.) I had brought four remaining pigeons to Harvard for a final test six years after conditioning. They all pecked the target accurately and gave small extinction curves.

It was an approach to the study of memory which I thought should be carried further. Pigeons could be exposed to a number of schedules, under different kinds of stimulus control, and then put aside to be tested years later. It could only be done by someone with an assured future and space for a colony of pigeons. I had the future but not the space. When I asked local breeders or fanciers about boarding pigeons, they were all worried about infection from strange birds, and I dropped the project.

*   *   *

DURING THE THIRTIES I had quite deliberately paid no attention to politics. A better understanding of human behavior was needed if we were to be more effective, and I would devote myself to that. But the Second World War was a war that had to be fought, and I played my ineffectual part—though not, as in 1918, to make the world safe for democracy.

Psychology 7 dealt in part with governmental practices. I did not like a political science that appealed to historical analogies or to absolute moral or natural laws. Instead, I wanted to know what those who governed actually did. In general, they suppressed unwanted behavior with punitive measures, which often led instead to escape, revolt, or apathy. As to wanted behavior, governments left that to their citizens, which meant leaving it to ethical, religious, economic, or educational forces. Punishment was "justified" by pointing to the resulting security and justice, but I thought it would be better if those conditions could be achieved with positive reinforcement.

I considered a practical example when I was asked to speak at the Mount Holyoke Institute on the United Nations in the summer of 1950. As Jack Volkmann, a former fellow graduate student in the Department at Harvard, then at Mount Holyoke, wrote, "Policy toward the Germans and Japanese is one of the topics of the week. Probably you can think of some appropriate things to say about that (like the inadvisability of beating people up if you want to live in the same world with them afterward)." Under the title of "Reward and Punishment in Occupation Policies," I compared punishment and its disadvantages with what we had recently learned about the power of positive reinforcement. The Marshall Plan and the Point Four Program were hopeful signs that positive measures were being recognized. (But North Korean forces invaded South Korea on the day the conference opened, and the newspapers merely reported my warning against using the A-bomb.)

MY HARVARD SALARY HAD NOT GONE as far as expected, and after taking Eve and the girls to Monhegan I taught summer school—a course on verbal behavior and an improved version of NS 114, with a graduate student, Herbert Jenkins, as my assistant.

On Monhegan the preceding summer, we had met Zero and Kate Mostel. Zero and I had talked about Molière, and that fall I had tried my hand at a free translation of *Le Malade Imaginaire*. Now I found Zero playing Molière at the Brattle Theater in Cambridge. The translation made little difference, because he was playing it (as Molière probably intended) in the *commedia dell'arte* manner.

WHEN PROJECT PIGEON CAME to an end, Keller and Marian Breland continued to work for General Mills, Inc., training animals to entertain people at state fairs where the company's products were advertised. Using the shaping technique that we had discovered on the top floor of that flour mill in Minneapolis, they trained a hen to play a five-note tune on a small piano and another to tap-dance in costume and shoes. When the audiences grew so large that the chickens were not easily seen, the Brelands changed to pigs. "Priscilla the Fastidious Pig" turned on a radio, ate breakfast at a table, picked up dirty clothes and put them in a hamper, ran a vacuum cleaner, and chose Larro food in preference to the products of other companies. In 1948 the *Wall Street Journal* published an article on this ingenious form of advertising, and in 1951 the Brelands called attention to their "new field of applied psychology" in the *American Psychologist*.

IN A STUDY OF American scientists, Anne Roe gave me a number of tests. I responded so rapidly to the Rorschach cards that she could not keep up with me, but I could say nothing at all on Harry Murray's Thematic Apperception Test, evidently because I had been involved in its construction and knew what it was said to reveal. My own thematic apperception test, the "verbal summator," was languishing. I still received an occasional request for the records supplied by the Audio-Visual Department at Indiana University, but they were not being as widely used to "locate complexes" as I had hoped.

*   *   *

WE HAD TROUBLE FINDING a house of our own. Eve had known the disadvantages of living in a suburb, and I hated commuting, but the houses for sale in Cambridge were overpriced and not exciting. In the spring of 1950 a piece of land about a mile and a half from the university came on the market and we bought it and hired an architect. On November 1 we moved into a new, small contemporary house. Behind it was a fairly large garden, which we neglected for many years because we spent our summers on Monhegan.

Soon after we came to Cambridge I bought Julie a rather primitive model of the new long-playing phonograph, together with a few records. Better models were soon available and I had a loudspeaker built into the top of one corner of our new living room and assembled a radio receiver and phonograph. Stereo was coming in, and I soon added another speaker. The range of pitch, volume, and timbre intrigued me, and I turned to the romantic composers. On Sunday mornings I would lie on the sofa and listen to things like Tchaikovsky's *Romeo and Juliet Overture* or Schönberg's *Verklärte Nacht*.

I WAS INVITED TO GIVE one of three major lectures at an International Congress of Psychology in Stockholm. It was a chance to show the children something of Europe, but it would be expensive, and we turned to my mother. She was only too glad to pay for the trip if she could go too. The result was disastrous. We covered too much territory— London, Paris, Copenhagen, Oslo, and Bergen, on the way to Stockholm, and Scotland and England on the way back. At seventy-three my mother tired easily and was impatient with the children, and the children in return were less manageable than usual. In Stockholm we found the new hotel in which we had made reservations only half completed, and were forced to live in inconvenient quarters for several days. When a young woman took the children to a park, Deborah fell and broke off a front tooth.

After the meetings we flew to Glasgow and came down through the Lake District. With several hours to wait for a train in a small

Scottish town, I took the girls for a walk. We stopped to buy balls of shaved ice treated with a dash of colored, flavored water. They were not very good, and when Debbie, then six, refused to leave the shop until she got something better, Julie and I left and walked down the street. Debs followed in a small rage. She came up to me and swung her foot in a half-intentional kick. I started to show her how silly she looked, but she suddenly moved and my shoe struck her smartly on the shin. She howled. People came to the doors of the shops. "You kicked me!" she cried. Was there a law in Scotland against kicking children? A jail sentence?

Eventually we reached London and Southampton and the *Queen Mary*. Before we docked in New York, my mother removed the cabin-class stickers from her luggage. She had thought that I would naturally order first-class passages, and she did not want her friends to know that I had not done so. (She was trapped when one of them asked whether men still wore dinner jackets in first class, and she later asked me whether she had been right in hazarding the guess that they did not.)

Eve and I enjoyed some pleasant moments. We dined and spent a rather alcoholic evening at the famous Gyllene Freden, discovering as we came home that it was never really dark in Stockholm in the summer. We attended a concert at the Drottningholms Theater, built in the eighteenth century but closed and forgotten throughout the nineteenth, and we were graciously entertained by several Swedish psychologists and their families.

MUCH OF THE RESEARCH I reported in Stockholm was done in collaboration with Charles B. Ferster. With extra support from the Office of Naval Research, I had been able to take on a full-time assistant, and Fred suggested Charlie. He had completed a thesis on operant conditioning and would receive a degree in June 1951. He came to work at the beginning of that year.

My lecture, called "The Experimental Analysis of Behavior," was held in the hall of the House of Parliament. I used forty slides, almost all of them showing cumulative records. (Aware that I should be giving the audience all too brief a look, I posted photographs in one of the quarters of the Congress. They were there for several days, but I never saw anyone looking at them.) One slide testified to the importance of rate as a datum; it reproduced records of pigeons responding at constant rates ranging from 300 responses per hour to 18,000—a sixtyfold difference. Inflections in a five-hour curve for extinction showed the importance of the pigeon's "internal clock." Another curve showed the effect of an external clock, which I had described in a letter to Fred:

> . . . *Our latest gadget: a device which introduces an external stimulus which changes* pari passu *(as Sherrington was always saying) with a hypothetical proprioceptive stimulus. For example, on fixed-interval reinforcement (Charlie has persuaded me to use fixed and variable interval, fixed and variable ratio) it is possible the organism uses an internal clock. So we simply let a small spot of light on the key grow slowly with the passage of time, going back to the smallest size at reinforcement. Or the spot can grow with an internal counter (fixed ratio) or vary as a function of the momentary rate (proprioceptive stimulation from rate).*

I reported a study of variable-ratio reinforcement—the powerful schedule used in all gambling devices which Fred* had said was "more like human prayer." We had used it on Project Pigeon, but it had never been systematically studied. In extinction after variable-ratio reinforcement a pigeon emitted nearly 50,000 responses in two and a half hours. Other experiments were on generalization, choice, preference, color matching, motivational and emotional effects, and punishment.

These were the "kinds of results which followed when one took probability—or, more immediately, frequency—of response as a subject matter." As to practical results, "what we transfer from the laboratory to a world in which satisfactory quantification is impossible is the knowledge that certain basic processes exist, that they are lawful, and that they probably account for the unpleasantly chaotic facts with which we are faced." My paper was published in the Proceedings of the Congress and, shortened, in the *American Psychologist*.

I had covered some of the same material earlier that year, when, as a new member, I was asked to speak at a meeting of the American Philosophical Society. When Benjamin Franklin founded the Society, it was not unreasonable to take all knowledge for one's province, and the papers still covered a wide range. I spoke on "Schedules of Reward and Their Effects on Behavior." The Society was "held [and housed] in Philadelphia for the promotion of useful knowledge," and Philadelphians were mentioned whenever possible, but I could think of none who had contributed to our knowledge of schedules. Fortunately, on my way to the meeting I passed a Horn and Hardart Automat—a kind of room-sized vending machine in which one inserted coins to gain access to sandwiches, pies, and other foods. According to an inscription, the first Automat had been opened in Philadelphia, and I could therefore acknowledge the contribution of those great Philadelphians, Horn and Hardart, when I described the automatic food dispenser in our experiments.

I could also speak of "useful knowledge." With men and women, as with rats and pigeons, schedules could, for example, be "stretched" to generate a great deal of behavior in return for very little reinforcement. Stretching was opposed for good reason in industry, but less often in gambling. We had learned enough about the variable-ratio schedule found in all gambling systems to design machines which would more rapidly empty the pockets of visitors to Las Vegas and bring the pockets back again as soon as refilled, but I did not say how it could be done. *Newsweek* picked up the story and ran a picture of me examining one of our relay panels as if I had never seen it before.

WHILE I WAS A Junior Fellow, I had served as a subject for Hallowell and Pauline Davis in their studies of the newly discovered Berger rhythm, and at a meeting of the Society of Experimental Psychologists I talked with John Kennedy of Princeton University about the possibility that "brain waves" were due to eye movements. If the retina and the sclera acted like a capacitor, tremor of the eye muscles might vary the capacitance and generate electrical changes closely approximating the alpha rhythm. Paul Schiller had used a small pump to aerate the water in his experiment on *Betta splendens*, and when I connected it to a small balloon strapped over my eyes, it delivered rhythmic pressures to the eyeballs which should have much the same effect as the tremor. M. A. B. Brazier, one of the more stimulating people in the Boston area, was working on brain waves, and she tried the balloons on some of her subjects. Alas, she was unable to detect a corresponding rhythm in their electroencephalograms.

*　　*　　*

A LARGE CHART drawn up only a few months after the Stockholm meeting shows how fast Charlie and I were moving. In addition to the four standard schedules, we listed the following: tandem, alternating, interpolated, interlocking, adjusting, multiple, mixed, and concurrent. External clocks, counters, and speedometers were to be added to all of them, and a performance could be "probed" at any point with a single reinforcement or a time-out.

We had discovered multiple and mixed schedules in an unusually haphazard way. We first tested the pigeon's "internal counter" by reinforcing either the twentieth or the hundredth response. The pigeon was soon beginning with a curve appropriate to twenty but, when that was not the schedule in force, it broke and gave a curve appropriate to one hundred. We called this a "two-valued" schedule. Then we found that if there were different colors on the key corresponding to the schedules in force, the pigeons simply gave appropriate curves. As we said in a paper called "Stimulus Control of Alternating Schedules of Reinforcement" at a meeting of the Eastern Psychological Association, "the pigeon developed the characteristic performance appropriate to each schedule under the control of the corresponding color of the key." In another paper called "Alternating Schedules of Reinforcement without Stimulus Control" we reported that "with no stimuli present, the bird's own behavior . . . provides effective discriminative control for the two schedules."

With improved automation, Charlie and I were able to run nearly a dozen experiments twenty-four hours a day. Each morning we made our rounds, moving from apparatus to apparatus, unrolling the records which had collected in baskets below the recorders, discovering occasional failures in the apparatus or in our planning, and making changes in the contingencies. There were many exciting moments, and scarcely a week passed without a surprise.

In March 1951 I reported to Fred:

> *Charlie Ferster has worked out wonderfully. In his quiet way he has vastly improved the basic design of most of our equipment. I have found it profitable to give him a full share in the design of experiments, too.*

We're starting to work up material for a long monograph on intermittent reinforcement—a subject I'd like to have done with.

We did not always agree. A well-designed variable-interval schedule gave a stable rate for many hours. The cumulative records were straight lines, and they seemed like ideal baselines in evaluating the effects of drugs or other variables. But there was a hitch. When a pigeon responds steadily for many hours at the same rate, the rate itself becomes an important controlling stimulus. A deviation from it is like a change in the color of the key, and returning to the rate is like a return to the original color. Such a return is reinforcing, and a given rate therefore becomes "locked in." Charlie always shook his head when I used that term.

In 1939, at a meeting of the American Psychological Association in San Francisco, two undergraduates from the University of Washington, Eleanor Maccoby and Fred Sheffield, had talked with me about *The Behavior of Organisms*. Eleanor went on to graduate work at the University of Michigan, and when she then moved with her husband to Cambridge, she asked if she could finish her research in my laboratory. She was testing my interpretation of a fixed-ratio schedule; was it true that reinforcements set up by a counter actually tended to reinforce relatively fast responding? She was planning to record ratio performances and look at the intervals between responses, but I persuaded her to see what happened when reinforcements necessarily occurred only when the pigeon was responding rapidly. We had used a device having that effect on Project Pigeon.

Eleanor and I designed a much more effective device, and it did, indeed, generate high rates of responding. It was the first careful study of what we eventually called *drh*—the differential reinforcement of a high rate. Doug Anger, who had become a Junior Fellow in the Harvard Society of Fellows, was doing something of the same sort by differentially reinforcing short interresponse times.

Ben Wyckoff, a former student at Indiana, was working on a discrimination in which reinforcement was contingent upon the presence of two properties of a stimulus, and he spent the summer of 1950 at

Harvard on a related project. Alfredo Lagmay, a graduate student in the department from the Philippines, made a classic study of pacing, in which reinforcement was contingent upon pecking at a steady rate. When the schedule would otherwise have generated a higher rate, the pigeon would break through and "get rid of extra responses" in a sudden burst. George Heise, another graduate student, tested the auditory sensitivity of the pigeon.

At Columbia, Fred's students were developing new methods. Donald Cook modified the old discrimination procedure, using intermittent reinforcement in the presence of the positive stimulus. James Dinsmoor, with a rather similar arrangement, found that the ratios of rates under positive and negative stimuli were not changed by a change in deprivation (as they were not in my extinction curves after intermittent reinforcement). Murray Sidman devised a new way of studying avoidance.

THE TAUT-STRING RECORDERS were not working well. The ratchets jammed, the paper crept sideways, pens skipped when moving fast and left blobs of ink when standing still, and we lost many valuable records. Charlie and I designed a new model but ran into another problem. The stepping switch which moved the pen was rated for only a few hundred thousand operations, and pigeons responding at high rates for as much as ten hours a day soon wore it out. We eventually found a switch that would operate many millions of times, and, meanwhile, in the department's Machine Shop, Ralph Gerbrands was working on a better model with a Telechron motor and a pen that reset when it reached the top of the paper. As early as 1952 he shipped a lever, a food magazine, and a "kymograph for obtaining cumulative response records" to a Japanese psychologist, paid for by the Japanese government.

A MAN NAMED Nanavati came to America to promote research on human behavior. In India, he said, it would be possible to get a fairly large number of newborn human babies and carry out some dramatic social experiments. I thought immediately of an archetypal question: What would happen if a group of babies grew up completely out of touch with older human beings—cared for, but only when necessary, by silent people dressed in, say, robot costumes? Would they develop a language? Teach each other? Form social classes? Would they eventually set up some kind of government? A religion? The experiment might tell us a good deal about human nature, but the ethical questions were unanswerable. No doubt a bleak future lay ahead for the babies in any case, but it was unlikely that they would ever find a place in the world when the experiment was over. They might remain feral children.

I gave Nanavati a copy of *Walden Two*, and after he returned to Bombay he wrote me enthusiastically. It was just the kind of thing he had been thinking of. Why not design a culture like Walden Two and construct the personal histories needed to make it work? I thought it was still too much of a gamble. I was not sure of the stability of the Indian government, I had a relatively sure thing in hand, and such a drastic intervention in human lives would still raise ethical questions, no matter how acceptable and useful the result.

OUR SOCIAL LIFE expanded slowly. In the Christmas parties in Memorial Hall, lavish as ever thanks to the profits from Smitty's Coke machine, and in play-readings we saw mostly other psychologists, but we became affiliates of Moors Hall at Radcliffe and we occasionally saw Ivor and Dorothea Richards and the Bridgmans. When a local representative of *Time* magazine, William Lang, interviewed me, we began to see him and his wife, Louise. Louise had a beautiful voice, and I played her accompaniments in Schumann and Schubert *Lieder*.

JOHN HUTCHENS AND I had nearly missed getting our degrees from Hamilton College because of our prank about a lecture by "the famous cinema comedian Charles Chaplin," but when our class held its twenty-fifth reunion, we both received honorary degrees. It was peony time at the Saunderses', and Professor Fancher, the butt of our prank, was still drawing beautiful music from the college choir. Edward and Grace Root asked me to come for Black Velvet under their trees after the exercises, and Professor and Mrs. Chase invited me to a very early buffet supper.

The two invitations drew me again into a conflict that I had first known a quarter of a century earlier. Members of the Root family had taught at the college for three generations, and Elihu Root was Chairman of the Board in my day. With Percy and Louise Saunders, Grace and Edward Root represented culture on the hill. Mrs. "Trot" Chase, the wife of the professor of Latin, was equally well educated but had no following, in part because she was a militant Catholic in a Protestant community. (Trot himself eventually converted to Catholicism.)

The division became sharper than ever when, under a *nom de guerre*, a Hamilton graduate, Paul Coonradt, published a scurrilous *roman à clef* about the Hamilton community. No key was needed to identify members of the Root family or to see that Alfie Frisby was Percy Saunders or Deborah, Louise, though Alfie played the flute where Percy played the violin, and the famous Saunders peonies became Frisby irises. (A vase of peonies made a brief appearance in the Frisby music room, possibly having escaped editorial excision.) Jack Chase, Trot's son and my classmate, was on the staff of Longmans, who published the book, and later told me that he had edited the manuscript. He said he had done so because he felt he could temper the blow, but it was significant that none of Coonradt's keys unlocked a closet of the Chase family, although Jack's mother would have been particularly good material.

I told Mrs. Chase that I could come to supper if I might be a little late, but what with Black Velvet and good company at the Roots', I was so late that I was not offered any supper at all, though the remains of a buffet were still to be seen.

I had not known how painful it would be to relive a bit of my Hamilton College experience, and a few months later, writing to Hutch on other matters, I said, "I hope I never have to go through an emotional wringer like that again. I don't know why the whole thing got to me as it did. Perhaps one can't, after all, just walk off and leave such a batch of mistakes behind. Jesus, what an experience. I would like to restore order by taking time out for a drink and will call next time I am in New York. . . ."

*   *   *

IN THE SPRING TERM of 1951, I gave Natural Sciences 114 for the third time. Kay Montgomery had gone on to a more promising job at Cornell, and Charlie Ferster took his place. Psychology 1 was still in trouble, and I was considering a more ambitious plan. As I wrote to Fred,

> Garry's course is languishing. He has three reasons why it is losing students—not including the real one. He may be amenable to a blended course incorporating mine and some other stuff running a full year. He's trying at the conscious level to adopt a hands-off, "it's-up-to-you-younger-men" policy—but it just isn't in him. Bill Verplanck [who had joined the department as an Assistant Professor] is doing wonders as an overall peacemaker.

In June I presented a plan to the Committee on General Education in which Natural Sciences 114 would be moved into the fall term and another course, given during the spring term, would cover much of the material of Psychology 1, which would simply be dropped. The committee said it would agree if the department agreed. But by September I was writing that "it now appears that sentiment in this direction was not quite as unanimous as I had been led to believe."

Upon request, the Harvard Testing Office would tell you how your grades compared with the other grades your students received during the same term. In 1950 I was grading low—by a rather wide margin. In 1951 I cut the curve more generously, giving more A's and B's and fewer C's and D's, but my average was still relatively low. Students were looking elsewhere for a gut course, and those who now chose Natural Sciences 114 were better students. I continued to move in the direction of more generous grades but never caught up. When, some years later, *Esquire* cited my course as one of the gut courses at Harvard, along with Chinese 10 and Fine Arts 13, I could have replied with convincing statistics. Students liked the course and were not under heavy punitive control, but they were not getting high grades for nothing.

*   *   *

IN A SHORT ARTICLE in the "Amateur Science Section" of *Scientific American* called "How to Teach Animals," I explained how one conditioned a reinforcer (the sound of a "cricket," for example) so that it could be made instantly contingent upon a bit of behavior, and how it could be used to get a dog to lift its head or turn around or a pigeon to peck a card that read "Peck" while ignoring one that read "Don't peck."

Shortly after my article appeared, a writer for *Look* magazine, Joseph Roddy, turned up at my office. As a poker player might have put it, *Look* was calling me. If I could teach a dog as easily as that, they wanted pictures. It was a reasonable challenge and I accepted it. Roddy bought a beautiful Dalmatian (to be given to his children when the project was finished) and persuaded Charlie to let him keep it in the Fersters' apartment on Beacon Hill.

I decided to use the photographer's flash as the conditioned reinforcer, and I told Roddy how to give the dog small pieces of hamburger just after occasional flashes (but never when the dog was begging for food or even looking toward him). When it was responding to the flash by quickly coming to be fed, it would be time for pictures.

Zero Mostel was in a play, *Flight into Egypt*, being tried out in Boston, and Eve and I were invited to a party after the show. Earlier in the evening I went to Charlie's apartment and saw the dog for the first time. We had agreed that I would teach it to stand on its hind legs (a more dramatic bit of behavior than any mentioned in my article). I took the switch that operated both flash and shutter and told the photographer to keep his camera on the dog. I had put some horizontal lines on one wall, and I waited until the dog went near them before triggering a flash. The dog came for its bit of hamburger and almost immediately went back to the wall. I waited until its head had reached a slightly higher line and again reinforced. Then I chose still higher lines, and under this "differential reinforcement" the dog was soon raising its head as high as possible. As I continued, its forepaws began to come up off the floor, and soon it stood straight up. Eventually it began to jump, and before the hamburger was gone, it was jumping so high that its hind feet rose a foot off the floor. A photograph had been taken of each stage. I had put my cards on the table and won the pot, and I joined Eve and went on to the party.

I had carefully explained the process to Roddy: the trick was simply to reinforce slight variations in the direction of the desired behavior.

But when the tear sheets arrived, I found that he was telling the readers of *Look* how I had put the idea of jumping into the dog's head. In class the next day I warned my students not to take the article seriously. As they well knew, to report that I had talked about putting an idea into a dog's head was "nothing short of libelous." Unfortunately, one of my students, Michael Maccoby, a reporter for the Harvard *Crimson*, took me seriously and called that evening for a few last-minute details about my suit for libel. Nothing I could say seemed to shake him. He changed the story only slightly: I had "considered taking libel action" but had decided instead to "write a scathing letter to Gardiner Cowles, publisher of the magazine." I did indeed complain to Cowles, but I soon had his answer, which, as I wrote to the *Crimson*, proved "that he was at least unscathed enough to express a friendly concern for reportorial accuracy —which," I added, "is quite fitting in a former editor of the *Crimson*."

IN 1952 I went back to Hamilton College to talk to students about college teaching and research as a career and called on Percy Saunders, who was seriously ill. Louise met me at the door and took me into the little room where, nearly thirty years before, I had tutored the twelve-year-old Blake Saunders and a boarding student, Cynthia Ann Miller, preparing for Radcliffe. Louise asked me to wait, and a few moments later called me upstairs. I sat on the edge of Percy's bed, and Louise handed us small glasses of sherry. We talked and laughed, and then we shook hands and said goodbye, both knowing that we were seeing each other for the last time. The doctors were soon proposing to take Percy into a Utica hospital for a few last desperate measures, but Louise had the courage to say no, her husband would die in his bed. And he did, at the age of eighty-four. As a young agricultural chemist he had, with his brother's help, developed Marquis wheat, a strain which greatly increased production in Canada, but his great love was hybrid peonies. He left records of more than seventeen thousand plants, among them some of the strains most highly prized by fanciers. I was one of his hybrids too. The way of life I found in the Saunders household had been grafted onto the life I had known in Susquehanna and Scranton.

*　　*　　*

WHEN I WAS SENDING the manuscript of *The Sun Is a Morning Star* around to publishers, I said I was planning "a book for the educated layman on the implications of a science of behavior—with enough on such a science at work to serve as an introductory text." Harcourt Brace, the fourth publisher to return the manuscript, said they would like to see the text, but Charles Anderson of Macmillan went further: he would publish the novel (renamed *Walden Two*) if I would give him first refusal on the text. He pictured a tantalizing financial future, citing the most popular current texts. When I called some of them "pot-boilers," he said, "Yes, but they boil an awful lot of pots." The book I had planned would not boil many.

In Psychology 7, face to face with more than four hundred educated laymen (and -women), I saw more clearly what such a text would mean, and I set about writing it. For the first two hours of each day I shut myself in my office, and my secretary took phone calls and shielded me from visitors. I wrote against a supporting background of clicking relays heard through a cinderblock wall. A visiting statistician once listened to the clicking for a moment and said, "Random." It was not as random as the clicking of a Geiger counter, but it was free of the beat of background music, and it reassured me that another kind of progress was being made.

In March 1951, I sent Fred three hundred mimeographed pages of *Science and Human Behavior*. To some extent they covered the same material as the Keller and Schoenfeld text, but, as I explained, "I don't see how I can write the latter half of the book without at least this much factual buildup." By 1952 I had a completed mimeographed manuscript for my class, and sent a copy to Anderson. I knew it was not the book he wanted. One of his readers, he wrote, had called it

"*a thoughtful, thorough, and logically consistent presentation of Skinner's psychological thinking and an application of his system to a number of extremely important social problems. . . ." [But] now let's review the debit side of the ledger. As an introductory text people are going to find a number of things wrong with it. There is not a single figure, table, or other detailed presentation of experimental results in it. There are no chapter summaries, or other customary textbook paraphernalia. [He might have added there are no pictures, no color charts, no optical illusions, no cross-sections of eye or ear, no mazes (not even a picture of Pavlov's dog in its stand), no learning or forgetting curves, no discussion*

of chromosomes or genes or neurones or reflex arcs, nothing about matu-
ration or development, nothing about intelligence tests, and no statistics.]
. . . It simply does not look like an ordinary textbook and that will de-
tract from adoptions for ordinary classroom use. . . . The appearance and
style are those of a trade book [but] the ideas are too closely reasoned and
the subject matter not sufficiently spectacular to justify the expectation
of a large trade sale. In short, some of the very features which to you
are virtues are likely to limit the general use of the book. This, of course,
is no surprise to me. I had not expected your book to be another Munn
or Ruch [the two best-selling texts at the time] and you may be right in
your opinion that psychologists will use it because it is not written for
psychologists. To a mere layman like me these things are unpredictable.
I mention the liabilities not to indicate a lack of enthusiasm on our part
but rather to prepare you for a realistic appraisal of sales potentialities.

I sent a copy of the manuscript to Mike Elliott, my old boss at
Minnesota, and an advisory editor at Appleton-Century. He wrote:

At all stages in reading, my background refrains have been two: "This
is Fred's best writing yet" and "How definitely this belongs with the
Behavior of Organisms *and Keller and Schoenfeld in the Century Psy-*
chology Series!" *I am really depressed that Macmillan should have strings*
on it [but Appleton-Century had had the first chance at Walden Two
and had turned it down]. . . .

The book was essentially an elaboration of my lectures in Psychology 7 and Natural Sciences 114, but here I could give more space
to difficult issues and add examples which I had turned up or my students had given me. I added one bit from my own history: My decision
to go-into psychology had been confirmed when H. G. Wells compared
Pavlov with George Bernard Shaw, to Pavlov's advantage. Shaw may
have been replying with a passage in *The Adventures of the Black Girl*
in Her Search for God, in which the girl tricks Pavlov with several verbal
stimuli. I wanted to use the passage, but Andy said that Shaw's American
publisher could not grant permission and that Shaw himself was difficult. When I wrote to Shaw, I received a postcard, the address composed
of bits carefully cut from my letterhead and, on the back, some excerpts
from the Copyright Act of 1911 with a conclusion: "*In view of the above,*
Mr. Bernard Shaw begs writers, publishers, and managers not to ask him
for unnecessary authorizations." In fewer words, the answer was no.

But within the year Shaw had died, and the Society of Authors gave me permission, in return for a small fee.

ONE OF THE FIRST PEOPLE to build another baby-tender was John Gray, an engineer with the Airborne Instrument Company. He was soon interested in producing a commercial model. I gave him the names of people who had written to me about the ones they had built, and he sent out a questionnaire which brought reports on 104 babies. They had been "freer to move about, more comfortable, quieter, happier, healthier (with fewer rashes and colds), and easier to keep clean" than babies in standard cribs. None developed rolling, head bumping, rocking, or any other compulsive crib behavior. Their parents worried less about smothering and inadequate covering and enjoyed greater privacy and quiet when the babies needed no attention.

I referred Gray to a research and development company in Boston which had some Harvard connections, and he tried several manufacturers, all without success. An unexpected patent problem arose. I had asked two neighbors to sign a description of our baby-tender, but my friends at General Mills, Inc., thought there was no point in applying for a patent. The device was, after all, nothing more than a small heated and humidified room, and patented features could easily be "designed around." In 1946 I sent specifications for switches, thermostats, and so on, to a young couple in Minneapolis, former students at the University, who were building a baby-tender. Two years later they wrote that a friend was manufacturing a model to be used in hospitals in which newborn babies were kept in their mothers' rooms. Now Gray discovered that the friend had taken out a patent on a larger model very much like mine. Since my article had put the device in the public domain, the patent had no legal standing, but it made it hard for Gray to interest manufacturers.

MY COLLEAGUES IN the Department of Psychology were ethical and moral men, but they seldom thought of how their science could be used to improve the world. In the Department of Social Relations, however,

Gordon Allport and others were studying social issues, and Harry Murray and his colleagues at the Clinic were helping people solve their problems. It bothered me that their graduate students were credited with a kind of accomplishment denied to ours. Pigeons were behaving in more complex ways than ever before in the history of the species simply because they had been exposed to more complex contingencies than ever before. What might human beings do if we could build a more favorable environment for them? Any progress a student might make toward that environment should be more clearly reinforced.

In December 1950, I gave a lecture at Mount Holyoke College called "How to Help Billions of People." I said that we quite justly admired those who went into social and clinical practice, but that even a slight advance in a science of behavior could eventually mean a far greater personal achievement and should be reinforced accordingly. The gratitude lavished on the clinical or social worker should be shared with the behavioral scientist.

An operant analysis moved directly into a form of behavioral engineering because it pointed to conditions that could be changed to change behavior. In the classical experiment on reaction time, for example, subjects were asked to respond to a signal as quickly as possible, but the reasons why they did so were lost in their personal histories. One could not ask a pigeon to respond as quickly as possible; one had to construct rather subtle temporal contingencies of reinforcement. The "reasons for responding quickly" were then clear and could be immediately used for practical purposes. (I had in fact designed a series of devices to teach quick responding—one of them a complex punching bag to improve a boxer's speed.)

Walden Two was an exercise in behavioral engineering, and I discussed a few traditional practices in Natural Sciences 114. A drop of honey on a religious book, tasted by the child when kissing the book, conditioned a favorable response. A young boy frightened by a dog could be given a harmless puppy, and as it grew older the frightening features of a large dog would appear so slowly that the fear would extinguish in easy stages. As I wrote in *Science and Human Behavior*, "an analysis of the techniques through which behavior may be manipulated shows the kind of technology which emerges as the science advances."

My students did not overlook the possibilities. Two of them once came to talk about a problem: They liked modern art and had acquired some good pictures and sculptures, but they had also acquired a new roommate who had no interest in art and was changing the character of their room. Did I see any reason why they should not apply a few behavioral principles to convert him to modern art? I said I saw no harm if they agreed to tell him afterward what they had done.

They began by paying attention to him only when he mentioned their pictures or sculptures. They held a cocktail party and primed an attractive young woman to ask him about them. They sent his name to art galleries in Boston, which began to send him announcements of exhibits. A month or so later they came to report progress: he had suggested that they go to the Museum of Fine Arts on the following Sunday! At the museum it just "happened" that he found a five-dollar bill on the floor below a picture he had been looking at. It was not long before they came again in great excitement—to show me his first painting!

Another student, Joel Wolfson, invented what would later be called a token economy. He had worked as a counselor at a boys' camp in Pembroke, Massachusetts, and had found the boys hard to manage. The next summer, though skeptical, he decided to try operant conditioning. He bought ten dollars' worth of dime-store novelties and mimeographed some paper money which he called "Klugies." On the first day of camp he showed the boys the novelties and said they could be purchased with Klugies at a weekly sale. Then, in a casual way, he occasionally gave a Klugy to a boy who had done something useful—made a bed, carried out the rubbish, or hung up a sweater. Within a few days he had an almost perfect bunkhouse. The other counselors, envious of his easy life, tried their versions of reward. One of them promised his boys that if they behaved themselves he would take them to the village for ice cream sodas—predictably, without success.

With one exception, Joel made no contract with the boys; he simply dispensed a Klugy from time to time. The exception was a boy who, the preceding summer, had wet the bed every night. (His mother had sent thirty-five sheets to help solve the problem.) Joel told the boy that whenever he found his bed dry in the morning, he was to help himself to ten Klugies. He wet the bed only once that summer (possibly significantly, the night before his parents came to visit him).

*   *   *

AFTER THE KOREAN ARMISTICE in 1953, it was reported that many Americans in the United Nations forces had not fired at the enemy when they had had the chance. A soldier might hold his fire to avoid drawing fire in return, of course, but the problem seemed more serious. A psychiatrist consulted by the Army said that a soldier should be under the command of a strong father figure who told him to shoot. In a talk before the Connecticut Valley Psychological Society I had made fun of that solution. There was, I said, a better one, though I should not wish to participate in putting it into effect.

My scruples soon weakened, and I sent a white paper to Franklin Taylor. The training procedures were at fault because, strange as it might seem, they used positive rather than negative reinforcers. Instead of firing as accurately as possible on a rifle range for commendation or medals, trainees should fire to avoid aversive stimulation. For example, a soldier standing on a small platform would be pushed off into ice water if he did not stop an approaching object by hitting it in a vulnerable spot. As training proceeded, the spots would become smaller and the object would move faster and more deviously.

I did not hear from Franklin, but I learned later that the paper was taken seriously and was sent around to many people. Nothing was done, in part because, in April 1956, a Marine drill sergeant marched a group of recruits into a creek in South Carolina, killing six of them. It was not the time for a closer simulation of the battlefield.

SHERRINGTON, MAGNUS, AND PAVLOV, the physiologists I had chosen as models, had looked at the behavioral effects of a few well-known drugs, such as ether, caffeine, nicotine, strychnine, curare, and the bromides. At Minnesota, W. T. Heron and I, and a student of Heron's, Elaine Wentink, tried a few of the newer drugs, such as Benzedrine (which, like caffeine, greatly increased the rate of responding during periodic reconditioning and extinction) and phenobarbital (which, like the bromides, greatly reduced it).

49

In 1952 Henry Meadow, Executive Secretary of the Committee on Research and Development at the Medical School, introduced me to several people with whom he thought I might have interests in common. One of them was Otto Krayer, head of the Department of Pharmacology. Krayer was interested in the effects of bromides, and a young man in his department, Peter Dews, came to work in my laboratory. He fed pigeons a special diet in which sodium bromide replaced sodium chloride. He put them on a multiple FI5 FR50 schedule; when the key was red, the first response after five minutes was reinforced ("FI 5") and when the key was green, the fiftieth response was reinforced ("FR 50"). As the bromide became more concentrated, the pigeons began to stagger about the box. They seemed unable to respond to the red key, but they rapped out normal ratio curves on the green. There were similar effects with barbiturates and scopolamine. Within the year Krayer wrote that he was "anxious to make a more long-range commitment" for Peter Dews, and with one of our graduate students, William H. Morse, Peter was soon planning an extensive program at the Medical School. He continued to come to our Pigeon Staff meetings.

Charlie and I did a few drug experiments on our own. When a pigeon was showing a stable performance at the end of an experiment, it was easy enough to inject a drug and see what happened. When, in an experiment with rats, pressing a lever occasionally produced food and continually avoided a shock, chlorpromazine suppressed the food-reinforced responding but left the avoidance unaffected.

We tried to keep a pigeon at a constant level of sedation by using two food dispensers, in one of which the grain had been infused with sodium pentobarbital. We chose a criterion rate of responding on a variable-interval schedule. When the pigeon pecked faster than the criterion, it received food containing the drug at each reinforcement and soon began to peck more slowly. When its rate fell below the criterion, it received untreated food and soon pecked faster. Unfortunately, the drug did not act fast enough and the rate oscillated widely.

At the Boston University Medical School, the Atomic Energy Commission was supporting research on X-radiation, and Ogden Lindsley made an operant analysis of the effect on behavior. The subjects were beagles and, as with any new species, there were engineering problems to be solved. Dogs gnawed a lever (Clark Hull's "anticipatory goal response"?), but a panel pressed by nose or paw worked well.

After stable performances were reached under a few schedules of reinforcement (and suppressed in what Estes and I had called "anxiety"),
the dogs were given LD-50 doses of X-radiation and changes in their
performances were recorded.

SHORTLY AFTER the initiation of ORCON—the Navy's experimental
project on the use of pigeons for missile guidance—someone at General
Mills wrote that Project Pigeon had been declassified; could they at last
run the story in the company magazine? I checked with Frank Taylor.
Should I not also write an article for a national magazine as a smoke-
screen? No one would think the government was taking the thing seriously if it were published. But Frank reported that only the contract had
been declassified; the nature of the project must remain secret.

I continued to act as a consultant. I would go to Washington on
the sleeper, and Frank would join me for breakfast at the station. We
would spend the day at the Naval Research Laboratories, where an
engineer, R. M. Page, had invented a better way of picking up the
signal. A small gold tip was fitted to the pigeon's beak (refitted each
week as the beak grew), and the target was projected on a plate of
semiconducting glass. The position of each peck was instantly reported
on polar coordinates by electronic equipment, far from miniaturized. The
system was later used in the so-called Pick-Off Display Converter, with
which a human operator reports the position of a blip on a radar screen
simply by touching it with a stylus (held in the hand). Moving pictures
were taken from the nose of a plane diving toward a ship at sea, and
pigeons kept a simulated missile on that target quite satisfactorily.

Since other ways of controlling a missile were being discovered,
ORCON was discontinued in 1953. Frank's final report was sent to the
Boston Office of Naval Research to be forwarded to me, but Harvard
was having Joseph McCarthy trouble, and the Technical Information
Officer wrote, "This office has received classified printed material to be
forwarded to you at Harvard University. However, due to the present
security situation at Harvard, this activity is unable to effect transmittal."
I went to the office of the Inspector of Naval Materials in Boston and
read the report with a guard standing by. Years later, *The New Yorker*
got an endpiece out of it:

ORCON—U. S. Navy acronym for Organic Control, a program which would employ pigeons sealed inside a missile to guide the missile to its target. A re-inforcing reward mechanism would be used so that the pigeon would peck at a particular spot on a glass plate. An electrode on the bird's beak would complete an electrical circuit and furnish correction signals. Abandoned.—*Code Names Dictionary, published by the Gale Research Company, Detroit.*

Always somebody who's faint-hearted.

FOR MANY YEARS I had thought of studying the behavior of psychotic people. In the early thirties I had planned some research with David Shakow and Saul Rosenzweig at the Worcester State Hospital, but it was never finished. (Later they reported interesting results with the verbal summator, which they renamed the "tautophone.")

Soon after I returned to Harvard in 1948, I was asked to lecture at the Worcester State Hospital, and Dr. Jacob Finesinger invited me to participate in the Grand Rounds of the Department of Psychiatry at the Massachusetts General Hospital in Boston. Finesinger was a psychiatrist who had known both Pavlov and Freud. Dr. Raymond Adams, a neurologist at the Hospital, also said he hoped I would have some contact with his department. Unfortunately, I was too busy with other things to take advantage of these opportunities.

In 1952 Henry Meadow introduced me to Harry Solomon, Head of the Department of Psychiatry and Director of the Boston Psychopathic Hospital, where he had pioneered in advancing the freedom and dignity of psychotic patients. Doors were left unlocked wherever feasible. If patients could not be given matches, they could at least be spared the indignity of having to ask for a light if electric lighters were installed. I told Dr. Solomon about my interest in experimenting with psychotic subjects, and he persuaded the Superintendent of the Metropolitan State Hospital in Waltham, Massachusetts, to give us space for a laboratory. I asked for a small grant from the Office of Naval Research, which was then supporting the pigeon work, and one of our consultants from the Boston office, Roy Hoskins, who had been in charge of the Worcester State Hospital when Shakow and Rosenzweig were there, put in a word with Washington. We also received small grants from the Rockefeller Foundation and the Milton Fund at Harvard.

Og Lindsley had finished his work on irradiated dogs and joined the project. We installed modified vending machines in two small rooms, with cumulative recorders nearby. The patients assigned to us were men, from twenty-three to sixty-three years old, who had lived in the hospital for an average of twelve years. We offered each of them a tray containing candy, cigarettes, or coins, and put whatever he chose in the machine to be dispensed as a reinforcer. He was either allowed to explore the room and discover that pulling the plunger was reinforced or shown how it worked, and plunger-pulling was then reinforced. A variable-interval schedule gave fairly steady rates ranging from ten thousand responses per hour in a manic subject to none in a catatonic. A fixed-ratio schedule yielded cumulative records very much like those of lower organisms. Some patients gave an interval performance in one room and a ratio performance in another, a crude version of the multiple schedules that Charlie and I were studying.

Our first report appeared in November 1953 as "Studies in Behavior Therapy" (the first published use of the term). One page was devoted to Plans for Future Work. We could test hearing loss or visual defects in mute patients. We could study problem solving, concept formation, and other kinds of intellectual behavior. We could study social behavior by observing the rate of work when another patient was present or absent, when another patient received half of each reinforcement, or when another patient was working on a similar apparatus, either cooperatively or competitively. When pictures of nude women were projected on a screen as reinforcers, some patients showed "guilt," and with a second plunger which turned off the experiment, we could follow them as they learned to "avoid temptation."

A last item read as follows:

> Practically every one of these proposals is related to "therapy." . . . In a broad sense we have already produced the kind of change required. . . .

As our experiments are extended to more and more complex behavior, we should be in a position to undertake in many cases the particular kinds of change in behavior needed to bring about recovery.

We reported our results in a paper called "A New Method for the Experimental Analysis of the Behavior of Psychotic Patients" at a meeting of the Massachusetts Society for Research in Psychiatry the following April. A psychiatrist, asked to comment, agreed that we had definitely shifted the "ratio of non-psychotic to psychotic behavior during a one-hour period," and that our research was a "magnificent pilot study that initiates a long and promising research program," but he had reservations:

> The experimenters use the terms "organism" and "control" quite as though they were still dealing with lower animals—or at least with an isolated nervous system. Personal elements are reduced as close to zero as possible. Presumably, the machine in the patient responds to the machine in the environment. Since we do not know what the patients *think* or *feel* in the process, the graphs, curves and other methods of quantification have little meaning in terms of *human* response as compared to lower animals.

Another psychiatrist thought that much of what we had demonstrated could be seen in current practices in psychiatric hospitals, and since patients would be going out into the real world where "monetary incentive" was important, "its use as a reinforcing agent was important," but "the incentives of normal social living" should also be provided.

In reply, Og pointed out that we had constructed simplified contingencies to shape effective behavior but that once the behavior had been set up, it should work in more complex settings. We also had plans for studying social behavior. People *were* different from rats or pigeons, but we should never know how different until we had studied them as we studied the other species. There had been a suggestion that we were working with our subjects without their permission, but Og made it clear that not only were they never coerced, they often hurried to the experimental quarters.

We were not the first to try operant reinforcement on a defective human organism. In 1949 a graduate student at Indiana University,

Paul Fuller, had successfully conditioned a fifty-pound "vegetative idiot," which had lain on its back and been fed only liquids and semi-solids for eighteen years. It could open its mouth but could not swallow well; it blinked and moved its arms, head, and shoulders slightly. At irregular intervals, it had clonic seizures.

With a warm sugar-milk solution injected into the mouth as a reinforcer, Fuller shaped lifting the right arm to a nearly vertical position, beginning with slight movements and reaching the final topography through successive approximation. The subject eventually responded about three times a minute, immediately opening its mouth for the reinforcer after doing so. When injections were stopped, responding continued at the same rate for thirty minutes and then declined; at the end of seventy minutes extinction was essentially complete. According to the attending physician, it was the first thing the creature had learned in eighteen years. When Fuller published his report, the editor deleted the section on shaping through successive approximation as an irrelevant detail.

In 1953 the Boston Society of Biologists organized a symposium titled "A Scientific Approach to Human Behavior." Smitty Stevens was master of ceremonies, and I was on the panel with Lawrence Kubie, Mark Altschule, and Norbert Wiener, whom I had met when we appeared together on a Lowell Institute radio program called "What Is Mind?" We were to have dinner at the Faculty Club to plan the evening, and when I arrived, Wiener, Stevens, and Altschule were waiting in the lobby. Kubie soon joined us. He greeted Wiener warmly.

"I suppose you will soon be off to the meeting of the Cybernetics Society," he said.

Wiener drew himself up, inflated his chest, and shouted, "I will not! I will not associate with bounders!" He turned away and started to go home. (The Cybernetics Society had been formed without consulting him.) Smitty took him aside and pointed out that the auditorium would be full of biologists who had come just to hear him, and it would be unfair to disappoint them. Wiener agreed to stay, but ate his dinner sullenly.

Kubie was shaken, of course, and he was to suffer further vexations. He had come up from Yale by train after an exhausting day, and during Altschule's paper he dozed off. At one point the audience laughed. Kubie woke up and seemed to think that they were laughing at him. He was in no mood to hear my presentation. It was a standard behavioristic line: We were looking in the wrong place for explanations of human behavior—in mental or psychic states rather than in genetic and environmental histories. Since those histories were needed to explain the mental states, nothing was gained. Freud had made a contribution in showing the relevance of early events in a person's history, but "by emphasizing an inner life as the object of study he put science back fifty years." When I finished, Kubie jumped to his feet.

"I am distressed," he said, "to think that this is the kind of thing that is told to Harvard students!" And he sat down, to a stony silence.

I tried to make a joke of it. "I don't know how Dr. Kubie finds students at Yale," I said, "but we have learned that it doesn't much matter what we tell Harvard students."

He was not to be appeased. He jumped up again. "That confirms my belief," he said, "that every professor should be forced once a year to read Stephen Leacock's essay on 'The Misuses of Academic Humor.'" And he sat down again. The audience was stunned.

I refused to bail him out, and after an awkward pause the symposium continued. When it was over, a member of the audience said to me, "I want you to know that I think the chairman should have reproved Kubie for that remark." Kubie left the meeting without saying goodbye to anyone, but he regretted the lapse. A week later, he sent me a copy of a letter to Smitty Stevens reading in part:

A discussion of what each discipline could contribute to the scientific techniques of the other would make a less entertaining cat and dog fight; but as you may have gathered from my irritation at academic humor (God save the mark) I am not impressed either by public caterwauling nor by wisecracking as devices to seduce the immature mind instead of informing it.

This was scarcely an apology, but whenever we met afterwards, he recalled that evening, and he sent me copies of his subsequent books. By 1961, when he had become Director of Training at the Sheppard and Enoch Pratt Hospital, we were using first names. He invited Eve and me to visit him there and wrote to tell me how much he had enjoyed *Walden Two*, although he felt I had not considered "the fate of the indigenous components of the neurotic process."

CHARLES ANDERSON SENT ME my first copy of *Science and Human Behavior* in January 1953. I had dedicated the book to Fred Keller, but rather ungraciously I wrote him: "The publishers seemed willing to give you a copy, so I let them pick up the tab. I wish you would bring the copy to Cambridge when you come in April, however, because I should like to inscribe it appropriately." Fred wrote back: "Our desk copies of *Science and Human Behavior* came today. George Renaud, one of our assistants, brought my copy to me on his way home from the lab. As he ran up our front steps, I asked him how it looked. He said he didn't know, that he had seen only one page—which he then showed to me. When he left we all looked at it, including John and Anne, until Frances told me to stop crying! Then I gave a lecture on *What a wonderful book this is* to all who would listen. It *is* a fine book, Burrhus, and I'm proud to be in it. I'll never receive a greater honor. Thank you very much." I replied: "Your note will go in a very special file where it will keep company with half a dozen letters I have received over the past twenty-eight years. The first in the series was from Robert Frost and somehow or other yours gives me the same kind of feeling. I have a little amplification of the dedication which I want to write in your copy when you come up."

Not everyone shared Fred's enthusiasm, but Frank Finger, reviewing a current crop of introductory texts, treated *Science and Human Behavior* well as a surprise entry. It was "unacceptable for widespread classroom adoption," but "its consideration should force us to scrutinize closely whatever faith underlies our practice in the first course. . . . What happens to all the time-honored observations and principles that we have come to know as general psychology? If the unsupplemented classroom use of *Science and Human Behavior* is precluded by limitations of curriculum and clientele, its assimilation by the serious teacher is most appropriate. . . . When the student finishes Skinner (or vice-versa), he will be aware that he has been up against something, whether good or bad."

57

Other friends rallied around. Herbert Feigl, one of the "philosophes" I had known at Minnesota, reported that he was reading the book "with genuine excitement, delight, and enormous intellectual profit." Charlie Curtis, characteristically rhapsodic, wrote:

> . . . All I am quite sure of as yet is that if I prayed I'd raise my head instead of my hands and [say?] that you are God (may He save the mark!) when you push the button and let drop the manna. You are an intellectual therapist and I am sweating out more tautologies than I ever thought I had. You are a Hume to the believer, a Holmes to the lawyer. . . .

Leonard Carmichael (about to move from the presidency of Tufts University to the Smithsonian Institution), writing in the *Boston Sunday Post*, called it "a landmark in the study of human behavior. Future historians of this aspect of science are almost certain to refer to it when most other books in psychology published in the last ten years have been forgotten."

A reviewer in the journal *Ethics* said that *Science and Human Behavior* was "a splendid example of the truly vast extent to which a behavioristic approach to human behavior and action can deal with the subject," and a sociologist writing in the *American Journal of Sociology* called it "an important book, logically consistent with the basic premise of the unitary nature of science."

Garry was helpful. He wrote:

> Because SCI & HUM BEH seemed so important to me, I wrote Girden to urge him to give it a specially competent reviewer for the Psychol. Bull. and to let it have lots of space. This got him and Wayne [Dennis] excited over the book. I suggested Hilgard, but Girden says he is doing some other big job for the Psychol. Bull. Girden assures me that they now have a competent reviewer. He does not say who.

Garry was nevertheless unhappy about the language of the book. For him the issue was not mentalism but determinism, and he wrote:

> I think it would be good for me to say here in writing what I am thinking about the freedom-determinism antinomy, especially in respect of you. I want to get myself clear, and this will help me. I am not trying to influence you, but I do want you to have me clear.

Your SCI & HUM BEH seems to me to be ever so important because it is the first book to put this deterministic view clearly all through—except that it is not written in deterministic language. I hope it gets reviewed thoroughly, and I hope also that this basic point of mine does not get missed entirely. I think of the book as like Hume's positivistic account which awoke Kant later to lead philosophers away to the a priori and moral responsibility. I'd like to see a Kant try you, but better to have someone try the synthesis that I try to get here—someone who could do it better than I can.

As an example, he sent me dittoed sheets that he was passing out to his seminar. I had begun by quoting Francesco Lana's belief that God would not permit the invention of an airship because it could be used to destroy cities. Where I then went on: "Contrary to his expectation, God has suffered this invention to take effect," Garry wrote: "Contrary to his expectation, history now records the fact that this invention was finally made." Where I continued: "And so has Man. The story emphasizes the irresponsibility with which science and the products of science have been used," Garry had: "Man made it. The story shows that not every bit of historical advance is such as to benefit man and favor his survival." And where I had: "Man's power appears to have increased out of all proportion to his wisdom," Garry had: "Social evolution increases man's power out of proportion to its increase of his ability to use those powers only for his own good."

It was the behaviorist's dilemma. If I had confined myself to terms and locutions which not only did not imply freedom of action but also did not allude to mental processes, the book would have been awkward and almost unreadable for purposes of normal discourse. I had learned to say "What do you have in mind?" without wincing. Why should I bother to ask the question in behavioristic terms? The physicist who talks with his machinist about the construction of an apparatus refers to physical things in terms which raise the ghosts of old theories, but to do anything else would be foolish. Terms referring to mind and its attributes should be redefined in a science, but they were still useful in daily life. Garry continued:

Mike [Elliott] wrote me one sentence about Sci & Hum Beh. It's hardly fair to quote it since it needs a context he did not supply, but it was this. "Did you ever know a perfect solipsist, except Fred Skinner?"

And that's it. You write as if you felt free and as if you did not feel you were expressing a delusion. The book could be redone in the language of determinism, and most of the excitement would leave it. That's why I amused myself awhile trying to get clear on this matter by translating sentences or paragraphs into deterministic language.

I had learned my operationism from Percy Bridgman, but evidently not well enough. When he saw the manuscript of *Science and Human Behavior*, he caught me up on two subtle points. He wrote:

> *I think it would be better in discussing the principle of indeterminacy to say that relevant information does not exist than to say we cannot put ourselves in possession of it. And I would not like to say, as seems implied, that science has to assume that the universe is lawful and determined, but rather that science proceeds by exploiting those lawfulnesses that it can discover. Anything smacking of faith I think we can get along without.*

As I wrote to a friend, I had "not had the nerve" to use *Walden Two* in my classes as she had done, but after putting *Brave New World* and *1984* on my reading list for a year or two, I added my own projection of the future. And now *Science and Human Behavior* was ready as a text, and I was embarrassed by asking my students to read (if not buy) two of my own books. When I assigned them, I read a paragraph from Max Shulman's *Barefoot Boy with Cheek* in which a professor of sociology named Schultz gives his students a list of the eight books they will need for the course—all of them by Schultz, including A *Bibliography of Schultz's Treatises on Sociology for College Freshmen.*

My multiple-choice examinations were still causing trouble, but reading blue books exhausted me, and I knew that my standards changed as I read them, and so I continued to use multiple-choice questions. Over the years I had prepared 299 of them and I now gave them all to the students before the final examination, with a warning that half the items on the examination would be new. As a result, as I wrote to Fred, "My students are going over the text more thoroughly and mulling over the main points more energetically. Whether I get a discrimination remains, of course, to be seen."

* * *

I SUMMARIZED MY LECTURES in Psychology 7 (the course that later became Natural Sciences 114) in this way: "Many people feel that a scientific interpretation damages the dignity of man—and contradicts any larger purpose in human behavior. But we have always succeeded in adjusting to new facts which question the pre-eminence of man. The application of science to the field of human behavior may place the human intellect in a very different light, but we may be consoled by the fact that it constitutes still another achievement of that intellect."

Not all my students made the adjustment or found consolation. Were people not free to determine the course of their own lives? Did they not deserve credit for their achievements? Some students were seriously troubled, and, as the issue became clearer, a few of them turned up each year at the Health Services—where, I learned later, a "Natural Sciences 114 Syndrome" was identified.

My treatment of religion was part of the problem. The summary of my lecture in Psychology 7 read in part:

> We may discuss the practical techniques of religion without questioning the authority of any religious agency or the truth of any claim regarding the nature or destiny of the soul. In general, religious control is exerted to weaken "selfish" behavior. Gluttony is classified as a sin, chastity as a virtue, poverty as better than riches, the modest man as preferable to the Pharisee, passivity as better than aggression. . . . [Controlling techniques include:] physical restraint (Moslem control of the behavior of certain classes of women) and the elimination of stimuli responsible for objectionable behavior (the cloistered life or censorship or prohibition in the world at large). Drives are reduced through permissible activities (for St. Paul, marriage . . . for the YMCA, sports). . . . The principal technique of control, however, is punishment or the threat of punishment. Desirable behavior is positively reinforced by a release from threat (absolution, being "saved").

At one time I heard that Catholics in the Boston diocese were advised not to take my course, and those who took it sometimes let me know what they thought. One of them wrote:

May I be permitted to make a few remarks privately regarding your lecture on religious control and the techniques employed? . . . By making this excellent exposé, what ultimate good, in the way of human action or of enhancement of knowledge, can be achieved? Or is it possible that more harm may be produced? . . . My observation of possible harm is substantiated in part by the number of hard-boiled cynics I have met, who have evidently gone through your mill, or of those of a similar mode of thinking. And we know too well what often happens to such people in later life—witness your disloyals and sex perverts in the State Department, to cite only one problem. [Those were McCarthy days.]

I preferred a letter like this:

After learning that I had passed your course (it was nip and tuck all the way) I had a talk with you about your theories. You might possibly remember that as a Catholic I opposed many of your ideas. Yet I have remembered them and discussed them with a number of people, 99% of whom either looked aghast, swore, ended the conversation, or else wondered what Harvard was coming to. . . .

. . . Call this a latent letter of appreciation. I believe your course to be one of the top courses offered at Harvard. I must admit that if I had failed it, then the stimulus would have probably evoked a different response.

The conflict was usually resolved without too much trouble. When I once saw two of my Radcliffe students coming out of the basement of Memorial Church after a service, I pretended to be shocked. "*What* have you been doing?" I demanded. "We've been *singing!*" said one; "We get *paid* for it!" said the other.

And I could tell my critics that Natural Sciences 114 was said to send more students on to the Divinity School than any other undergraduate course.

IT WAS SAID that prisoners of war in Korea were being "brainwashed." The term was apparently a translation from the Chinese, but as a Communist practice the press quickly associated it with Pavlov and coined the term "pavlovize." I drafted a letter to the *New York Times*:

As scientists actively engaged in the study of conditioned reflexes, we wish to protest the current misuse of the name of I. P. Pavlov. The greater part of Pavlov's work on conditioning was done prior to the communist regime, and he was frequently called to account by that regime for expressing unsympathetic views. It is only within the last two or three years that the Soviets have attempted to make a Russian hero of him and this has been done for obviously nationalistic purposes. Although we can do nothing to change their policy, we can make an effort to prevent a similar misrepresentation elsewhere in the world. . . . Communist techniques in dealing with military and political prisoners (in particular, the so-called "brainwashing") have nothing in common with the experimental procedures of Pavlov, or the processes discovered by him. . . . If Pavlov had not been Russian, or if his name were not now used politically by the Russians, it would never occur to anyone to think of his work when presented with the facts concerning the treatment of prisoners. . . . To make a Communist hero of Pavlov is absurd and unfair. It is equally absurd and unfair to make him a scapegoat.

I sent the letter to Howard Liddell, and he signed it and sent it on to Horsley Gantt, at Johns Hopkins, who added a quotation in which Pavlov disclaimed any application of his results to human behavior. I sent it to the *Times*, but they did not publish it. Instead, a few months later, they published an article by a psychiatrist, Jan Meerloo, called "Pavlov's Dog and Communist Brain Washing," which only made matters worse. I wrote to ask whether they would like an article "giving a rather different slant on Pavlov and his work." They suggested, instead, a Letter to the Editor.

IN PSYCHOLOGY 7, I summarized my lecture on education in this way:

Some agency (parent, group, school) provides an arbitrary reinforcement for behavior which is later to be followed by "natural" or at least "noneducational" consequences. . . . Marks, grades, promotion, diplomas . . . are made contingent upon behavior which (it says here) will eventually be useful [for other reasons]. . . .

That parenthetical "it says here" reflected my unhappiness not only about my course but about education as a whole. I had failed to apply a technology of behavior to my own field.

My own education had been uneventful. I studied most subjects because I liked them, and a disciplined childhood saved me from trouble with the few I studied "because I had to." I did not look back on that history as ideal, and education in Walden Two was different; the community was a teaching environment. "The motives in education," says Frazier, "are the motives in all human behavior. Education should be only life itself." My chapter on education in *Science and Human Behavior* began: "In an American school if you ask for the salt in good French, you get an A. In France you get the salt." And the A was probably reinforcing only as an escape from a threat of punishment. Students studied to avoid the consequences of not studying.

I knew how true that was of my daughters, but I had never felt that I should interfere in their schooling. I once wrote to the director of the Shady Hill School to protest a new assignment of homework: "It was something of a blow to learn that Julie will be expected to put in on the average two hours every evening. This extends her [school] day to nearly nine hours, or something over a forty-hour week. I cannot believe that the work of the ninth grade requires that much time. . . ."

On November 11, 1953, I made a more positive move. It was Fathers' Day at Shady Hill, and with a few other fathers I sat in the rear of Debbie's fourth-grade arithmetic class. The students were at their desks solving a problem written on the blackboard. The teacher walked up and down the aisles, looking at their work, pointing to a mistake here and there. A few students soon finished and were impatiently idle. Others, with growing frustration, strained. Eventually the papers were collected to be taken home, graded, and returned the next day.

I suddenly realized that something had to be done. Possibly through no fault of her own, the teacher was violating two fundamental principles: the students were not being told at once whether their work was right or wrong (a corrected paper seen twenty-four hours later could not act as a reinforcer), and they were all moving at the same pace regardless of preparation or ability.

But how could a teacher reinforce the behavior of each of twenty or thirty students at the right time and on the material for which he or she was just then ready? I had solved a similar problem in the laboratory. When I was a graduate student, almost all animal psychologists watched their animals and recorded their behavior by hand. They could make only a few observations, many of them not too reliable. Mechanization had made a great difference. Charlie Ferster and I could have done only a small fraction of our work on schedules if we had not used instruments. If students were to learn at once whether their responses were right or wrong, and if the responses were to be those for which they were best prepared at the moment, instrumentation was needed.

A few days later, I built a primitive teaching machine. Problems in arithmetic were printed on cards. The student placed a card in the machine and composed a two-digit answer along one side by moving two levers. If the answer was right, a light appeared in a hole in the card. In a second model, the student moved sliders bearing the figures o through 9, a figure on each slider appearing through a hole in the card. If a composed answer was correct, lights appeared in a corresponding row of holes when a lever was pressed. (To make sure that the student would not move the sliders to search for the right answer, pressing the lever locked them in place.)

In a still more sophisticated model, problems were printed on a pleated tape and appeared one at a time in a fixed order. Again, figures could be exposed through holes by moving sliders. When all the holes were filled, a knob was turned and if the answer was right, a new frame moved into place. If the answer was wrong, the knob would not turn and the student had to return the sliders to zero and start again. I listed the features of the machine in a note:

> The student composes rather than selects the answers. Unlike flash cards, the machine reports the correctness of an answer without revealing the answer. The student must solve one problem before moving on to the next. The student cannot look back or forward to get help from other problems. The principal reinforcing consequences come from being right and making progress. [I had added a bell which rang as a new frame moved into place and I noted that this event could be scheduled.] The student must stop at the end of the tape for a teacher's review and for the loading of a new tape.

These were not my first teaching machines. At a Christmas party in the Department in 1950, I produced a play in the tradition of the travesties staged by the graduate students. My characters were perfectly cast: Stanley Smith Stevens played Stanley Steamer, E. G. Boring played E. G. Roaring, and so on. Act II, Scene I went as follows:

Professor Skinneybox is at his desk, reading a copy of *Esquire* [twenty years later it would have been *Playboy*]. Barrelbottom, a new graduate student, enters and clears his throat as Professor S. goes on reading. Professor S. sees him, puts down *Esquire*, takes a form and writes as he asks questions.

Professor S.: Your name?

Barrelbottom: Barrelbottom.

Prof. S.: Sit down, Barrelbottom *(points to chair in middle of stage. Barrelbottom sits down, lets out a yell and jumps up again.)* Oh, sorry *(flicks a switch on his desk)*, didn't know it was on. Sit down, it won't hurt you now. *(Barrelbottom tenderly sits down.)*

Prof. S. (in a smooth, professional manner, and operating a couple of switches on his desk from time to time): Now, Barrelbottom, we are here to learn psychology, right?

Barrelbottom: Right. *(A vending machine on the wall makes a noise. Barrelbottom jumps and then regains his seat.)*

Prof. S.: It's quite all right, Barrelbottom. Peanuts. Help yourself. *(Barrelbottom takes a couple of peanuts from the machine and eats them.)* You want to be a graduate student in psychology, right?

Barrelbottom: Right. *(The vending machine operates and Barrelbottom takes another peanut.)*

Prof. S.: What are your interests?

Barrelbottom: Well, sir, I want to be a psychologist.

Prof. S.: You want to be a psychologist?

Barrelbottom: Right. *(The vending machine makes a noise; Barrelbottom looks in, but finds nothing. Slightly embarrassed:)* I guess it isn't working, sir.

Prof. S.: That's what you think! Now what particular branch of psychology?

Barrelbottom: Well, I'm sort of interested in clinical . . . *(He lets out a whoop as he jumps into the air.)*

Prof. S.: Sit down, Barrelbottom, sit down. Now let's see, what are your fields of interest?

Barrelbottom: Well, sir, I've always thought education was kind of . . . *(lets out another yell and jumps up again.)*

Prof. S.: Sit down, sit down, Barrelbottom.

Barrelbottom: Then there's what they call this Experimental Psychology.

66

(The vending machine makes a great noise and Barrelbottom eats about five peanuts.)

Prof. S.: Good, Barrelbottom, that's excellent. You're making progress. Now I am going to make a little change in the situation. *(Carries a typewriter over and puts it on a table in front of Barrelbottom.)* So far, you've been talking to me, but that's expensive. You don't really need me. The whole thing can be done by machine. I want you to type out the next answer. What particular field of Experimental Psychology are you interested in? *(Prof. S. goes back to his desk: Barrelbottom pokes about seven or eight letters with his right hand only. Then he jumps up a bit and says "Sorry," moves the carriage back and strikes out seven or eight letters, then types another word, whereupon the vending machine rattles, and he eats a couple of peanuts.)* Now let's see if we can't bring that left hand into it. *(He takes a rubber hose connected with the vending machine and puts it in Barrelbottom's mouth. Barrelbottom now starts to type, rather hesitantly, with both hands. Occasionally he bounces off the chair; occasionally he stops to chew a bit. Prof. S. goes back to his* Esquire.)

IN 1948 the American Psychological Association had met in Boston, and I had arranged a special meeting of the Conference on the Experimental Analysis of Behavior, in Memorial Hall. The following year we met in June at Columbia. Just before the Boston meeting of the Eastern Psychological Association in April 1953 I arranged a somewhat more formal "Seminar in Procedures and Methods in the Study of Operant Behavior." About 150 people attended. The program gives a fair idea of work at that time. Charlie Ferster discussed "Techniques in the study of schedules of reinforcement," Lawrence Weiskrantz, "Problems connected with the use of monkeys as subjects in operant conditioning," Og Lindsley, "Quantitative aspects of a time sample of behavior in the dog," Floyd Ratliff, "Operant techniques in studying perception in lower organisms," James Anliker (a new graduate student in the department), "Experiments involving monkeys as subjects," Edward Green, "Operant behavior in human subjects," Joe Brady and Murray Sidman, "Monkeys and cats as experimental animals," Sidman, "Procedural problems in the study of avoidance behavior," Herb Jenkins, "Human operant behavior," Doug Anger, "Measures of activity and their relation to operant behavior," Joe Antonitis, "Operant behavior in children," and I, "The effect of the apparatus in selecting properties of operant behavior."

THE UNIVERSITY OF PITTSBURGH invited me to speak at a conference on the practical applications of behavioral science and, excited about teaching machines, I asked whether I could discuss education. My paper, called "The Science of Learning and the Art of Teaching," began with a review of the achievements of the experimental analysis of behavior. We had taken the Law of Effect seriously by making sure that effects *did* occur and in such a way that behavior was changed. "From this exciting prospect . . . it is a great shock to turn to that branch of technology which is most directly concerned with the learning process—education."

The reinforcers in education were still aversive—not necessarily the birch rod or cane, but "the teacher's displeasure, the criticism or ridicule of classmates, an ignominious showing in a competition, low marks, a trip to the office 'to be talked to' by the principal, or a word to a parent who might still resort to the birch rod." The consequences were predictable: truancy, school vandalism, and stubborn inaction. Fortunately something could be done. Effective positive reinforcers were available. The sheer control of nature (as in getting a right answer) was reinforcing. It might not be too powerful, but even a weak reinforcer was tremendously effective when properly used. The process of becoming competent in a given field could be divided into a very large number of small steps, and if almost every step were correctly taken, the positive reinforcement derived from success would be raised to a maximum.

There was a practical problem. Since many pupils were taught by the same teacher, the total number of contingencies which could be arranged during, say, the first four years, was of the order of a few thousand. "But a very rough estimate suggests that efficient mathematical behavior at this level requires something of the order of 25,000 steps." The result was well known: even our best schools were being criticized for their inefficiency in teaching drill subjects such as arithmetic.

The solution was instrumentation. "We have every reason to expect . . . that the most effective control of human learning will require instrumental aid." As a mere reinforcing mechanism, the teacher was out of date. "Marking a set of papers in arithmetic—'Yes, 9 and 6 are 15; no, 9 and 7 are not 18'—is beneath the dignity of any intelligent person." With the help of a machine, the teacher would begin to experience "the distinctive intellectual, cultural, and emotional effects which testify to her status as a human being."

My machine was on the platform, and I explained how it worked. A graduate student in the audience heard a professor of education say to a colleague, "He's kidding!"

My paper was published in the *Harvard Educational Review*, and that summer, at a conference on policies governing the study of education, I was asked to debate the issue with Howard Mumford Jones, professor of English at Harvard and author of several books on education. Our title, "Human Education and the Science of Learning," was not far from that of my paper. Jones was on the side of art; machines could never have the "gusto" of good teachers. I agreed that *de gusto non disputandum est* but insisted that most teachers needed help, and that a science of behavior could supply it. The moderator, Francis Keppel, Dean of the Graduate School of Education, had already given me support for the teaching machines, but the discussants, Max Black and Israel Scheffler, were clearly on Jones's side.

That figure of 25,000 steps was a guess, but it was not an unreasonable one, as I discovered when I began to program arithmetic in earnest. As I wrote to a friend, Julian Stanley, in July:

> . . . I have constructed experimental frames beginning with the numbers o and 1, then constructing the numbers 2, 3, 4, and 5, one at a time, and working out the notions of adding, subtracting, multiplying, and dividing with spatial arrangements for the concepts of more and less, the notions of odd, even, and prime numbers, and so on. In constructing such a series, one discovers that what seems like a single step can be broken into several, and one turns up with perhaps 300 or 400 frames before reaching the stage of constructing the number 6—and all of this without any repetitive drill.

Sidney L. Pressey, of Ohio State University, read about my teaching machine in *Science News Letter*, and wrote: "It has long been my belief that mechanical devices in schools were as feasible as in banks, and when I saw your pigeon demonstrations at the Cleveland meeting last year, I wondered if something of this sort was not in the offing. I shall expect to see a busy child in a similar display case in New York this September." He also sent a package of reprints. The first, published in 1926, was called "A Simple Apparatus Which Gives Tests and Scores —and Teaches." The student was rewarded for right answers with candy. A second article, published in 1927, was called "A Machine for Automatic Teaching of Drill Material." The student read questions and selected multiple-choice answers by pressing numbered keys. "When he presses the right key, the drum revolves and turns up a new question; the question is kept before the subject, however, . . . until the right answer is found." After the subject has gone through the series twice, "the apparatus skips the questions which on both first and second trials were answered at once—without the pressing of a wrong key. . . . After every item has been mastered to this point, the apparatus automatically stops and releases a small coupon, indicative of the fact that the exercise has been mastered." In "A Third and Fourth Contribution Toward the Coming 'Industrial Revolution' in Education," published in 1932, Pressey described a simpler self-scoring device and reported that a "commercial testing machine for testing and teaching" was being manufactured.

I had not known of Pressey's work. Obviously, he had been a generation ahead of me in saying that machines would help both the teacher and the student—particularly the student, who was "automatically rewarded for good scores" and for whom "the amount of practice on each item was adjusted to the extent of the student's mastery." At the meeting of the American Psychological Association that fall I had breakfast with Pressey and his wife, and we had an exciting discussion. In the last of his papers on teaching machines he had reported his discouragement and his decision to withdraw from the field, but we agreed that a brighter future lay ahead.

IF TEACHING MACHINES were to be used in schools, a company would have to manufacture them. Frank Keppel spoke to a Harvard officer, who suggested that an alumnus, Sherman Fairchild, might help. (The officer was interested in Fairchild because he was a wealthy man without heirs who had never done much for Harvard; it was not until twenty-five years later that Harvard got five million from the Fairchild Foundation for its biochemistry laboratory.) The approach was made through another prominent alumnus in New York. Fairchild was a member of the board of IBM, and he simply turned the matter over to the company. In September I received a letter expressing interest in the machine, with a form routinely sent to those who wished to disclose ideas or inventions. Since they were coming to me, I saw no reason why I should sign it, but I was told that I should have to do so unless I intended to file a patent application, in which case they would wait.

I had taken a model of the machine to the most prestigious firm of patent lawyers in Boston. The man I showed it to could scarcely conceal his amusement, and he turned me over to a younger colleague, who set about drawing up an application. I did not want to wait until it was ready for filing and therefore agreed that any ideas at a meeting with IBM "would not create a confidential relationship." Two officers came to Cambridge, and by November an oral agreement had been reached: the company would look into the possibilities of manufacturing a machine (suitable for spelling as well as arithmetic), and I would try to find a foundation to support the development of programs.

Charlie and I were working hard on our book, but in November I found time for a lecture called "An Experimental Psychologist Looks at Education" and later that month spoke on "The Machine Age in Education" at Northwestern University (where I had planned to speak on "The Ethics of Controlling Behavior"). In December the *New York Herald Tribune* listed teaching machines among the achievements of the year.

SHORTLY AFTER MY fiftieth birthday I wrote a note:

> May 5, 1954, 10:30 A.M. Home with a cold, listening to Bruckner's 4th, in a mood for inventory.
> *Family.* Relation to *Eve* never better. Mistakes have been made by both of us. These have led to better understanding. Eve's life becoming more interesting with children growing up. Less distrust of assertion of

our own interests. Growing mutual tolerance of foibles, interests, etc.

Julie seems in fine shape. Putney has been just right. Quite mature for a high school sophomore. Intellectually adequate(!) Musical interests. Adjusted socially.

Debbie improves rapidly. School difficulties question of motivation not intelligence. Gradually coming through. Immature socially. Too dependent on me. But prognosis good.

Mother: Increasing difficulty in maintaining good relations but not very large part of my time.

Finances: Salary not enough for educating girls at present standard. College will be costly. Hence dependent upon mother. Alternative: more writing that will pay off, or lower standards for us all. Retirement provisions not adequate because of late start. Plan to retire early depends upon mother. Alternative: stay on as long as possible. Job elsewhere after forced retirement here. Or—successful writing.

Profession: Three well known & respected books. Two more in process. Prospects of research funds for future excellent. Preferred field: Education. (Medical [psychotherapeutic and pharmacological] aspects are in good hands.) Other preferred areas: complex arrangements of responses in HMP [Higher Mental Processes] with implications for epistemology & personal dynamics.

Department: No longer of interest as result of recent appointment. Doubt whether [psychology] will be important at Harvard. Possibly blessing in disguise. Better to emphasize non-local issues. Relative isolation, possibly in Education, can be arranged. [I had asked Frank Keppel about moving to the School of Education. He did not think I would like it.]

Teaching: Enjoy and believe in Nat Sci 114. Question of [General Education] up in air, however. Not interested in Psych 1. May drop all undergraduate teaching. Interest in developing post-doctoral apprenticeships.

Broader interests. Interpretation of human behavior in ethics, government, religion, law. Growing interest in this is clear. Fictional treatment possible. Articles for Harper-type publication, etc.

Recreation: Has suffered because of fast pace recently. Piano only occasionally of interest. Listening to music still reinforcing but unresolving. Might go back to painting or sculpture. Sailing satisfying but limited to 1½ months. French novel [Constant, Stendhal, Balzac] still of special interest.

Social: Heavily professionally oriented; possibly as result of rapid pace also. Easier contacts. Much larger circle of professional acquaintances. No interest in other social contacts.

*   *   *

SURPRISES WERE still turning up in our research. In *The Behavior of Organisms* I had pointed out that interval schedules tended to reinforce when the rate of responding was low and ratio schedules when it was high. Interval schedules therefore generated moderate rates, ratio schedules high ones. (It was this explanation that Eleanor Maccoby had checked with her experiment on "drh"—the differential reinforcement of high rate.) Charlie and I missed the point when we incorrectly predicted the effect of what we called a "limited hold." On a variable-interval schedule a pigeon responds fairly steadily, and occasional reinforcements are set up by a slowly moving tape. Suppose, now, that a reinforcer remains available for only a few seconds. If the pigeon does not respond during that time, it will miss the reinforcement. The rate of responding should then drop and that would mean even more misses. We predicted a kind of prolonged extinction in which "the schedule would lose the pigeon." The result was very different. The pigeon missed a few reinforcements, but *only when it was responding rather slowly*; the reinforcers it did receive were therefore contingent on relatively high rates. It began to respond more rapidly. A limited hold was a kind of *drh*.

PART OF THE TIME Charlie and I worked as Baconians. On large sheets of paper we drew up tables showing schedules programmed by clocks or counters, the ratios or numbers fixed or variable, with two or more schedules in effect simultaneously or in succession, correlated or uncorrelated with colors on the keys, and so on. We strove for a fairly systematic coverage. If we added *drh* to a variable-interval schedule with good results, it was time to add it to a fixed-interval.

At other times we were Galileans; we had a theory. Unless our pigeons had extrasensory perception (a possibility we dismissed), their only contact with the programming equipment came at the moment of reinforcement. But a number of stimuli were acting at that moment corresponding to readings on a speedometer (the bird had been responding at a given rate), a clock (a certain amount of time had passed since the last reinforcement or some other event), and a counter (a given number of responses had been made since the last reinforcement). We designed our experiments to give these stimuli a chance to make their presence known.

Békésy had developed a method of testing auditory sensitivity in which subjects reported whether or not they could hear a faint tone as it changed pitch slowly over a wide range. Floyd Ratliff, a physiological psychologist in the department at the time, and a graduate student, Donald Blough, adapted the Békésy technique to pigeons. Their pigeons drew dark-adaptation curves showing the transition from cone to rod vision.

Two graduate students, Bill Morse and Richard Herrnstein, were exploring many new lines. They found that intermittent schedules of reinforcement could be aversive and that a pigeon would terminate an experiment if it could do so by pecking a second key. (Why did it not simply stop responding?) Another graduate student, Edward Green, did his thesis on operant behavior in human subjects under Bill Verplanck's direction.

At the meeting of the American Psychological Association in Cleveland in 1953, Charlie and I set up the demonstration mentioned by Pressey in which a hungry pigeon could be seen pecking a key, its behavior reinforced with food and recorded cumulatively. Observers could push buttons to select any one of three performances—a fixed interval of five minutes, a fixed ratio of forty, and *drl* (the differential reinforcement of a low rate). Three pigeons kept the demonstration running a dozen hours a day. The following year we were asked to bring the exhibit to the spring meeting of the National Academy of Sciences in Washington, and that summer it was shown at the International Congress of Psychology in Montreal. (James Olds was at the Congress. He was using electrical stimulation of the brain stem to reinforce behavior in a maze or discrimination apparatus, and I urged him to try lever pressing.)

THE UNITED STATES INFORMATION AGENCY heard about teaching machines, and someone in the French Service of the Voice of America called to ask if I would be in New York in the near future with time to spare for an interview with Monsieur Robert France. During a meeting of the American Psychological Association, an interview was arranged.

I was received by a "special events officer" who explained that M. France might be a little late. It then appeared that the interview was to be in French. I said that I was afraid my French might not stand the strain; I could manage a conversation with a visiting Frenchman, but I scarcely felt up to *ex tempore* public speaking. The officer suggested that we prepare a few questions and answers in advance, and as we walked toward his office, he began speaking in French with some care. French was not his first language either, and when I answered in kind, he brightened. Notes would not be needed; we should go directly to the studio. If I needed help, I could ask for a word in English and my inquiry would be cut out of the tape. A young woman behind a glass panel connected our microphones with a tape recorder in a distant room, and we got off to a promising start.

We did not get very far. After two or three minutes, M. France dashed into the studio, dismissed his assistant with a wave of his hand, took the place opposite me, and broke into a torrent of French. *Real* French this time. I protested feebly, without effect. I found myself composing schoolbook sentences which I hoped were reasonably appropriate to what I took to be the gist of M. France's remarks. The assistant had joined the woman behind the glass panel, and after watching for a moment he tore his hair symbolically and departed.

French was not only M. France's first language, it was to some extent his only one. I tried to describe the operation of my machine, but what the devil was the word for "slider" or "ratchet" or "cam"? Some of my English did less for M. France than his French for me. We appealed to the woman behind the glass, who replied helpfully through a loudspeaker. It was soon clear that I had lost M. France and with him, I suspected, my French audience. He began to do almost all the talking himself, and his paraphrases of what he thought I was trying to say became longer and longer. I was reduced to a series of "Oui, monsieur" or "C'est ça!" Finally, in evident relief, he embarked upon a standard peroration—thanking me for my cooperation in bringing French listeners up to date on an important subject.

He seemed happy about the whole thing. A fine interview, he assured me, though it would take some cutting. A tape of the finished product would be sent to me. Fortunately I have never received it. Nor, so far as I know, have the French people ever heard it. When the young woman behind the glass joined us as we left the studio, I tried to smile, and then shrugged my shoulders. "It's all right," she said quietly. "You should hear some of them."

AT LEAST ONCE A YEAR I still went straight through the Mozart Sonatas in a kind of ritualistic tribute to the woman who, when I was a boy, sent me a copy of the Third Sonata to improve my taste in music, but I had played no chamber music since leaving Minnesota. At Indiana I was too busy, and at Harvard I was afraid that the string players would not be tolerant of my shortcomings as a pianist. In the fall of 1954, however, Stanley Sapon, a linguist interested in my analysis of verbal behavior, came to spend the year in Cambridge, and I discovered that he was a cellist. Dick Herrnstein, then a graduate student, played the violin, and the Harvard library had all the scores. We were at about the same level of competence and we spent many happy Sunday mornings playing piano trios.

Record companies were selling surplus stock at bargain prices, and I made discoveries. I bought Bruckner's First Symphony and within a short time I had all the Bruckner symphonies, as well as the scores. (I first listened to the Eighth when I was reading a racy novel by Cécil Saint-Laurent called *Le Fils de Caroline chérie*, about the Napoleonic campaign in Russia, and it became absurdly bound up with that wonderful symphony.) A good discount recording of *Lohengrin* soon led me to all Wagner's operas.

We continued to see friends in the psychological community—Robert and Pauline Sears, whom Frank Keppel had lured to Cambridge for a few years before the call of California became irresistible, Duncan and Gay Luce, Smitty Stevens and Didi Stone (especially at Smitty's farm in New Hampshire), Walter and Judy Rosenblith, and Bill Verplanck. Elsewhere in the Harvard community we saw something of Ken and Kitty Galbraith, George and Nancy Homans, Ben and Felicia (Lamport) Kaplan, Van and Marge Quine, and Harry and Elena Levin. Friends outside Harvard included Edwin and Terry Land (of Polaroid fame), Al and Kathy Capp (of Li'l Abner fame), and Arthur and Jean Brooks. (Arthur had designed our house.) Together with

Julie and Deborah we often spent a day in Wakefield with our old friends Lou and Ken Mulligan and their three daughters, until they moved to Washington. Eve joined a Cambridge Home Information Center, a group of women bent on self-improvement, and found herself president for one year.

I READ NOVELS, in English and French, in part because of Eve's interest. When some of Fred's students arranged a debate with Lionel Trilling at the New School in New York, I took a rather philistine position. My "revolt against literature" was still unresolved. Literature gave us useful terms and interesting case histories, and it recognized a measure of lawfulness in human behavior in its archetypal patterns and its concern for consistency of character, but that was short of "understanding." I quoted Chesterton's comment on a character of Thackeray's ("Thackeray didn't know it, but she drank"), which had figured in my revolt twenty-five years earlier, and contended that "the consistency of Alyosha, Dmitri, Ivan, and Smerdyakov was not due to understanding but to the fact that Dostoevski was merely being himself—a part of himself—in each case." The devices of poetry also gave the reader a false sense of understanding; one agreed not because a point was made but because the line scanned or rhymed. The attractions of literature could not be denied, but in the long run a scientific analysis told us more about human behavior.

I RECOVERED VERY SLOWLY from my failure as a writer of fiction. In the thirties and early forties I wrote two or three short stories (unpublished) and in 1945 *Walden Two*, but I had been too busy to do anything more. In 1955, with a sabbatical term coming up, I wrote to Henry Allen Moe, head of the Guggenheim Foundation, about a fellowship which would let me write a novel. I quoted Robert Frost's appreciation of my short stories and said that I thought *Walden Two* was

an interesting and challenging book, though I would not argue strongly for its artistic merits. It was written rapidly and its very nature greatly restricted my freedom in character creation and the development of incidents. I hope to write a novel on a much broader canvas—a fusion of scientific and literary approaches to the problem of human behavior. My plan is simply to get off by myself and probe my verbal behavior with all the devices at my disposal, away from all my academic and scientific commitments.

It was soon clear that I could do nothing of the sort. I desperately wanted to finish *Verbal Behavior,* and I had agreed to write a chapter for a study of psychological theories edited by Sigmund Koch. I still hoped to get away from Cambridge and find a spot where I would be undisturbed. That would not be much of a sabbatical for Eve, and she chose to spend the term in Europe, with a brief tour of Egypt. Julie was in her junior year at Putney, Vermont, and we found that Deborah could board with a staff family and attend fifth grade in a school run mainly for the children of the Putney faculty. I looked for quarters not too far from them. I had once visited the MacDowell Colony with a friend who had spent a year there (he had played pool with Stephen Vincent Benét, who was writing *John Brown's Body*), and I asked if I might come for the spring term. Unfortunately, the colony was then open only in the summer. I looked at hotels in Vermont and New Hampshire (they were not yet full of skiers) and in the end I chose the small Putney Inn, run by the school.

I had a large room with a single sunny window. It was over the kitchen and warmed mainly by the kitchen stove. On cold evenings I sat around in my overcoat or simply got into bed. I had breakfast and lunch in the dining room with a few regular patrons or an occasional visitor, and in the evening ate snacks in my room. I drank no alcohol. Charlie and some of the graduate students gave me a turntable with headphones, and before going to sleep I listened to Bruckner. (Invariably, I noted, the themes that occurred to me the next morning were from the symphony I had played the night before.)

On my first day I wrote a note:

If not Walden Two, at least a reasonable Walden One. I am resolved to construct a mode of living which will keep me in top condition for (1) finding out what I have to say and saying it and (2) enjoying music, literature, etc. Fatigue is a ridiculous sort of hangover from too much reinforcement. As soon as I rest up—as I did last night, going to bed at 8 o'clock—I begin to bubble over with things to say, with leads to follow. Why isn't this the optimal life? Two things [would be needed when I returned to Cambridge]:

(1) Some way of controlling the strength of my own behavior. How to stop work before the optimal condition fades? This might be automatic if it were not for leftover compulsive effects of aversive control. Exhausting avocations are a danger. No more chess. No more bridge problems. No more detective stories. When I am not working, I must relax—not work at something else!

A good measure of fatigue would be helpful. I can tell how tired I am when playing the piano. Early in the morning, well rested, I surprise myself. Later in the day, I accept my errors as inevitable. My handwriting is also a gauge. It would be nice to have a shibboleth—a passage to be written in ten seconds, the errors to determine whether I work or relax. . . . I *must* keep busy? Then relax profitably. The books I brought with me were so selected: Hawthorne's *Blithedale Romance* (a. question of technique of the novel; b. *Walden Two*); Courant and Robbins' *What Is Mathematics*—relaxing, profitable for my research and my analysis of verbal behavior; *Les Misérables* (in French—somehow [like the heroine of Gide's *La Porte Étroite*] I feel good about bettering my use of a foreign language, and I certainly like the French flavor of books in French); Lecky's *History of European Morals* (if you're going to argue with historians!).

(2) Careful planning to avoid labor which cannot be postponed and is aversive. I must review my teaching. Is Nat. Sci. 114 worth it? A good part of a term goes that way. My research: simply a question of money; I can get excellent help there. No more building of apparatus by me. Committees: avoid them. I will have served Harvard on the Committee on Educational Policy for a five-year term by June '56. That's enough for a while. National organizations? No. Department? No. Lecturing elsewhere? I can see this building up. Northwestern [lecture] leads to Ohio State (and that immediately to Denison). I hate to think of giving one or two lectures again and again. Acres of Diamonds! But if I can integrate lectures with my current thinking, they may be worthwhile. Publishing articles or even books makes very little impression on the people I ought to be reaching, especially since my main audience may lie outside psychology.

In sum: the optimal use of my energy will require a lot of planning.

How many irons in the fire? The psychotic project has set an excellent pattern: Promote, get in a good man, keep an eye on it for a year, gradually withdraw. (Break, to set up my phonograph, lie down and listen to Bruckner.)

A later note:

There is no question of the efficiency of a life of this sort. Out of bed whenever the spirit moves me—6 o'clock or 8 if I feel like staying in bed. Breakfast on schedule, but no preparation and no cleaning up. Back to work immediately—no trip to the office, no settling down to work in a different place after saying hello to new people. Work interrupted at any time—for a brisk walk, instantly in a pleasant countryside, or a bath as an intervocation, and lunch by myself with the mail by my plate. Early afternoon hours for routine—the least productive hours of the day. An interlude with Debs at three, but back by five o'clock to a comfortable room. Time out for a glass of milk at seven, then reading during the evening, a spot of Bruckner and bed. What is wrong? Possibly too little companionship for a permanent schedule.

But how much must be sacrificed to key such a life into a similar life for someone else? In other words, is this a selfish existence? In terms of actual cash I am spending the smallest portion of my income on myself at the moment, but that is not fair because Eve's current expenses are unduly high. But I am not leading an expensive life. I am not neglecting the children. My work I like, and that is lucky, but a considerable share of it is work, even so, and necessary if I am to support the family.

But what about Eve? How could my life be changed if she were here? How much would it need to be changed to give her a fair break? There is a problem in doing things together. I walk faster and longer than she. She needs entertainment (movies, TV, plays) that I can do very well without. What is a fair deal then? How much should be done to make her happy in spite of the fact that it will make me less happy? Without any change whatsoever I could have breakfast and lunch with her, have her come along with Debs, spend some time with her reading or talking in lieu of reading in the evening, spend the night in bed with her. That would undoubtedly be a better life than this, and the sacrifice in return for this would still bring me out even.

The only way to arrive at a reasonable arrangement is to plan things frankly and explicitly. We are both getting mature at last [I was fifty-one!], and I really hope and expect that an intelligent design for living can be worked out.

* * *

I WAS, indeed, not neglecting the children, although Julie was not too happy at having a father so near. When she told me that she and another girl had violated a rule and had gone to meet two boys after lights out, I sent her a letter: Putney gave her freedom, and she should abide by the rules if she wanted to enjoy it. The next day she refused to see me, but the matter was soon forgotten. She was taking violin lessons and once or twice I played the piano with her.

I wrote a note about an archetypal question: What do parents who have had premarital affairs tell a seventeen-year-old daughter?

1. Lie for the sake of a good example. "We never went all the way. Be like us, and be happy." That will probably not work as a lie, and anyway what is the point? Do the parents wish they hadn't?

2. Admit similar actions but point out health dangers. Pregnancy, abortion, disease. Instruction in contraception? Is this not encouraging the behavior by making it safe? Fact is, parents don't want children to do what *they* did. But why?

3. Point out *social* dangers. Bad reputation. Comes to same thing as health dangers. Can you honestly say that men play around with free girls but marry the other kind? The "right man"? Do you get the wrong man by playing around? Interesting men are probably in general sexual.

4. Personal danger. Letting these powerful reinforcers play too great a role in your life. But, except for real nymphomania, probably less interference from moderate sexual indulgence.

I think I am for honesty all the way. Tell the whole story? No, any "whole story" told all at once is an inaccurate account. Some things should go untold. But admit the kinds of facts, point out all *honest* consequences.

As FOR DEBBIE, I realized that I had "a very practical problem in human engineering at my very doorstep":

D. has not done well at school. She learned to read very late. The school made no move to help until we complained when she was in third grade. Very little improvement in fourth grade. I worked steadily with her last summer and she made considerable progress in both reading and writing, but her reading with me now is only a little better than it was last fall. From the beginning the school has complained of poor work habits, lack of application. In other words, it has never solved the problem of motivating her; it has simply complained that she doesn't do as well as she could. Along with this has gone a poor social adjustment. She has no close friends her own age. She tends to boast, compare things to the disadvantage of others, is easily hurt.

I would say that she needs success. She lacks confidence in almost everything she does. Exceptions: music (good pitch in singing), drawing (above average), riding (not really good but loves it). She needs success in (1) her school work, (2) her relations with friends. So far my plans are pretty vague. I hope to:

1. have her come to my room and read into my Audograph. She finds this reinforcing and can spot her mistakes upon listening back. She also seems to want to repeat a passage until it is correct. I should keep this up.

2. get her to talk maturely about mature things. I emphasize words and their meanings. She is interested in double meanings, conundrums, etc.

3. get her to verbalize social relations. I have got her talking about what she doesn't like in others and what she does like. I plan to turn this around and see if she knows what she does which others like and don't like.

I began to go with Debbie to the horse barn to watch the students ride. I wrote a note:

There is definitely something wrong with the way the horses are handled. Even though no one is hurt, and the students (all girls, I notice) ride when they please, the horses are jumpy, mean, and, I should imagine, hard to care for. The control is almost exclusively aversive. I am going to talk to the teacher in charge of the horses and unless she thinks it likely to "spoil" the present training, I'll try to . . . shape some behavior.

I bought a small aluminum frying pan, in which I could offer a horse oats or chopped hay, and a bicycle horn, the sound of which I conditioned as a reinforcer. I first taught a horse named Mama to turn her head to one side. Later I reported that I was ready for, say, holding the head for bridle and bit. We soon ran into trouble:

Some of the girls have been circulating word that we are violating a fundamental rule. If you want to be nice to a horse and give it something special to eat, hide it in the hay so the horse doesn't know it comes from you. There seems to be a belief that you must *not* be nice to a horse. Today a girl named Sarah tried to get Mama out of her stall. She whipped, tugged, slapped, and swore. When she went to get a rope, Debbie led Mama out of her stall, I tooted the horn, and gave her a carrot. When Sarah returned she was furious. We were spoiling Mama. She would henceforth come only when you gave her a carrot and that was that. Mama must go back and come out when told to. So Mama went back in. More tugging. Then Sarah tied a rope around the horse's head, passing it over the upper gums and back of the ears. This was supposed to "press on a nerve." Whether it worked or not I don't know because I left. If Debs is going to be permitted to ride, I'll stay away to avoid trouble. Little use in explaining to Sarah how the carrot can eventually be omitted.

Except for Julie and Debbie I saw almost no one. I went for long walks through the Vermont countryside, even during that month when Vermont means mud. I saw the trees tapped for maple syrup. Occasionally I drove into Brattleboro for supplies; otherwise, I confined myself to quarters.

I HAD TIME TO DREAM, and a favorite theme was an experimental community. As a child I had particularly liked a song called "Beautiful Isle of Somewhere," which my grandmother and grandfather Burrhus played on their phonograph. It was the utopian dream—of an ideal world, not yet realized. Walden Two was different; it was, I thought, plausible here and now—more so, in fact, than when I had written the book.

There had also been a stir of interest in experimental communities among psychologists. Jack Vernon, an old friend of Bill Morse's, now at Princeton, wrote that he had been on a utopia jag since reading *Walden Two,* and sent me a bibliography. I had, of course, begun to hear about the kibbutzim in Israel, and members and former members had come to tell me about them.

I wrote a spate of notes. People get trapped in "unprofitable, unsatisfying, insecure, and even injurious ways of life. Only by taking thought can life be designed in terms of ultimately 'good' consequences." Scattered remedial changes are unprofitable; change is needed in the whole pattern. "No one knows the 'good' ways of life which will effectively exploit the best in men. . . . Experimentation is the only way to find out." There will be problems: "Economic (starting capital, for example), incentives (profit motive out, aspirations), leisure activities, security for the future (relaxation and reduction of anxiety), personal relations (how to be liked, problem of group contacts), living arrangements, and education." I drew building plans and worked out a way of manufacturing thermally efficient, double-walled concrete blocks which could be locked together to form walls.

I HAD TOLD FRED KELLER that the William James Lectures would be the final draft of *Verbal Behavior*, but it soon became clear that I could not say all I had to say in ten lectures. When Natural Sciences 114 demanded a text, I postponed the completion of a manuscript. I was in no hurry, because copies of my lectures mimeographed at Columbia and of Ralph Hefferline's notes of my summer-school course were being fairly widely distributed. A flyer for *Science and Human Behavior* referred to "another book, *Verbal Behavior*, . . . to be published in the near future," and at Putney—more than twenty years after the exchange with Alfred North Whitehead which had led me to start writing it—I put essentially a final version on the disks of my Audograph and sent them off to be typed in Memorial Hall. I was soon writing to Fred, "I have written 12 chapters. Now I'm running into less well-prepared material, but even so, if I can hold to my present standard ('The important thing is to get it *published!*') I may have it ready by fall. With luck we ought to be able to give you proofs of both [*Verbal Behavior* and *Schedules of Reinforcement*] by winter."

I had not lost my faith in the importance of the field. The human species had taken a gigantic step forward when, through evolutionary changes in its nervous system, vocal behavior came under operant control. Mating calls and cries of alarm had evolved because of their survival value, but vocal behavior was acquired because of its consequences during the lifetime of the individual. Verbal behavior as we know it then followed, and in turn the rapid evolution of cultural practices, including "rational thought."

I HAD CALLED the formulation of verbal behavior "inherently practical," with "immediate technological applications at almost every step." Some of the applications were in education, and I wrote about one in a note:

> Debbie has been raised with nearly a minimum of aversive control. She is seldom made to do anything she doesn't want to do. She is well enough behaved as children go. She seldom gets obnoxious, is nice to little children, gets on well with adults. But she has never had the chance to acquire techniques of self-control—to control rage, resentment, a sense of being unfairly treated. . . . Techniques based upon punishment do not teach these things directly, but they permit some people to learn them.
>
> Is the alternative explicit instruction in self-control? I think so, but I am aware of how pathetic my efforts at this junction may seem. However, a start must be made. I have begun to make sets of cards with material which could be used on the [IBM] spelling machine but which, for the time being, must be on flash cards. The first set (15 cards) deals with procrastination. Other sets might treat

> Haste makes waste
> Winning friends
> Solving simple problems
> Controlling emotions [In another note: "Pathetic as it may seem, I
>   am going to make up a series of cards on 'Count ten in anger.'"]
> Silly jealousy
> Reasonable attitude toward mistakes.

> I believe she will at least go through this material. It will improve her verbal skills, engender some mature thinking, and possibly help in school and social situations.

There was a technical problem. I did not want Debbie simply to choose answers from a set of alternatives; I wanted her to compose sentences. But if I asked for whole sentences, they would not always be like the sentences supplied for self-evaluation. I therefore asked her simply to complete sentences by filling in blank spaces with an important word or two.

*   *   *

IN 1953 the National Science Foundation gave the American Psychological Association a contract to evaluate scientific psychology. Sigmund Koch was appointed director of the section on the methodological, theoretical, and empirical status of the science. In the fall of 1954, in a bar near Washington Square in New York City, he quizzed me about my early research, and then asked me to write the story for the project. I wrote it at Putney and gave it as my Presidential Address at a meeting of the Eastern Psychological Association in the spring of 1955.

The contributors had been asked to make a "systematic formulation," defined as "any set of sentences formulated as a tool for ordering empirical knowledge with respect to some specifiable domain of events." Topics to be covered included Background Factors and Orienting Attitudes, Initial Evidential Grounds for Assumption of System, Degree of Programmaticity, and Intermediate and Long Range Strategy for the Development of the System.

What I wrote instead was an account of my life as a behavioral scientist. It was also a kind of parody. Sentences like "The first thing I can remember happened when I was only 22 years old" or "The major result of this experiment was that some of my rats had babies" suggested that I was not taking the assignment seriously. The seventeen illustrations were crude line drawings. As to methodology I listed a few of my own principles: "I. When you run on to something interesting, drop everything else and study it. II. Some ways of doing research are easier than others. III. Some people are lucky." I never

behaved in the manner of Man Thinking, as described by John Stuart Mill or John Dewey or in reconstructions of scientific behavior by other philosophers of science. I never faced a Problem which was more than the eternal problem of finding order. I never attacked a problem by constructing a Hypothesis. I never deduced Theorems or submitted them to Experimental Check. So far as I can see, I had no preconceived Model of behavior—certainly not a physiological or mentalistic one and, I believe, not a conceptual one. . . . If I engaged in Experimental Design at all, it was simply to complete or extend some evidence of order already observed.

When I submitted the paper to Koch, he wrote that it was "simply not on the same editorial continuum as are the other contributions. . . . The other contributors have uniformly taken great pains to analyze their positions in accordance with the intentions of our discussion outline. In such a context, your own contribution can create a feeling that the issue has not even been joined." My reply was crotchety: "Why don't you just leave me out of it? My article will eventually, I assume, appear in the *American Psychologist*, and as you have noted, I acknowledge my indebtedness to Project A in an early paragraph."

A year or so after my paper was published, W. H. Kruskal, a distinguished statistician, wrote that he had read it "with delight."

Your remarks about the role of statistics in scientific methods are clear and stimulating, whether or not one fully agrees with them. In any case, all those who, from pompousness or ignorance, claim for statistics more than its proper place should read your article. So should graduate students of statistics.

I do hope, however, that readers of your article are not left with the thought that professional statisticians think of statistics as synonymous with scientific method, or that statistics is to be damned because it can be and often is wrongly applied in the most horrendous cookbook way.

There was a practical side to the issue. My laboratory was being generously supported, but other operant conditioners were in trouble. Operant research was not really planned, and we could not honestly tell a granting agency what we would be doing after the first few weeks of a project. Our "N"—the number of subjects—was always shockingly small and control groups were often lacking. Supporting funds were also likely to be small and often lacking too.

As a graduate student I had enjoyed great freedom. Assistant Professors Pratt and Beebe-Center were deferent to a fault, and I argued with them man to man. Boring was clearly of higher rank, but my fellow students Keller and Trueblood knew more about behaviorism than he, and I rejected his criticism of my thesis out of hand. Crozier, in General Physiology, was occasionally didactic but always treated me as an equal in discussing my experiments. No one played the Herr Professor of European graduate schools.

My own students made it easy to return that freedom. John Carroll came to work with me on language and technically took his degree under me, but when he became interested in factor analysis, about which I knew nothing, I sent him to Thurstone's people in Chicago. W. K. Estes finished his doctoral research before we discussed it. When Norman Guttman returned from the war for graduate work at Indiana, he was simply an old colleague from Project Pigeon. I had only one or two other graduate students at Indiana and was too busy with administration to give them much time. Charlie Ferster was still a graduate student at Columbia when he came to work as my assistant, but we instantly became colleagues. Since I had never really been taught, it never occurred to me to teach.

Years later, Charlie recalled one example of my indifference. Nate Azrin, a graduate student whom Og Lindsley had spotted at Boston University, came to Harvard and when he was ready to do research for his thesis, he asked for a "box." I told Charlie that "Nate needs a pigeon box." I had meant a box with keys, food dispenser, and a programming panel, but Charlie misunderstood me and gave him a new Sears, Roebuck ice chest, from which our boxes were made. Nate was left to beg or borrow all the rest. As Charlie reported, Nate "went on to complete an experiment which was an original departure from the main experimental program of the pigeon laboratory and which still remains in the literature as a basis of much research and thinking."

Unfortunately, freedom could look like neglect, and when I returned from Putney I found that I was seriously in default. Five of my graduate students had finished their work, written their theses, and come up for their oral examinations without my help. It was the largest number of graduate students ever to take their degrees under me in one year. Even so, the protest came mainly from the staff, who were pressed into reading theses and conducting examinations in my absence.

I WAS NOT UNCONCERNED about graduate teaching; in fact, I wanted to see more of it. But Smitty Stevens, who had been closely associated with William Sheldon, was arguing that we should select our students according to body type and leave them alone. Karl Lashley, a member of the department stationed at the Yerkes Laboratories in Orange Park, Florida, agreed: any student worth teaching did not need to be taught. I found it hard to argue for instruction as such. I had wanted the department to be as good as it could be and I took an active part in staff meetings, but a change was setting in. "My interest in the department and the University," I wrote at Putney, "is now at a low ebb. There are several reasons for the extinction. I have carried very few points, and the issues on which I was on the winning side were not won for that reason."

When I came back to Cambridge I made one more effort in a white paper, parts of which read as follows:

> I do not believe that the Harvard department is making a significant contribution in its program of graduate instruction.
> Our students have two strikes against them because of the split between psychology and social relations. [The split had long since lost its point. Social Relations had never functioned as intended. Its courses attracted large numbers of undergraduates, but its graduate students kept their separate identities as social psychologists, sociologists, and social anthropologists. Moreover, the social psychologists, possibly to prove that they were not going soft, took on members who obscured any useful distinction. I had given the William James Lectures on verbal behavior, had published a utopian novel, and was giving a course on human behavior at least half of which was "social," yet I was not a social psychologist. Richard Solomon, in Social Relations, was working on the autonomic nervous system of dogs.] No matter how well our students do with us, they turn up on the market as extraordinarily narrow specialists.
> The department should offer three or four one-term basic courses which will guarantee that our students are at least familiar with the content of the narrow field locally defined by the term "experimental psychology."

I thought we were vastly overdoing statistics, and I saw no reason why we should continue to require French and German.

> Naturally I would be delighted to have all our students speak German, French, and Russian fluently, as I would be delighted to have them all expert statisticians, but we face a very real problem in furthering other important aspects of graduate instruction, and I am confident that it is only by reducing the emphasis upon *requirement* as a technique of edu-

8 9

cation and by doing some teaching instead that the reputation of this department can be salvaged.

THE WILLIAM JAMES LECTURES, established by an affluent alumnus, Edgar Pierce, were given every two years. The departments of Philosophy and Psychology took turns in selecting the lecturer. In the fall of 1953 I suggested that my old friend Herbert Feigl be appointed. With a psychologist, Paul Meehl, and two philosophers, Michael Scriven and Wilfred Sellars, he had been working on basic concepts in psychology, and a series of lectures might be just the right place for a report. The two departments could join in appointing him without prejudice to the alternating schedule. (I was hoping that the Department of Philosophy might take Feigl on as a permanent member. Percy Bridgman had mentioned that possibility to me.)

I was on sabbatical when action was taken. The notion of a joint appointment was viewed favorably, but my candidate was not. There was some interest in Gilbert Ryle from Oxford, but Quine felt he might have said all he had to say in *The Concept of Mind*. Ernest Nagel at Columbia would be good but aroused no enthusiasm. Someone suggested Norbert Wiener, but Wiener's views were already well known in the community. John von Neumann was a possibility, but he might not be available because he had recently become a member of the Atomic Energy Commission.

Another candidate was available because he had *not* become a member. Robert Oppenheimer's loyalty had been questioned by Senator Joseph McCarthy, and in turn by the government, and it was felt that Harvard should now pledge its faith in a distinguished alumnus. I thought he would have less to say than any of the others, but he was appointed. Fred also had reservations:

See by the Times *that Mr. Oppenheimer is doing the W. J. lectures. And that some folks don't like it! I have not understood him or his great allure for psychologists. Is he* really *good? I heard him once on TV and he sounded confused. If I hadn't known his name I would have said worse— that he was a ham actor or something. But I am sure I got a bad sample. Or couldn't follow the complications of really meaningful stuff. I shall be very interested in your response to him.*

*   *   *

WHEN I WAS A GRADUATE STUDENT, W. J. Crozier had helped me in many ways. He passed on Jacques Loeb's conception of the organism as a whole and the possibility of studying its behavior apart from the rest of its physiology. He had sustained my faith in a quantitative analysis of behavior and had given me unlimited support during five postdoctoral years. I saw little of him after my return to Harvard, however. His star had fallen when Conant became president, and his closest associates had left Harvard. During the war he served as an operations analyst for the Twentieth Air Force, and afterwards confined himself to the study of human vision, in which I was not interested. I once joined in nominating him for election to a prestigious association, but he failed to make it. In 1955 he died. His dream of a science of General Physiology had died long before.

THESE WERE OUR HAPPIEST and most productive years on Monhegan. Debs and I built a tubby boat, which she rowed around the harbor, the gunwales nearly awash, and I tried to use our kite to pull the Folbot. (In Widener Library I had found an account of a Frenchman who had crossed the English Channel in a boat towed by a *cerf volant*.) A very large kite should move the boat faster than my little lateen-rigged sail, and if the strings came to a point below the center of gravity, it would not tend to tip the boat over, as a sail necessarily did. With our steerable kite, I might even be able to tack. I managed to get the kite up when I was in the boat. The strings ran forward over the bow and it did pull me forward but, alas, only in the direction of the wind. When I steered the kite to one side, the strings came around the wind as around a great pulley and into the boat straight over the bow.

One of the dogs that survived Og's experiment on radiation was a beautiful beagle named after Og's old professor of psychology, Walter S. Hunter. Hunter came to live with us. He particularly liked Monhegan, and one summer as we drew close to the wharf he began to pick up the scent. He dashed to the side of the boat and without waiting for the gangplank leaped toward the wharf. He was pulled out of the water by a helpful Monhegan boy. We made a small dog cart with which he helped us carry groceries and mail, and Julie and Debbie were soon teaching him circus tricks. Debbie had only to say "Stay" and he would sit quivering until from a distance she gave a high-pitched signal, whereupon he would dash off and, good hound that he was, have no trouble in finding her. Charlie Ferster and I once had better evidence of his tracking skills. Charlie was spending a few days with us, and one day we locked Hunter in the cottage and walked to the eastern side of the island. We climbed down from a headland and made our way over heavy boulders to a spot near the surf, where we sat and talked. Suddenly we heard baying. Someone had let Hunter out. He came over the headland on the run and tracked us accurately over the heavy rubble.

AT THE END of the summer I wrote a note called "Julie at Seventeen":

Everyone seems to agree that Julie is something special. Physically she is strong, healthy, a little too heavy for the current fashion but well built. Not a classical beauty, she is nevertheless clean-cut and (yes) radiant. A man stopped her in the road and said "Have I told you that you are the most beautiful girl on the island?" She fled in embarrassment. She will use no makeup and dresses very simply. She is self-conscious of her figure and will not swim on the beach. In a spirit of self-flagellation she will go without food for a day—only to eat a huge meal or a whole box of cookies the next.

She made an impossible list of things to be done this summer and felt guilty at having done so little. Nevertheless she learned to cook and got most of our meals. She baked pies, cakes, bread, made jam of berries which she picked, and gave some to friends and the church bazaar. She read a book or two in French and a Jane Austen and learned touch-typing up to a fair speed. She learned to play the alto recorder quite well and progressed more on the violin than she realizes. She "hacked" a lot with Debs, with only a moderate amount of friction.

She has high ideals for herself and for people in general, though she still fools herself. (E.g. one day she was "having" to practice—i.e. practicing because she felt she ought to—when Debs began to bother her. This was quickly converted into "If you are going to do that, I can't practice," and the violin was put away.) She is tolerant, friendly, a little diffident, ambitious ("Play in orchestra and be on Student Council"). She is possibly in love with Arthur and talks of the fairly distant future with him. It seems to be an uneven relationship, with Julie adjusting sensibly to a rather difficult but likable boy.

There were signs of change in Debbie. A few days after her eleventh birthday, I wrote a note called "Solitary Journey":

After supper two days ago, D. started out with Hunter on the road to Burnt Head. (She later commented on how beautiful that road is.) From Burnt Head, she went down to the rocks and along the shore all the way to Gull Cove. It was getting dark as she came back on the Gull Cove path. She arrived quite calmly although she said it was "scary" in the woods.

This was quite dangerous because it is easy to sprain an ankle or break a leg on the large jumbled rocks between Burnt Head and White Head, and the path back is hard to follow even during the day, and getting off can be a very rough experience. At this season there is no one to see her, and we should have had great trouble in finding her. Neverthless, I merely asked her to be sure to let us know when she went again and later suggested that if she were ever lost she should tie something of hers to Hunter's collar and send him off. Because this was a great step for Debs. I hope it shows, as I think it does, that the spring term and summer have greatly strengthened her confidence. She has:

a) stayed with a new family several weeks without seeing her parents. [After Putney she had stayed with Eve's sister, Tick, and her husband.]

b) become part of a new school group.

c) learned to handle horses.

d) got her own boat and covered the harbor alone.

e) learned to play the recorder.

f) acquired some facility in arithmetic.

All of this, I think, combined to set her off on her solitary journey.

A few months later I was writing to a teacher at Shady Hill:

I don't need to tell you of the great change which has come over Debbie during the year. She has matured rapidly, and has developed a growing confidence in herself, although she still has a long way to go. She is taking the responsibility for her homework and for getting off to school in an almost amusing way. Her "new handwriting" will doubtless

93

settle down to a more acceptable form, but some of my psychological friends would, I am sure, be most impressed with it as an expression of her new personality. Her old hand was angular and cramped, but the new one, which she herself apparently decided to adopt, has a vigor and flow to it which, if she can bring it under control, will be quite refreshing.

LIKE PRESSEY, I had seen that teaching machines were needed for immediate reinforcement and individual pacing, but "programming," as it emerged from my analysis of verbal behavior, was something more. Soon after coming back from Putney I wrote to Robert Gagne, who was at the Personnel and Training Research Center at Lowry Air Force Base in Denver, Colorado. Gagne had been a student of Walter Hunter's at Brown and (with Leslie Briggs, a student of Pressey's) was working on a multiple-choice Subject Matter Trainer. (A similar device used during the Second World War had been sent to me by the Navy, at the suggestion of Roy Hoskins.) To Gagne I wrote:

Following the pioneer work of S. J. Pressey in the field of mechanized education there has obviously been a broad realization of the need of mechanical devices to simplify and extend the educational process. However, these seem to me to be based upon rather outmoded theories of learning. They all assume that you need simply chop a given task up into small parts, each of which is learned separately along the lines of recency and frequency theories. In fooling around with a teaching machine myself, I have been impressed by the fact that such machines make it possible to approach the matter of teaching in an entirely new way. As you know, we have had a lot of practical success in shaping up and maintaining the behavior of an organism under a variety of schedules. [My use of "up" after "shaping" was a vestige of the verbal behavior of my childhood, and I soon dropped it.] As I vaguely indicated in my Pittsburgh lecture on "The Science of Learning and the Art of Teaching" . . . these principles can be applied to classroom education. I have just arranged to have some work done during the coming year in re-analyzing the behavior involved in grade-school arithmetic, and in the construction of a very long sequence of steps through which the average, or even below-average, child can be put in possession of this behavior. . . . I have a hunch that the more complex instruction in which you and your colleagues are interested could also be approached in the same way. What the teaching machine does is to permit the experimenter or teacher to arrange a very much larger number of contingencies for the student than is possible in personal instruction. . . . [One can then] analyze the nature of the behavior to be taught and . . . design an entirely new type of educational program. . . .

I had become so accustomed to speaking of "shaping" behavior that I was surprised when I heard Eddie Newman refer to it as something new in learning theory, but he was right. And it raised an important behavioristic issue by identifying a different initiator of the change called learning. The pigeon or student acquired behavior, but it was the *experimenter* or *teacher* who arranged the conditions which shaped and maintained it.

One kind of program consisted of a series of steps of increasing difficulty. One could teach high-jumping simply by raising the bar a millimeter after every successful jump, and I had once programmed a bit of verbal behavior in essentially that way when Debbie brought home a worksheet in arithmetic. There were twenty or thirty problems designed to teach the equivalence of different expressions for the same operation. Debbie was to add, for example, when she saw "the sum of ____ and ____," or "____ plus ____" or "____ added to ____." But the blanks contained two- or three-digit numbers, and in her concern for correct calculation, she was missing the point about equivalence. I wrote the expressions on a sheet of paper in ink and inserted the figures 2 and 3 in the blanks in pencil. Debbie had no trouble with "the sum of 2 and 3," "3 plus 2," or "2 added to 3." She obviously knew what the expressions meant. Then I erased the numbers and put in slightly larger ones, and again she had no trouble. After two or three revisions, she did the original sheet effortlessly.

Even in high-jumping, however, the best form is not shaped simply by raising the bar, nor was arithmetic or reading taught by a series of passages arranged in order of a carefully measured difficulty. My analysis of verbal behavior pointed to the essential steps. Students must first engage in the behavior they are to acquire. If they are good imitators, the teacher may serve as a model and "show them what to do." If they have learned to follow directions, the teacher may "tell them what to do" or let them read directions. Their behavior is thus "primed"—that is, made to occur for the first time. After being sufficiently reinforced, it occurs without priming.

Once primed, behavior often needs to be *prompted*. One prompts an actor by supplying *part* of a forgotten line; supplying the whole line is telling, not prompting. The adjectival meaning of prompt—"on time" —is close; a prompt *hastens* the recall of a response in the presence of a stimulus which will eventually exert full control. In my analysis of verbal behavior I called the kind of prompt supplied to an actor "formal." A "thematic" prompt was called a hint.

Primes and prompts are temporary aids. They can be withdrawn most efficiently through a process I began to call *"vanishing"* or *"fading."* I used it one day when Debbie came home from school unhappier than usual because she had been told to memorize fifteen lines of Longfellow's *Evangeline*. I printed the passage on a blackboard and asked her to read it aloud slowly and carefully. Then I sent her out of the room and erased a few of the letters. I called her back and she read the passage again—correctly, although many words were incomplete. I sent her away again and erased more letters, and she was still able to read what was left. After five or six erasures, there was nothing on the board, but she "read" the passage without a mistake. At first the whole text was a prime, but as I "vanished" it (the magician's transitive use of the verb), parts of it became prompts, and eventually no text was needed. (The behavior was a chain of responses but, of course, the first word did not then elicit the second, the second the third, and so on, as critics have supposed "chaining" to imply.) When, a month later, Debbie reported that she was the only one of her class who could still recite the poem, I was alarmed; what would fifteen lines of *Evangeline* do to a child if permanently implanted?

The process could be used with other materials. As the name of a pictured object was vanished, the student came to "know what the object was called." As the picture was vanished, the student came to "know what the name meant." In teaching a vocabulary in another language, the words in either language could be vanished. A word could be vanished by slowly putting it out of focus, making it smaller, or reducing its contrast with the background. I made several pocket teaching machines in which a passage to be memorized could be covered with sheets of lightly frosted plastic or clear sheets with obscuring spots or lines. The passage became less and less legible as additional sheets were placed over it. Later that year with Fletcher Watson of the Graduate School of Education I discussed the use of these principles in teaching thinking.

THE MACHINE THAT IBM was to produce could not be used with the programs I had written at Putney or with others I was writing, and by April I had built a different kind, which I described in a letter to Tom Gilbert. Tom was teaching an introductory course at the University of Georgia, using Keller and Schoenfeld's *Principles*, with readings from *Science and Human Behavior*. He was interested in teaching by machine and had asked about the machine described in my paper. I wrote that IBM was working on a better model, but that he might want to try a different type which I had just built:

> The material is printed on twelve-inch disks exposed one sector at a time. The pupil writes an answer on an exposed strip of paper, then moves a lever which covers his answer with a transparent mask, and reveals the correct answer. If he is right, he moves the lever in a different direction. This punctures the paper to record his judgment, and moves a detent so that the material does not appear again, or will appear only once again as the disk revolves. [When the lever was moved back in place, a new frame appeared.] After finishing the disk, the student tears out the strip of paper and puts it in a file to record his progress.

I was hoping to develop a program in physics or chemistry, but if funds were not available, I might be "forced back upon my own course based upon *Science and Human Behavior*."

IBM had assigned the construction of my machine to its Electric Typewriter Division and in August I met with two of its officers. I was not surprised to learn that they thought material could be presented on punched cards. Shortly afterward, back on Monhegan, I sent some specifications: We could anticipate from twenty-five to fifty frames per lesson and about two hundred lessons per term. The machine should stand rough handling, students should be able to load it themselves, and it should not be possible for cards to get out of order. Material could be more easily improved if items on which errors were often made were marked in some way, such as by a smudge on the backs of the cards. Progress would be more reinforcing if the cards told the students how far they had gone through a set; some kind of jackpot payoff might even be arranged. That fall I looked at a card verifier in the Boston office of IBM to see whether it could be used as a teaching machine, at least for experimental purposes. When I wrote to say that I did not think it could, I pointed out that more than a year had passed since my first meeting with IBM and very little had been done. A tentative schedule was then drawn up. Ten trial models of a machine were to be ready by fall 1956, to be installed and tested in a school by spring 1957. Preparation of materials would begin by summer 1957, and the device would be for sale in the fall of 1958. We had not yet signed a contract.

ALTHOUGH OUR PIGEONS never guided missiles, our efforts to show that they could do so were not wasted. The project would be supported only if we could prove to some very skeptical people that pigeons would peck steadily at the image of a rapidly changing target undisturbed by accelerations, buffeting, and flak. To make sure that they did so, we adapted them to many simulated distractions and reinforced correct responses on the powerful variable-ratio schedule. My colleagues and I were impressed by the control we achieved and began to look closely at its implications. I talked with my friends the *philosophes* about a "technology of behavior" and the ethics of control. Those were the main issues in *Walden Two*, and I discussed them at length with my Harvard students. I summarized a lecture in May 1950 as follows:

> The issue is not between *planning* and *laissez-faire*. The laissez-faire political design of Jefferson was itself a plan—which assigned control to extra-governmental agencies. The main question, aside from that of the best plan, is who is to do the planning. Our own culture is strongly opposed to excessive control by individuals. We have repeatedly acted to diversify and limit control. A characteristic feature of the contemporary scene is the refusal to accept control when it is available. Excessive personal influence is branded as Machiavellian. The powerful control acquired by the psychotherapist is repudiated in "client-centered" therapy. Educators adopt philosophies which conceal control, and they refuse to

accept techniques which would make their practices more effective. But in the long run the issue cannot be decided by refusing to face it. To refuse to control is simply to allow the control to fall into other hands. A science of behavior is already in position to give substantial aid to men of good will in any field of human affairs. The difficulty is that it is likely to be seized by those who would control with respect to special interests and advantages.

There is only one answer to the question Who is to control? He will control who controls. The prospect need not be frightening. . . . Physical restraint and the use of the power to punish are not ultimately advantageous and they are the forms we most object to. Alternative techniques can only be implemented when a scientific understanding of human behavior is well advanced. One hopeful possibility is that only the culture which fosters an energetic science of behavior will be in a position to control. . . . It can also be argued that the best techniques of control are those which work to the advantage of the controllee. This fact in itself is some guarantee against misuse.

In a paper at the New York Academy of Sciences titled "The Control of Human Behavior," I reviewed many of the ways in which behavior could be controlled. A priest told me afterward that I should not have been allowed to speak, but my point was a warning, not a recommendation. Punitive and aversive forms of control naturally led to escape or revolt, but techniques like emotional conditioning, positive reinforcement, and drugs might not be resisted.

IN MY PAPER at the New York Academy of Sciences I went so far as to say that we were "entering the age of the chemical control of human behavior. Drugs have been used for this purpose ever since the first man was deliberately made drunk, but better drugs are now available. . . . In the not-too-distant future, the motivational and emotional conditions of normal daily life will probably be maintained in any desired state through the use of drugs."

That rash contention was due in part to a meeting earlier in the day with Dr. Karl Beyer of the Research Laboratories of Sharp and Dohme, a large pharmaceutical company. At lunch in the Oak Room at the Plaza he had told me that the company was setting up a program to study drugs bearing on mental illness. He had visited half a dozen laboratories, including Clifford Morgan's at Johns Hopkins, Richard Solomon's in the Harvard Department of Social Relations, Neal Miller's at Yale, and Harry Harlow's at Wisconsin. He had also talked with Peter Dews at the Harvard Medical School and with Charlie and me, and he saw certain advantages in operant methods: standard equipment was available, the experiments required little attention, and some research on drugs had been done, with more underway. He had also talked with Joseph Brady at the Walter Reed Army Medical Center in Washington. Brady and a colleague, Howard Hunt, had worked with the conditioned suppression that Bill Estes and I had called "anxiety," in which a stable rate of responding on an interval schedule was suppressed by an otherwise innocuous stimulus which on a number of occasions had been followed by a shock. Electroconvulsive shock, then widely used in the treatment of depression, eliminated the suppression, and Brady had found that reserpine, an antidepressant, had the same effect. (A former student of mine at Indiana, Harris Hill, with two colleagues at the NIMH Addiction Research Center in Lexington, Kentucky, had found that morphine also eliminated conditioned suppression.)

Beyer told me that Sharp and Dohme would be installing operant equipment in their laboratories at West Point, Pennsylvania, and that John Boren, a student of Fred Keller's then working with Brady, would take charge. Could I visit the project four times a year as a consultant?

I went to West Point to discuss the program further with Beyer, Brady, and Boren. (A liveried chauffeur met me at the station in Philadelphia, took my bag, and led me to an air-conditioned limousine—a touch of affluence for which life in the academy had not prepared me. We followed a picturesque route to West Point, where at the gate of a large tract of land a guard examined my credentials.) The short-term objective of the program included a search for tranquilizing agents having the same effect as chlorpromazine, reserpine, and meprobamate, and stimulants similar to the amphetamines but without serious effects on the cardiovascular system. Long-range objectives included compounds useful in treating schizophrenia, obsessive-compulsive neuroses, depressant states, and other "clinical entities," as well as compounds possibly useful in everyday life that would increase attention span, improve discrimination, relieve mental fatigue, increase speed of learning, and control appetite. Boren, working with rats or monkeys, would screen compounds with performances on multiple fixed-interval fixed-ratio schedules, differential reinforcement of low rates, conditioned avoidance, and conditioned suppression. He would also have time for his own research.

In October, as an official consultant, I attended another meeting to learn more about the chemical and pharmacological work of the laboratories. Joe Brady and I met at a rather posh hotel where rooms had been reserved for us, and as we drove out together, again in a limousine, we were not unaware that an operant analysis had rather conspicuously arrived.

I suggested to Karl Beyer that we try some promising compounds on a number of psychotic subjects in our program at the Metropolitan State Hospital, but he said that such compounds were strictly controlled and elaborate tests of toxicity would first have to be made. Within a month, however, I was writing to alert him to the fact that a representative of "our distinguished Philadelphia competitors" (Smith, Kline, and French) had visited the psychotic project and had been so enthusiastic that the company was sending a three-man visiting committee.

BRITISH BIOLOGISTS, particularly Julian Huxley, were promoting the new science of ethology. Bill Verplanck spent the spring term of 1953 at Oxford with Niko Tinbergen, met Konrad Lorenz several times, and came back full of the new discipline. Later that year the Chairman of the Dunham Lectureship at the Harvard Medical School asked whether I thought Lorenz should be invited to give three lectures. I said that he seemed to be "immensely stimulating," though I was not sure he would have any important effect "upon behavioral research in this scientific community." He was invited and came to see my laboratory.

Bill Morse and I had just discovered a beautiful demonstration of the power of stimulus control, and we thought Lorenz would be interested. When pecking a green key has been reinforced but pecking a red one extinguished, a pigeon will stop midway in the act of pecking if the color changes from green to red. When the color is quickly changed back to green and then to red, it starts and stops. By changing the color at just the right speed, we could move the pigeon's head back and forth as if it were a mechanical toy. Lorenz was not impressed. A pigeon in a box was not a real pigeon.

Though I objected to "born that way" explanations of behavior, as I objected to the physiology of taut nerves and brain fag, I had been interested in the genetics of behavior for a long time. My first experiments were ethological, and I used relatively pure strains of rats, looking for behavioral differences among them. In *Science and Human Behavior* I argued that a tendency to behave in a given way was no more remarkable than any other feature of the anatomy and physiology of a species. In 1954 one of my multiple-choice questions in Natural Sciences 114 began: "The evolutionary development of reflex behavior resembles operant conditioning because . . . ," and the following continuations were called right: "(1) In both cases a form of behavior is selected because of its effects. (2) The characteristic which the processes have in common is the principal reason why behavior is often called purposive. (3) In neither case is a particular instance of behavior which achieves a consequence altered by that consequence." In a question on susceptibility to reinforcement, a correct item read: "Sweet foods are usually highly reinforcing because it must have been highly advantageous to the organism in an earlier epoch in human history to ingest as much sugar as possible."

In "A Case History in Scientific Method," I published three cumulative records under a multiple schedule—one for a pigeon, one for a rat, and one for a monkey. They were very much alike, and I commented: "Pigeon, rat, monkey, which is which? It doesn't matter." That was enough to revive the myth that behaviorists did not believe in species differences. But I went on to say that, "of course, these three species have behavioral repertoires which are as different as their anatomies. But once you have allowed for differences in the ways in which they make contact with the environment and in the ways in which they act upon the environment, what remains of their behavior shows astonishingly similar properties." I saw a bearing on a current issue: "When organisms that differ as widely as this nevertheless show similar properties of behavior, differences between members of the same species may be viewed more hopefully."

I was also misunderstood when, in *Science and Human Behavior*, I compared operant conditioning to shaping a figure from a lump of clay; although the final product appears to be unique and new, "we cannot identify any point at which these characteristics emerge." That looked like complete environmentalism with no regard for genetics, but I went on to say that "in such a bird as the pigeon the pecking response has a special strength and a special coherence as a form of species behavior. . . . The parallel does not take account of some units of behavior which appear to have emerged from an earlier evolutionary process."

I remained, of course, primarily an environmentalist. No matter how important the heredity of an organism in determining its behavior, it could not be changed after conception.

JULIE AND DEBBIE WERE environmentalists, too, and they became experts in shaping behavior. For a science project at Shady Hill, Julie trained a parakeet to do tumbling tricks, and Debbie taught a pigeon to play scales on a toy piano. The keyboard of the piano was inserted into one end of the pigeon's cage, and striking the keys in a descending scale was reinforced with food. When the experiment was over, Debbie sometimes left the pigeon free in her room, and one day, spotting the piano on a dresser, it played a few notes although it was probably not hungry. (A child would have been said to have acquired a love of music for its own sake.) Debbie also taught a parakeet to say a few words, including "Bonjour," evidently with a good accent, because my secretary, who was French, took care of the bird when we were away for a week, and when we returned she said, "I think that bird speaks French."

WHEN THE DEMONSTRATIONS in Natural Sciences 114 were picked up by the newspapers, I began to get letters from people who said I was mistreating my pigeons. I told a reporter that they were treated better than pigeons had ever been treated before; they were having fun. But I was disturbed by a letter to the editor of the *New Statesman and Nation*: "Any adult capable of thought and imagination must be disgusted by the sight of animals compelled to perform 'tricks' in public for their owners' profit." Circus animals were conditioned in secrecy, he said, but there was evidence of the most hideous cruelty. A trainer had reported that he incited a tiger to attack him "and then broke clubs over its head and used the whip—'lashes came down like an avalanche, each cutting deep into the tiger's shining coat.' " Even Dr. Goebbels was said to have complained that the method was "too brutal."

The phrase "performing 'tricks' in public for their owners' profit" bothered me; my demonstrations were done for a kind of profit, and in Keller and Marian Breland's new field of "applied animal psychology," the profit was money. But we did not use punishment, and that made a difference. In a letter to the editor of the *New Statesman and Nation*, I agreed that punishment was often used: "One has only to watch circus animals closely to see that they are often performing because they are afraid not to. But the circus is not the only offender. The well-trained saddle horse or hunting dog has probably been through a similar experience. As for our own species, I am told that there is a company in London which still sells birch rods (junior and senior size), canes, and multithonged whips. Fortunately, none of this is any longer necessary, for recent experimental studies of behavior have revealed powerful alternative methods with which it is relatively simple to 'shape up' the behavior of an animal without using any form of punishment whatsoever. It is to be hoped that the greater efficiency, if not humanity, of this method will soon appeal to all trainers of performing animals."

As further proof that cruelty was used, the letter of protest to the *New Statesman* said that no one had ever accepted the offer of the Performing Animals' Defence League to pay a reward of one thousand pounds "to anyone who succeeds in training without cruelty any untrained animal to perform a simple circus 'trick,' " and in my response I added that "if the offer is intended to stimulate the search for humane methods, I should have no hesitation whatsoever in arranging to teach an untrained lion to jump through a hoop, say, without the use of even the mildest punishment. I should have to ask the League to arrange for the use of a lion and the space necessary for the experiment."

When the *New Statesman and Nation* failed to respond, I wrote directly to the author of the letter, asking for his help in promoting humane methods. Would he send me the address of the Performing Animals' Defence League or, better still, forward my letter? There was no reply. Twenty-five years later I received a better reply when *The New Yorker*, describing the current circus in Madison Square Garden, said, "Ever since the advent of B. F. Skinner . . . animals have not been beaten; it has been discovered that beating is unnecessary, and that animals will learn more quickly under the reward system alone."

JOHN HUTCHENS WAS EDITOR of the *Sunday Times Book Review* when *Walden Two* was published, and he put it on the list of "Should-Be Best Sellers," a feature he had added to the *Review*. The philosopher's distinction between "should be" and "is" was never better illustrated. In 1951 the last eighty-six copies were sold, and the type distributed. Andy Anderson then induced the College Department to offset the book in a small reprinting but only at a short discount, which meant that it was carried only in bookstores near colleges where it was "adopted."

References to the book occasionally appeared, but they were not the kind to encourage a publisher. In *Quest for Utopia*, for example, Negley and Patrick expressed their horror at the "psychological conditioning" I described:

Of all the dictatorships espoused by utopists, this is the most profound, and incipient dictators might well find in this utopia a guidebook of political practice. . . . In nauseating conclusion, the perpetrator of this "modern" utopia looks down from a nearby hill on the community which is his handiwork and proclaims: "I like to play God! Who wouldn't, under the circumstances? After all, even Jesus Christ thought he was God."

The book represented, in their view, a descent "from the heights of confidence in man's capacities and noble aspiration for his progressive betterment to a nadir of ignominy in which he is placed on a par with pigeons."

In 1954, *Walden Two* was severely criticized by Joseph Wood Krutch in *The Measure of Man*. I had met Krutch three years before when Hiram Haydn, editor of the *American Scholar*, asked me to participate in a recorded discussion of the question "Is There a Social Science?" Krutch and I sat around a table with Crane Brinton, the historian of ideas, and Alfred Krober, the anthropologist. What we said was relayed to a tape recorder by a man wearing a muffled microphone —an early electronic improvement on the stenographer—and published in the *American Scholar*, spring 1952. When Brinton told me that Chester Barnard was to write a comment on the issue, I wrote to Barnard:

> *I am so unhappy about what we achieved that evening that I have not been able to bring myself to read the published version. Naturally I must take responsibility for what is said under my name, and this letter is by no means a plea for mercy. However, if you are interested in the point of view I was representing, you might want to see part of a book which I am just completing and which Macmillan will publish next year, probably under the title of "Science and Human Behavior."*

Krutch was unhappy, too, and in 1954, in *The Measure of Man*, he attacked my position, mainly as set forth in *Walden Two*. I represented, he said, a prevailing determinism derived from Darwin, Marx, and Freud. In *Walden Two*, people are "managed" in such a way that they live in perfect harmony with one another, but as human beings they have lost their grandeur, along with their social friction.

Hamlet, said Krutch, had exclaimed of man, "How like a God!" but Pavlov had said, "How like a dog!" I was said to see in man only those features which were common to rats and pigeons. But I had defended the study of lower organisms only as a necessary first step. Should we ever know what was unique about man until we knew as much as possible about other species? Two of the three books I had published were about human behavior. They would have been different books if I had not studied rats and pigeons, but I had not neglected the differences. As the last part of *Science and Human Behavior* made clear, the human species had moved into its unique position with the evolution of verbal behavior and, in turn, the development of cultural practices.

I replied to Krutch in a paper written on Monhegan the following summer in response to an invitation to join George Shuster, Krutch, Erich Fromm, and Reinhold Niebuhr in another issue of the *American Scholar*. I called the paper "Freedom and the Control of Men." Krutch had argued that in an engineered culture it was "impossible for the unplanned to erupt again." *Walden Two* was wrong because it left no room for accidents. But I pointed out that we "no longer wait for immunity to disease to develop from a series of accidental exposures, nor do we wait for natural mutations in sheep and cotton to produce better fibers."

A planned culture, according to Krutch, was degrading, and *Walden Two* was an "ignoble utopia"; an engineered society left nothing for which the individual could take credit. But should the practice of giving credit not be examined? We admired Lincoln for rising above a defective school system and did not "give Franklin Delano Roosevelt the same credit for becoming an educated man with the help of Groton and Harvard, but was that important?" Krutch quoted T. H. Huxley's famous confession: "If some great power would agree to make me always think what is true and do what is right, on condition of being turned into a sort of clock and wound up every morning before I got out of bed, I should instantly close with the offer." I could not agree with Krutch that the decision was "scarcely credible."

The democratic concept of freedom was also an issue, but was it any longer relevant? To refuse to control was to leave control to other sources. "Unless there is some unseen virtue in ignorance, a growing understanding of human behavior should make it all the more feasible to design a world adequate to the needs of men."

My paper was widely reprinted. It appeared as an example of contemporary writing in *An Approach to Literature* by Cleanth Brooks and Robert Penn Warren. Miss Graves would have been proud of me.

FRED KELLER WAS PROBABLY the first to try an operant analysis of human behavior. As he once reported it:

In late summer of 1939, I took my apparatus home, to study the lever-pressing response in my 17-month-old daughter, under several conditions of reward with bits of chocolate. Within a two- to three-day period she provided me with cumulative records of conditioning, satiation, intermittent reinforcement, and extinction. I made slides from the curves I had collected, and showed them at some professional gathering (I can't remember where), but I never tried to publish. The study was dead, for me, before it was done. I had known in advance what would happen, that the child would behave like a rat! And so she did, except for one small difference. In extinction she held on to the bar of the lever and shook it, in little volleys of response. It even seemed a sign of weakness to have carried out the study, or to have thought that it was needed. It was like doubting evolution!

When Debs was nine months old, I had easily shaped the response of lifting an arm by turning a light on and off as a reinforcer, but when she was four or five I tried something of the same sort with a different result. I was talking with her at bedtime. She was lying face down and I was rubbing her back. I stopped rubbing until she lifted a leg and then rubbed briefly. After two of these reinforcements, she lifted her leg in a great arc and began to laugh. "Whenever I lift my leg," she said, "you rub my back." She had discovered and stated the contingencies.

Serious work with children began in the fifties. Sidney Bijou, a student of Spence's at Iowa and hence in a way a second-generation disciple of Clark Hull's, had been a colleague of mine at Indiana, and when he went on to the University of Washington, he began to teach operant behavior and to inspire research, particularly on children. One of his graduate students, Montrose Wolf, had already done some operant research on children with Jack Michael and Arthur Staats at Arizona State University. Marbles were used as conditioned reinforcers in teaching reading. The child dropped them into a transparent tube, and when it was full, the child was given a toy. Sid wrote to me about his current research in March 1955:

1. *Performance . . . is related to age but not to sex.*

2. *Functions pertaining to strengthening and extinction are fairly stable. Studies (using small groups) repeated after 10 days on the same subjects give substantially the same results.*

3. *With 100%, 40%, and 20% schedules of reinforcement, strengthening rates and resistance to extinction functions are relatively consistent with those from animal studies.*

4. *A Ph.D. study on 100% reinforcement varying the number of trinkets [used as reinforcers], showed that resistance to extinction increases as a function of number of trinkets within the limits of the range employed.*

5. *An auditory stimulus immediately preceding the presentation of the trinkets increases resistance to extinction. . . .*

At the Presbyterian Medical Institute in San Francisco, Thom Verhave, a former student of Fred Keller's, used operant reinforcement to induce children to hold still for inspection and treatment.

* * *

SO MANY INTERESTING THINGS were happening in our research that Charlie and I had little time to write reports. We gave a few papers (a joint one on a sustained performance under delayed reinforcement in 1951) and discussed our work at the Conference on the Experimental Analysis of Behavior, but unreported cumulative records and protocols were piling up. Obviously we should write a book. Neither of us liked the prospect, and we took steps to strengthen the necessary behavior. Into a large freshly painted room, we moved tables, chairs, filing cases, a dictating machine, and a drafting table to use in preparing figures. Thousands of hours of data meant thousands of feet of cumulative records, but we worked out a way of cutting much of the white space out of a record and nesting the remaining segments. Duplicating systems were not yet well advanced, and after microfilming our figures we sent the originals to the publisher.

We worked systematically. We would take a protocol and a batch of cumulative records, dictate an account of the experiment, select illustrative records, and cut and nest them in a few figures. In the end we had more than 1,000 figures, 921 of which went into the book.

If Charlie had had another year or two at Harvard, with the help we were getting from our graduate students, we might have reached and tested a comprehensive theory of schedules. As it was, we had to be content with a kind of atlas showing performances under many different contingencies of reinforcement.

We finished the manuscript in a final burst of activity in the summer of 1955. Since our house in Cambridge was rented until the end of summer, Eve and the children went directly to Monhegan and I took a room near Harvard Square. It was on the top floor and unbearably hot. Memorial Hall was hot too, and Charlie and I worked in shorts. We set a quota: Each day we would put the finishing touches to the text for fifty figures. When that left an evening free, I spent it practicing on a new tenor recorder.

I had told Andy Anderson, at Macmillan, that Charlie and I were going to write a book (we were calling it *Schedules of Reward*, lacking the courage to impose the term "reinforcement" on the reading public or even the profession), and he planned to publish it. (In 1954 someone at ORCON reported that "the person handling the advanced publicity for your book has been discussing some of the classified aspects," and I told Andy to be sure that "everyone who knows about our forthcoming manuscript is warned not to refer to any applications.") But the manuscript was not immediately forthcoming, and when Andy learned more about it, he lost interest. The Harvard University Press also turned it down after investigating ways of reproducing those hundreds of cumulative records. At Appleton-Century, Dana Ferrin said he would publish it (the Harvard Press added an inducement by releasing its rights to *Verbal Behavior*, which had fallen to it as the William James Lectures), but unless we could find a subsidy the price would be very high. Fortunately, two of the drug companies with operant laboratories—Merck, Sharp, and Dohme and Smith, Kline, and French—made generous contributions, and *Schedules of Reinforcement* appeared at the relatively low price of ten dollars.

Cooperative research sometimes raises a question of credit. When reporting our experiments in Stockholm, I had listed myself as director of the project, but had said that "Dr. Charles B. Ferster has served as principal investigator." Nevertheless, I was sole author of the paper and got credit for it. In 1952 Charlie submitted a paper of his own called "The Use of the Free Operant in the Analysis of Behavior." The editor liked it but wanted some additional information. What part had I played in it? I was sent a copy of his letter and asked to comment. I replied:

> *Ferster and I have worked very closely together on this project for nearly three years. Before that I had the good fortune to have had a series of stimulating co-workers all the way back to the old Project Pigeon in 1942. It is simply impossible to establish credit for all the ideas which have gone into our present practices. If I had helped write this paper I should have got credit for much more than I deserve. . . . We are following standardized practices which are quite different from most animal experimentation and which are leading to data of an entirely new order of rigor. Some account of this in a journal is badly needed. When Ferster proposed doing an article along these lines, I was delighted to find such a simple solution.*

The book that we had discussed with publishers was "by Skinner and Ferster," but I was a professor of psychology and Charlie a mere research fellow, and if my name came first, he would be cast in the role of an assistant. I had planned to offset this by making a last-minute change so that when Charlie saw his first copy he would read "by C. B. Ferster and B. F. Skinner." But there were signs that he was unhappy about his share of the credit, and it was unfair to let him wait, and so I told him that his name should come first.

We were aware of one kind of criticism our book would receive, and we thought of anticipating it with a dedication, modeled after one by P. G. Wodehouse: "To the statisticians and scientific methodologists with whose help this book would never have been completed." But there was a real debt that demanded acknowledgment, and we dedicated the book "To the Pigeon Staff."

By 1955 Charlie had received a grant, but it could be given only to a holding corporation rather than to him directly. He had hoped that it might go to the Yerkes Laboratory in Orange Park, where he would be able to work with chimpanzees. Karl Pribram had been trying to get Yale and Harvard to take over the Orange Park laboratory but nothing had been done that would give Charlie a chance. For a time he planned to work with Walter Rosenblith at MIT on the operant conditioning of nerve impulses from the brain of various preparations, allowing efferent impulses to operate the programming equipment normally operated by pecking a key or pressing a lever. But eventually the Orange Park job came through.

For years my handwriting had been a problem, and when Charlie and I read an article in the *Christian Science Monitor* on italic, we sent for instructional cards and chisel pens. I joined the Society for Italic Handwriting, and was soon studying the works of the great Arrighi. A friend who was promoting the use of italic organized an exhibition at MIT and asked me for a sample. It was not, I am afraid, up to standard, but even a rough italic hand made a great difference. As I put it in a note:

1) I write more slowly and hence—
   a) more economically. Details omitted if not relevant; super-fluous adjectives dropped. [And I began to use "Notehand" abbreviations.]
   b) with less fatigue. I write more on a given point before escaping to something else.
   c) more deliberately, with much more planning.
2) I write more clearly. Hence—

a) I reread, or otherwise use, my notes more readily.

b) I take pleasure in the sheer appearance of my notes and with this added reinforcement write more of them.

c) I make fewer mistakes. "What is worth doing is worth doing well." At least I am kept from doing worthless things, and the energy I save may indeed mean that what I do I am more likely to do well.

A very curious byproduct—I play the piano more slowly, with much more attention to accuracy, completeness, fingering.

But I noticed a great increase in solecisms, malapropisms, and the kinds of errors one makes in taking dictation. I would write *or* for *are*, for example. My old hand was evidently a kind of primordial verbal behavior whereas, with italic, I first spoke covertly and then transcribed what I had said.

ANOTHER ONE OF THE PLANS drawn up at Putney read:

Research. Project pigeon. At current level. Support assured for 2 years. [The Office of Naval Research had continued to support my research for two or three years after ORCON was discontinued, but in 1955, the National Science Foundation had taken over, with a grant of $32,000 for two years.] Bill Morse all set. Round out Schedules, where necessary. Then analyze complex cases, thinking, and self-control.

William H. Morse was one of the five graduate students whom I had neglected in their ordeal by fire. Shortly after I returned from my sabbatical I went with him to a baseball game. The next day I wrote a note:

I brought Bill back to the laboratory at 5 p.m. This morning at 11 a.m. he is still here. He spent the night working out interresponse-time probability curves with Nate Azrin. This work is almost too reinforcing. The immediacy of experimental results is part of it. The gradual coming-together of diverse phenomena is another. Horizons get broader every day. Control of the organism becomes more effective. . . . We have passed the realm of intuition. We can deal with, predict, and control behavior very much as physicists do parts of the atom—and with as little appeal to what we would do if we were a pigeon or an electron.

Clare Marshall, a psychiatrist whom I had met when I spoke at the Boston Psychopathic Hospital, spent a year in my laboratory working on the reinforcing effects of sexual contact in rats. When a male rat pressed a lever, a receptive female dropped into the experimental space. The event could be scheduled in various ways and proved to be, to no one's surprise, highly effective.

One of the students in my first seminar at Harvard, Leslie Reid, took a teaching job in New Zealand. As a member of a committee that administered a small scientific foundation, I had been able to send him a cumulative recorder and a few other bits of equipment. By 1956 he had returned to the University of Aberdeen and I wrote to tell him that another one of our students, Lawrence Weiskrantz, had taken a job at Oxford and was using operant methods with monkeys. Larry had written:

> You might be interested to know that English monkeys are bar-pressing (to determine the reinforcing strength of various concentrations of saccharine solution), and everything was going beautifully until a new batch of baboons arrived in the Lab. Currently all monkey behavior is suppressed! They are terrified!

In September Larry moved to the University of Cambridge.

OPERANT INSTRUMENTATION was being improved. Ralph Gerbrands had formed a company and was making standard equipment for psychological laboratories. With Charlie's help, he built a highly reliable cumulative recorder, and by 1955 he had one machinist working full time on them. Rufus Grason and Steve Stadler, who had helped set up my laboratory when they were in charge of the Electronics Shop in the Psychoacoustics Laboratory, had also formed a company and were supplying standard prewired relay panels with snap leads. An early technical advance was the commercial production of pellets of food as reinforcers. The Noyes Company was supplying various kinds and sizes.

Our Pigeon Staff meetings were now an established institution. Murray Sidman often came over from Massachusetts General Hospital, Peter Dews from the Medical School, J. M. Harrison from Boston University, and Og Lindsley from the Metropolitan State Hospital. Half a dozen graduate students were bringing cumulative records to be reviewed, and new discoveries and new solutions to problems were discussed, often with great excitement.

Late in 1955 I gave a lecture sponsored by the scientific society called Sigma Xi at twenty-one centers on the eastern seaboard of the United States. It was called "The Experimental Analysis of Behavior" and showed the progress we had made since my lecture in Stockholm five years before. I used one of Charlie's curves from the Yerkes Laboratories in which a chimpanzee operated a switch with its right hand on a fixed-ratio schedule and another switch with its left hand on a variable-interval schedule. I showed "stimulus generalization gradients" obtained by Norman Guttman and his students at Duke University, and an experiment by Don Blough in which spectral sensitivity curves for scotopic and photopic vision in the pigeon were very similar to those of human subjects. I reported an experiment by James Anliker showing ingestion curves from normal and obese mice, one by Peter Dews on the effects of chlorpromazine on a multiple fixed-interval fixed-ratio schedule, one that Charlie and I had done on concurrent fixed-interval and Sidman avoidance schedule, one by Joe Brady on the effect of a tranquilizer on conditioned suppression, and one by James Olds in which for twenty-four hours a rat responded almost continuously to give itself shocks to the anterior hypothalamus. As to human subjects, I compared the performance of a pigeon on a fixed-interval schedule with one for a human subject in some work by James Holland, and other performances by pigeons on a fixed-ratio schedule with those of psychotic subjects.

HARRY SOLOMON AND I had received a grant of $50,000 from the National Institutes of Mental Health for the project at the Metropolitan State Hospital, and we were planning to turn it over to Og, but Og could not take it officially, because he had not yet got his degree. He had passed his orals but still needed to pass a German examination. Once a month he came to Memorial Hall, took a different version, and failed. I discovered that there were reasons: he had been shot down on a bombing mission over Germany and had spent many months as a prisoner of war—an experience not likely to condition positive responses to the German language. The issue became critical when the Dean of the Graduate School heard that he was claiming to have the degree. (In a hospital setting, along with medical students who had not finished their internship, he was called "Doctor" for the sake of the patients.)

I solved the problem when I learned that as an undergraduate at Brown University he had passed a two-year German course. I moved that the department accept that achievement in lieu of a German examination. Garry was furious: I was allowing personal relations to enter into an administrative decision. But the motion passed (by one vote) and Og got his degree and took over the project.

By the end of 1956, he had set up five new rooms and had recorded 1600 hours of patients' behavior. The daily lives of some of the patients were showing improvement. In one case, Og reported some effects of 600 hours of reinforcement with candy, cigarettes, and pin-up pictures on a one-minute variable-interval schedule:

> Rate of response increased steadily from 30 responses per hour to over 8,000 responses per hour. Patient placed on parole, for first time in 19 years of hospitalization, when rate had reached 2,000 responses per hour. Catatonic and hallucinatory behavior subsided, only to return when rate dropped to 300 responses per hour after 70 hours of extinction.

A year later, Og could begin a status report: "We have completed the methodological phase of our research and are now ready to spend our full research time on the analysis of psychosis."

I showed something of the same confidence when I gave a paper at the dedication of the Renard Hospital in St. Louis. Although all the other speakers were psychiatrists, I was brash enough to call my talk "What Is Psychotic Behavior?" It was straight-from-the-shoulder behaviorism: Behavior should be studied as a function of hereditary and environmental conditions. These were external to the organism, but for two millennia internal surrogates had taken their place; species status had been treated as instinct, hereditary differences as traits of character and abilities, personal history as memories, and the physical setting as perceptual experience. Behavior itself was internalized as an act of will or a wish, its probability of occurrence as psychic energy, and changes in its probability as thinking, discriminating, repressing, and so on. If all that were changed, progress could be made, and as an example I described the research at Metropolitan State Hospital.

* * *

THANKS MAINLY TO Joe Brady, who was actively promoting the experimental analysis of behavior in the assessment and study of drugs, almost all the large ethical pharmaceutical companies had set up operant laboratories. Advertisements for new drugs began to show cumulative recorders, and *Life* magazine ran a full-page picture in color of an unboxed rat pressing a lever surrounded by racks of relays and timers. Since departments of psychology were not yet hiring many operant people, a number of new Ph.D.'s turned to the drug industry for well-equipped laboratories and a reasonable amount of time for independent research.

At the New York Academy of Sciences in 1956, Peter Dews and I organized a conference on the effects of drugs. Howard Hunt, from the University of Chicago, talked about classical conditioning, Helen Nowlis from Wendt's laboratory at Rochester on the analysis of moods in human subjects, and Neal Miller on the value of using a variety of measures, but even so it was pretty much an operant affair. Peter talked about the different sensitivities to sedatives on interval and ratio performances, Bill Morse and Dick Herrnstein, in a joint paper, about certain effects on complex schedules, Don Blough, who was then at the National Institutes of Health, about sensory processes, and Murray Sidman, then at the Walter Reed Army Medical Center, about drug-behavior interactions. (Howard Hunt was the only one to use the expression "Skinner box," and I wrote to ask him to substitute "lever box" in the published report. He had already sent the manuscript off to the Academy, but the Executive Director made the change.)

At a Conference on the Evaluation of Pharmacotherapy in Mental Disease, sponsored by the National Academy of Sciences, Seymour Kety, a psychiatrist, took issue with what he called "a doctrinaire segment" of the paper I gave. "Why does the behavioral psychologist appear to belong to the one group which feels the necessity to deny other aspects of the problem, the mentalistic ones, which may be tremendously important? . . . It is one thing to say that I will study what I can measure; it is another thing to say anything that I can't measure isn't important, especially in this field of psychopharmacology. . . . Some people believe that feelings and sensations are important and until the time the mind can be resolved into neurophysiological or biochemical mechanisms it at least is not unnecessary and certainly not undesirable to include them in the discourse." And he cited the effects of LSD, "only about 10 percent of the total phenomena being behavior. . . . One can still create a mental science, so to speak, which deals with subjective phenomena, even though they may be reported through behavior, as still being things which exist and as still being things which are within the domain of scientific discourse."

I was not denying the existence of any event within a person's body; the important thing was not the act of feeling but what was felt. Dentists worked on the tooth, not the toothache, and psychiatrists on the condition of a patient, not on how that condition felt. Just as a dentist did not need to have a toothache, so the psychiatrist did not need to "share the feelings" of the patient (or take LSD, as was being suggested, to know what it felt like to be psychotic). We did not need to wait for neurophysiology or biochemistry to explain why people felt what they felt without talking about a mind.

Feelings were getting medical attention. Like the unfelt unconscious in psychoanalytic theory, they were held responsible for headaches, fatigue, allergies, ulcers, and other illnesses. In the thirties, Hallowell Davis had called my attention to psychosomatic medicine, but I had dismissed it as the institutionalization of mind over matter: the illnesses in question were due to environmental histories rather than the mental states said to result from those histories. The psychosomatic argument was incomplete: If a chronic anxiety explained ulcers or asthma, what explained the anxiety? If it was some part of the patient's history, then that was the explanation of the ulcers or asthma. The only way to get at a supposed psychic condition was through the environment, and that was where an experimental analysis of behavior came into play.

SOON AFTER MY Pittsburgh paper was published, a teacher in Surrey, England, wrote: "Machines such as you envisage for teaching both spelling and number are bound to come one day. How relieved teachers will then be of unnecessary burdens, how much freer to get to *know* their pupils." Machines would mean other differences in classroom practice. For example, students who were absent for a few days could take up where they had left off. (The person who is not good at mathematics may have been the student who was out with the measles when fractions were first taken up.)

Classroom practices could be improved in another way. Joel Wolfson had gone on to teach in a school in California and in January 1955 he wrote:

> I am using a system similar to the Klugy system which has been so successful year after year at the summer camp. My store this year is named after the school, the Driffill Dollar Store. I'm sending a sample of the reward coupons. The reward system has made discipline in the overcrowded classroom a pleasure. The children also regard the bills with more respect than the monthly report cards. They are rewarded according to the progress they show in their work.
>
> We also have the embellishments that my system so adequately provides. We have regular banking accounts with interest, raffles, deflations and inflations, etc.

Nothing could have been more appropriate to a system that would soon be called a *token economy*.

THE FORD FOUNDATION had set up a Fund for the Advancement of Education which, "in view of the impending steep rise in college and university enrollments," had in turn formed a Committee on Utilization of College Teaching Resources. McGeorge Bundy was a member, and at a meeting of the Committee on Educational Policy early in 1956 he told us that the Fund was ready to support research on teaching. I asked for a grant to build ten of the disk machines, rather cautiously described as "mechanical devices adapted to college teaching in elementary language and science" which permitted "immediate grading of multiple-choice answers [but also required] the student to compose answers, thus demanding creative activity rather than mere recognition." In April the Fund gave Harvard a grant of $25,000, and on Monhegan that summer I made elaborate mechanical drawings of a better model of the disk machine. That fall I hired a machinist, and the machines were ready by the late summer of 1957. One of them was demonstrated, with a program in geography, at the APA meeting that fall in New York.

One of the first government agencies to support automated instruction was the Office of Human Resources (HumRRO). I went to Washington to see Meredith Crawford, the director, was fingerprinted (and no doubt investigated), and eventually received a small grant. The Milton Fund at Harvard also gave me some money with which I was able to hire a colleague on the teaching-machine project. I chose Lloyd Homme, an imaginative, if undisciplined, young psychologist who could take a year's leave from the University of Pittsburgh. For space I turned to the Graduate School of Education, where John Carroll, who had worked with me at Minnesota twenty years before, was Director of the Laboratory for Research in Instruction. He and Frank Keppel gave me a large room in Batchelder House, a frame building recently acquired by the University.

That fall Lloyd and I moved in, joined by Sue Meyer, a graduate student from the University of Buffalo whom I had hired to write the arithmetic program for IBM; Irving Saltzman, who was spending a year in the department on leave from Indiana University; Douglas Porter, a graduate student in the School of Education; and Matthew Israel, a graduate student in psychology. There are several contemporary accounts of that year. Sue, in the secretarial role which fell to her according to the standard of the time as the only woman in the group, kept notes, and we sent reports to HumRRO and the Fund for the Advancement of Education.

We had, of course, never seen an instructional program. How much of a subject should it cover? How much in a single session? How much in each "frame" (as we began to call each presentation)? If frames were to reappear for review in later parts of a program, how should they be distributed? How much could we assume students already knew, and where were we to find students who were at the right point to test a program?

We explored various techniques of priming, prompting, and vanishing. As we reported to HumRRO:

> The student is first asked to talk about familiar things—for example, dots, lines, distances, directions, angles, and so on—using his everyday vocabulary. He is led—much as a lawyer "leads" a witness—to discuss

relations among these, many of which he has probably not previously noticed. Technical terms are then slowly inserted. For example, in geometry, the student first discusses dots; a dot then comes to indicate merely a point in space and the discussion proceeds in terms of points. Within a short time, and with little effort, the student finds himself discussing many of the materials of geometry or trigonometry in technical terms. His behavior may begin to "pay off" in the discovery and demonstration of unexpected properties or relations.

A new response could be primed, for example, by letting a gratuitous, unfamiliar synonym used in one frame replace the familiar one in the next. In general we moved from examples to principles (a practice which came to be called the "egrule"). Although we approached a final performance through successive approximation, we knew that knowledge was not linear and that programs would necessarily have branches. We explored ways of letting students skip sections when they were making very few errors, and we considered writing two programs, a long one with small steps in which even a mediocre or poorly motivated student would still make few errors and an abbreviated version for better students. But what was the "optimal density of errors?" After testing a program, on our one machine, we replaced a step which proved to be difficult with several smaller and hence easier ones.

By the end of the year we had constructed short programs in kinematics, trigonometry, coordinate systems, basic French words and material to teach French dictation, phonetic notation, vocabulary and rudimentary grammar, as well as single demonstration disks in geography, anatomy, and poetry.

One of the last taught a poem, as I had taught Debbie those lines from *Evangeline*, by vanishing it. Another was intended to teach "literary appreciation." I had read an article by a professor of English literature in which he reported how discouraging it was to lecture on literary appreciation to thousands of freshmen in a large state university. He was not sure that he could really help them appreciate a poem like Housman's "Loveliest of Trees." I wrote a short program on the poem for the disk machine. A few frames were about meter and rhyme scheme, the rest about content. Which stanza was about things, which about the poet, and which brought the two together? And so on. Perhaps it would not lead to a deep "appreciation," but I thought it would give students some respect for the poem as a structure and as the expression of an idea. If the professor was right, it could be as effective as his lecture and take much less time.

WHEN CARL ROGERS WROTE for a reprint of my paper on the control of human behavior, he added: "I don't know any American psychologist today with whom I feel a deeper philosophical disagreement, but I have a hearty and general respect for you because you are forthright and honest in stating your views. I wish that some time we might have a chance to talk together and explore what I believe are our differences." I suggested a public debate, and we arranged one at the annual meeting of the American Psychological Association in 1956. My paper was along familiar lines:

People . . . conform to ethical, governmental, or religious patterns because they are reinforced for doing so. The resulting behavior may have far-reaching consequences for the survival of the pattern to which it conforms. And whether we like it or not, survival is the ultimate criterion. . . . As science points up more and more of the remoter consequences, we may begin to work to strengthen behavior, not in a slavish devotion to a chosen value [I had in mind "happiness"], but with respect to the ultimate survival of mankind. Do not ask me why I want mankind to survive. I can tell you why only in the sense in which the physiologist can tell you why I want to breathe.

What Rogers seems to me to be proposing . . . is this: Let us use our increasing power of control to create individuals who will not need and perhaps will no longer respond to control. Let us solve the problem of our power by renouncing it. At first blush this seems as implausible as a benevolent despot. Yet power has occasionally been foresworn. A nation has burned its Reichstag, rich men have given away their wealth, beautiful women have become ugly hermits in the desert, and psychotherapists have become nondirective. When this happens, I look to other reinforcements for a plausible explanation. . . .

If the advent of a powerful science of behavior causes trouble, it will not be because science itself is inimical to human welfare but because older conceptions have not yielded easily or gracefully. We expect resistance to new techniques of control from those who have heavy investments in the old, but we have no reason to help them preserve a series of principles which are not ends in themselves but rather outmoded means to an end. What is needed is a new conception of human behavior which is compatible with the implications of a scientific analysis. All men control and are controlled.

The issue was treated a year later by John Hollander in a poem called "Science and Human Behavior" in the *Partisan Review*. It ended:

> I once saw Dr. Johnson in a vision;
> His hat was in his hand, and a decision
> Of import on his lips. "There is," he said,
> "Free Will, and there's an end on't." All the same,
> Atropos and her sisters, overhead,
> Grinned at this invocation of their name.

EVE AND I FIRST read plays at Indiana in a manner devised by members of the faculty of the University of Chicago. When interest in playreading in the department flagged, we found a few other people in Cambridge who had belonged to the original Chicago group—among them Amos and Katherine Wilder and John and Babette Spiegel. A new group, the Cambridge Playreaders, was born. The first performance, staged in our living room, was *The Long Christmas Dinner* by Thornton Wilder, Amos's brother. A real turkey was on the table in the set, and we ate it afterwards in a late supper. Monthly meetings soon became a standard part of our life.

We also saw something of the legitimate theater. In New York, Max Shulman, whom I had known as a student at Minnesota, had invited us to dinner with the composer and librettist of the musical made from his *Barefoot Boy with Cheek*, and we saw Max again when his *Tender Trap* was tried out in Boston. Clifford Odets, whom we had met on Monhegan, invited us to a theater party after a performance of his *Country Girl*.

THE EXPERIMENTAL ANALYSIS of behavior was "single-organism research." We seldom used statistics, and that meant trouble. I was once challenged because I called four of the more than four hundred curves in *The Behavior of Organisms* "typical." Typical of what? I had meant typical of all the curves obtained under the same conditions. A cumulative record for one rat told us more about behavior than a curve in which data for many rats were averaged, and it was not true that an averaged curve told us more about what another rat would do. Cumulative records often showed significant local changes in rate which disappeared in an average. At one time those who submitted papers for meetings of the American Psychological Association were asked to say how many subjects they had studied. In two sessions on animal learning in 1955, the average number mentioned in the abstracts was more than sixty. When I reported an experiment that Bill Morse and I had done on concurrent activity under fixed-interval reinforcement, I described the results for one rat and then said, "In deference to the standards of this Association, I will now report on the other rat."

I had made some of these points at a Conference on Psychophysiology at the United States Air Force School of Aviation Medicine at Randolph Field, Texas, in August 1951, but the paper was never published. (Paul Fields, who had organized the conference, later explained that the Military Chief in the Department of Psychology had taken offense "at the way the conference was run, and at some of the papers" and had ordered "that the preliminary report . . . could not be sent to you or even to the Commanding General." Fields was "ordered not to write or communicate in any way with the various members of the conference.") I made some of the same points again in a memorandum to the Harvard department. The statistics examination taken by our graduate students covered more ground every year as members of the department added topics in which they had become interested. Almost none of it was important for my students, and I myself could not have got a passing grade. In my memorandum I compared the equipment with which we programmed contingencies of reinforcement with the "sample space" of probability theory, as well as the more complex spaces of decision-making and game theory. It was impossible to account for the effect of the contingencies, as Charlie and I had found, without following the interaction between organism and space. A formal analysis of the contingencies or the sample space alone was worthless.

In 1955 the issue came closer to home when Robert R. Bush and Frederick Mosteller, both in the Department of Social Relations, published *Stochastic Models for Learning*. The publishers had asked me about their proposed book, and I had said that "it would be well-received," though "I would not see much hope for progress in the field of learning from this direction." Boring asked Bill Estes and me to write reviews for *Contemporary Psychology*.

Six years earlier, Fred had written: "What's all this stuff about 'stochastics'? Nat says Fred Frick is steamed up, and Nat himself is queasy about it. I never heard of the word, even, but it sounds quite esoteric and highfalutin." Bush and Mosteller had an answer to Fred's query; they used the word "stochastic" to emphasize the temporal nature of the probability problems they considered, but in my review I argued that they were using it in at least four different ways.

Statisticians were trying to help psychologists make the most of a "large bulk of empirical information on learning," but a more attractive possibility would be to discard all early work as crude exploration and "proceed to the collection of fresh data with new instruments and more rigorous methods." By showing that "*something* may be significantly inferred from a set of data," statistics encouraged psychologists to continue with poor methods. In a note I added that Bush and Mosteller had wasted "vast quantities of impeccable mathematics on vast quantities of peccable data."

I was bothered by the unwarranted prestige of mathematics in a field which I did not think was ready for it, but I hesitated to criticize it because of my own incompetence. To my students in Natural Sciences 114, however, I used the Borsuk-Ulam Theorem to show that mathematical certainty was not enough. I struck the lecture table with a piece of chalk and proved that at that very moment there were two points one hundred miles in opposite directions with precisely the same temperature. The statement was perfectly true but perfectly useless, because the points could not be located.

FOR A NUMBER OF YEARS my name had appeared on the ballot for President of the American Psychological Association. The Association was changing its character, and the elections were affected. Each year four experimental psychologists (Harry Harlow, Arthur Melton, Kenneth Spence, and I, representing the old order) were on the ballot with a "sociotrope"—a social, clinical, or educational psychologist. Each year the four experimentalists divided the experimental vote, and the sociotrope was elected. Because a similar issue had split the Harvard Department, Garry wrote to the Executive Secretary: "Every man who has been elected President of the APA during the last few decades has the right to feel honored because he was in that year the choice of a majority of the voters among a number of nominees who had been picked under a democratic procedure," but something should be done to get a better representation of fields.

The President served on the board of directors for three years, one of them as Chairman. An account of one meeting, published in the *American Psychologist*, was a frightening picture, and in 1954 I wrote to Fill Sanford, the Executive Secretary:

> *I am willing to have my name appear on the ballot for President of the APA, but I have the impression that the existing structure of the Association makes this merely a formality. If there is any danger that I may be elected, I would like to have it understood that my ex officio membership on the APA council [I should have said board] would be regarded by me as purely nominal. I will be away next year and in any case do not feel that I am the kind of person who should serve on such a council.*

Fill replied that the bylaws had something to say about the duties of the President, and that I ought to be willing to follow them. There was, however, some feeling that "the APA presidency should be more of an honor and less of a chore," and perhaps my stand would encourage the Association to change.

Eddie Newman knew a great deal about the Association, and I asked him whether the presidency was as burdensome as it seemed. He said it was. Indeed, the issue had been discussed, but no change had been made, in part because no one had refused to serve. It was then that I decided not to let my name stand.

The following spring, at Putney, I received the usual invitation and replied that I could not agree to serve. I soon received a desperate call from Fill. If I ran, they would have an all-experimental ballot! I let my name stand and, indeed, an experimentalist, Harry Harlow, was elected.

When I wrote to congratulate him, he replied that he was sorry to be deserting the little group which had stood together so long and so valiantly.

I never ran again. In a note I confessed that

> I do feel that I am letting some of my friends down and possibly forgoing the opportunity to give some of them a boost. . . . But personal considerations must prevail. I am planning to retire from psychology fairly early and have quite explicit plans for the remaining years. Serving as President of the APA would really upset the apple cart. . . . I believe the presidency of the APA is a very great honor, but I have already received more than one man's share of honors and in the long run I will look back with greater satisfaction upon the scientific contributions I hope to make in the next four or five years before retirement if I stick to the kind of job which, experience has shown, I seem to do best.

I HAD BEEN LUCKY in the university presidents under whom I served—at Minnesota, Guy Stanton Ford, and at Indiana, Herman Wells. I had never liked Conant, but he was not my president for very long, and in his absence Paul Buck, the provost, was almost faultless. The appointment of Nathan Pusey in 1953 disturbed many of us. In an address at the American Academy of Arts and Sciences, Percy Bridgman, one of my few heroes, commented on "a growing anti-intellectualism . . . the manifestations of which on the political stage [Eisenhower and Nixon] are too clearly before us to require further comment. Anti-intellectualism may be only one symptom of something more deep-seated. I must confess that the recent change of emphasis at my own university introduced by the new administration gives me misgivings in this direction. The emphasis is on a return to humanistic attitudes which we are forgetting in the hurly-burly of our technology, but without, as far as I can see, any notable revitalization of these humanities themselves in the light of our recent intellectual experiences."

Soon after his arrival at Harvard, Pusey made several tactless remarks about religion. He was not roundly applauded when he said he felt that all members of the faculty of the Divinity School should be Christians (its most distinguished scholar, Harry Wolfson, was Jewish), and he raised a storm when he announced that Memorial Church should be regarded as essentially Christian. The building had been given by Harvard men of all faiths or none in memory of those who had died in the war. Pusey contended that "true learning requires fundamental spiritual commitment or it is nothing." "The total college experience of each undergraduate will help him again and again in years to come to realize the enlightenment and joy of belief." In February 1956 I wrote to him:

> For some time I have felt a growing concern about statements appearing in the press which seem to reflect an official attitude toward religion at Harvard. Several paragraphs in your current Annual Report were particularly disturbing, and I have been wondering how I might make my reaction clear to you. Recently Mr. E. B. White, writing in the New Yorker, has expressed a similar reaction to statements of President Eisenhower's. Several paragraphs from his article seem so apropos that I venture to bring them to your attention. Mr. White writes:

>> The matter of "faith" has been in the papers again lately. President Eisenhower . . . has come out for prayer and has emphasized that most Americans are motivated (as they surely are) by religious faith. The Herald Tribune headed the story, "PRESIDENT SAYS PRAYER IS PART OF DEMOCRACY." The implication in such a pronouncement, emanating from the seat of government, is that religious faith is a condition, or even a precondition, of the democratic life. This is just wrong.
>> I hope that Belief never is made to appear mandatory. . . .
>> . . . When I see the first faint shadow of orthodoxy sweep across the sky, feel the first cold whiff of its blinding fog steal in from sea, I tremble all over, as though I had just seen an eagle go by, carrying a baby.

> I believe these paragraphs mutatis mutandis [Mr. Pusey was a classical scholar] speak for many devoted members of the Harvard Faculty, and I have thought it worth while, in the interests of good faith and intellectual honesty, to bring the matter to your attention.

Mr. Pusey replied:

> I am grateful for your letter and happy that you wished to express your concern to me. Let me say in reply that I feel confident no one need worry that anyone is ever going to suggest here at Harvard that "belief" be made "mandatory!"

* * *

I HAD HAD SOME CONTACT with Logical Positivism and the Vienna Circle. Through Van Quine I had met Rudolph Carnap, whom I saw again when he was ill and staying with the Feigls in Minneapolis. With Feigl himself I discussed behaviorism and the logic of science at length. I was particularly pleased that he liked my "Operational Analysis of Psychological Terms."

Philipp Frank, another member of the Circle and one of the great philosophers of science, directed the General Education program which included Natural Sciences 114. He was also chairman of the Unity of Science Committee of the American Academy of Arts and Sciences and asked me to be a member. I attended some meetings, but it was soon clear that I sought unity in a different direction—in an analysis of the behavior of the scientist—and I resigned. Frank was also President of the Institute for the Unity of Science. When he asked me to discuss the problem of privacy at its annual meeting, I was too busy to accept; but later that year, at the request of Herbert Feigl, a member of the Institute, I discussed psychoanalysis at the annual meeting of the American Association for the Advancement of Science.

In *Science and Human Behavior* I had argued that the Freudian dynamisms were not stratagems with which a repressed wish evaded punishment but products of the conflict between positive and negative consequences. The behavior at issue was "the responses of a person who had had a particular history, rather than the symptoms of a psychological struggle." I thought Freud's achievement lay in showing that many features of behavior were due to circumstances in a personal history, although that was evidently not Freud's own view. At the age of seventy he had said, "My life has been aimed at one goal only: to infer or guess how the mental apparatus is constructed and what forces interplay and counteract in it." But Freud had *invented* his mental apparatus, he had not *discovered* it. It was not a useful model in explaining behavior and certainly not in changing it. Freud's distinction between a conscious and an unconscious mind misrepresented the role of introspection. All behavior was unconscious; it was only when social contingencies, primarily verbal, led one to respond to one's own body that one could be said to become conscious of it. Freud believed that the mental apparatus would eventually be explained by physiologists, but the behavioral facts were much easier to bring into contact with natural science.

Harry Murray wrote that my paper was "well considered, well ordered, and well delivered," but he did not say "correct." He added a reassuring plea for help: "You may be surprised, or you may not be surprised, to find yourself cast in the role of Bad Habit Therapist, but I cannot think of anyone else who can come to my rescue at this moment." A patient, a twenty-year-old woman, had been wetting the bed without interruption since infancy. Harry had not found any indication of "the usual psychological determinants of enuresis," and it seemed "that a three-year analysis to discover some event that occurred in 1936 or thereabouts would not be the best way to spend her time or a doctor's time." He recalled my mentioning that Hobart Mowrer's device to correct bedwetting was being marketed. Where? I was able to give him professional advice: the Wee-Alert was sold by Sears, Roebuck for $18.95.

SOMEONE IN THE CIA sent me a page from a report reading in part: "The concept of feedback was reintroduced into Soviet behavior theory during 1955. . . . The technique is called 'operant conditioning' by Western psychologists. [According to a footnote, even less accurate, 'Operant conditioning involves the production of behavioral responses by stimuli not under the direct control of the experimenter.'] Operant behavior is elicited by the consequences produced by the environment as a result of previous responses which are 'sent back' in the organism. . . . There is no doubt that the possibility of operant conditioning combined with the renewed interest in feedback phenomena has opened up vast new possibilities for the analysis of behavioral phenomena in terms of a 'science of man.' . . . Such behavior raises most of the practical problems in human affairs, whereas classical Pavlovian conditioning has only limited laboratory applications."

The concept of feedback was emphasized in Norbert Wiener's science of cybernetics, but the Greek root of *cybernetics* meant merely "guidance" or "control." A guided missile was held on target, for example, by feedback from the target. That was very different from operant conditioning which, although it required feedback from the consequences of behavior, had the effect of increasing the probability that the behavior would occur again.

WHEN JULIE GRADUATED from Putney, Eleanor Roosevelt was the commencement speaker. Eve and I had always admired her, Eve especially, and we had a chance to talk with her. (Later I would protest to Dean McGeorge Bundy that Harvard had never given her an honorary degree.) Eve drove Debbie and me to Monhegan and then she and Julie put the car on a boat for Veracruz and spent much of the summer in Mexico. Julie entered Radcliffe that fall. She had planned to concentrate in mathematics but changed to music and from violin to viola.

I FINISHED *Verbal Behavior* twenty-three years after starting it. Two months later I wrote a note:

> The whole thing is aversive. I avoid using terms like tact, mand, autoclitic, though they would be useful. I am anxious to see the book appear but I seldom think of it or mention it. It will be interesting to see whether, when it finally appears after so much travail, I will find it reinforcing. I can understand how a mother might hate a baby who caused great pain or other trouble.

There was little if any of this left when the book appeared. It was the sixtieth volume in the Century Psychology Series, and as a graduate student I had written an (unpublished) review of the first—Boring's prestigious *History of Experimental Psychology*. The whole series had been edited by Mike Elliott. As Eddie Newman pointed out in a review of the series, it had contained "the basic trilogy on learning, Tolman, Skinner, and Hull," but had never had an introductory textbook as a money-maker.

The book went beyond the William James Lectures at many points, developing among other things (1) the autoclitic and its relation to primordial verbal behavior—especially in the interpretation of grammar, (2) the difference between scientific verbal behavior and poetry or fiction and their respective audiences, and (3) the analysis of thinking and knowing. I sent copies, never acknowledged, to Bertrand Russell and Joseph Wood Krutch.

SHORTLY AFTER THE START of the new year I wrote to Mac Bundy:

The more we go into the potentiality of instructional devices, the more exciting the whole thing seems. The Army, Navy, and Air Force are all alert to this and keeping in close touch with us. The Army is going to test one of our devices at HumRRO, and the Special Devices Section of the Navy at Port Washington has asked permission to duplicate the device in quantity for immediate research purposes. Meanwhile an extensive memorandum on teaching machines describing our work is being circulated among Air Force personnel and training people. Unfortunately there is no one to pursue the extension to academic instruction quite so aggressively. That may explain why I sound so aggressive myself.

The armed services and industry were looking for better ways to teach; the educational establishment would have to have them thrust upon it.

Lloyd and I had not gone very far with programs in introductory physics and French, mainly because we could not afford to hire people who knew the fields well, and I therefore decided to put teaching machines into Natural Sciences 114. Lloyd's leave of absence from the University of Pittsburgh was coming to an end, and I was looking for a replacement. At a meeting of the American Psychological Association I had met James G. Holland. It was late in the evening, and people were moving from party to party in the hallways of a hotel. Through an open door I saw cumulative records spread out on a bed, and a young man explaining them to a few people. A party-goer who had been watching him turned to me, shook his head, and said, "You operant people are crazy!" The young man was Jim Holland, and the records were from his research on vigilance.

"Looking for something" is a good example of behavior which seems to be directed toward the future. It is often said that a rat presses a lever "in order to get food" or with the "purpose" of getting food, or that food is its "goal." I had argued that "no current goal, incentive, purpose, or meaning [need] be taken into account," and I had used "looking for something" as an example. Suppose you teach a pigeon to peck a spot on a wall and then remove the spot. The pigeon moves its head back and forth as it "looks for the spot," but it is simply doing the kind of thing that has previously brought the spot into view.

Jim was studying that kind of behavior at the Naval Research Laboratories in Washington. Radar operators often sat "looking for" the blip of, say, an enemy plane on a small screen. Under what conditions would they look carefully for long periods of time? Jim was asking enlisted men to report the movements of a pointer on a dial which they could see only by illuminating it with flashes of light. The pointer moved on various schedules—fixed-ratio, multiple fixed-interval fixed-ratio, differential reinforcement of low rate, and extinction—and the resulting cumulative records of flashing had familiar features. I had used one of his records in my Sigma Xi lecture.

I persuaded Jim to take Lloyd's place on the project. By fall the new machines were ready and the University gave us a "self-instruction room" in the basement of Sever Hall in the Harvard Yard. We installed ten booths with sound-absorbing walls, each with space for a disk machine and a phonograph when available. During the fall term we tested short programs on miscellaneous subjects and parts of the program we were writing for Natural Sciences 114.

Teaching machines and a self-instruction room could not be kept secret, and the press came around. I worried about how Harvard would view the publicity, and put the question to Mac Bundy. He replied:

> I think it is high time that public attention was given to your teaching machines—and I myself propose to have no truck with circumlocutions. Moreover, since each Harvard professor is traditionally free to decide on his own methods of instruction, I see no reason at all why we should conceal the fact that you will be doing some teaching with machines next year. Finally, subject to your approval as Instructor, I have no objection to photographs of students working on these devices.

IN A NOTE DATED October 4, 1957, I reported that Eve and I and the girls

> got up at six and went out on the terrace. At 6:20 the Russian satellite Sputnik appeared in the North, crossed the Northeast sky passing the Big

Dipper, and disappeared into the dawn. Newton's theory of celestial mechanics has been experimentally confirmed!

An appraisal of American education quickly followed. How could the Russians have beaten us? It was not long before the National Defense Education Act was passed; money would at last be available for research on teaching.

I HAD LOOKED UPON my years of collaboration with Charlie Ferster as my Golden Age as a behavioral scientist, but Bill Morse came up to the same mark. In one experiment (which I reported in my Sigma Xi lecture), we studied the differential reinforcement of very low rates of responding: a peck was reinforced only if the pigeon had not pecked for a number of *minutes*. The pigeon responded steadily day and night for weeks. If it slept at all, it must have been in very short catnaps during the required intervals of no responding.

In some early experiments on that schedule, the pigeons surprised us by filling their crops with water. We had to lift them out of the box very carefully to avoid spilling. I thought I knew why. Hungry pigeons had once become similarly waterlogged when I gave them food whenever they drank, and in the present case a response to the key was more likely to be reinforced if the pigeon had just spent some time drinking. But other examples of "schedule-induced polydipsia" soon turned up to which that explanation did not apply.

In another experiment, Bill and I put a lever and food dispenser alongside a running wheel. Standing in the wheel, a hungry rat pressed the lever and received pellets of food on a five-minute fixed-interval schedule. During each interval it went for a brief run, presumably when the schedule was least in control. It was at about the same point in the schedule at which Bill and Dick Herrnstein had found that a pigeon would peck a second key to turn off an experiment, and at which Og had found that psychotic subjects would engage in bizarre behavior, much of it verbal. It appeared to be a kind of escape from aversive features of the prevailing contingencies.

In another experiment, we reinforced pecking one key with water, another key with food, and a third key with one or the other in an unpredictable order. When we changed food or water deprivation, the rates on the appropriate keys changed, and the rate on the third key was always an average of the other two.

We were puzzled by the fact that extinction curves following continuous reinforcement contained very different numbers of responses. One possibility was that some of the pigeons were not always pecking the key accurately enough or strongly enough to operate the food dispenser. If that were so, the reinforcement was intermittent, and more responses should be expected to occur during extinction. To be sure that every response was reinforced, we made an extremely sensitive key and evoked a strong exploratory peck with a technique prompted by my old experiment on the moving spot of light. We occasionally lighted the key for a few seconds and then operated the food dispenser. The pigeon soon began to peck the lighted key. We called the procedure "conditioning a 'hot' key." The result of the experiment (never published) was important: extinction curves recorded after many thousands of really continuous reinforcements contained fewer than a hundred responses.

When Bill moved to Peter Dews's department at the Medical School, one of our recent graduate students, Lewis Gollub, took over the pigeon lab. It was being well supported by federal agencies, but I was spending most of my time on teaching machines and programmed instruction. Taking stock in April 1958 I wrote, "Operant program does not move very fast. Retooling begins in three weeks. A more photogenic lab (danger!), more units, more time for active participation by me. Work on: attending, observing, choosing, etc. Self-controlling processes plus repeat on reaction time." By September I could add, "In full swing," but distractions were mounting, and our collaboration suffered. Lew carried on pretty much on his own, and we never published any papers together.

Dr. Henry Beecher, at Massachusetts General Hospital, was exploring the use of hypothermia in surgery, and one of our graduate students, Tom Lohr, set up operant equipment to check on possibly damaging after-effects, using rats as subjects. Two or three days after recovery from either ether anesthesia or hypothermia, runs of hundreds of responses broke through the interval performances on a mixed fixed-interval fixed-ratio schedule. They were attributed to "stress," possibly due to an accumulation of carbon dioxide. (Fred Keller had already studied oxygen deprivation, in which similar consequences had been taken into account.) Unfortunately, it was hard to induce hypothermia in rats, and the research never went very far.

For many years a biology teacher in the Plymouth, Massachusetts, high school brought a few of his students to my laboratory, and in 1958 one of them was a finalist in the State Science Fair. In an exhibit at MIT her pigeons successfully "named colors."

The Pigeon Staff meetings, still completely informal, were flourishing. In 1958–59, Nancy Mello, Tom Gilbert, and Howard Gilhousen were spending the year in the department, and Jim Anliker from Massachusetts General Hospital, Peter Dews from the Department of Pharmacology at the Medical School, Og Lindsley from the Metropolitan State Hospital, and John Falk from the Department of Nutrition at Harvard were also, so to speak, in residence. In addition, we often saw Don and Patricia Blough from Brown University, Marc Waller from the Jackson Memorial Laboratories in Bar Harbor, Maine, J. M. Harrison from Boston University, and Barbara Ray and Paul Touchette from the Fernald School.

In March 1940, *Science* had published a letter from my old friend Pei Sung Tang. He had helped to found a medical school in Kweiyang, where physicians were trained to be sent to the front against the Japanese. He and his colleagues had begun with "nothing—absolutely nothing, except a 'hospital' of four beds and a group of determined men. But those months were the happiest of my life. . . . Of course we are missing a great deal—the fine things that science and industry can give us, the music, the arts, and the theater—but I can sincerely say that we are having an experience that you all may envy, for as in a football game, we are the players, and you are the spectators." In 1946 from the National Tsing Hua University in Kunming he had replied to a letter I had written from Indiana. He was in touch with the world, thanks to a radio supplied by the U. S. Army, and was about to move to Peiping (now Peking), where he would be dean of a new agricultural college.

In 1957, Pei Sung wrote to several of his American friends. He was establishing an Institute of Plant Physiology in Peking and would welcome books in that field. I sent him some technical books, including *The Annual Review of Plant Physiology*, for which I placed a standing order at the Harvard Coop. He also asked for old magazines, and I began to send him copies of *Time* and the *New Statesman*, to which we then subscribed. (He soon asked me to stop. The magazines, he said, were making him "too conspicuous.")

THE REVIEWS OF *Schedules of Reinforcement* were mixed. In the *Annual Review of Psychology* for 1957, Howard Kendler wrote that

> to those psychologists who are starved for facts, this book will satisfy their hunger for many a moon. To those psychologists who are interested in controlling behavior, this book will offer both exhilaration and example. To those psychologists who are interested in quantitatively expressed empirical laws, this book will be a source of frustration. . . . [If] the behavior theorist . . . can control his temper he will realize that many interesting theoretical problems remain hidden and unanalyzed within its covers. . . . In short, *Schedules of Reinforcement* will sicken the statistician, puzzle the philosopher of science, and challenge the non-Skinnerian psychologist.

David A. Grant was one of the sickened statisticians. In a lengthy review in *Contemporary Psychology*, he wrote:

> From the standpoint of the efficient communication of scientific ideas, *Schedules* is a mighty noisy device. The reviewer cannot believe that all 250 million of those pecks are signal. Since statistical summarizing is disdained, the alternatives are to report all data or to select representative examples. Ferster and Skinner are forced to do the latter. Assuming that they passed the tests of genius and character prerequisite to presenting the "right" 5–10% of their findings, the authors must then leave to their readers the frustrating task of attempting any summarizing. Clearly, Ferster and Skinner believe it cannot properly be done, so that the culmination of all their program is indeed a bulky, cumbersome atlas and a crude one at that.

But Robert Ammons, in *Psychological Reports* for 1957, said that "For one who has patience to read carefully and to examine the many graphs the result will be rewarding in ideas as well as in information. The book provides a fine illustration of the fruitfulness of an integrated program of research no matter how initially irrelevant-looking the data."

In return for its share of the subsidy, the Merck Company got a few free copies, and I sent them a list of people who might like to have them. One was Donald Broadbent in Cambridge, England. He was interested in signal detection, and in thanking us for the copy he said he was having "an apparatus for human operant performance of the [Jim] Holland type" constructed. He wanted to look more closely at the inter-response times and at the effect of reinforcing one response on the incidence of another response. He thought our data on concurrent schedules showed an effect on one response of reinforcing another, "and it is certainly true in the human case that detecting signals of one type affects the detection of signals of another type." Jerzy Konorski in Warsaw acknowledged receipt of a copy, calling it "a magnificent present. We shall all study this book most carefully in our laboratory." He was sorry he had not been able to visit us on a recent trip to America.

My own comment after the manuscript had gone to the publisher's: "*Schedules of Reinforcement* never clinched the analysis. Crucial experiments needed, not to identify correct theory, but to gain greater control. Design all research in this direction."

DURING THE SUMMER OF 1956, several versions of a formal agreement with IBM had gone back and forth between New York and Boston, and eventually my lawyer sent one which he advised me to sign. We had reached Phase I in the program outlined a year before, two years after our first contact. Sue Meyer had been writing programs in arithmetic, but nothing was being done about a machine. The company assuaged my impatience by sending an artist to Cambridge, who sketched a machine as I described its probable features. When in April I wrote to point out that if I were to test a model in a school that fall I should have to make arrangements soon, I was told that a test by that time was unlikely. In August I reported that *Life* magazine was going to run a story on the disk machine; should I mention the IBM machine? Since the machine was not yet completed, I should not. Early in the fall I asked whether a classroom test might begin in February, and that was also said to be unlikely.

IBM finally turned the development of the machine over to a private model builder, and in the company's plant I saw draftsmen at work. By the end of the year a date was set for the inspection of a plaster model, and by the end of February I was to have a prototype to which I could adapt our program. (Meanwhile I had received an inquiry from a different division of IBM expressing an interest in teaching machines.)

THE SUBTITLE OF *The Behavior of Organisms* was "An Experimental Analysis." I had not attached any special significance to it, but the conferences which Fred, Nat Schoenfeld, and I arranged were said to be on "the Experimental Analysis of Behavior," and that was the title of my address in Stockholm. The phrase began to identify a field, distinguishing it from the animal psychology of Watson, Hunter, and Lashley, and in particular the work of Hull and his students at Yale.

Operant conditioners were finding it hard to publish their papers. The editors of the standard journals, accustomed to a different kind of research, wanted detailed descriptions of apparatus and procedures which were not needed by informed readers. They were uneasy about the small number of subjects and about cumulative records. (The cumulative record was, in fact, attacked as a "subtle curve-smoothing technique" which concealed differences between cases and should be abandoned in favor of "objective statistics.") At our Conference in 1948 we considered several solutions. Nothing was done until the spring of 1957, when the *Journal of the Experimental Analysis of Behavior* was planned and a Society for the Experimental Analysis of Behavior incorporated as publisher. Five of the first board members were students of Keller and Schoenfeld; seven were mine. Charlie Ferster, who had left the Yerkes Laboratories and was studying the behavior of autistic children at the Indiana University Medical Center, was appointed editor, and the first issue went to its 333 subscribers in 1958. Fred had been elected President of the Eastern Psychological Association, and his Presidential Address, "The Phantom Plateau," a delightful assessment of the "learning curves" which had appeared in textbooks of psychology for nearly half a century, was the first paper.

*　　*　　*

When I went back to Pittsburgh in 1957 for a second Conference on Current Trends in Psychology, I found myself among friends who called themselves social, clinical, physiological, genetic, and mathematical psychologists, one or two of the latter concerned with "the simulation of human thought." There was very little of the old experimental psychology, and in my paper I explained this "flight from the laboratory" by pointing to the reinforcers which lay in wait elsewhere. The Albert Schweitzers of psychology, working with real people in daily life, were yielding to the "blandishments of gratitude." Mathematical psychologists turned to unreal people, showing a preference, as a popular song had it, for "a paper doll to call their own" rather than a "fickle-minded real live gal." A flight to the inner man, mental or physiological, had the advantage that one's assertions were not easily checked. A flight to laymanship was attractive because one could then talk about almost anything, using "common sense." I did not expect to recapture "the interest and enthusiasm of those who have fled from the laboratory to pleasurable dalliance elsewhere," but "the possibility of an adequate theory of behavior, together with its enormous technical potential, would [I hoped] interest young psychologists." I found room for a reference to Sputnik: "The methods of science no longer need verbal defense; one cannot throw a moon around the earth with dialectic. Applied to human behavior, the same methods promise even more thrilling achievements."

I was more than ever aware of my position as a maverick when I spent a month at a lodge in Estes Park as one of a committee of psychologists who were to review graduate teaching in psychology. My colleagues represented many fields, and talking with them strengthened my feeling of isolation. (Our families came with us, and it was a pleasant month. There was square-dancing in the evening, and Eve and I had become good square-dancers at Minnesota, but there was a difference between altitudes of 800 and 6000 feet, and we danced briefly if at all. Eve and Debbie did a good deal of riding. For some reason I drank no alcohol.)

When my class in Natural Sciences 114 met that February, Jim and I had written 49 segments of a program, and they had been put on disks and duplicated. News of the teaching machines had raised the registration from 115 to 187 students. I met them on the first day of the term and explained the plan. During February and March they were to go through the programmed material. They would find machines available at almost any time of day, and an attendant would give them disks and collect and file their answer strips. If they put off the assignment, I could not guarantee that the room would not eventually be crowded. Most of the students paced themselves well and from those who did not we learned how much could be done in a short time. One of them worked through 31 disks in a single session, and another did the entire set of 49 in only two days, their performances apparently not impaired. On the average, a student went through the set in about 14½ hours. The easiest disk took 8 minutes, with a range from 5 to 13 minutes, and the hardest 28 minutes, with a range of 17 to 80 (the last figure atypical).

When I saw my students again near the end of March, I was sure, for the first time, that they understood the principles I would use in the course. I lectured with greater confidence and, I think, more effectively.

By the end of March, we found ourselves in possession of several hundred thousand responses. They were extremely valuable data. A program had the advantage over a textbook that weak spots could be found and strengthened. We could also compare the effectiveness of priming, prompting, and vanishing, and ways of avoiding unwanted responses. We had for the first time a clear picture of what it meant to teach part of a college course by machine.

I HAD USED A DISK in the teaching machine for the sake of the detent system, which made it easy to give the student a second or third chance at a correct response, but I had very little faith in classical research on verbal memory, and I do not know why I thus encouraged "memorization." Pressey's machine quite properly allowed for it, but behavior shaped by successive approximation was not learned by trial and error, and in a well-constructed program students made very few errors. The disk had room for only twenty-nine frames and no room for graphs or tables. The brevity required in writing each frame had a salutary effect on our style, as Jim later pointed out, but that did not offset the limitations. A better machine was needed.

One day I was showing Edwin Land the self-instruction room. When I said that the detents were not working well, he said, "You need a detent engineer." That was the way he would have solved the problem in improving a camera, but it was not within my reach. I would have to find a company, and on my next trip to New York I took a disk machine to show to a few people at IBM, hoping they would be interested in developing a better model. I used a disk which taught a short poem by progressively dropping out more and more words. It was a convenient example because it did not require any particular preparation, and I had been impressed by the speed with which Debbie had learned those fifteen lines from *Evangeline*, but it was a bad choice because, again, it suggested nothing more than memorization.

When IBM decided that it should not spread itself too thin and would concentrate on one machine, I took the disk machine to McGraw-Hill. I thought the company might be interested because it was already marketing a device using cards with magnetic recordings on their backs to teach foreign languages. They, too, turned it down.

There were, of course, simpler ways of presenting frames of material and exposing acceptable responses. Doug Porter built one of the first for some research on teaching reading, and Stanley Sapon and Charlie Ferster built another for a program to teach German. Later Charlie produced the "Ferster Tutor," made of heavy cardboard. Programs began to be published in workbooks in which students uncovered correct responses by moving sliders or turning to other pages. I did not like devices of that sort, because it was too easy to look at correct responses and other frames of material.

In OCTOBER 1958, *Science* published my paper "Teaching Machines." It began with a review of Pressey's work, with a photograph of a recent model of his machine, but went on to criticize multiple-choice testing. Recognizing a right answer was a superficial kind of knowing. (I might have added an example from my own experience: When the department was considering a new multiple-choice examination in French for our graduate students, a few of us took it to see how valid it was. My score was in the 99th percentile—and I could have argued about the point or two I missed—yet I did not *speak* French fluently. A similar difference in physics would be harder to spot.) We are all better listeners than speakers. For example, we know a name is right when we are told it, although we could not recall it. What, then, does "knowing the name" mean? I also pointed out that wrong answers must be plausible if a multiple-choice item is to be effective, and that they may teach errors.

In my paper I described the IBM machine and gave two frames of a program designed to teach spelling. I also described the disk machine, with frames from a program to teach incandescence. I discussed techniques for shaping verbal knowledge, the move away from aversive practices in the Western world in favor of other kinds of "motivation," the role of the teacher, and the economics of teaching machines. Requests for reprints came in a flood.

My friendship with I. A. Richards was still spiced by some basic disagreements. Soon after I returned to Harvard, he asked me to speak to his class in General Education. He called the class to order, made an announcement or two, and then said, "I now present the Devil," and sat down. (A decade later at a conference at the American Academy of Arts and Sciences he demoted me: I was simply "spiritual enough to be *advocatus diaboli.*")

Programmed instruction brought us closer together. Ivor was interested in teaching English as a second language to new Americans, and with Christine Gibson he had organized a company to publish paperback texts illustrated with stick figures. When my paper appeared in *Science,* he sent me some questions: What did "size of step" really mean? Could steps be measured? Would the vanishing technique conceal the value of the poem being memorized? But he concluded, "On the whole loud long cheers! Doubts chiefly as to how you can keep programming out of the hands of mere memorization routineers. I have known and admired your stuff so long I can say anything to you about it." And he asked whether he or Miss Gibson could come along to one of our meetings to give us a "generalized account of their *sequencing* as it bears on programming."

*   *   *

I WAS HOPING TO RENEW our Ford Foundation grant for three years at $50,000 a year. We particularly needed an indexing phonograph for a new kind of language instruction (a favorite post-Sputnik field). But Clarence Faust, the Vice-President in charge of education at the Foundation, said he could not support us. Nor could the National Science Foundation expand its support of the pigeon laboratory to include an analysis of the acquisition of knowledge. I tried John Gardner again at the Carnegie Corporation. He was generously supporting Conant's study of American high schools, but, again, the answer was no.

In March I had lunch with William Jovanovich, President of Harcourt-Brace, who was interested in publishing programmed materials at the high school and college levels, and within a month we reached an understanding: Harcourt-Brace would cooperate with any company manufacturing my machine and publish programs for it. They would start with high-school grammar, and I began to work with a consultant on a program eventually published in workbook form as *English 2600*.

I had had some discussions with the Comptometer Company, but during the summer Harcourt-Brace investigated Comptometer and found that it was not a very big company and was losing money. IBM was much more promising, and John McCallum, the Treasurer of Harcourt-Brace, went to see several of its officers. They agreed that they had been seriously at fault in their arrangement with me but would shortly move faster. They also intended to manufacture other types of machines, among them one for which Harcourt-Brace would be glad to publish programs.

A PLASTER MODEL of the IBM machine was eventually ready for inspection, and I later attended a meeting in which a young man from the office of a prestigious industrial designer told us what was wrong with it and what a teaching machine should look like. Target dates for a completed model were set and postponed, and eventually the project was assigned to a new IBM factory in Kentucky, where a working model was produced within a month.

I brought it to Cambridge, and we took it to a school in Somerville, where the superintendent had agreed to let us test it. Sue Meyer tried several tapes with a few children. IBM had asked for an elaborate report covering testing principles used, the optimal length of lesson, and the optimal length of time students worked productively, but when I pointed out that our agreement specified several machines, I was told to do what I could with just one. The evidence was clear: The children liked the machine and learned quickly. Their responses were rather like that of one of the first students to work on my earlier model, as Doug Porter reported it: "Are you sure this is arithmetic? This is fun." Nevertheless, early the following year I was told that IBM would terminate our agreement. My patent would be reassigned to me, and I would be given the rights to Sue's programs. I could keep the machine, and they would send the plaster model.

It was not quite over. An IBM engineer, Harold Robson, phoned me to "hold everything." The decision to drop the machine had been made by the director of the Typewriter Division, who preferred to use any available money to keep the IBM typewriter ahead of its competition, but the Data Processing Division might take over. An effort would be made to have the young children of Thomas J. Watson, Jr., President of IBM, try the machine.

When that failed, Robson looked for money outside the company. One prospect was a good Catholic who, after consulting two of the leading educators in the Church, agreed to subsidize the machine if Catholic schools could have exclusive use of it for three years. When I would not agree, Robson took the machine to a company in marketing, with whose help as "finders" I met several potential investors. (I came away from one meeting with a copy of Otto Weininger's *Sex and Character*, inscribed "from the brother of O.W.") In the end, nothing was done about a machine.

We had explored three conditions under which students learned rapidly: immediate reinforcement, freedom to work at their own pace, and a minimizing of errors through priming, prompting, and vanishing. We discovered another gain: frequent reinforcement maintained behavior in strength. On a good program students worked easily and well. Many of them spontaneously reported the absence of any feeling of effort while they were at work, although they might be tired when they finished.

It was a welcome change. Throughout history, students had studied to avoid the consequences of not studying, and in spite of a recent move toward permissiveness they were still doing so. That was why they worked hardest just before an examination: the subject had not suddenly become interesting; the threat of failure was then greatest. And that was why they drank coffee and took amphetamines when cramming and tranquilizers during the examinations. (Some teachers objected to programming just because it made subjects too easy. They were using a threat of failure for disciplinary purposes and lost control when their students were almost always right.) The three principal by-products of aversive control, as I described them in *Science and Human Behavior*, were never clearer: education had its own name for *escape*—"truancy"; attacks on teachers and vandalism of schools and school property were forms of *revolt*; and the apathy and stubborn inaction of many students exemplified *passive resistance*. These were among the major problems of education, and to a large extent they were created by education itself.

BEFORE WE WENT to Monhegan in 1955, I bought a little book of recorder duets called 4 × 6. It was a beautiful example of programming via graded difficulty, and I wrote to the composer, Hilda Hunter, to report its effect:

> *Deborah is easily discouraged. The fact that her older sister, Julie, is reasonably skillful musically is a problem. Last summer she watched as Julie and I played recorders or violin and recorder together. We were obviously having fun, and that made Deborah's frustration all the deeper. Fortunately, I had picked up a copy of your 4 × 6, and one day I managed to persuade Deborah to play the top part of the first piece. She was pleased with herself, but when she glanced through the rest of the book she said, characteristically, "Oh, I can never do that." As the days passed, however, we moved on to more and more difficult pieces with growing success, and within two weeks she was doing the whole book, playing either part with great éclat.*

*   *   *

SINCE STUDENTS who were "paying attention" listened to their teachers and looked at their books, it was easy to suppose that the task of the teacher was simply to guarantee listening and looking. The ubiquitous "Pay attention!" was supposed to have that effect, but physical restraint was more effective, and a remedial reading teacher at Shady Hill proudly told a group of parents that, since students who paid attention did not look out of the windows, she met her class in a windowless room. A young woman told me that she had invented a teaching machine, the only function of which, I discovered, was to hold her motionless while facing a book. A rather elaborate, nationally advertised, "teaching machine" simply held the student's head between earphones, facing a brightly lighted page.

One alternative to coercion or restraint was attraction. Educational television was defended on the grounds that the brightly lighted screen and the exciting events there portrayed *held* the child's attention. But looking, listening, and reading were "signs of attention" only if they occurred for a special reason: students paid attention when listening and looking were reinforced. Materials which strongly attracted attention deprived them of the chance to discover that paying attention could be worthwhile. Span of attention and distractibility were not traits of character; they were products of instructional contingencies.

I saw how important interesting material could be when Debbie was preparing for her first year at Woodstock Country School. She was to read *Vanity Fair* during the summer and take a test at the school in the fall. As I wrote in a note:

> Debs could not have read the book in a normal way (I found it hard to sustain as a sophomore at Hamilton), and so I have been reading it with her. She reads a page aloud, then I read a page. (We change readers in midstream, even in the middle of a word.) She has learned to read even Thackeray's tortured sentences with fair skill. (We came upon a sentence yesterday with a parenthesis between adjective and noun.) We have talked over the characters and the action, and I have discussed *autres temps, autres moeurs* and the battle of Waterloo. Still, the fact that the book has not been reinforcing is evident in the ease (!) with which she does other things while reading. She will: (1) stop to count the pages

left in the chapter; (2) leaf through the book, comment on the illustrations (bad); (3) go back to see if a word was spelled the same way before; (4) ask questions—"Why does he call her Becky sometimes and Mrs. Crawley sometimes?"; (5) ask my opinion of the characters; (6) anticipate the plot—"Does Rawdon really kill himself?" (7) look for the place; (8) simply sit silently looking at the page; (9) bring up other subjects—"I wish I had a such-and-such"—and two minutes later, "You can get them at the Coop."

My impatient "Go on, read"s irritate her. Sometimes I time her delays, or the reading of a page, to prevent myself from hurrying her. God knows what her teachers do. The solution is to give her a reinforcing text—something very different from *Vanity Fair*.

I HAD HAD TROUBLE with patents. The arithmetic machine was not taken seriously by my lawyer, and the patent finally issued (and assigned to IBM) protected only a piece of machinery with no feature that could not be "designed around." A report of the patent in the *New York Times* was reprinted in the IBM *Daily Newsletter*, and that was that. For a patent on the disk machine I turned to another firm and an equally useless patent was issued. The baby-tender patent was still causing trouble for John Gray in promoting the Aircrib, and I became unduly sensitive to possible competition in the field of teaching machines. In February 1958 I talked to a group of Regional Vice-Presidents of AT&T and showed them the disk machine. Herb Jenkins and Oliver Holt were psychologists at the Bell Labs at the time, and they asked me to suggest someone who might come to work on programming. I suggested Tom Gilbert, and he spent the summer there. He had designed a simple machine, of which Bell Labs made copies. "Enthusiasm," Tom reported, "borders on the unrestrained." One high official was "so excited he sent out a general notice to engineers announcing the arrival of the machine age in education and pointing out that the Bell Telephone Labs were in the vanguard of this development." Bell Labs then hired a man who had spent the summer on my project, borrowed Sue's master sheet of the arithmetic program, and offered her a job without telling me, in what I described to an acquaintance as "an all-out effort to invent the teaching machine."

Two professors at Hamilton College were programming a number of courses, and in February 1959 the college received a grant from the Ford Foundation for about $200,000, with a small grant to Harvard to support my role as a consultant. I soon heard that a company was planning to build machines for the project and presumably to market them. The president of Hamilton, Robert MacEwen, was an old friend (he had given me the honorary Sc.D. in 1951), and I wrote to say that I thought his people were showing unseemly haste. "My only reason for holding to any rights I may have in the design of the machine is to offer some *quid pro quo* to a company, so that it will put in the time and money needed for an adequate development without being faced with the possibility that, as soon as an excellent machine is developed, others may build and sell without having to pay for development." And I withdrew as a consultant. Later the president of the company building the machines wrote to the president of Harvard. I have forgotten the nature of his complaint, but the score was then even: each had complained to the other's president. By this time I had matters in better perspective. I made sure that the Hamilton men were invited to a conference in New York in June, 1960, and turned them over to reporters who wanted to know more about teaching machines.

A CONFERENCE ON TEACHING MACHINES, organized by Eugene Galanter and sponsored by the Air Force Office of Scientific Research, was held at the University of Pennsylvania in the fall of 1958. Five of the participants were from the Harvard project and their papers give a good account of our work at that time. Jim reported on the use of teaching machines in Natural Sciences 114, Sue discussed the IBM machine and the future of programs in arithmetic, Doug Porter described his year-long project in teaching spelling to second- and sixth-grade students, Tom Gilbert (who had come to spend the year at Harvard after his summer at Bell Labs) talked about analyzing and revising instructional programs, and I discussed the programming of verbal knowledge. *Verbal Behavior* was now in print, and in the presentation I could use rather sophisticated examples of priming, prompting, and vanishing. In a set of frames designed to teach the Greek prefixes used in chemical notation (*mono, di, tri, tetra, penta,* and so on), the student first went from Greek to English ("The Decalogue is another name for the ⸺

Commandments" or "A *monocle* is a lens for use in only —— eye")
and then completed familiar (and later unfamiliar) expressions by adding prefixes ("The *five*-sided building in Washington used by the Army
is called the ——gon" or "People who make a practice of having only
one wife or husband are called ——gamous.) Eventually the student
gave the names of chemical compounds ("CF_4 is carbon ——fluoride")
and wrote symbols ("Osmium octafluoride is written ——"). And all
of that on one disk.

A report of the conference was published the following year as
Automatic Teaching: The State of the Art.

When Robert Hutchins was brought into the new Ford Foundation,
he proved to be something of a problem, which was solved by giving
him a few million dollars to set up his own Fund for the Republic. It
supported a Center for the Study of Democratic Institutions in Santa
Barbara, where I spent a weekend during our stay at Estes Park. It was
rather like the Last Judgment. I was seated at one end of a long table
with Hutchins at the other end. On my right was I. I. Rabi, the Nobel
Laureate chemist, and around the table were half a dozen other distinguished scholars. Hutchins believed that truth about the human species
and its destiny was to be found in conversation, and we were there to
converse.

I had been asked to begin with my views on freedom, a subject in
which I had a vested interest. Operant behavior was traditionally called
"voluntary"—defined in one dictionary as "proceeding from the will,
produced in or by an act of choice." In my thesis I had reviewed the
history of the reflex as the steady attack on, and capture of, territory
once assigned to volition and, as an amusing coincidence, my first
appearance as a colloquium speaker had been as a replacement for
Leonard Troland, who had been scheduled to speak on "The location of
the will in the brain."

Mortimer Adler, a close associate of Hutchins's, had just published
a book in which he listed five basic ideas of freedom, four of which were
traced to the Greeks, and in my paper at Santa Barbara I argued that an
idea which had remained essentially the same for more than two thousand years was a failure. What could be said for the idea of a "natural

freedom of self-determination" when forty-four men of genius (from Anselm to Whitehead, in alphabetical order) had never been able to make it march? Effective ideas bred replacements. Aristotle, the leading scientist of his day, would not understand a single page of modern physics, but Plato would have little difficulty in understanding current discussions of freedom. It was not a welcome theme at the Center.

The Fund also had a Center in New York, and one of its committees was chaired by Halleck Hoffman. Possibly because of *Walden Two*, Halleck asked me to join a group concerned with voluntary associations. Among the other members were Harvey Wheeler, Eugene Burdick, and Stephen Bailey. We met once a month, with occasional guests—among them Beardsley Ruml, William Lederer, and Aldous Huxley. One day we took up the question of the President's gatekeeper: who gets to see the President, and why? Another day we considered using Kinsey's technique in other fields than sex (Halleck and Gene Burdick had held confidential interviews with known gangsters about their criminal behavior).

Most of the members were political scientists, and only at Halleck's request did I say very much. On one occasion, however, when Halleck tried to paraphrase my position, I prepared (in the middle of the night at the Biltmore) an axiomatic statement of principles, which was copied and circulated the next morning. Was "intention" needed in defining political activity? Was the hired hack carrying a political poster engaging in political behavior? A structuralist might say yes, but an operant analysis brought the consequences of the behavior into the definition, and the consequences for the hack were wholly economic.

Though I did not try to impose an operant analysis on the group, I once demonstrated its effectiveness. A guest for the day, Erich Fromm, proved to have something to say about almost everything, but with little enlightenment. When he began to argue that people were not pigeons, I decided that something had to be done. On a scrap of paper I wrote "Watch Fromm's left hand. I am going to shape a chopping motion" and passed it down the table to Halleck. Fromm was sitting directly across the table and speaking mainly to me. I turned my chair slightly so that I could see him out of the corner of my eye. He gesticulated a great deal as he talked, and whenever his left hand came up, I looked straight at him. If he brought the hand down, I nodded and smiled. Within five minutes he was chopping the air so vigorously that his wristwatch kept slipping out over his hand.

William Lederer had seen my note, and he whispered to Halleck. The note came back with an addendum: "Let's see you extinguish it." I stopped looking directly across the table, but the chopping went on for a long time. It was an unfair trick, but Fromm had angered me—first with his unsupported generalizations about human behavior and then with the implication that nothing better could be done if "people were to be regarded as pigeons."

The Committee never issued a significant report, but as a member I saw more clearly the contribution that an experimental analysis of behavior could make to the social sciences. I thought political science leaned too heavily on historical evidence, which in Natural Sciences 114 I had dismissed as "not easily integrated into a science of behavior." In its place we should analyze the behavior of those who govern and its effects on the governed. That was a view that did not please the Harvard Department of Government. Eddie Newman once heard the Chairman, William Yandell Elliott, refer to me as a "theoretical madman," but when he went on to ask whether anyone took me seriously, a tutor in government broke in, "My students do!" (I was told by someone who knew the field that my position was actually rather close to Elliott's.)

I had had one exchange with Elliott's protégé, Henry Kissinger. At a dinner meeting of the General Education Shop Club, Kissinger discussed current relations between Russia and America. America, he said, had a democratic type of government, Russia a revolutionary. I said I thought typologies were dangerous; in psychology they had been devastating. Could any existing government fit such a *pattern*?

Thinking it over afterward, I felt my remarks had been a digression, and I wrote to Kissinger to apologize. But I then developed the idea further, and referred to an article in the *Nation* by C. Wright Mills which "seems to me to make excellent sense precisely because the ultimate appeal is to practices which influence human conduct rather than to governmental types." Kissinger replied that he was "in complete accord with everything you say about stereotypes." He had not attached any particular value to the term "revolutionary." "The difficulty of our relations with the Soviet Union has nothing to do with the fact that the

Soviets are revolutionists domestically. In many respects they may well be more conservative than we are. It is rather that their philosophy has tended to make them look at the outside world with so much hostility and even apprehension that relations have become very difficult indeed. I wrote once that the distinguishing feature of a revolutionary power is not that it feels threatened, for a measure of threat is inherent in relations of sovereign states, but that nothing can reassure it. Perhaps we could have a chance to talk this over at greater length. I would welcome it very much."

Unfortunately, we did not talk further, and I cannot claim to have influenced Kissinger, although a story told many years later may be relevant. It was said that once when Kissinger was talking with President Nixon, Nixon's dog began to chew the rug. Nixon pushed him away several times and then, when he persisted, threw him a dog biscuit to stop him. Kissinger is said to have remarked, "Mr. President, you have just taught your dog to chew carpets."

Political scientists were usually committed to given ideologies and institutional practices; one could not get outside a political system to look at it with full detachment. But that was not true when governmental practices were interpreted with principles derived from an experimental analysis of behavior. The analysis itself was part of a natural science—in a broad sense, biology—and free of ideology to the extent that the results followed from the experimental setting, not from a bias of the experimenter.

It could still be argued that experimenters chose the conditions they studied and could abort work leading in a direction contrary to ideology or bias. It was said, for example, that operant conditioning was a peculiarly American process, studied only because of a fascination with individual achievement. Later, it would be called "factory psychology"; pressing levers or pecking keys was production-line work. But the original research had not been conducted because of an ideological bias. To Thorndike, a reinforcer had been "satisfying" (scarcely a conspicuous feature of work in factories), and I had run onto operant conditioning by accident. I knew of no research that had been stopped because the results were running counter to the experimenter's views.

We were also relatively free of ideology in interpreting religion, economics, education, and psychotherapy. By using behavioral principles, theologians could be freed from their own religious histories, and economists from their own economic sanctions. Teachers could begin to teach as they themselves had *not* been taught, and psychotherapists could minimize their personal involvements.

Verbal Behavior received a few favorable reviews. In *Science* Don E. Dulaney, Jr., called it "a distinguished book that makes an enormous contribution to the psychology of language. It is a rich and difficult book. But there is material here to influence all of the disciplines with a claim to the study of language."

I first received a very different opinion in a fifty-five-page manuscript by a linguist whom I had never heard of named Noam Chomsky. The first pages were not reassuring. An early footnote reported a "prevailing note of skepticism with regard to the scope" of the experimental analysis of behavior. (I could not take that seriously when work in the field was rapidly expanding, a new journal had just been founded, and many practical applications were beginning to be made.) My description of the causation of behavior was said to be "of a particularly simple nature." (Operant reinforcement was perhaps simple, but the contingencies of reinforcement were quite complex.) I was said to regard "the contribution of the speaker [as] quite trivial and elementary." (As an initiating agent, yes. As a behaving organism, far from trivial.) Linguists and psycholinguists dealt mostly with the effects of verbal behavior upon a listener. Their own responses to verbal stimuli—as in answering such a question as "Is this sentence grammatical?"—were among their data. They were unprepared for an analysis of speaking. I was said to claim that precise prediction involved only the specification of "the few external factors that [I had] isolated experimentally with lower organisms." (I did not claim to be able to predict verbal behavior precisely. I was *interpreting* it, using terms and processes derived from work in which a fairly precise prediction *was* possible.) I could not see how a review beginning that way could be of any value, and I stopped reading. A year later I received a thirty-two-page version reprinted from the journal *Language*. When I saw that it was the same review, I put it aside again.

It soon began to receive far more attention than my book. Chomsky, along with anthropologists like Lévi-Strauss, was looking for explanatory principles in the structure of behavior rather than in the conditions of which it was a function. The role of contingencies was assigned to intentions, ideas, meanings, and so on. Psycholinguists were taking the same line, following the development of more and more complex forms of behavior while paying little or no attention to the developing verbal environment.

A crucial issue concerned rules. As two psycholinguists put it, a child composes a noun phrase like "A coat" by following the rule: "Select first one word from the small class of modifiers and select, second, a word from the large class of nouns." This was called a "generative rule," used by children whose "average utterance is approximately two morphemes long." I could not believe that a child ever spoke in that manner. So far as I was concerned, the utterance was "generated" by the contingencies maintained by the verbal community. They could be described in a rule, but the rule was not *in* the contingencies. In arguing that rules of grammar are innate, Chomsky pointed to certain universal features in all languages. But take a baby boy from Peking to New York and he will grow up speaking English rather than Chinese. True, there will be common features—universals—but they will be due, not to inborn rules of grammar, but to the fact that both languages serve the same functions. In all languages people ask questions, state facts, describe objects, give orders, and so on, and "use grammar" in doing so.

It was said that a behavioral interpretation of language could not explain the infinite number of sentences which a speaker could compose (given infinite time); a creative intelligence must be recognized. But the same thing had been said about natural selection and the creation of a potentially infinite number of species. The origin of behavior was comparable to the origin of species: variations, quite possibly random, were selected by their effects on an environment—in this case, on the verbal community.

I had pointed out that when a young child is learning to talk, his first verbal responses are reinforced even though they are not well executed or precisely contingent upon stimuli. This suggested that I was arguing that children always had to be taught to speak. But many of the contingencies of reinforcement maintained by a verbal community were quite unrelated to instruction.

The reappearance of mentalism in the guise of cognitive studies supported Chomsky's position. My former student John Carroll is said to have begun a speech by saying, "Behaviorism is dead and it was a linguist [Chomsky] who killed it." It was not the first time the death of behaviorism had been announced.

HARLEY HANSON, a student of Norman Guttman's, had joined John Boren at what had become Merck, Sharp, and Dohme, and my visits continued to be stimulating. In September 1958, John submitted to the company a report of a brainstorming session in which we discussed drugs classified as stimulants, depressants, antianxiety, antidiscouragement, antidepressant, anaphrodisiac or sex depressant, appetite stimulant or depressant, analgesic, euphoriant or anti-"guilt," emotion suppressant or stimulant, and antifatigue. We also discussed drugs which simulated or suppressed psychotic behavior and made stimulus control more or less precise and behavior more orderly. Merck manufactured streptomycin, an antibiotic that often worked where penicillin failed but, when taken chronically in high doses, produced deafness. I thought an adaptation of the Békésy technique as developed by Ratliff and Blough could be used to study the hearing of rats in looking for an alternative drug.

Side effects were a serious problem with most of the psychotropic drugs, and although I still talked about "the exciting possibility of the chemical modification of behavior," I was growing less sanguine. Behavior could be changed, after all, in better ways. Schedules of reinforcement had many of the effects we considered in that brainstorming session.

Because I was badly overworked, I was especially interested in the possibility of a drug that to some extent offset fatigue or had the same effect as sleep; and I both discussed and exemplified the problem when, in December 1958, I gave a Vice-Presidential Address on "The Effects of Drugs on Behavior" at the annual meeting of the American Association for the Advancement of Science. The next day I wrote a note:

> I did a poor job. It was a good audience, an honored occasion, an interesting subject on which I had something to say, but I was tired and bored and could scarcely force myself to compose the sentences needed

to put an end to it. In the first place I did not want to give the lecture. If I had seen the office coming, I should have refused to serve. Secondly, it was not a sharply characterized occasion—a miscellaneous group with varied or unknown interests, some there because of the announced title, others because they were psychologists attending the AAAS. I had given the same lecture to the Pharmaceutical Manufacturers at Sea Island and was killing two birds with one stone. I thought I had something to say and still feel I ought to publish an article about operant research in pharmacology and the field in general, but I didn't catch fire.

Fortunately, Joe Brady had organized a livelier session in which John Boren, Bill Morse, and Don Bullock gave papers. Murray Sidman and I were discussants.

WHEN I EXPLAINED to the staff at Shady Hill how I would teach a child to spell a word, a teacher said, "Yes, but can you teach *spelling?*" When I asked a colleague, "What do you expect a student to do as the result of having taken Physics 1?" he replied, "I guess I've never thought about it that way," but he would settle for "a general knowledge of physics." When I asked a friend who was working on the new math, "what do you want the student to do?" he said, "Just follow a logical argument." Behavior was one thing; spelling, a knowledge of physics, or following a logical argument was something else. (The something else was often used to cover failure: a child who could not read well could still be said to have been "given the experience of reading.") In 1957 Carl Rogers wrote: "If learning could be arranged in the ways I believe you are trying to do, then from my point of view that would leave room for education to take place on top of it."

In our report to HumRRO, we had said:

What is needed is nothing less than an analysis of various forms of knowledge. . . . It does no good to say that we are interested in setting up "mathematical ability" or "artistic appreciation" or a "language skill." We must identify relevant behaviors. [Those who] suggest that we are neglecting "abilities" or "understanding" or "insight" . . . should be asked to specify the behavior which they would accept as indicating a successful realization [of these goals]. If among the specifications there are kinds of behavior which have not been taken into account, further programming will be needed.

Ben Wyckoff and Roger Kelleher, among others, had demonstrated a kind of "intellectual self-management" by arranging contingencies under which a pigeon responded in one way to improve its chances of responding successfully in another. Something of the sort happens when children are taught to look carefully at a problem before trying to solve it or simply to put objects side by side in order to compare them more accurately. Jim Holland, working with Eugene Long, began to teach inductive reasoning. Small geometric forms were arranged in a series according to some principle; the child was to extend the series by choosing the form which came next. Sequences became more and more complex, and verbal analyses leading to correct choices were primed and prompted. The children made few if any mistakes, yet they could be said to have solved a problem in much the same way as those rare children who discover a solution for themselves. They would be much more likely to go on to solve other problems.

Jim had turned his attention to the proper construction of items. Priming, prompting, and vanishing could work too well. An item could essentially *tell* a student the answer, in which case little learning would take place. An example of a bad frame from a program published by Harcourt-Brace was used in an editorial in *Science*:

"Even Frost would probably not have forced so much rhyme on himself if he had planned a long poem. Since he doubtless had a hunch that this was to be a —— rather than a long poem, he decided to increase the difficulties of his rhyme scheme still more."

The word *short* is missing, but so is something else. What is also missing is the careful analysis that should go into preparing these items.

WITH SANFORD AUTOR, and later with Charlie Catania and George Reynolds, I studied aggression. When a hungry pigeon attacked another, we gave it food. At first, it simply moved so close to the other pigeon that an exchange of pecking occurred, but later a fairly standard attack emerged: the aggressor, but not the aggressee, cooed, paced back and forth, and ruffled its neck feathers. As I said in a note, "The ethology rides in on the operant behavior." The other pigeon remained relatively quiet, and in its living cage afterward behaved in a way which could be called a "funk."

When we reinforced attack in white light but not in green, the ethological pattern continued to be displayed in white light but disappeared in green. We could turn aggression on and off by changing the color of the light. With a touch of whimsy, we tried music as the peaceful stimulus; it soothed the savage breast.

There was an obvious bearing here on human aggression. The characteristic display, and presumably the feeling, of emotion, followed rather than caused the behavior reinforced as aggressive. I noted that "the question of why hurting someone is reinforcing to an angry man is not answered," though I would soon be arguing that a susceptibility to reinforcement by signs of damage presumably evolved because of its survival value in shaping effective aggression.

Later we designed food dispensers which could be operated only by a pigeon which "knew how to operate them," and could then selectively reinforce either pigeon and bring its aggression under the control of a special stimulus. By reinforcing going to opposite corners when not fighting, we staged a kind of championship bout.

In May 1958 a representative of the Rheem Company came to see me. The company manufactured steel drums, which were losing out to pipelines, and was planning to diversify. It was interested in teaching machines. I met one of its officers, who painted a glowing picture of the financial rewards which lay ahead. A lawyer whom I had met on the Committee of the Fund for the Republic, Don Rivkin, helped me with a preliminary agreement, and in June 1959 the Rheem board of directors approved a plan to develop an improved model of the machine I was using in Natural Sciences 114 (with paper tapes replacing disks), a "preverbal" panel-pushing machine, and (if IBM dropped it) a machine in which answers were composed by pressing keys. In August I signed a formal agreement, the terms of which were much less opulent than those we had first discussed. It would be my last commercial venture. As I wrote to Rivkin, "If Rheem wants out in eighteen months, I will stop trying to promote teaching machines."

A trade name was needed, and I spent many hours combining and recombining *self-* and *auto-* with all the words and roots I could find associated with teaching or learning. For IBM I had proposed "Auto-structor," which unfortunately suggested a traffic accident. I rather liked the Greek root *didaktos*, and "Auto-Didak" would have served if *autodidact* had not become slightly pejorative as the word for a self-taught person. I suggested "Didak," not entirely free of the overtones of *didactic*, and the company registered it as a trademark.

Early versions of the machines were to be exhibited at the APA convention in Cincinnati in September, along with a machine which taught typewriting and a recent model of the Air Force Subject Matter Trainer. I began to worry about my place in the exhibit. No doubt machines would have to be produced commercially if they were to be widely used, but how far could I go in promoting them? I went over the APA statement on ethics and, from Monhegan, wrote to Smitty Stevens and Eddie Newman for advice. To Rheem I wrote: "(1) I assume these are to be Rheem's teaching machines, not Skinner's. 'Rheem' is to become the household (or schoolhousehold) word. (2) My name will appear in the early development simply as a guarantee of up-to-date design to early users. (3) There will be no point in stating our association once it is generally known that the Rheem machines have my blessing—and this should be the case fairly soon. (4) In the general distribution to schools there will be no reason to bring my name in at all. Eventual users won't know me from Adam, and there is no reason why they should."

No particular problem developed at the meeting. A press conference for Rheem was inevitable, but I refused to pose with the machines. I mentioned them in a symposium on Methodology in Education, in discussing a paper by Simon Ramo on possible contributions of the electronics industry, but I carefully avoided saying that they could be seen at the meeting.

The machines had been thrown together in a hurry, and more work was needed. As I wrote to my contact at the company, a change in one of them made on the advice of another consultant was wrong and should be corrected, and many things needed to be done with the other. I hoped the company would organize an advisory council on teaching machines, and as members I suggested Leslie Briggs, Fred Keller, Howard Kendler, Arthur Lumsdaine, Arthur Melton, Neal Miller, and Sidney Pressey.

A month or so later the president of Rheem told me that, to accelerate the project, they were buying a language-laboratory company with suitable manufacturing facilities, and in December I dined with Rheem's board of directors at a private club in New York. I could report many auspicious signs. Harvard was setting up a Center for Programmed Instruction, and within the week I would be filming a prime-time television special with Charles Collingwood in which teaching machines would be featured. (The film opened with a demonstration of one of the Rheem machines.) In a few days I would be meeting Conant's prestigious group. I thought I could say that the company was on to a good thing at just the right time.

The machines on display at the dinner, however, were the defective ones I had seen in September, and the next day I wrote to my contact that nothing seemed to have been done "in spite of the fact that literally hundreds of people are waiting for models. Three valuable months have been wasted. I had the impression that the Board of Directors were in favor of quick action, but the market is not going to stand around and wait."

THE CONQUEST PROGRAM with Charles Collingwood would be sponsored by the Monsanto Chemical Company, and although the Harvard administration was unhappy about involvements in commercial television, Mr. Pusey granted an exception because Monsanto was supporting the program as a public service (and research at Harvard as well). The corridors of Memorial Hall were filled with photographic equipment for a week. A window between my office and the hall was removed so that Collingwood and I could be filmed in conversation at a slightly greater distance. Dick Herrnstein and I were filmed as we shaped responses in a pigeon, set up a discrimination, reinforced responses on fixed-interval and variable-interval schedules, and differentially reinforced a low rate. We taught a pigeon to match to sample and demonstrated pigeons which attacked one another whenever a green light was on but remained peaceful when it was off. I lent them a film of pigeons playing Ping-Pong, and one from Project ORCON showing a pigeon pecking the image of a ship during two diving approaches, with a gold contact on its beak. They photographed a friend's child matching words with objects and thus learning to read on the Rheem machine, and Charles Collingwood going through several frames on the machine in the self-instruction room in Sever Hall. The program, called *What Makes Us Human*, was aired on March 6, 1960, and was shown on the BBC and in Canada.

THE BOARD OF DIRECTORS of Harcourt-Brace was to review the question of teaching machines and programmed instruction, and I was asked to send the IBM machine to be shown to them. Early in March, Jovanovich wrote that the meeting had run a long time and that another would soon be held. A week later, the company treasurer walked into my office and handed me a letter from Jovanovich, regretting that the board had refused to back the project and that Harcourt-Brace was withdrawing from the teaching-machine field. They would do whatever seemed to me reasonable, and I suggested that they pay me the balance of my small consulting fee for the current year. They would keep all rights to the grammar program (they did not tell me that they were planning to publish it in workbook form), but I could have an elaborate machine that a model builder had made for them.

THE MEAD-SWING LECTURES at Oberlin College were "designed to keep Oberlin students informed of significant developments in science, in religion, and in the relations between the two fields." In October 1959 I gave four lectures on "The Design of a Culture." Before I arrived, a professor of political science attacked my ideas as either unworkable or dangerous. In a radio broadcast he said that if the science I represented were really feasible, he would be "in favor of calling out the firing squad."

Oberlin's Department of Psychology was one of the oldest behavioristic departments in the country, and some of its students were also taking political science. They decided to demonstrate the power of a behavioral analysis by shaping the professor's behavior. They would get him to stand on one corner of the platform for a few minutes and then to face the blackboard. They began the class period with deadpan indifference. When the professor moved toward the chosen corner, they nodded and smiled. He was soon teetering on the edge. A signal went out, and the nods and smiles were withheld until he turned toward the blackboard. I was told that he finished his lecture facing the board and talking over his shoulder—arguing meanwhile that operant conditioning worked with rats and pigeons but not with people.

The Chairman of the Mead-Swing Committee, Professor Walter Horton, a theologian, was sympathetic and helpful. When he disagreed with me, he confined his criticism to recommending a relevant book or two.

In my lectures I argued that man, both as a species and as an individual, was the product of his environment and that, contrary to common belief, that was an encouraging view because the environment could be changed much more easily than man himself. In 25,000 years the species had probably undergone very little genetic change, but it had built a world in which it was able to behave in much more effective ways. It had done so largely because various cultural practices, quite possibly arising by accident, had been selected by their contribution to the survival of the practicing group. The explicit design of better practices was now possible. The good of the culture was the ultimate value, and to the question, "Why should I care whether my culture survives?" one could only reply, "Perhaps there is no real reason, but if your culture has not given you one, so much the worse for the culture."

Would-be designers of cultural practices were accused of intervening in a natural process, but they also had evolutionary histories. When they intervened, they were simply acting in ways shaped by their cultures. Our own culture had reached the stage at which explicit design was common. We invented new forms of education, new kinds of industrial incentives, new methods of taxation, new forms of social security, and so on. We might even have reached the point at which a science of behavior would yield new ways of designing practices.

*   *   *

For years I had had a sublime faith that the truth would prevail. I was quite content to get my papers into print somewhere; those who needed them would find them. (It was a useful principle, for it permitted me to continue working in isolation when isolation was probably more valuable than being influential.) I may have been right about a future historian of ideas grubbing about in a library, but I was wrong about my contemporaries. They were not reading all my work, and in taking stock during my Putney sabbatical I considered putting together a book of collected papers. I could think of eighteen that could be included, but when the manuscript went off in October 1958, it contained thirty. I called the book *Cumulative Record*.

When I asked Garry if I could dedicate it to him, he was immensely pleased. No one had ever dedicated a book to him. My request was more than a gesture of departmental solidarity. Garry and I had at last begun to understand each other, and our antagonisms had given way to something close to affection. When he retired in 1957 and the Edgar Pierce Professorship passed on to me, his response was typical:

It may make but little difference to you, but I want to tell you that I get pleasure and satisfaction (reinforcement? but what for?) out of the fact that the University has now tacked the Edgar Pierce label onto your title. . . . Of course I was it first. Is it immodest of me to congratulate you? Well, I had been around and identified with Harvard's Edgar-Pierce kind of psychology, laboratory psychology, and I had one foot on the brink of retirement, and I do think that made sense too, though I should hate by my incumbency to have lessened in any way the significance of the distinction for my successors. But all I am saying is the simple thing: I think that, by and large, algebraically, Harvard appreciates you, and it pleases me that it says so, even when its huzzah is only whispered.

I thought the rapprochement was due largely to a change in Garry. In editing *Contemporary Psychology*, a journal of reviews, he had been brought into contact with much more of the field of psychology than he had covered in his *History*. He had more or less escaped from Titchener and had even begun to understand behaviorism. No doubt he would have seen a change in me.

Perhaps because I was getting a book "for nothing," I went about preparing *Cumulative Record* in a curiously debonair way. The very title was a pun. My preface contained a cumulative curve showing the number of words in the papers plotted against the year of publication (and the publishers put it on the cover above my name). I wrote a brief introduction for each paper and added "A Word about Boxes."

When I saw my first copy, I knew that something was wrong: I had been boasting! I had told the reader that "Freedom and the Control of Men" had been reprinted in the French and Italian editions of *Perspectives U.S.A.*; that Gertrude Stein had said of me as a psychologist that . . . when he is not too serious he is a pretty good one"; that although my chapter in *The Behavior of Organisms* on "The Conceptual Nervous System" had been "interpreted as showing an anti-physiological or anti-neurological bias," I believed the book was "a positive contribution to physiology"; that when a questionnaire was sent to seventy-three couples who had used baby-tenders for one hundred thirty babies, all but three had described the device as "wonderful . . . with physical and psychological benefits [which] seemed to warrant extensive research." "A Word about Boxes" read as follows:

The title "Baby in a Box" was not mine; it was invented by the editors of the *Journal*. Nevertheless, the Air-Crib is a sort of box, and this is also true of the apparatus known as the "Skinner Box"—an expression which I have never used and which my friends accept as *verboten*. (I believe the term was first popularized by Hull and his students in the form "Modified Skinner Box.") Helplessly, I have watched the teaching machines gradually assume the form of boxes. (There is consolation in the fact that in this case the organism remains on the outside.)

I confess to one extension of the term, though I plead irresistible circumstances. At the dedication of the Renard Hospital in St. Louis . . . there was a summarizing round-table discussion. Someone mentioned the "Skinner box" and a discussion ensued. I took no part in it, and Alan Gregg, sitting next to me, evidently shared my discomfiture. Finally he leaned over and whispered, "Box et praeterea nihil." It was doubly appropriate: (1) we had been hearing about "nothing but boxes" for several minutes, and (2) the gist of the argument had been that one could have an effective science using the facts observed in the box *and nothing more.*

At that point someone asked me to comment on the way in which my utopian novel, *Walden Two*, had been received. I could not resist the variables, intraverbal and otherwise, which were playing upon my behavior and therefore replied that I had evidently been accused of wanting to build a *box populi*. I do not believe the remark has seriously damaged the notion of an experimental community. Nevertheless, it is surprising how often a proposal to remedy some defect in current cultural designs is brushed aside with a reference to boxes.

I was dismayed. I was advertising the "Skinner Box," dropping names, and showing off my Latin and my wit by *punning* in Latin. What would the many friends to whom I had sent copies think of me? Dick Herrnstein was one of them, and my anxiety was somewhat assuaged when he was surprised to hear that I was concerned. Had anyone criticized me? He thought the material was charming. But I suffered acutely, and within a year I had persuaded the publishers to bring out an enlarged edition. It was "enlarged" by the addition of only three papers, added without repaginating, but with most of the offending material removed. As I wrote in a note: "Gone are the personal touches . . . gone is my acute shame in thinking about them."

A year or two later, reading something by Diderot, I found myself envious of his freedom in speaking about himself, and it occurred to me that I should write under another name. Fiction under my own name was a possibility, of course, but it was not concealing enough. I needed to let go completely, and a truly anonymous book might be the solution.

THE DEPARTMENT OF PSYCHOLOGY had in a sense retreated to the basement of Memorial Hall, where it was rather isolated. It was only slowly that I came to meet other members of the Harvard faculty. Beginning in 1951, I served for five years on the Committee on Educational Policy, which met once a month under the chairmanship of the President or the Dean of the Faculty of Arts and Sciences and brought important policy decisions to the attention of the faculty. For five years I was also a member of the Council of the American Academy of Arts and Sciences. Kirtley Mather was President, and some of the other members of the Council were Harvard people. (I played only a small part on these committees. It was not the kind of thing I took any interest in or did well.)

My only other contact with the Harvard community was the Shop Club, a group of twenty or thirty professors who met once a month to have cocktails and dinner and hear a member talk about his work. Garry proposed me for membership. Percy Bridgman was another member, and among the older men I got to know Howard Mumford Jones, Harlow Shapley, and Sidney Fay. Fay, the author of *The Origins of the World War*, lived near me, and as he grew old and nearly blind I began to drive him to the meetings. L. J. Henderson had never liked him; "He whitewashed the Germans," he said. Among the younger members I got to know Evan Vogt, the anthropologist, and Zeph Stewart, in Classics, a moderating influence on my anticlericalism and always helpful with a reference or a bit of Greek or Latin grammar. When Vogt ended his year as Steward, he asked me to take over. At the time I was seriously overworked, and often struggled not to doze off after presenting the speaker for the evening.

JAMES BRYANT CONANT HAD RETURNED from service as High Commissioner in Germany to embark upon a study of the American high school. Under the auspices of the Carnegie Corporation he visited schools, talked with administrators, teachers, and students, and published a series of books. In general, he thought there was nothing wrong with the schools that could not be corrected by good intentions and good judgment. He was asking questions such as: How many class periods were needed for flexible schedules? What ratios of pupils to teachers and counselors were acceptable? What subjects should be taught, and when? How much homework should be required? But he was not asking what I thought was the important question: How can teachers teach better?

I wrote to ask if I could come to New York to talk with him. He replied that he would be interested in knowing more about my "so-called 'teaching-machine'" and that if I would inform him of any "probable appearance in this city," he would try to schedule a meeting. He added, however, that "it is certainly not worth your while to make a special trip for the purpose of instructing us." Eve and I were taking Debbie to New York between the holidays, and a meeting was arranged for the morning of Thursday, December 31, 1958. We would have a discussion and then Conant would take me to lunch.

Before the meeting, I sent him a copy of the first chapter of my manuscript on teaching machines and programmed instruction. We were faced, I said, with a consumer's revolt:

> Parents, employers, the military—these are the disaffected and they are complaining of the products of education. They demand better schools and more skillful teachers, they want students to work harder and learn more about subjects which bear more directly upon their place in the world. But it is not enough to attract better teachers by raising salaries and improving working conditions, to regroup students according to ability, to make curricula more or less specialized and more or less professional, to build more and better schools, and so on. We need a careful study of *teaching*. No enterprise can hope to improve itself without a close look at its own technology. We should not expect much help from the past. Theories of education have never been technically productive. . . . For every authority in educational philosophy whom we may now call right, we shall probably have to call an equally distinguished authority wrong. Indeed, it is possibly not unfair to say that they have all been right or wrong by chance.

It was not an argument likely to appeal to a former college professor and president, for whom, according to hallowed tradition, the classroom was the teacher's castle, never to be invaded, and Conant opened our meeting by handing the chapter back to me with the comment: "This is pretty shrill." The meeting continued in more or less the same spirit, and when it was over Conant turned to me and said, "Well, do you *want* to go to lunch?" I said yes and he took me to the Century Club.

I had not convinced him or his staff that teaching could be improved, but, as I reported to the Rheem Company, I did get some advice:

> *He thinks that we are trying to do too many things and that the whole feasibility of the machine program could be demonstrated with a single project. He suggested that we go into the schools of Harlem or a Negro district in Chicago and teach beginning reading. At the moment, these students simply do not learn to read and the NAACP, a very powerful pressure group, is raising the devil with everybody concerned. They would certainly back a large-scale project, Conant believes. His proposal is that we select about a thousand elementary grade students, give them all intelligence tests, and then see how far we can go in a matter of two or*

three years in teaching them to read. At the moment, these students hang around school, sleep or raise hell, and never do learn basic reading skills. As Conant put it, if you could carry that group of students through sixth grade reading you would have produced a miracle, and the world would be yours with respect to the further development of teaching machines. He considers this entirely a matter of strategy. If we try to support research in a great number of lines, as we are almost necessarily obliged to do, we may not make the kind of noise a single experiment of this sort would make. Conant kept referring to the parallel with the atom bomb. People in the field in the early days kept pointing out the uses of nuclear energy in industry, transport, and so on, but it was Conant who insisted that they bear down on a single objective and devote all their powers to achieving it.

To Conant I wrote that I recalled his suggestion that

an important and quite dramatic test of our proposal [would be] to go into school systems where there is at the moment a real problem in the teaching of reading, and see what we can do with machine instruction. I have in mind putting an excellent man on such a job and giving him the staff necessarry to carry it out, perhaps on the scale of a thousand students for a period of five years. It is possible that I could find support for such a project by diverting a grant from the Office of Education which is at the moment waiting for a decision about Harvard policy with respect to patents and copyrights. . . . I greatly appreciate your offer to sound out people who might be involved in such a proposal and would be happy to learn whether Harvard is indeed a spot where such an experiment would be likely to be received with understanding or possibly more active support.

Conant replied that he was "not in a position to be of help to you along the lines you suggest." I had misunderstood him. He had asked me to submit evidence "that something could be accomplished by the use of teaching machines in connection with reading in the first three grades," which he would then "submit to a reading specialist in another city where there is a large Negro population." If the reaction was favorable, he would then suggest something on the scale I had mentioned, but without that first step "I do not feel I am in a position to be of much assistance to you. . . . I am wondering if you do not underestimate the resistance to new and novel procedures on the part of those who have the responsibility for the education of young children. After all, if a new idea involving reading should turn out to be highly unsuccessful, the official who had authorized it would have the permanent damage to his 1,000 pupils very much on his mind!"

(Three years later a young writer on the *Boston Globe*, Ian Menzies, reviewed one of Conant's books unfavorably, and I dropped him a line: "You will probably be criticized for your review . . . but I think you were much closer to the truth than Hechinger's accolade in the *New York Times*. It is just too bad that Conant has not found a better use for his enormous prestige in improving education in America."¹ Menzies soon called me. The *Globe* was being severely criticized, and his editor had, indeed, had him on the carpet. He had defended himself by showing him my letter. Could they publish it? I saw no point in a public quarrel with Conant and said no. Instead, the *Globe* published a fulsome apology for Menzies's review.)

In 1958 I received the Distinguished Scientific Contribution Award of the American Psychological Association, and in return I was expected to give a lecture at the next annual meeting. Project Pigeon and ORCON had at last been declassified, and I called my lecture "Pigeons in a Pelican." It was "the history of a crackpot idea, born on the wrong side of the tracks intellectually speaking, but eventually vindicated in a sort of middle-class respectability." Something had happened on the project which had taken me a long time to realize. The practical task before us had created a new attitude toward behavior. I thought I could trace a connection with *Walden Two*. Project Pigeon was "a declaration of confidence in a technology of behavior. Call it a crackpot idea, if you will; it is one in which I have never lost faith. I still believe that the same kind of wide-ranging speculation about human affairs, supported by studies of compensating rigor, will make a substantial contribution toward that world of the future in which, among other things, there will be no need for guided missiles."

*   *   *

MONHEGAN WAS LOSING its appeal. It was too small a community for an adolescent girl, and Julie began going elsewhere—to the Aspen Music Center in Colorado one year, to Yugoslavia with an old school friend the next. In 1959 we decided to sell the house and make other plans for our summers. The last day on the island I wrote a note:

My mood is a sustained sadness, not in leaving the scene of former pleasures but in recapitulating the dominant mood of my life in this cottage. It has been the scene of rather compulsive activities, half enjoyed, half merely discharged. In the beginning the house was the promise of great things to come. I recall, but can now scarcely believe, that I plucked grass away from small yew beds, foreseeing a luxuriant growth, and spread spruce branches under the trees in anticipation of a pleasant grove where one might sit in cool shade. There was always something to do about the house, again half pleasure, half compulsion. The kite, the boat, some work in the shop, were pretty straight fun.

It is the sadness of failure. I have known my children in this house and have shared their failures. Last year Debbie wholly failed to understand her relation to other children and as the summer ended she paid a wholly disproportionate price for a fib, telling a neighbor's child that one of the boys had tried to kiss her. I have seen Julie try to paint and fail, and I have seen her master the guitar. I have seen them both start and stop projects in the shop, with little accomplished, and I have watched myself, helpless, handle it all the wrong way.

At the end of the second summer Eve was visiting her sister, and in a steady rain, the fog horn blowing, I closed the house alone. That year the girls sang "You are my sunshine." Four years ago Debbie and I were alone, and that year she sang "Go on with the wedding/Don't bother about me/Let me be forgotten/Or just a memory." These tunes still touch me. I was lonely and didn't know it.

I bought the house as health insurance; no matter how much I overworked during ten months of the year, two months on the island would put me back together physically. At first, it worked; if I did not really relax (and the island did what it could because of my summers there in the early thirties), I was at least distracted. But my work became more and more reinforcing and took more and more of my time. Writing "Freedom and the Control of Men" one summer and designing the disk teaching machine another had set a pattern: I could do profitable things, and relaxation became more and more a prescribed medicine. Work encroached, and in the end I was not on vacation at all. Our social life was not up to that in Cambridge and daily life was inconvenient. The island had never provided a really good summer for Eve. Like a hooked gambler, I was staying on although reinforcements were spaced farther and farther apart.

Before we left, we bought two small gouache paintings from Reuben Tam.

SHADY HILL SCHOOL WAS still telling us that as soon as Debs learned to make use of her natural abilities she would do good work. I did not reply, as I thought I should, that she would do good work as soon as Shady Hill's teachers learned to teach. And now we discovered that in eighth grade she was to have "four 40-minute periods each week of Latin . . . the four conjugations of verbs complete in the indicative including *eo, io* verbs of the III Conjugation and *sum*; adjectives of the I and II Declension," and so on. I had enjoyed my four years of high-school Latin but I had a very different home discipline, and I could imagine Debs's despair.

So far as I was concerned, teaching Latin could be defended mainly for its effect on English usage, and my analysis of verbal behavior suggested a different way to get the same effect. The school agreed to excuse Debs from Latin if she studied material on Greek and Latin roots and affixes on the new teaching machine. Sue Meyer and I wrote a program in which Debs, given a list of roots and affixes, discovered the meaning of, or invented, standard English words which she had probably never seen. Sue later expanded the program for publication.

A note written during the summer of 1959 is a fair recount of my relations with Debbie at the time.

As a boy I was extraordinarily forgetful. "You'd lose your head if it weren't fastened on," said my parents. Possibly that is why I'm not angry with Debs for losing an orthodontic "retainer" which may cost fifty or seventy-five dollars to replace—why, in fact, I merely feel sorry for Debs. Her crime has the classical features: She was warned that it would be easy to lose, that it would be expensive to replace, and that its loss would somewhat delay the end of her orthodontia. And it was "sheer carelessness." She sat down with a friend to eat a candy bar, put the brace in her lap while she ate, and forgot it when she got up. Later she searched without success. When I came home last night there was a note by the light: "Daddy, I have lost my braces."

What can be done to "make a young person remember?" Punishment? Should the cost of replacing the retainer come out of her allowance or money she has earned? That would make her more careful, more anxious—actually more fearful—whenever she took the retainer out. Would that generalize to other situations? Would it possibly generalize too broadly—to a general anxiety about making mistakes? There is already too much of that in Debs now.

Are there positive measures? The fact that we knew there was a danger of forgetting, that we warned her, shows that we knew conditions were favorable for forgetting. A retainer is aversive; there is only a weak tendency to replace it in the mouth. It is rather distastefully aversive out of the mouth; we have frequently asked Debs not to leave it in sight at meals. Also, there is resistance to putting it in a pocket—moist and with wires which pick up dirt and lint. The dentist supplied a blue plastic box, but it is unnecessarily large and a nuisance to carry for only occasional use. A pocket especially lined for the purpose in every garment would have prevented not only this small catastrophe but many small annoyances and anxieties.

So much for the environment. What about behavior? This kind of forgetting involves "holding on to a stimulus"—remaining under the control of the retainer-in-the-lap until the time comes to get up, while scarcely responding to it meanwhile. A set of materials for teaching machines might be designed to encourage: (1) remembering what it is you are looking for, (2) remembering several things at once, any of which may suddenly be important (cf. the card game "Concentration"), and (3) remembering directions until the opportunity arises to follow them.

DURING HER SENIOR YEAR at Radcliffe, Julie broke her leg while skiing. As I wrote in a note:

She behaved rather typically during the first week of her hospitalization in Burlington, Vermont. She had made a mistake—first, in going skiing against a recommendation made for a reason I have forgotten and, second, in skiing dangerously. She has almost never been ill, and the broken leg with the heavy cast was something of a shock. It led to a sort of manic compensation: playing her guitar, moving about the hospital to "entertain" other patients. (Her first roommate asked to be moved to another room.) When she makes a mistake, she adopts a tight-lipped defense: Everything is all right or will come out right. A high-pitched modulated, "Oh, no" to explicit or implied criticism, followed by an often childish covering-up or disguising of intention. Later, an honest acknowledgment.

In another note I wrote:

> This morning Julie was very angry with herself and unhappy. She thought she had left her purse in a neighborhood grocery last evening. In addition to personal checks, money, and keys, it held her driver's license, social security card, and credit cards, and she would have to phone or write to get duplicates. I offered to drive her to the store as soon as it opened, but it was a tough neighborhood and we had little hope. Then we found the purse in our bedroom.
>
> The interesting thing was the speed with which we assumed she had left it at the store; it was "like Julie." And that was the source of her intense self-criticism: she was "always" doing things like that. There was some consolation. Perhaps it was a good set of contingencies to "improve" her—but was it, really? At least she plans to reduce contents to minimize the consequences of future loss, wisely working on the purse rather than on herself.

I had played recorders with Julie and Debbie, and they both played the guitar pleasantly, but I sometimes regretted that they had not spent more time in learning to play a standard instrument. In Indiana Julie had studied the piano, and both girls took piano lessons briefly in Cambridge. I had sent Julie to the Longy School for a course in solfege. She took up the violin and eventually the viola (in her senior year a newspaper photograph of the Harvard-Radcliffe orchestra showed her with her conspicuous hip-length cast), but she barely reached the keyboard skill necessary for her concentration in music.

I once pointed out to her that there had never been a great woman composer, and when Harvard gave Nadia Boulanger an honorary degree, I asked Julie if she had heard her speak. It was clear that I would be happy to see Julie become the next Nadia Boulanger. When she sang with the Harvard and Radcliffe choirs and the Boston Symphony in Bach's *St. Matthew Passion*, Debs and I went to hear her, and we went backstage afterward. With tears in my eyes, I said, "Julie, I have looked forward to seeing you here since you were that high." We both laughed at this "intervention" in her life.

I put on cap and gown to attend her commencement. I was sitting a few feet away as she came up to receive her diploma and she passed me without looking, characteristically both pleased and embarrassed, proud and diffident.

IN A LECTURE called "Men and Machines" at Denison University in 1960, I used Michelangelo's *Creation of Adam* to illustrate the "spark-gap" theory of creation, in which Life and Mind pass from God's finger to Adam's. (My slide was made from the tinted photograph I had brought back from Rome in 1928.) I sketched the history of automata which simulated Life and Mind. One which appeared to do so was the famous "mechanical Turk" exhibited by Mälzel of metronome fame. I had read about it in a chess magazine to which Eve and I subscribed shortly after our marriage. The Turk played excellent chess thanks to a small but human chess player concealed inside. I argued that computers which played chess also had people inside them—the people who designed the computers and wrote the programs.

I had been able to talk profitably about Mind with Herbert Feigl, who had come from the Vienna Circle and whose first paper, on probability and knowledge, had appeared in the first number of *Erkenntnis*, to which I was a charter subscriber. Logical positivism was not far from one kind of behaviorism, and Feigl liked my paper on private events. I could also talk with Willard Van Orman Quine, because, as an undergraduate at Oberlin College, he had taken a course using Watson's *Psychology from the Standpoint of a Behaviorist* as a text.

With philosophers in general, however, it was hard going. In 1959, when Sidney Hook asked me to comment on a paper by Stephen Toulmin at a conference at the New York University Institute of Philosophy on "Dimensions of Mind," I was not happy with the result. As I said in a note, *in the time available, and in the terms available, I could say nothing. The discussion ran riot in the use of apparently ultimate terms like intention, meaning, context, truth, and lying. Evidently there was solid satisfaction among the philosophers—including Ernest Nagel, Sidney Morgenbesser, Paul Weiss, Michael Scriven, Karl Popper, Max Black, and C. J. Ducasse—with a blend of logical, linguistic, and psychological terms.*

When Hook asked if he could publish my remarks, I demurred: I thought I had contributed little to the discussion. But he assured me that I "had some of the chief philosophical dualists in the country mumbling in their beards . . . they weren't convinced of course but they were strangely silent." Would I not also say something about Chomsky?

I wrote a short reply to Toulmin. He had used an example in which saying "Tea, please" had two consequences: a cup of tea for the speaker and, since it was the last cup, no chance for a friend to ask for tea. The strength of the verbal response was therefore a function of a history of two kinds of consequences and the episode could be analyzed accordingly, but, as I said in my comment,

since we have not actually deprived or satiated the speaker with tea or altered his attitude toward the friend, we have no quantitative measure of his tendency to say "Tea, please." Nevertheless the analysis is not therefore meaningless or "spuriously" scientific. We are not interested in predicting or controlling this particular instance of behavior, but merely in treating it as if we were. That is what the physicist does when he offers a casual explanation of some occurrence in daily life.

IN WRITING THE Mead-Swing Lectures and trying them out on my class in the analysis of behavior, I was aware that I was challenging entrenched views in philosophy, history, letters, and religion, and I was all the more aware of it as I gave the lectures at Oberlin. My lack of expertise bothered me, as did a good deal of early conditioning. The night after my last lecture I had a violent nightmare, and when I checked out of the motel the next morning, the clerk looked at me curiously, and I wondered if I had been heard by other guests.

I was soon asking myself, "Are the humanities worth saving?" and writing several aggressive notes in what I called an attack on the humanities. "We have reached a stage in the experimental analysis of behavior at which we can say to philosophers, men of letters, critics, and others, 'unless you are willing to inform yourself of current facts and formulations you must simply shut up.' "

I felt the same way about many of the scientists who wrote about the humanities. In a book called *Science and Human Values*, Jacob Bronowski explained how we arrive at a concept. "We see the head of a penny and then the tail, we put the head and the tail together. We see that it makes sense to treat them as one thing. . . . We have a symbol or a name for the whole penny. . . . The data of the senses [are] put together to make a thing which is held in the mind." I was outraged: "There was no suggestion that there is a science to deal with this, no questioning of the usefulness of lay terms, no hint of the improvement needed in such a formulation, no plans for further research." Scientists were conceding the value of humanistic wisdom "either because of the prestige of 'culture,' or from guilt at their own greater prosperity, or as an easily afforded indulgence, but to get down to brass tacks, what *is* the wisdom which can be communicated only by history or letters?"

In Natural Sciences 114 I had taken a strong line against the usefulness of history. How well could one describe a period? Could one even describe the present time adequately? The past seemed easier because we had forgotten most of it or because it had been deliberately rewritten. A recent move toward the quantification of historical facts was only a beginning, and even if we could characterize an epoch, did history really repeat itself? Many historians disavowed any ability to predict the future and some, like Reinhold Niebuhr, made a virtue of unpredictability.

I reminded my students that predictions sometimes came true, or were proved false, through deliberate action. Someone had predicted that Caligula could no more become Emperor of Rome than ride across the Bay of Baia on horseback, and when he became Emperor he had boats lashed together across the bay and rode back and forth all day.

History was like developmentalism in psychology. One could identify patterns, cycles, and sequences (a Munich or a Versailles was as much an archetypal pattern as the personal archetypes of Jung), but, once identified, nothing could be done about them or with them.

As to letters,

there are more useful observations of human behavior page for page in the Goncourt *Journal* than in Montaigne or La Rochefoucauld, because the Goncourt brothers describe behavior rather than generalize about it. They imply principles but relate facts, where the others usually leave their readers to find the facts in their own experience. But how many of their generalizations can be supported? How many contradictory principles could be made equally plausible with a different selection of cases? Why not throw it all out? Great instances of human nature are useful only for illustrative or persuasive purposes.

From time to time I get expansive glimpses of how an extensive work might be reinterpreted. At the moment I am reading Bréhier's *Hellenic Age*—the chapter on Plato and his rhetoric and verbal devices. Should I analyze the verbal contingencies? Could I rewrite ["translate"] Plato? Given how many years?

Eight months after giving the Mead-Swing lectures, I wrote:

I have read the transcript and dipped into it for short talks; otherwise it has lain fallow. And I am less and less inclined to publish it in its present form. The main points need to be made—and again and again—but I am not sure how many of them are mine. I prefer to take time to find out and to publish only what I myself have to contribute rather than a general picture. As to the picture—I may use the American Academy paper to organize it.

The following year a two-day conference at the American Academy of Arts and Sciences was devoted to Evolution and the Individual. I gave the keynote paper on the first day and Harry Murray on the second, and our papers were published in a special issue of *Daedalus*. My topic was "The Design of Cultures." Why was it so hard to improve the social environments in which people lived?

It is easier to demonstrate the right way to build a bridge than the right way to treat one's fellow men (the difference reducing to the immediacy and clarity of the results). Even though relatively disinterested, the cultural designer has found it necessary to appeal for support to secular or divine authorities, supposedly inviolable philosophical premises, and even to military persuasion. Nothing of the sort has been needed for the greater part of physical technology. The wheel was not propagated by the sword or by promises of salvation—it made its own way.

Our cultures had been designed largely by guesswork, with some very lucky hits. We could now better ourselves and our world through a science of behavior.

By 1960 *Walden Two* was beginning to be used as a text in several different kinds of courses, and two or three companies asked about paperback rights. Macmillan eventually brought out its own edition, printed from the same plates and sold at a short discount. In 1960 about two thousand copies were sold.

The book was still causing trouble at Harvard. A student told me that William Yandell Elliott broke into a lecture with an angry, "Walden Two, Walden Three, Walden Four—who does the man think he is?" There was a more tolerant reception in a course on utopias at Boston University Junior College, where I gave a lecture every year for a number of years.

My mother outlived my father by more than ten years, but they were not happy ones. Her friends were dying, and to those who remained she could find no comforting answer to the question, "Why don't you go and live with Frederic?" A week with us at Christmastime was almost more than she or we could bear. In desperation, we took her to Cinerama, the *Ice Capades,* almost anything to fill the time. She suffered from acute neuritis and had a breast removed. She continued to believe in service and remained a Gray Lady at a hospital, but in the hotel she began to act the *grande dame.* With little jokes about the stock market, she gave the employees the impression that she was far richer than she actually was.

Shortly before she died she said, "If I had it to do again, I would remarry." She was thinking, I am sure, of a man who lived for a time in the hotel, and on whom I called at her request when I was once in Scranton. He would, indeed, have made a great difference. A pleasant, outgoing man with a great sense of humor, he was everything my father was not. Unfortunately he lacked the thing my father could boast of:

success. He was dependent upon his children for support, and it was soon necessary for him to join one of them in California.

Like my father, my mother developed heart trouble, and like him was assured by the doctors that it was indigestion. During a week in late January 1960 she gave a small luncheon and attended a bridge party, but at night she suffered. One night she wrote in her daybook: "Is this the end?" On the Saturday morning, February 1, a doctor called to tell me that she had had an attack, and she died within the hour.

I went immediately to Scranton, hoping to settle her affairs over the weekend, but for some legal reason the manager of the hotel could not let me into her room. On Monday the friends who managed my mother's affairs got me permission to go through her things. I had phoned the old friend whom I called Aunt Harriet, and she came and took my mother's clothes, as she had done for almost seventy years. A few other friends and relatives came for the funeral, and my mother's ashes were buried beside the graves of my father and brother. Though my mother had a simple faith that she would see my father and brother again, she was not a church-goer, and there was no reference to God in the notes she wrote during her last few days.

IN FEBRUARY 1960 I attended a small conference arranged by the American Cancer Society. Paul Lazarsfeld was chairman and George Gallup was one of the other members. How could young people be made aware of lung cancer and the other dangers of smoking cigarettes? Afterwards I sent Lazarsfeld a rather detailed memorandum: long-deferred aversive consequences could never be made effective, and emphasizing the dangers in smoking might do little more than add psychosomatic problems. Instead, I suggested that special programs in grade and high school ("but possibly helpful for the whole population") should be set up to:

a) emphasize the *immediate*, positively reinforcing consequences of giving up smoking or never smoking.

b) condition other positively reinforcing consequences—as by "glamorizing the non-smoker, publicizing testimonials of non-smokers."

c) teach alternative behaviors (a short course in what to do with your hands, for example).

d) oppose the symbolic use of smoking as a sign of contentment or friendship—"possibly working through the entertainment industry."

e) point up the *immediate* harmful effects of smoking. Survey annoyances.

f) teach self-management, such as "arranging situations to avoid temptation."

g) show those who are giving up smoking how to make their progress clear.

h) supply cigarettes with graded amounts of nicotine for those who must break a physiological addiction.

i) make clear to young people that not starting is easier than giving up.

j) make clear that the supposed satisfaction and lift from smoking is merely a return to the normal state enjoyed by non-smokers.

So far as I know, few if any of these steps were taken for many years.

SHORTLY AFTER *Walden Two* was published, someone asked me about my motivation in writing it, and I said that "it was a kind of self-therapy as the Burris side of me struggled to accept the Frazier side." As I put it in a lecture at Columbia Teachers College in 1960, "Frazier soon started to say things I should have been surprised to hear from my own lips . . . but once I had put down the whole pattern of his thinking, I saw the connections among its parts, and I became, a year or two after I finished, a thorough-going Frazierian." I reported another visit to Walden Two, though not as a character from the book.

[When I told Frazier that I was to give this lecture,] he said, "You must call it *Walden Two Revisited.*" I must have looked puzzled, for he added at once, "Huxley, man! Aldous Huxley! Haven't you read *Brave New World Revisited?*" When I said I had not, he swung into an obviously prepared review. *Brave New World*, published in 1932, was committed to a few selected techniques of behavioral control. The genetic problem was solved by the as yet fanciful breeding of large numbers of identical twins. The behavioral techniques were reducible mainly to the Pavlovian conditioning of attitudes and to the allaying of all needs and desires through massive gratification. That was the Sybaritic solution in cultural design: complete satiety. Fordian productivity was to make most of it possible, and the rest could be achieved by a reversal of sexual conventions which Huxley borrowed from the Marquis de Sade. If satiation failed, stultification could be completed with the help of drugs. Huxley himself described the object of this engineering in his preface to the paper edition of *Brave New World* in 1946 as "making slaves love their servitude." A decade or so later, in *Brave New World Revisited*, he has not gone much farther. He is still talking about the engineering of attitudes (with subliminal perception as a new threat) and other techniques of inculcating acceptance on the part of the ruthlessly governed. But there is something new in the *first* chapter of *Brave New World Revisited*, and . . . Frazier read me a passage with obvious glee: "In the light of what we have recently learned about animal behavior in general, and human behavior in particular, it has become clear that control through the punishment of undesirable behavior is less effective, in the long run, than control through the reinforcement of desirable behavior by rewards, and that government through terror works on the whole less well than government through the non-violent manipulation of the environment and of the thoughts and feelings of individual men, women, and children. Punishment temporarily puts a stop to undesirable behavior, but does not permanently reduce the victim's tendency to indulge in it. Moreover, the psychophysical by-products of punishment may be just as undesirable as the behavior for which an individual has been punished. Psychotherapy is largely concerned with the debilitating or anti-social consequences of past punishments."

"Where do you think he got that?" Frazier shouted, and he turned to the end of the book where *Walden Two* is described as:

a self-sustaining and autonomous community, so scientifically organized that nobody is ever led into anti-social temptation and, without resort to coercion or undesirable propaganda, everyone does what he or she ought to do, and everyone is happy and creative.

"That might have been written with tongue in cheek," I said.

"No," he said, "he means it."

When I asked Frazier whether he had not been wrong about the sustaining function of the pictures of Lenin and Stalin in Russia, since nothing happened when Stalin's were taken down, he evaded the question by turning to China. Burris had received a letter from an old friend who was a professor at the University of Peking [it was a letter I had received from Pei Sung Tang]: "I can write a *book* commenting on your book! And a larger book than the original. But not necessary because what is considered Utopia, that is your *Walden Two*, is an *accomplished fact* (only in the embryonic stage of course) here! Not in a hypothetical group of 1,000! But in an actual soc. of 700,000,000! Dear friend, you must make a trip here, if possible, *now* to see your 'Utopia' *in the making* (with its unavoidable defects of course), if you can stand the hardship in building an 'Utopia' out of virtually 'nothing'! Or you may come to live with us (as *my guest*) ten to fifteen years from now! And you do *not* need to walk all the way here either, as a 'pilgrim' as in your closing chapter! Everything is as you visualized (as I say, we make some technical errors in minor places, but soon rectified). *We do experiment!*"

THROUGHOUT THE Eisenhower regime, particularly in reaction to McCarthyism, I had had some sympathy with Communism. The stronger advocates I knew (I was not sure how many of them were card-carrying members) were decent people. When a cartoon in the *Christian Science Monitor* in 1954 implied that the movement headed by Ho Chi Minh had something in common with the Japanese seizure of Manchuria and Hitler's march into the Rhineland, I wrote to protest.

At a meeting of the Eastern Psychological Society, Gregory Razran described the vagaries of psychology in the Soviet Union and the difficulties and indignities to which our Russian colleagues were subjected, and when I was asked to comment, I pointed out that science in America was not free of similar pressures. A physiologist from Minnesota had just told a meeting of doctors that people would live longer if they ate fewer dairy products. "Minnesota is a liberal state, but it is also a dairy state, and the physiologist may not have heard the last of it." A group of scientists had just debated the causes of lung cancer, and "it was no reflection on their integrity to point out that their positions were related to the sources of their funds. . . ." *Science and Human Behavior* was the only well-known textbook that analyzed religious rituals or practices, and some Razran of the future would point to the omission in other texts as an example of "thought control." Pavlov was once called before the Russian equivalent of a Senate Investigating Committee to explain why he had criticized the regime. At one point he looked at his watch, said "Gentlemen, I have an experiment," and was allowed to walk out. "A member of this association is still paying for a similar act of 'contempt' and would, except for a technicality, be in jail. . . . Two years ago, a great American university gave a medal to a psychologist [it was Carl Rogers] and commended him for having developed a theory of human behavior consistent with a democratic philosophy. To those who cherish democracy this may seem innocent enough, but fundamentally it is as dangerous as the Nazis' exaltation of Jaensch for his racial theories."

One of my sophomores at Minnesota, Orville Freeman, who was then Governor of the state, made the nominating speech for John F. Kennedy at the Democratic National Convention in July 1960. (When the lights went out halfway through his address, he carried on as if nothing had happened.) I wrote to congratulate him, and in his reply he said that he had read my books "with very real interest" and hoped to discuss them with me. He thought that the Democrats had a good ticket; he knew they had an outstanding platform. (Was there a point in that distinction between "think" and "know"?) In the election he lost the governorship, and I wrote that I hoped he would do something of an international character in the new administration, but he accepted the post of Secretary of Agriculture.

A year or two later, the Fund for the Republic invited him to speak in Los Angeles and Halleck Hoffman reported, "he gave a great speech. You'll be pleased to know that he still considers you one of his mentors, was delighted to hear me speak of you, and wondered how you are and when he would have a chance to see you. I gather that the door is wide open for you at the Department of Agriculture if you care to walk in." I was in Washington shortly afterward and made an appointment, but a cabinet meeting was called unexpectedly and our meeting was canceled.

A few years later, an English graduate student at McMaster University said he hoped that I would talk to Labor Party people in London on Utopian planning. He was a member of the party and was going to send a copy of *Walden Two* to Harold Wilson. I said I would be glad to talk with anyone interested in anything I had to say, but in a note I asked:

What *do* I have to say? Nothing immediately relevant to British problems—about which I know very little. But hopefully [the word was just coming into vogue and I was not yet sick of it] something about (a) incentives and the shortcomings of "welfare," (b) leisure and enjoyment, (c) small productive units.

DURING THE FIRST five months of 1960, I spoke to organizations of secondary school teachers, graduate students in education, school administrators, textbook publishers, school psychologists, boards of higher education, deans and other officers of large universities, school boards, college presidents, and congressmen and -women at the Brookings Institution in Washington. The people who came to see me showed the same range.

They were not always worthwhile:

My daybook said "Jones and Robinson at 2 p.m." Mr. Robinson was announced. Short, dark, about 30. A dark business suit with a patterned blue handkerchief ballooning from his breast pocket, his tie a bad match. He grasped my hand, held it firmly and just a shade too long, looked me straight in the eye on principle.

He made it clear that his trip to Cambridge was not just to see me. He had been seeing friends and now had got around to keeping his appointment. Did I know Mr. Jones well? (Not at all, so far as I could recall, but I remembered that it was Jones who had made the appointment by telephone.) Mr. Jones sang. He made records for children. A few names were dropped.

And now to business. Mr. Robinson had heard a good deal about teaching machines. He felt he might be of some help. His plan was to get together some of the outstanding people in the field, get capital, organize a company. Among the people he was anxious to help were "gentlemen like yourself" who needed management to develop teaching machines, educators who needed to be told what machines were all about, and the American public who needed a chance to invest in teaching machines.

He knew almost nothing about the field. When I mentioned a man or a company, he struggled to find a scrap of comment. He was surprised to learn that I had designed machines. A few days later he wrote to thank me for seeing him and to express his pleasure in knowing that if I had not had other commitments I should have been glad to work with him. Is he telling himself that palpable lie? Is he telling others? Or did I tell it to him to get rid of him?

Nevertheless, he had had his ear to the ground. In June 1960, *Control Engineering* published an article on "The Coming Boom in Teaching Machines" in which it was said that "a $100 million a year market for automatic teaching machines is predicted within the year." I had demonstrated my model at the University of Pittsburgh only six years earlier.

I had often said that a good program in a good machine could teach twice as much in the same time and with the same effort as classroom instruction, and I soon had proof. In 1959 I had given the Page-Barbour Lectures at the University of Virginia—a series of four lectures on teaching machines and programmed instruction. Nearly one hundred students in a class in introductory psychology at Hollins College had attended. They had missed my lecture on "Cane Kills Able" (an attack on punitive sanctions), and Allen Calvin, their instructor, asked me to give it again at the College.

Calvin had been interested in programmed instruction for some time. His colleague, William Sullivan, was writing a program to teach French. They had asked about the Harcourt-Brace machine, and when I reported the breakdown in my negotiations, they turned to Rheem. Calvin was soon writing that three requests for quotations on seventy-five machines had gone unanswered. He and Sullivan then bought machines from a company which made operant equipment, and in the spring of 1960, Calvin took me to see an experiment in Roanoke, Virginia, in which thirty-four eighth-grade students were studying ninth-grade algebra. A former high-school mathematics teacher was barely keeping ahead of them in writing the program.

The students were at work on the machines when we came in, and when I commented on the fact that they paid no attention to us, Calvin went up to the teacher's platform, jumped in the air, and came down with a loud bang. Not a student looked up.

The class completed a full year of algebra in that one term. They scored at least average on ninth-grade norms, and twenty-five who were available for a retest a year later showed an average retention rate of slightly more than 90 percent, where the normal rate was 70 to 80 percent. (Years later, when I told a physicist friend about the experiment, he asked, predictably, "But did they really learn algebra?" For him algebra was not the solving of certain kinds of problems; it was a mental faculty.)

The program had not only taught algebra in half the time with half the effort, it had done so in a lower grade. Where schools were postponing instruction, machine teaching could advance it. When Layman Allen designed a program to teach mathematical logic to students at the Yale Law School, he found that it could be used in college and even in high school, and by 1960 the Carnegie Corporation had given him a grant to adapt it for elementary schools.

Not everyone was pleased. For administrators, the consequences of any improvement in teaching were frightening. As Sidney Pressey wrote to me in October 1960, "Before long the question will need to be faced as to what the student is to do with the time which automation can save him. More education in the same place, or earlier completion of full-time education?" If what was taught in the first and second grades could be taught in the first, what would the second-grade teacher do? What would happen to the traditional pattern of eight years of elementary school, four years of high school, and four years of college?

And, of course, what would happen to the teacher? In October 1958, *Fortune* published an article on the productivity of the education industry. It pointed out that teachers were becoming less efficient. "There is now one teacher for every 26 students, in 1928 there was one for every 30 students, and in 1900 there was one for every 37." The "most radical proposal" for raising educational productivity, *Fortune* said, was to let machines do some of the work presently assigned to teachers. But did that mean replacing teachers? One of the best popular articles on teaching machines (by Gay Gaer Luce in *The Saturday Evening Post*) was unfortunately called "Can Machines Replace Teachers?" At the time there was a shortage of teachers and few were worrying about their jobs, but technological unemployment was a threat.

We had prepared an answer in our request for an extension of our grant from the Fund for the Advancement of Education:

> We visualize a very considerable change in the status of introductory teachers, whose lives will be freed of the burdensome chores which can be handled as well by instructional devices and whose economic status, speaking of the country as a whole, should be improved by their greater productivity. It should be possible to recruit better instructors when their duties are consonant with their status as human beings, and it should be

possible to bring many more students to a given level of competence with a given supply of teachers.

It was said that machines lacked "the warmth and personality of the inspired teacher," but by taking over the heavier chores of the classroom, machines gave teachers a better chance to *be* warm and personal. It was certainly not true that, as one writer put it, "learning cannot take place without the teacher-student relationship." We learn a great deal under nonsocial contingencies in nature.

I once spoke to a class in child psychology at Occidental College on "The Non-Freudian Nursery." Many of the problems which took people to psychological clinics were due to inept personal attention, including loving care. Young children should have highly reinforcing *physical* environments. As a child, I myself had been exposed to enormously varied practical contingencies in the kind of world that promoted Rousseau's "dependence on things."

MANY THINGS WERE HAPPENING at Harvard. Jim was analyzing the importance of words in a frame by comparing versions of our program in which different, especially less relevant, words were supplied by the student; by blacking out different parts of an item he could identify the parts which were controlling most of the behavior. He made a study of errors and revised the items in our program on which more than five percent of the students made mistakes. With Bruce Chalmers, Professor of Chemistry at Harvard, he wrote a successful program on crystallography, in part of which students arranged marbles in plastic matrices to show how molecules could be packed.

Matt Israel, for his thesis, explored the use of variably blurred prompts in teaching an English-German vocabulary. Words in either language were made less and less distinct as students learned equivalent words. Harlan Lane and John Martin used the matching-to-sample machine in some experiments with retarded children at the Fernald School in Waltham, Massachusetts, and with music or candies as reinforcers they tested successfully for color blindness and taught simple reading. (When the dispensing mechanism broke down, they found that success in operating the machine was enough to keep the children at work.) Wells Hively, who had developed a matching-to-sample machine using a slide projector, worked with Helen Popp on teaching reading. When I demonstrated the disk machine to the Boston Society for Psychiatry and Neurology at Massachusetts General Hospital and discussed its possible use in medical education, I could cite a program on neuroanatomy which Murray Sidman and his brother Richard, a neurologist, were then writing.

IN THE SPRING OF 1960 Howard Aiken, who had designed the first large-scale computer, the Mark I, and who was then director of the Harvard Computation Laboratory, told me that Charles Mott, one of the largest stockholders in General Motors, was interested in supporting the use of teaching machines in an adult-education program. I said that Jim and I could use some help, and I mentioned the indexing phonograph. Language laboratories, strongly supported by the federal government after Sputnik, were based on outmoded learning theories. Jim and I wanted students to compare recorded passages with one another, transcribe passages in phonetic symbols (to develop a good ear), translate passages, and immediately check all their responses. I had made a crude model of a suitable phonograph, using a four-inch magnetic belt, but the technical problems were beyond me.

Dr. Frank Manley, Director of the Mott Program of the Flint (Michigan) Board of Education, came to see me with the general manager of the AC Spark Plug Division of General Motors. The Wakefield, Massachusetts, plant of the AC Spark Plug Company could put its sophisticated electronics laboratory at my disposal. I was soon in touch with its manager. I visited the plant in Wakefield and invited one of the engineers to spend the summer at Harvard. He designed two machines: an audio-playback device which gave students access to sixty channels of recorded speech or music, and a channel on which they could record their own speech, and a portable version of our multiple-choice panel machine using a slide projector.

A report was sent to Michigan, but there was no reply, and in December I was asked to call Manley about it. The general manager came to Cambridge and, in obvious embarrassment, told me that General Motors would build the machines but only if I could find a foundation to pay for them. Mott was interested only in teaching children who needed special help and then only in Flint, Michigan. Moreover, he was eighty-five and quite ill. I later heard that he had been enraged by the election of John F. Kennedy and refused to support any work at Harvard. Once again, Jim and I had wasted a lot of time.

By SUMMER I was complaining that I had given Rheem the names of more than six hundred people who had asked about teaching machines and that the company had not written to any of them. As a result, I was receiving letters which were almost abusive, and people who had wanted my machines were buying other models. The company had also not done anything about an advisory council, although I had written to possible members. I had refused several invitations to work with publishers of programs, but Rheem was not acquiring any rights. To assuage my impatience, I was asked to visit a plant in California, where I was put up at the Beverly Hills Hotel, given the use of a large company car, and taken to an excellent dinner. But nothing was done about machines. The manager of the old language-laboratory company was in charge, and he was promoting language laboratories. (He was not interested in an indexing phonograph, but asked me not to take the idea to another company.) He thought simpler teaching machines would be adequate. When I pointed out that they had agreed to develop my machine, I was given a drafting table and permitted to draw plans.

In August, a Rheem attorney admitted to Don Rivkin that reorganization had put the company nine months behind schedule, but insisted that they were still interested in teaching machines and were enthusiastic about working with me. Many of the Rheem officers were asking, however—and this was a new and ominous note—whether this was the time to embark upon full-scale production. In October, I wrote to an officer of the company:

> I'm on a speaking tour of the midwest, talking on Teaching Machines. Denison U., Ohio State, U. Wisconsin at Milwaukee so far; Western Michigan (Kalamazoo), Michigan (Ann Arbor), Lexington, Kentucky, Missouri, Louisiana, Texas, Rochester, Skidmore still to go. Interest in machines is terrific. Students, teachers, administrators crowd the auditoriums and questions and answers go on for hours. The main question:

Where can we get machines? And what programs are available? Naturally I'm urging them to wait for a good machine.

I was told that the machine I had designed in California was nearly ready, and that by February I should have enough for Natural Sciences 114.

TEACHING COULD BE CALLED information-processing, and computer companies began to buy up publishers. A new era in communication was at hand and teaching would be part of it. But I was not happy about the early uses of computers as teaching machines. According to the *New York Times*, one program called students by name, spurred them into action with martial music, and reprimanded them for poor work: "Listen, son. You are being very careless. You really should study a lot harder. Careful study habits will help you make your own way in the world." If there was ever a "robot teacher," it was the computer programmed in that way. As I said in commenting on Simon Ramo's paper at the Cincinnati meeting of the APA, little was gained from simulating traditional classrooms or traditional exchanges between students and teachers.

To many educators, television also seemed the answer. In 1959, Purdue University began to broadcast courses from a high-flying plane, to be received over much of the Middle West, but, as with any mass medium, the students all moved at the same rate, and their behavior had no reinforcing consequences. They simply looked and listened.

WATSON's *Behaviorism*, the book which brought me into psychology, had long been out of print and when the University of Chicago Press asked whether I thought a paperback edition would sell, I said it would. Watson was still alive, and he dedicated the new printing to the American Psychological Association, which had recently awarded him its Gold Medal, citing him as "one of the vital determinants of the form and substance of modern psychology."

When he died, on September 25, 1958, the editors of *Science* asked me to write his obituary. In it I traced the origin of behaviorism in three names: Darwin, Lloyd Morgan, and Watson. Darwin, looking for continuity among the species, pointed to signs of reasoning, sympathy, and even artistic enjoyment in lower animals. Lloyd Morgan contended that the signs could be explained in other ways. Watson took the inevitable next step: if mental processes could be explained in other ways in lower animals, why not in man? Unfortunately, his only evidence of the role played by the environment was the reflex and the conditioned reflex, which made an uneasy marriage with the concept of habit, which he also used. He was drawn into several digressions: a superficial interpretation of introspection and thinking, questioning the importance of many genetic factors, and warning parents against displays of affection. As a result "his brilliant glimpse of the need for, and the nature of, a science of behavior was all but forgotten. Perhaps history is ready to return to a more accurate appraisal."

(I had, of course, begun as a disciple of Watson's, but in reporting his death, *Science* reversed the direction of influence and called Watson "a founder of the 'reinforcement theory' which holds that the response of the higher species, including human, is guided by the presence or absence of a reward or reinforcement." Watson had, in fact, rejected Thorndike's Law of Effect, with its references to satisfying and annoying consequences.)

I THOUGHT IT WAS IMPORTANT to translate mentalistic expressions "into behavior." When La Rochefoucauld, for example, spoke of feelings and states of mind acting upon each other as if they were physical objects, it was easy to describe the facts in other ways. I cut up a copy of the *Maxims*, pasted one at the top of each page of a notebook, and under each one wrote a "translation into behavior." Here are two examples (in F. G. Stevens's English):

"The clemency of princes is often nothing more than a political artifice designed to secure the goodwill of their subjects." Translation: Rulers often withhold or moderate punishment because their subjects are then more likely to support them and less likely to revolt.

"Such clemency, though hailed as a virtue, is the product sometimes of vanity, sometimes of indolence, not infrequently of timidity, and generally of all three combined." Translation: They sometimes withhold or moderate punishment because they are then praised, sometimes because they thus avoid work, often because punishment would have aversive consequences for them, and generally for all three of these reasons combined.

I thought the translations were as close to what La Rochefoucauld was saying as the English versions, but the apparent wisdom and profundity had vanished. Compared with the human mind and character, human behavior was superficial stuff. And that was doubly unfortunate because, where La Rochefoucauld's inner forces remained forever out of reach, my translations pointed to things that could be changed. Translation soon became perfunctory and I lost interest. La Rochefoucauld's insight into the causes of human behavior had, however, impressed me.

I carried on with what I called "The Dictionary," a collection of behavioristic definitions of words referring to feelings or states of mind. A few entries under S: *sacrifice, sarcasm, satisfy, search, seduce, shun, sorry for, stoical, stress, stubborn, suggest, supercilious, surrender, suspect.* I also listed useful alternatives to the jargon of a behavioral analysis. For example, to describe people no longer under the control of a particular social environment I liked *disaffected* and *disenchanted,* in spite of the original references to feelings. I also looked at etymology: Why had *docile,* which first meant "easily taught" or "ready and willing to receive instruction," eventually meant "submitting to punitive control"? Or, contrariwise, why had the Latin *minari,* meaning "to drive cattle by threatening," eventually come to mean "to lead" (Fr. *mener*), as if the stick had become the carrot?

I objected to the lay vocabulary for practical, as well as theoretical, reasons. From a single issue of the *Boston Globe* at commencement time in 1961, I collected three examples:

Pusey, at Harvard: "The confidence and hopefulness and eagerness to proceed, which historically have been the fruits of faith, are now too frequently simply not there—or too feebly there."

Riley, at Boston College: What this country desperately needs is a "totality of outlook that will put a spiritual face upon American society."

Griswold, at Yale: America has yet to release her moral power, "the animating force that is necessary to galvanize all the other kinds of power."

The preoccupation with confidence, spiritual commitment, and moral power obscured the social conditions responsible for current problems and offered no help in solving them.

JOHN GARDNER, of the Carnegie Corporation, had said he could not support my work in the analysis of behavior, but he was soon supporting a venture at Harvard that covered much the same territory in a different way. George Miller and I had seen eye to eye on the shortcomings of the department, and a year or two after I submitted my white paper he wrote to me suggesting changes which would "give Harvard an active, vigorous, scientific Department of Psychology." It included a joint concentration in Psychology and Social Relations and a one-year introductory course combining Psychology 1 and Natural Sciences 114.

But George was moving in a new direction. In 1960, with Eugene Galanter and Karl Pribram, he published *Plans and the Structure of Behavior,* and with Jerome Bruner in Social Relations he was proposing to found a Center for Cognitive Studies at Harvard, supported by the Carnegie Corporation. In March 1961 I reported

a very discouraging meeting yesterday with the visiting committee of the Board of Overseers. George Miller reported on progress of the Center for Cognitive Studies. It epitomized the current scurrying about to get something done in psychology. A separate building [an architect was at work], a staff, invited "scholars"-in-residence for a year or so at a time, colloquia, and—I suppose—reports. All in the interests of "higher mental processes." John Wilson of the NFS, one of the big money givers, lapped it up. The invitees? Barbel Inhelder—carrying on for Jean Piaget. A mathematician—"sort of fun to have around." Somebody with a theory of how to teach mathematics—"It doesn't seem to work too well."

There were interdepartmental, if not quite internecine, issues which had become clear when George and Jerry offered Social Sciences 8 as a replacement for Boring's Psychology 1. Suspiciously like Natural

Sciences 114, it was to be "a bridge between biological and social sciences" which would cover language (in lieu of my treatment of verbal behavior), learning and teaching (in lieu of operant conditioning and programmed instruction), and cognition (a fancy word for "knowing" or "thinking," which I had defined in *Verbal Behavior* and treated elsewhere in some detail as one kind of "behaving"). I never discussed these matters with George or Jerry, but their students took my seminars, and in 1963 I noted:

> There is no doubt that my seminar in Psychology 207 has forced me to think more deeply about the behavioristic formulation. Yesterday I clarified several points, for myself if not for my students. I also discovered how deep-seated mentalism is among our graduate students—supported, I am afraid, by the positions of Stevens, Bruner, and Miller. This is all to the good so far as the course goes. It is good for me, too, in clarifying a broader audience.

The rise of cognitive psychology was by no means a local phenomenon. For centuries mentalism had permeated the everyday languages of the world and the technical languages of philosophy, theology, literature, history, and more recently many of the social sciences. For a long time "experimental psychology" had resisted out of a concern for some kind of scientific rigor, but when the computer emerged as a possible model of human behavior, the restraint was broken and mentalism returned in a flood. Psychologists no longer needed to worry about the difference between a perception and the world perceived; the mind simply processed information. Memory was no problem; information was simply stored in various compartments of the mind and classified and organized by various cognitive processes to facilitate its eventual retrieval. Some processing involved cybernetic feedback. The brain was a great computer, and the neurophysiologists would answer questions about the stuff of which it (and hence the mind) was made. It became fashionable to insert the word "cognitive" wherever possible.

My objections were in part standard behaviorism. Cognitive processes were inferred from the changes in behavior they were said to explain. They could not be directly observed through introspection because "there were no nerves going to the right places." They lacked physical dimensions. Information was, as I had said in *Verbal Behavior*, a newcomer as a replacement for idea or meaning. It could not be given the physical dimensions of what it was said to be about, any more than a word could be given the dimensions of its referents. It was impossible to define knowledge in a way that would fit all the expressions in which the word was used—such as acquiring knowledge, possessing knowledge, and communicating knowledge.

I BEGAN TO WORRY about overwork. A note written in 1960:

This summer I have made a steady effort to reduce the time I spend on correspondence, interviews, "duties" to my students, etc., with the result that I am beginning to have time to think in the old way. I am amazed at the fatigue shown in some of the things I wrote a few weeks ago, and am resolved to avoid that degree of exhaustion in the future. Part of the trouble may be the techniques I have used to get the most out of myself; I may have ended by getting too much. Part is the effect of reinforcement—too many things have paid off for me; there is always something I want to do. But the biggest part is undoubtedly the invasion of intellectual privacy, particularly as the result of the teaching machines but also of "success." Letters of inquiry, visitors, papers with requests for comments, invitations to write, speak, or otherwise participate, etc.— these would be reinforcing if I worked for acclaim—and I am happy to say they are not, at least not to any great extent. I would undoubtedly miss them, and step up my activity to bring them back. I certainly want to be effective; and these are, if not the effects I want, at least the signs of them. But the cost is great.

I think of the unreinforced years—particularly the Guggenheim year in St. Paul—the ideal condition of almost total professional neglect. I still don't know how I sustained so large a ratio; the conditions were obviously right for productive work. I should not have done that spade work on Verbal Behavior or written Walden Two if I had been as successful as my more distinguished contemporaries—for example, Hilgard, Marquis, Carlyle Jacobson, and Melton.

As to personal design (incidentally I have had the courage to use that expression on the analogy of cultural design for the first time today), the variable ratio reinforcement needed to sustain neglect must come early.

*　　*　　*

In May 1961, Eve and I were members of a delegation of behavioral scientists who visited Russia, Czechoslovakia, and Poland under the auspices of the National Academy of Science and the State Department. In Moscow we stayed at the luxurious Sovietskaya Hotel, saw *Swan Lake* in a box at the Bolshoi, visited the Kremlin, used the immaculate, often garish, subways, and visited institutes and experimental schools. We saw a good deal of Alexander Luria at the Neurosurgical Institute. (He was using behavioral tests to tell surgeons where tumors would be found. As he and I were walking through a ward, a nurse handed him a slip of paper. He smiled and said to me, "They found it where I said they would.")

One day Luria asked me if we could have a few moments together, and when I suggested that he come to our hotel for a drink, he called his wife, and we went to his home instead. Although he was the best-known Russian psychologist (Leontiev nevertheless outranking him in Russia for irrelevant reasons), he and his wife, together with his daughter and her husband and an older woman, lived in three small rooms. He explained that they were near his work and a library. He had a dacha.

When I lectured on teaching machines at the Institute of Pedagogical Science, the audience was attentive and, I thought, rather stunned. The first question afterwards was about regimentation; what would machines do to the individuality of the student?

I was asked to speak on Russian television. The young psychologist who was serving as our courier would translate, and he asked me to write out what I was going to say. I explained our mission and described my own work, with a brief reference to teaching machines. I closed by expressing our gratitude for the hospitality and friendship we had been shown. When I was asked to expand the remarks about friendship, Luria suggested that I do so by showing one of the small plastic trowels we had brought with us, inscribed "To Cement Russian-American Friendship, U. S. Behaviorial Sciences Delegation, 1961." I wrote a note about the broadcast:

We were supposed to arrive at the television station ten minutes after six but actually got there nearer the half hour. We were stopped at the gate by the only armed policeman I have seen, who eventually let us pass. Complete chaos followed. It appeared that the station preferred to have me read a first paragraph, then to have Yuri [our guide] translate it and go on with the rest of my manuscript, leaving the last sentence for me, which would then be translated in turn. Since this meant that Yuri would have to have a typed version, he rushed into a room with a stenographer and started to dictate. I was taken to a large studio, very much like those in America—a huge barnlike room, the ceiling covered with frames for lights, with cameras being moved back and forth.

I was put at a small table. Two men nearby were broadcasting a running comment on sports and news events shown on a monitor. I kept my eye on my watch and waited. At the very last minute Yuri dashed into the studio, sat down beside me, handed me my copy, and we were on. It was Saturday night and the program was microwaved to other cities in the Soviet Union. According to the manager of the studio approximately thirty million Russians saw it. I was paid a few rubles for my services.

In Leningrad we visited Pavlov's laboratory, talked with Anokhin, one of his students, went to the Hermitage and Peterhof. Then we invented reasons to fly to Tashkent and Samarkand. I was not impressed by Russian behavioral science. There was little or no interest in behavior as such. Psychologists avoided the risk of being called idealists by turning either to physiology or mathematical modeling and cybernetics. In Tbilisi and Kiev we found traditional brands of psychology. In Prague, Anatol Rapaport and I spoke to large audiences, and early the next morning he and I left for home to meet other obligations. Eve remained with the delegation and saw something of Warsaw and East Germany.

From Russia I sent "safe" postcards to Pei Sung, to which he quickly replied. Later I wrote:

I was glad to have your reply. My reactions to my recent trip are still unsettled and mixed. . . . I was pleased by many signs of progress and accomplishment, particularly when one recalls the devastation of the war and other starting handicaps. People were in general happy, and many of them quite enthusiastic. The cities are immaculate compared with ours. But as the weeks passed, I grew increasingly doubtful whether the full productive energies of the average man are being stimulated. "To each according to his need"—I was surprised to find the phrase in St. Augustine's Rules for Monasteries recently—is only half the story. It is the humane half, the just and fair half. What is left out is the reinforcing effect of the satisfaction of needs. Can you solve that problem? Under what conditions can we make sure that each man receives what he needs in such a way that he is inspired to live an enthusiastic and productive life? You and I may forget the importance of a purpose in life, because we have never lacked purpose and have enjoyed a life which others would call hard work. But this must come to be the case for everyone; it must be made the case for everyone by the culture in which men live.

My second reservation: I don't see what sort of good life the Russians have in mind. Their standards in architecture, painting, public parks, monuments, etc. are taken straight out of the nineteenth-century bourgeois culture. What are they being successful for? How do they plan to live? Like us!?

Maybe you have the answer. One of the hosts on my trip said, with a touch of envy—"Ah, China! There is pure communism!" I wish I knew more.

As you see, I am in a sober mood. And never have I valued our friendship more highly.

In 1959, Jim and I were supplying copies of what we called a "Self-Tutoring Introduction to a Science of Behavior." Jim had become a consultant on teaching machines and programmed instruction to the McGraw-Hill Company, and in 1961 they published the program, improved in the light of our experience, as a programmed text called *The Analysis of Behavior.* Each page was divided into frames on six levels and the student worked through the book one level at a time, the correct response appearing on the next page.

In an introduction, Jim and I recalled Edward Thorndike's remarkable speculation in 1912 that, "if, by a miracle of mechanical ingenuity, a book could be so arranged that only to him who had done what was directed on page one would page two become visible, and so on, much that now requires personal instruction could be managed by print." He and Arthur Gates had said the same thing in their *Elementary Principles of Education* in 1929. Gates wrote to me that he thought the miracle had not happened earlier because progressive education was hostile to any type of "alleged predetermined mechanical learning" and those in charge of school budgets "were disposed to scorn the idea that schools could afford such expensive materials, especially in the years following 1929." I was beginning to wonder whether the educational establishment was even now ready for a miracle.

*   *   *

EARLY IN 1960, I had talked with Dennis Flanagan, editor of the *Scientific American*, about an article on teaching machines. The trip to Russia delayed me, and when I finished the manuscript, Flanagan did not like it. Could one of their writers, Frank Bello, write a story to be published under my name? Probably because Bello had once told me that he liked my paper "Freedom and the Control of Men," I agreed. He interviewed the staff of the center, and a photographer spent a day with us. The article contained excellent pictures of the self-instruction room in Sever Hall, young people at work on machines teaching rhythm and musical behavior, the operation of Didak 501 (covering two full pages), and a page in color of some of the material Jim and Eugene Long were using to teach inductive reasoning. There were also pictures of pigeons pecking keys and several cumulative records. The text was, as I had expected, well written, but rather more critical of current education than I had allowed myself to be. It attracted a great deal of attention and reprints were widely sold, but I never felt that it was my paper.

IN 1962 an editorial in *Science* read:

By the end of this year, one will be able to choose among 250 programmed courses in elementary, secondary, and college mathematics, 60 in science, 25 in electronics and engineering, 25 in foreign languages, 120 in social studies, and others in contract bridge, parliamentary procedure, fundamentals of music, and even in chess and etiquette.

The list will grow; techniques will become more standardized; research and experience will bring improvements; emotional reactions against anything called a "teaching machine" will dwindle; and the devices—or, more important, the programmed materials—will come into widespread and effective use. . . . There are several reasons for watching this development with continuing interest. It is the first major technological innovation in education since the development of printing. It is based on theories of learning; the theory-to-practice sequence is not as rigorous as is common in the physical sciences and engineering, but a direct connection is nonetheless present.

A National Society for Programmed Instruction was organized. Pressey and I were elected honorary members and, the following year, life members, and I spoke on "What Is Programmed Instruction?" at the first meeting of a Greater Boston Area chapter. Conferences began to be organized in profusion. A "Second Conference on Programmed Learning" was held in Albuquerque, New Mexico, in January 1962, and on the following day a "Third Western Conference on Programmed Learning" at the Systems Development Corporation in Santa Monica, California.

Cartoons and jokes were inevitable: a drawing of a robot on the blackboard labeled "teacher," a boy holding up his hand asking the machine if he may leave the room; a meeting of the Parent–Teaching Machine Association. A widely quoted limerick ran as follows:

> The latest report from the Dean
> Concerning the teaching machine
> Is that Oedipus Rex
> Could have learned about sex
> By machine and not bothered the Queen.

Equally inevitable were misunderstandings. Many writers knew only the psychology they had studied in college and wrote about trial-and-error learning in rats in mazes or conditioned reflexes in dogs. When IBM's magazine, *Think*, ran a story on teaching machines, a great black-and-white maze on the cover was said to be the kind of thing "used to measure the learning rate of animals" and to reveal "the problems of learning. The mind takes many consecutive steps, some down blind alleys, others along winding paths of knowledge." A headline in the *Wall Street Journal* read: "Robot Teachers: Schools, Business Firms Spur Use of Machines to Drill, Test Students." Some machines—Pressey's, for example—did, indeed, "drill and test," but students working through a well-designed program were not being tested or drilled in the sense of being made to go over points again and again until they could do so without error.

Psychologists were among those who misunderstood. One of the most static views of the human mind was a by-product of intelligence testing. By processing scores in various ways, it was said to be possible to reveal the "structure of intellect." Theories of the sort had a certain grandeur beside which principles derived from animal research seemed little short of vulgar. J. P. Guilford, an authority in the field of intelligence, wrote:

> Education in this country has unfortunately been too much dominated by the learning theory based upon the stimulus-response model[!] of Thorndike, Hull, and Skinner. People, after all, are not rats (with a few exceptions), and they are not pigeons (with similar exceptions). Let us make full use of the human brains that have been granted to us. Let us apply a psychology that recognizes the full range of human intellectual qualities.

Arthur Gates suggested that I write a rejoinder. "It is no easy matter," he wrote, "to convince schoolmen of the subtle errors in statements of this kind." He was right. Professional educators were the most refractory in taking up a new point of view. Horace English had added a postscript to his letter to Garry Boring about the invention of the teaching machine: "In the main, the damn thing works to help form connections." "Forming connections" or associations was one of the cognitive processes most often assigned to the mind. The only real connections were made in the environmental contingencies.

In a letter to the *Saturday Review of Literature*, a distinguished professor of educational psychology said that psychologists had

> failed to make use of one of their important principles of learning; namely "reinforcement. . . ." Here is how it would work. Every time the pupil presses the lever of an incorrect answer, he will receive a mild electric shock. This can be arranged through a specially designed handle which he holds while taking the examination; or better still, by placing a metal grill on the seat of the chair. . . . The shock should not be so strong as to make the pupil jump; it should only startle him. This would be "negative reinforcement." Now, when the pupil selects the correct answer . . . the machine should eject a candy bar, or a piece of chocolate, or some other choice bit. This would be "positive reinforcement." I am really surprised that this principle has not been incorporated.

What was really surprising in this heavy irony was that it should so closely parallel my travesty of more than a decade earlier, and that a well-known educator should be so completely out of touch with what was going on.

My own musical education had been faulty. I had played the saxophone well, but the piano only passably. I could read music easily, but could not play by ear or memorize. I once spent a whole day learning the C-Major Prelude in the first book of the *Well-Tempered Clavichord* and could play only a few bars of it the next day. Obviously I had never learned to "think musically"—or, better—to "behave in musical ways." Was it a genetic limitation, or could that behavior be programmed?

Rhythm was important. In Debbie's nursery school, I had seen children clapping blocks of wood together as their classmates marched or sang songs, but nothing required a good rhythm. Yet pigeons could pace their behavior with great precision, as Fred Lagmay had shown. I designed a machine in which a child tapped a button in unison with a series of clicks presented at different speeds and in different patterns, unison being signaled by a flashing light. At first, the tolerances were generous; they were slowly reduced to shape precise behavior.

Intervals, melodies, and harmonies required rather more elaborate instrumentation, and I persuaded the Hammond Organ Company to give us an organ with a player attachment. It was a beautiful instrument and played beautiful music, but our efforts to adapt it as a teaching machine were disastrous. The electronics of the pitch-producing system were beyond us, and the punched-paper player never became the programming device we envisaged. Except for a keyboard which could be used to teach intervals, nothing soon remained.

I was asked to serve on a panel of the President's Scientific Advisory Committee, chaired by Robert Morison, on technological extensions of behavioral science. It was a chance to get some federal action on programmed instruction, and I accepted. Joe Brady was another member, and he and I prepared the part of the report dealing with education. In April 1962 I recorded our meeting with the President's top scientific brass:

We waited in the Music Room of the Rockefeller Institute until
2:15 and were then shown into the presence. The committee was sitting
around a long lozenge-shaped table. A coffee urn at one end of the room
was constantly visited. Someone raised the question of over-emphasizing
computer technology. (I had repeatedly raised it myself at our meetings.)
... When Morison asked me to say something about machines, Wiesner,
sitting next to Zacharias, cut me off. A special panel on Educational
Technology would deal with that. At 3:30 Det Bronk [President of the
Rockefeller Institute] came in, the meeting moved on to something involving the Institute, and we adjourned to the bar and game room to
"revise" our report. There was not much we could do. . . . Our report
will be published [it was not] and may have some effect. It had no effect
on PSAC and I'm not sure I should want it to have. What will the
President be told as a result of what we have done?

WHEN AN ARTICLE CALLED "Education ex Machina" in the *Economist*
for June 2, 1961, said that "This promising development is being
jeopardized by rank commercialism," I could only agree. My experiences with American companies had not been encouraging, and worse
was to follow.

Lloyd Homme had become President of Teaching Machines Incorporated, with Robert Glaser as a Director and Ben Wyckoff as
Chairman of the board. The company manufactured a simple machine
and wrote many good programs for it, but another company was selling
the machines and giving them away in connection with door-to-door
sales of an encyclopedia. Their salesmen were emphasizing my part in
their design and my Harvard connection. Whenever I protested, an
officer promised to take action, but incidents continued to mount. A
student told me that he had applied for summer work as an encyclopedia salesman for a subsidiary of the company in California and that
the sales manager used my name quite freely and instructed the applicants to do the same. When I complained, I was told that the sales
manager was flying East to be disciplined. Later, the Federal Trade
Commission asked me whether I had any connection with the company,
and whether I was aware that it was using my name. Still later, a young
psychologist in Bethesda, Maryland, wrote that he had been approached
by a salesman who showed him a plastic-coated blowup of a *Time*

magazine article about my work, told him about the Aircrib, and used my name in a "quite unethical way." When I again protested, I was told that the company had thousands of salesmen in several national organizations "each of which is beset by high turnover," and that some "eager salesmen go to the library to read about programmed learning and encounter your name and try to find a way of using it."

Another large publisher hired some of the best scholars in the field and began to market programs in spiral-bound notebooks with sliding masks. They soon decided that the scholars were not really needed, and fired them. An effort was even made to stop them from taking "company secrets" with them.

WHEN THE RHEEM MACHINES arrived, there were many things wrong with them, and a machinist spent a good deal of time putting them in shape for my course. The company was in trouble. Its stock was falling and sharp economies were imposed. It had paid too much for the language-laboratory company; concealed debts had been discovered, and there was talk of suing the public auditor. I could not yet recommend the Rheem machine and I had given up trying to answer inquiries. When I complained, I was sent again to California, where I enjoyed a dinner on the patio of another vice-president.

I WAS OFTEN TOLD that I should not have said "teaching machines." "Learning machines" would be better. But machines did not learn. Like books and teachers, they composed contingencies under which students learned, and that was teaching.

Other objections were raised. The famous "Hawthorne Effect" was invoked: machines would lose their effectiveness when the novelty wore off. But every step in a program was novel; new things were always turning up, and in fact good programs did not lose their power as students continued to work on them. It was said that students whose behavior was always immediately reinforced would be in trouble when the consequences were deferred. But that had been true for centuries under punitive control. Students could be weaned from immediate, contrived reinforcement in well-known ways. (They acquired a tolerance for delayed reinforcement, for example, when they learned to appreciate good literature. In cheap literature the reinforcers occur on every page, but in a great book one reads a long time before reaching a great moment.)

It was said that there was something slightly dishonest about contrived contingencies of reinforcement—as in the use of tokens in classroom management. Students should learn in a natural environment. But Socrates feigned ignorance and pretended to misunderstand his students, and traditional punitive contingencies were far from natural. Contrived reinforcers were justified if they were contingent upon behavior which would later have naturally reinforcing consequences. It was said that students would come to depend upon programmed material and never learn to read a book. But textbooks scarcely prepared students for ordinary books, either. As we reported to HumRRO in October 1957, the issue is raised by all education. "Teachers are to produce men and women who will continue to read, observe, and analyze with interest, skill, and profit after they have severed connections. Devoted teachers will be most missed, and they must be especially alert to making themselves expendable." Programs could be designed to wean the student by slowly withdrawing support.

Many people were afraid of programmed instruction just because it worked. They did not fear traditional education because they knew it was ineffective, and hence harmless. Poor teaching was also said to be good because it left room for individuality and creativity: if only part of what a student learned was due to teacher or text, the rest could be attributed to the student. But the variety of experiences required for individuality or originality should come from something more than defective instruction. With programs and machines, students had more time for personal instruction, and could take advanced courses for which a high school or small college could not afford to hire teachers.

Meanwhile, traditional theories continued to flourish. The report of a conference of experts called "Learning to Read," with an introduction by James Bryant Conant, asserted that "We hold that reading cannot be taught through 'sight-words' (look-say) alone. Such teaching would require our children to memorize, word by word, the mass of printed words. No reading authority advocates so impossible a procedure." But in *Verbal Behavior* I had shown how a repertoire of "atomic" verbal operants emerges from ordinary verbal behavior although no specific contingencies have been arranged to teach it. Many philosophers of education still insisted that knowledge was inside the student and had only to be relcased: it lay waiting to be born, needing only a midwife. In the *Meno*, Socrates claims to show that a slave boy already knows Pythagoras's theorem for doubling the square and needs only to recollect it. The boy makes some fifty responses, a few of which involve counting, the rest nothing more than assent. The list begins, *I do. Surely. Yes. Oh, yes. Yes. Yes, so it is,* and ends, *Two. Twice. Eight. This one. Yes. Certainly, Socrates.* The boy could not possibly then have gone through the argument by himself afterwards, as Socrates later admits. The passage was still widely quoted as a model of instruction, although it was one of the greatest of intellectual hoaxes.

IN 1959 I wrote a note:

> I want to prepare myself for deterioration, and to avoid its worst consequences by shifting to fields where it is less felt. Two warnings have appeared on the wall recently. In my new undergraduate course on the advanced analysis of behavior I have been reviewing *Schedules of Reinforcement*. Those were great years. I gave more of my time to the pigeon lab and I am doing more elsewhere now, but the fact is, my productive day is now shorter, including the meditating hours, which are probably less cogent or rigorous.
>
> A second shock came from rereading *Walden Two*. It was written fourteen years ago. How much of my thinking in social and political fields has really gone much beyond it? I have progressed mainly by becoming a convinced Frazierian and making some contribution to implementing a more effective social control.
>
> There is no doubt that the last year has not been productive. My dominant concern has been to recover from the strain of the preceding two or three years. My exchanges with American business must someday be recorded—even if the future is a lot better. So far the result has been frustration, sleepless nights, days and weaks [sic] of unproductive negotiations. I must have given 50 lectures on programmed instruction in the past two years, and answered more than a thousand letters. I gave the Page-Barbour and Mead-Swing lectures and carried on my teaching and research. It was much too much, and I have not escaped the conse-

quences. I am shocked at how badly I have been thinking and writing. The American Academy paper, *The Design of Cultures,* is an extract from the Mead-Swing lectures and not very good.

ETHOLOGISTS WERE STILL ACCUSING behaviorists of ignoring differences between species. At a conference on behavior genetics in August 1961, Daniel Lehrman recalled a visit to our laboratory. An authority on the behavior of doves, he had asked to see our fighting pigeons, presumably to discover whether the behavior was typical of the species. Dick Herrnstein, he reported, urged him to try shaping a pigeon's behavior, and "with no more than 15 or 20 reinforcements" he induced a pigeon to turn away from the food dispenser and stand on one leg—"a very unpigeonlike way to feed." The experience led to a "blinding insight": Why not get a ring dove to do a courtship bow that resembled the courtship bow of a rock dove? Could one not thus "study the ontogeny of instinctive behavior and the tie between instinctive behavior and the environment during development?" To his surprise Dick said he did not think it could be done; operant reinforcement did not readily change what you might call "bird behavior." But "if it is not successful with what you call 'bird behavior,'" Lehrman said, "what are you showing about birds by developing these data? You get the communality between birds and guinea pigs by ignoring everything that's important about a guinea pig."

That was the ethological dogma: "Everything that was important about a pigeon" was what a pigeon did as the result of natural selection. But the capacity to be changed by consequences during the lifetime of the individual was also part of the genetic endowment of a species, and in that capacity pigeons resembled guinea pigs, not to say people. By studying a convenient species one could learn as much about certain behavioral processes as about digestion, respiration, or reproduction. Much of what was then known about genetics had been learned from the fruit fly.

In simplifying the experimental space in laboratory research, we usually eliminated most of the releasers of ethological behavior, and it was then easy to call the space or the behavior unnatural. Nevertheless, what we had learned in that simplified space told us a good deal about genetics. If I had been given a pigeon which had no innate tendency to build a nest and in which nest-building was not automatically reinforced by its consequences, I should not have taken on the assignment of teaching it to build one. We knew enough about operant conditioning to know that pigeons did not build nests because of a series of accidental reinforcements.

A graduate student, Neil Peterson, showed the relevance of laboratory research to an understanding of the genetics of behavior when he found that the behavior of a young duckling in following an imprinted object was not necessarily innate; coming nearer to the object was a reinforcing consequence. A duckling would peck a key or even walk away if the object was then brought closer.

Keller and Marian Breland were caught up in the ethological attack on operant conditioning. Their "new field of applied psychology" was prospering. They had acquired hundreds of acres of land, were employing more than a dozen people, and had conditioned the behavior of thousands of animals. *Life* magazine featured their truly "animated" advertisements for the products of General Mills, and, in a later issue, their IQ Zoo. *Time* reported their work, as did *Reader's Digest*. In 1955 they were called in as consultants at Marine Studios in Florida. A German animal trainer had taken several years to teach a porpoise two or three simple tricks, but the Brelands quickly produced much more complex behavior, and other "marine lands" in Florida, California, and Hawaii soon adopted their techniques.

In March 1960, Keller wrote that he and Marian were looking forward to the *Conquest* program. They had found that businessmen simply would not believe, in the absence of a demonstration, "that the behavior of animals can be controlled to the extent we know is possible." They would be grateful if I referred any inquiries to them.

Later that spring Keller came East, and at a Pigeon Staff meeting he reported some surprising facts. A raccoon taught to pick up a coin and drop it in a box seemed, like Pliny the rat at Minnesota, unable to let go. In their natural environments, rats and raccoons evidently have little reason to "let go to produce an effect." In many of their demonstrations, an animal repeated a bit of behavior many thousands of times, and behavior which was pretty clearly phylogenic often broke through. For example, a chicken which delivered a small toy in a capsule when a coin was dropped in a slot began to treat the capsule as if it were a seed pod and, instead of delivering it to the customer, struck it against the floor again and again.

A lively discussion followed, and some experiments were suggested. For example, would the chicken strike the capsule if it were thirsty rather than hungry and the reinforcer were water? We urged Keller to publish as soon as possible, and he wrote that after the meeting "my head was buzzing with ideas so that I drove a hundred miles in the wrong direction on the turnpike."

A year and a half later, he and Marian sent the *American Psychologist* a paper called "The Misbehavior of Organisms." "After looking at the galley proofs," they wrote to me, "it occurred to us that it might convey impressions not intended. Perhaps we did not state strongly enough our feeling as to the efficacy of operant conditioning in the control of organisms. This conviction is so 'old hat' with us that I am afraid that we sometimes forget that it is not shared by all American psychologists."

Their paper did, indeed, convey some strange impressions. It gave a good account of the "breakdowns of conditioned operant behavior" which Keller had described to the Pigeon Staff, but it went on to argue that they "represent a clear and utter failure of conditioning theory." Behaviorism, they said, made three tacit assumptions: "That the animal comes to the laboratory as a virtual *tabula rasa*, that species differences are insignificant, and that all responses are about equally conditionable to all stimuli." I myself had never made any such assumptions and had, in fact, published data which contradicted all of them. I was only too willing to agree that "the behavior of any species could not be adequately understood, predicted, or controlled without knowledge of its instinctive patterns, evolutionary history, and ecological niche." The Brelands' data were simply interesting examples of phenomena which needed to be studied further.

They themselves were soon contradicting their claim that "ethological facts and attitudes in recent years had done more to advance our practical control of animal behavior than recent reports from American 'learning labs.' " True, the Men's Magazine, in a long article describing their company, reported that they had been the first to use for commercial purposes the principles we had discovered on the old Project Pigeon. The article cited my paper, "How to Teach Animals," on the importance of immediate reward, the use of a conditioned reinforcer, and the shaping of behavior through successive approximation. Marian was soon promoting the same principles in a handbook called "Shaping Behavior with Positive Reinforcement or Reward" for the use of those who worked with retarded children.

I MADE A SMALL CONTRIBUTION to the literature of ethology in a short paper in the *Harvard Alumni Bulletin*, reporting an episode I had witnessed when I was a postdoctoral fellow. Memorial Church in the Harvard Yard had been completed, and a bell was to be hoisted into its tower in a little ceremony. It was discovered, however, that a squirrel had begun to move her brood from a tree near the bell to a building a few hundred yards away, and President Lowell told everyone to wait until she had finished. There were more baby squirrels than anyone had expected, and their mother's heroic undertaking was watched by a steadily growing crowd. The bell was hoisted an hour late.

Kathy Safford and I had failed to strengthen a pigeon's cooing through operant reinforcement, and I had had no luck with a cat's meow, but to my surprise Harlan Lane successfully reinforced cheeping in young chicks and found that a fixed-ratio schedule yielded a characteristic curve, and Mark Molliver, at the Medical School, later successfully reinforced meowing in cats. Nevertheless, it was only the frequency of the behavior that changed, not its topography.

AT A PSYCHIATRIC HOSPITAL in Saskatchewan, Theodore Ayllon, a student of Lee Meyerson and Jack Michael at the University of Houston, explored the use of a token economy in managing ward behavior. Other work followed, and by 1960 the practical use of operant conditioning in psychotherapy was attracting so much attention that, at a meeting at the American Academy of Arts and Sciences, Lawrence Kubie, Carl Rogers, Erik Erikson, Abraham Maslow, and Harry Murray —all independently—proposed that we meet to discuss it, and the Executive Director of the Academy said he planned to organize an appropriate conference. Og, however, continued to find it difficult to work with psychiatrists, and since I was much too busy to help, our project was closed and Og moved into education.

HARVARD'S DEPARTMENT OF SOCIAL RELATIONS had never jelled. The sociologists were unhappy without a department of their own, the social anthropologists were drifting back toward the Peabody Museum and physical anthropology, and the original personal reasons for separating experimental and social psychology had vanished with the persons. Clinical psychology would soon be declared out of place in a graduate school of arts and sciences on the grounds that it was a profession. As a first step toward a return to the *status quo ante*, Mac Bundy appointed a committee of experimental and social psychologists to plan the future of the field at Harvard, and the architect Yamasaki was at work on a building for joint occupancy by the behavioral sciences.

A SOVIET DELEGATION of scientists came to Harvard to look at programmed instruction. I reported our exchange in a note:

In Russia we used to joke about our paranoia. Did they not want us to see their schools in action? If not, why did they put us off until the children had gone home for the day, or say that a school was closed to celebrate the founding of the Young Pioneers? Usually these excuses proved valid. Occasionally there was an obvious reluctance to show us something that was not wholly admirable, but no real sign of dissimulation. Now the shoe is on the other foot—and I am afraid no sense of humor will save us. Our Committee on Programmed Instruction took the four Russians to lunch at the Faculty Club, and they came to our house for cocktails later in the afternoon. We invited some of our Russian-speaking friends, among them Elena Levin. She and Harry took one member of the delegation home for the evening and, relaxed by a few drinks, he eventually told her that the delegation had appreciated our hospitality but had learned nothing. He was convinced that I was under State Department instruction to tell them as little as possible about teaching machines. Elena assured him that he was wrong and offered to call me to see whether I could meet with him before he left Cambridge late the following afternoon. When she asked, "What will you believe if it turns out that he is busy all day and can't see you?," he replied, "I will believe he does not want to see me."

Fortunately I was free, and he came to our house with an interpreter. I went through the outline of the book I was writing, *The Technology of Teaching*, chapter by chapter, and discussed every point he raised. When I finished, he said simply, "Will you make the manuscript of this book available so that a Russian translation can appear simultaneously?" I agreed to ask my publisher if that could be done.

I had already told Alexander Luria that I was sure my publishers would be glad to see a Russian edition, but it turned out that *simultaneous* publication would raise copyright problems.

As a graduate student I had answered an advertisement in the *Boston Evening Transcript* in which a Mlle. Angelie Chenel offered French conversation at 75 cents an hour. I looked forward to meeting a charming young woman but found instead a wretchedly poor spinster, who lived in a boardinghouse rather like Père Goriot's, which became our main topic of conversation. In the early fifties, when a good many foreign psychologists were moving about in the postwar world, I found French useful and occasionally paid someone to come in and converse with me. (A French industrialist came to talk with me about teaching machines. He brought an interpreter, but when he found that I could manage passable French we spent the afternoon talking, not about teaching machines, but about Stendhal, in whom we were both interested. When he returned to France, he sent me a five-volume set of Stendhal's *Journal*.)

When Professor Paul Fraisse asked me to lecture at the Sorbonne, I rashly suggested that I do so in French. Fraisse was *ravi*, and said that if I could be in Paris on the first Saturday of any month he would arrange a meeting of the Société Française de Psychologie. We agreed on the third of November 1962, and during the summer I wrote the lecture. I wanted to think it in French, rather than translate my own English, but I needed help. Claude Levy, a French member of the Play

Readers, introduced me to Margaret Brooks, whose husband, Peter, was finishing work for a doctorate in comparative literature at Harvard, and she and I wrote a draft. When I reached Paris, I found that I would not be breaking ground, because placards on the kiosks were advertising an article in the magazine *Sciences et Avenir* called *"Les Machines à Enseigner"*—an excellent article, well balanced and comprehensive. The Brookses had come to Paris, and Margaret and I made a few last-minute changes. (The Rheem Company, anxious to do everything it could except develop a good teaching machine, offered the services of its Paris office. The Director's charming secretary would be glad to type a final version on a proper typewriter free of penciled diacritical marks.)

On the morning of the meeting, Fraisse looked at my manuscript and suggested that an assistant could make a few useful changes. (He was equally exacting in other matters; at lunch he protested my choice of entrée as inappropriate to the soup I had ordered.) In the afternoon, at the Sorbonne, he introduced me to an alarmingly large audience, but the lecture went off without incident. A question period followed—also, of course, in French—but those who asked questions first made speeches, and the questions were mercifully brief.

I had a few friends in the audience, among them Ira and Shirley Hirsh. Ira had helped me with Psychology 7 when he was a graduate student, and he was then spending a year in Fraisse's laboratory. Debs came up from Grenoble, the Brookses were there, and when it was over, we all went out for a drink. The guarded opinion was that I had got away with it.

A week later, I gave the same lecture at Piaget's Institute in Geneva and met some of his students in a larger and much more serious question-and-answer period. Piaget and I sat side by side and spent part of the time talking to each other. He understood English perfectly, but refused to speak it. I was less cautious about my French, and the students were delighted. I used *étudiants* for children much too young to be called that, and in describing Piaget's famous experiment on the conservation of volume, I referred in my haste to glasses of different *grossesse*—pregnancy, not size.

*   *   *

I WAS ACTIVE in too many fields and badly overworked. I reported a sample day in my notebook:

Yesterday began with an hour and a half at my desk on the manuscript. I met my class on *The Technology of Teaching* from 11:00 to 11:50. I dashed to the Boston Psychopathic Hospital for what I had supposed to be a luncheon-discussion with the staff but found the Chapel filled and waiting for me. I improvised a lecture on radical behaviorism, and a very energetic discussion followed. I got away in time for a sandwich and cup of coffee with the Director, Jack Ewalt, and was then driven to Cambridge where from 2:15 to 4:15 I discussed Waldens I and II in a seminar on "Paradise" conducted by Harry Murray and Harry Levin. At a cocktail party later in the afternoon I was buttonholed by two people, one of them from MIT, and questioned closely about teaching machines. I felt no fatigue, even when forced to talk about teaching machines, and I was also, whatever it means, in good form. I see no after-effects this morning, except that I am writing notes instead of working on the MS. But I need to relax!

Eight months later I was making progress in what I called intellectual self-management:

I begin to see myself more clearly in relation to the daily environment in which I live from hour to hour. (Apostrophe: Am I now leading a more "rational" life? In the traditional sense, no. My behavior is still controlled by the same variables—mostly reinforcing consequences—acting through the same processes. I am arranging these variables rather than allowing them to turn up at random or from irrelevant sources, but that is not "reason." A weighing of consequences was certainly part of the "life of reason," and that is present now, but even a selection of goals does not change the nature of the effect of those selected. There is no issue of reason vs. emotion. Or vs. whim, impulse, fancy.)

My examination of my own life-sphere has been stimulated by two first-person accounts: Boring's autobiography and Stendhal's *Journal*. Boring tried a psychological analysis—the lonely Philadelphia boy, the overriding professional ambition, the Moravian-Quaker ethic—all with little insight. He believed in inner forces and took to psychoanalysis to learn about them. Stendhal, still in his early twenties, goes straight to the heart of the matter. What effects are his various daily contacts having on him? What does reading Shakespeare do? Or seeing Mme. T? Or gambling? What changes must he make in his *daily life* (not in himself)?

In the same vein, I look for, and find, the reinforcing contingencies which are operating from moment to moment.

I still accept aversive controls, and may be on the point of extending them. The White House Panel draws to a close; the final report and the place in it for an operant analysis will show whether it was worthwhile. A NATO conference may be worth the effort. I am caught by an Arden House symposium (at the request of Roy Larsen of *Time* magazine), but it will give me a chance to explain teaching machines to some important people. [It did not.] I could not get out of a visit to Maryland, but at least I will talk about an experimental community there. My graduate course will cover the MS of *The Technology of Teaching*— profitably, I hope. And so it goes.

Meanwhile, my day and how well I spend it is my first concern. Carlyle's lines,

So here has been dawning another blue day.
Think, wilt thou let it slip useless away?

which I learned in 6th grade, sets the Puritan pattern. Unfortunately, a high resolve does not guarantee effective behavior. Boring did not want to let a day slip useless away, either, but he tended to fill it with compulsive, made work. Like Stendhal, I am looking for another solution. How am I to find the conditions under which I will make the contributions which are most likely to be uniquely mine?

In *Age and Achievement*, Harvey Lehman had reported that people in the hard sciences did their best work when they were in their thirties. I thought my science was fairly hard; when would a decline set in? I asked Lehman himself during a visit to Ohio University. Should I change to a field in which I would be more effective? "To administration," he said, but my brief experience as a department chairman was not encouraging.

I was soon making a positive move. A Harvard professor may retire emeritus at the end of the academic year in which he reaches sixty, and for me that meant June 1964. I told the Dean that I would retire at that time. I would bring my research to an end by July 1962. The great days of my collaboration with Charlie Ferster and Bill Morse were over. I had been increasingly aware of how little attention I was giving to the laboratory. "My projects are no longer part of me," I wrote. "In spite of all my efforts I cannot find time for research. . . . If I were head of the National Science Foundation and knew the situation here, I would reject my applications for funds." Dick Herrnstein was back as an assistant professor and beginning to publish work he had done with Bill Morse at Harvard and at Walter Reed Hospital with Joe Brady and Murray Sidman, and he would take over the pigeon laboratory. I would leave it without regret. I had had more than thirty years of research, and I could not complain.

I would give Natural Sciences 114 for the last time in the spring of 1963. Sever Hall was to be remodeled (the old, deeply carved, benchlike desks would be sold to nostalgic alumni to be converted into coffee tables), and the Self-instruction Room would be torn up and the teaching machines put on tables in Lamont Library. Dick was not interested in taking over the course, and it would be dropped from the catalog. Had it been worthwhile? Harvard and Radcliffe students did not change as obviously as my sophomores at Minnesota, but an occasional letter pleased me (". . . it has been one of the most exciting educational experiences of my life"), as did word that a colleague in Social Relations had warned his students that if they had taken my course they would not do well in his. I myself had learned much. I had not greatly changed my position, but in restating it year after year to responsive students I filled in gaps, spotted inconsistencies, and developed implications which I had not at first seen. Among other things, the course had prepared me for a project which was emerging in my plans for retirement—an analysis of the evolution and design of a culture.

In a series of notes, I reviewed other reasons for retiring early:

> I used to feel that I wanted to quit before I lost touch with the best work in the field, before I began not to understand why younger men did what they did, before I failed to see that they were actually doing better work than I. But I am convinced that there is another reason: I must get out of the way of younger men! Operant behavior would be more effectively studied during the next decade if I were to die tomorrow. My continuing presence could:
>
> 1) keep excellent men out of a field in which it would be difficult to gain recognition because pitted, merely from the accident of age, against an entrenched figure.
>
> 2) substantially reduce the reinforcement of work already in the field by keeping alive the epithet "Skinnerian."
>
> 3) deflect research from its most productive course by setting an

example too tightly bound to the past and by commending and politically supporting what is now already traditional.

In another note I referred to "the situation at Harvard. I am no longer interested in the department. It has resisted all my efforts to improve it. It will be dominated for some time by the cognitive psychologists."

It was a decisive change but not a disturbing one:

> Though I have been (1) observing myself closely of late, (2) considering rather drastic changes in my life, including the termination of my research and teaching, (3) reviewing the disappointing status of the teaching-machine movement, (4) contemplating delays in finishing *The Technology of Teaching,* and much else with respect to a doubtful future, I have not been depressed. My mood is, if anything, one of fatigue—I am tired of some of the things I have been doing and physically less energetic. But I do not *suffer.* I seek rest and avoid exhausting labors, but I *enjoy* my life—not ecstatically but steadily and contentedly.

I was aware of certain dangers. My courses were providing

excellent audience control, under which I work much harder and longer to clarify my analysis, and not a day goes by when I do not improve it, often in a surprising way. How important is this? Can I work effectively without it? I could continue to give lectures, like the Page-Barbour and the Mead-Swing, but there is something to be said for a class in a well-defined and to some extent appropriately prepared environment.

I planned to take a sabbatical year in 1962 to "test myself on retirement."

DEBBIE HAD NOT DONE WELL at Woodstock, and the school seemed to feel that she should plan on no more than a two-year college. I was sure they were wrong. Born in August, she had always been slightly younger than most of her classmates and had matured slowly. A year off before starting college would help—in a school in Switzerland or England, perhaps, or with a French family, perfecting her French and taking a course or two at the University of Paris.

In August 1962 Eve, Debs, and I sailed from Montreal on the SS

Homeric. From Southampton we went directly to Manchester, where I spoke on teaching machines at a meeting of the British Association, and then on to Paris. I had written to several French families suggested by friends, but fortunately had made no commitment, because we found that the University had very little interest in its students and Debs would have had to be considerably more mature to survive in the life of the city. At Dijon all adequate living quarters were committed, but in Grenoble we found a pleasant apartment in which a Mme. Guillot who spoke no English took in two or three girls each year.

Debs signed up for courses at the University and then went with us to see the caves at Lascaux, Les Ezyies, and in Spain at Altamira. We spent some time in Basque country, and saw Lourdes on a particularly grim, rainy Sunday. Then Eve and I left Debbie in Grenoble and went on to Oslo, Göteborg, Lund, and Stockholm, and, again in Britain, to Aberdeen, Edinburgh, Sheffield, Nottingham, Birmingham, Bristol, Oxford, and Cambridge. At all these places I lectured on "The Future of Teaching Machines," and in London I discussed "Behaviorism Today" at a meeting of the British Psychological Society.

Before the term was over, I had given several other lectures in the United States—at the University of Minnesota on behaviorism (the R. M. Elliott Lecture, named for my old boss), in Denver on the nature of a society, and in Pittsburgh and at the University of Maryland on the future of teaching machines. It was scarcely an adequate test for retirement. I had not done any original thinking. I was repeating myself:

> I find myself coming up with points *as if for the first time* which I had made as long ago as the *Behavior of Organisms*. . . . My work is attracting wider attention and I am called upon to discuss it with new audiences, particularly with nonpsychologists or with psychologists in peripheral fields. . . . but I must not become a mere propagandist, a simple expositor. I believe I still have original things to say.

On January 1, 1962, I wrote another, more revealing, note:

> It is nearly nine o'clock on the first day of the new year. From a deep blue sky, sun streams into our living room. Outside, our lawn glistens with only slightly soiled crusty snow, broken by the frozen swimming pool, on the surface of which I can still see signs of yesterday's skating. My hi-fi is midway through the first act of *Tristan und Isolde*.

Julie and Deborah on Monhegan (appropriately, Deborah is painting and Julie is writing).

Reading the part of George Moore in Tom Stoppard's anti-Skinnerian play Jumpers, *with Eve as my secretary.*

Eve with Julie and Deborah.

In the laboratory with Richard Herrnstein.

*With Marian Anderson, receiving honorary degrees at
Hobart and William Smith Colleges.*

With Fred Keller, listening to Charles Ferster at my
Festschrift dinner.

Pigeon Staff meeting. At my right, Charles Catania, William H. Morse, and George Reynolds.
Behind Catania, Peter Dews. Others unidentified.

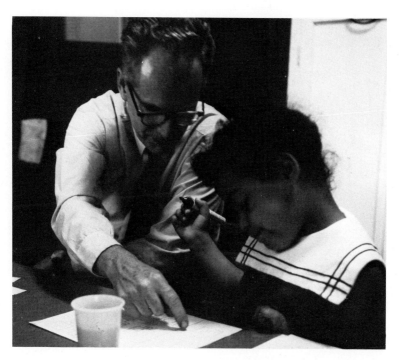

Testing the handwriting program with a student.

Shaping the behavior of a porpoise at Sealife Park, Honolulu.

Student using the teaching machine I demonstrated at Pittsburgh in 1954.

Deborah and Barry Buzan.

Granddaughter Justine with pigeon.

With Julie in a Learning Center.

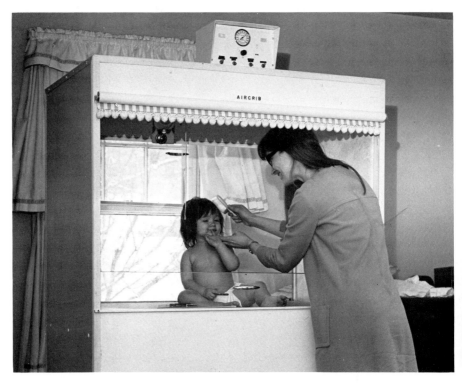

Julie with Lisa in the Aircrib.

Julie and Ernest Vargas just before their marriage.

A very pleasant environment. A man would be a fool not to enjoy it. In a moment I will go to my study, possibly—and if so, rarely—taking the Wagner with me for background music, where I will write for two or three hours (my daily average is now only two) on a manuscript which I think important and which may "help mankind." So my life is not only pleasant, it is earned or deserved. Yet—yet—I am unhappy.

It is not so much that, so far as the world goes, I am perhaps one in a thousand (a million?) to enjoy a life like this; it has always been thus. It is not entirely the realization that the world could not support this kind of life for everyone; birth control would remedy that by reducing the mass of "everyone." It is not wholly a belief that no man is an island; an enclave of misery elsewhere in the world may not affect me or my children, though I may feel guilty about it as my Puritan heritage.

It is the fact that so little is being done about it! We are trapped— in the love of a life like this, in false social science, in statesmanship based on historical analogies, in a network of pressure groups whose members (as in a lynching) become more violent just because they are acting together. Etc. Etc. Is it up to me? (A Wagnerian theme, if I ever saw one!)

When that note was published in a profile in *Harper's*, many friends wrote to me about my unhappiness. Was I no longer optimistic about the future?

WHEN DEBS WAS HOME during spring vacation in her last term at Woodstock, we had an argument, and later I found a note:

ODE TO A PROFESSOR OF PSYCHOLOGY

Our professor's named Skinner,
The likeable kind.
His upbringing's perfect!
A remarkable mind!

With him all goes well;
Now shouldn't it oughter?
But poor Skinner's damned
With a troublesome daughter.

She's spoiled and she's spiteful,
Her mind's but a blur.
"Psychology," Skinner says,
"Won't work on her."

My reply:

Here's to old Skinner—behavior he teaches,
But seldom practices just what he preaches.

For example, to cancel the gift of a horse meant
Punishment rather than real reinforcement.

His daughters are *not* the result of his system.
Its benefits? Maybe it's well that they missed 'em.

A year later another note:

At this moment Debs should be taking off for London from Geneva.
Somewhere I have a note on her first solitary journey. This is her first
solitary year—and I am equally proud of it. She has vast resources—but
they are not standard ones and they do not gain her the successes a girl
of eighteen needs.

I cannot honestly call her the product of nonaversive control. I have
been aversive at times, and so have others a good deal of the time. Shady
Hill school had no way of handling her except to pour on the guilt. She
has strong feelings of inadequacy.

Yet she draws with the true creative skill of the artist. Unpretentious,
imitative only of herself, she draws for the sheer pleasure of seeing the
pictures she produces. Her letters have a similar spontaneity, and she is
enough aware of their value to ask us (and her other correspondents) to
save them.

Both her drawings and her prose are worthy of the *New Yorker,*
say—or would be if they had more of a *point.* It is not discipline she lacks
but a sense of the function of a work of art. This can come nonaversively,
I think.

With it, I can imagine great creative energy—with joy. I wish her
that, as I wish her safe conduct at this moment.

BECAUSE SHE WANTED TO LIVE IN NEW YORK, Julie began to teach at a
private school for girls and rented and furnished a two-room apartment
on Riverside Drive—a second-hand piano finding space in the kitchen

Although she had lived with us only during vacations from high school and college, I missed her:

RIPPING OUT THE PAST

I am dismantling the combination desk, chest-of-drawers, and cupboard I built in Julie's room in 1951. It symbolizes my rather inept handling of Julie—and now my disconnection from her life. The rather cheap pine pieces, screwed together with a clear pine top, painted gray, with small "modern" shelves at one end, warping eventually, the drawers and cupboard doors sliding uncertainly. The desk never organized her life as a student. (The far edge has separated from the wall and in ten years the gap has received two Christmas cards, one made by Julie herself on a borrowed theme ["Humbug"], a penny, several hair-pins, and a little gold locket containing a picture of our beagle, Hunter.)

She came back from New York for the summer and I wrote another note:

MOTH DOWNWIND

Saturday night, and Julie was home doing nothing. In a good mood. I could see no tension, no irritation, no unhappiness. But when a sports car popped noisily in the circle, she moved quickly to the door and glanced out. No one for her, and I, at least, felt a sudden touch of sadness.

Julie has a distinctive beauty. She is well-educated, knows interesting people. She would be a wonderful mother. But she is in a way not good company. With me at least she too readily expresses impatience, contradicts too hastily. Sometimes she adopts a compensatory loftiness, almost amounting to "putting on airs."

What can I do? a) Let her see how she affects me? But she would mark that off as an old idiosyncrasy of our special relationship. b) Talk with her about personal relations? "Don't try psychology on me!" c) Help her meet a greater variety of men and lower her sights? There is danger there! A shoemaker's child?

The problem was soon solved. At Teachers College the following year, Julie met Ernest Vargas, another student, and she brought him to Cambridge to meet us. He was tall and handsome, with black hair and a beard. His parents were Mexican-Americans living in Los Angeles. He had left home when he was young and worked his way through college and on to Teachers College, and would be going on to the University of

Pittsburgh the following year to work towards a Ph.D. in sociology. They came a second time to tell us that they were engaged, and I opened a bottle of champagne. In spite of my protests, Ernie kept calling me "Professor Skinner" until I printed a sign, CALL ME FRED, and hung it around my neck. Later I wrote a note:

> I am obviously disturbed by Julie's coming marriage. She is probably right in her choice of a husband, but I know him scarcely at all and cannot be sure that she has not made this choice within a narrow part of her cultural environment and that much of her will not now be left behind when she enters her new life as a married woman. Aside from that, I suppose it is always a blow to have one's oldest child married, particularly when it is a daughter. How well have I known Julie? I might be surprised to find out. I remember that I expected to see more of her during the term I spent at Putney. She quite rightly kept me well out of her life there. I really saw very little of her at Radcliffe (somewhere I have a note to the effect that the Radcliffe quadrangle reminds me of the days when I *looked forward* to seeing her there—but seeing her I seldom actually did.) She stopped coming to Monhegan during our last summers there, and for two years she has lived in New York.
>
> How much has her behavior reinforced mine? How much has reinforcing mine meant to her? All in all, very little. It is almost as an abstraction that I love Julie so dearly.

We liked Ernie and Julie loved him, and a wedding was arranged for the thirtieth of June. Ernie's mother came to stay with us. A linguist friend of Ernie's, Paul Pimsleur, was best man, and Debs was bridesmaid. Babs and John Spiegel gave a wedding party at their house on the coast in Rockport. There was a simple nonreligious service in the Unitarian Church in Harvard Square. Our old friends, Lou and Ken Mulligan, came up from Washington, and Harry and Elena Levin were there. Afterward there was a reception in our garden, and Julie and Ernie drove off to spend their first married night together in the Levins' house in Wellfleet on Cape Cod.

In June 1962, Carl Rogers and I resumed the discussion of our differences in a two-day dialogue in Duluth, Minnesota. We had a large and appreciative audience, we were not pressed for time, and although I am afraid we came no closer to agreement, I thought we made our positions much clearer—even to ourselves. Gerald Gladstein, who had organized the conference, invited Rogers and me to his home to relax and dine. As he later reported: "Skinner was quite talkative, accompanied my wife's cello playing on the piano, chatted with our children (even made some origami pigeons!), and took a nap. . . . Rogers also socialized easily, enjoyed the meals, and was quite gracious. However, he seemed to be still concerned over some aspects of the first dialogue. This became clearer during the next day. As a result, he dealt with the feelings and made his public during the second dialogue. In effect, he and Skinner were behaving in ways that were quite consistent with their long-held views about human behavior."

Here are some excerpts from the notes I used in our discussions:

We agree that human behavior can be controlled and with greater and greater success as a science of behavior develops. Rogers fears 1) surreptitious control and 2) special kinds of power, such as brainwashing, judgments contrary to the evidence of the senses (Orwell's 1984), electrical brain stimulation, and hallucinogens and other drugs. I want to look at more traditional practices—in industry, government, education, and religion. . . .

Total control does not mean Krutch's "dead end." Genetic and environmental control may be complete but we can (and are disposed by our own genetic and environmental histories to) change the variables and we thus control ourselves. Self-control needs to be analyzed.

Cultural practices designed for purposes of self-control often seem to go wrong. Religious and governmental sanctions prove either crippling or the seeds of revolt. Even the most intelligent ethical practices may work for one person or a whole generation but not for another person or another generation. They may create either the straitlaced prude or the why-should-I-conform? beatnik. I shrink from writing on self-management because of the way in which the material will be received in some quarters. I have already been called a prude for having written Walden Two. But there is nothing wrong with self-control (it is man's only hope) nor with the techniques which have been worked out. What is wrong is education. People are said to be "too stupid to control themselves." [And, thinking of the Roanoke experiment, I added:] Or to learn algebra?

*   *   *

As A LABORATORY SCIENTIST I had been bothered by the special acclaim given to theoretical physicists and the corresponding neglect of the laboratory physicists whose work was essential to theorizing. The issue came closer to home when the department began to drift toward mathematical psychology in considering the appointment of new members. Decision-making was a favorite topic, and in 1962 I submitted a memorandum to the permanent members of the department:

> Theories of decision making are usually formalistic analyses of possible courses of action, to which are attached estimates of value or utility . . . [and they have] little or no relevance to the behavior involved in decision-making.
>
> Most of my professional life has been, in a sense, a study of decision-making—at the very least the decision "to press or not to press" but in many cases a choice among multiple operanda under multiple stimulus control. With respect to the resulting data, existing mathematical models simply do not "march." The assumptions which enter into them are too unrealistic. Assumptions about utility or net gain fail to come to terms with the immediate contingencies of reinforcement which are responsible for probability of action. The example of gambling should have taught both economists and psychologists a lesson; behavior can be generated without limit by a system with negative utility. To me, it is a gesture of voluntary bankruptcy to turn to mathematicians for the next advances in psychology. I am still getting too much reinforcement from current methods and the development of new methods which continue to enlarge the body of relevant psychological data through an intimate and rapid interchange with a subject matter.

I put the matter rather more roughly in a note:

LES CALCULATEURS

Békésy is urging me to attack the mathematicians. He is as unhappy about the situation as I am, but is not himself, or so he thinks, the one to speak out. Most of what goes on in "mathematical psychology" is sheer nonsense. It nonetheless astonishes the psychological bourgeoisie and, worse, draws off students. A letter yesterday informed me that not only computer time but research support [to go with it] might be made available for young psychologists at Harvard. Brains are not only being replaced; those which survive are being bought and kept.

The attitude of the nonmathematician [towards mathematicians] reminds me of an episode at the Conference on Basic Research at the Rockefeller Institute several years ago. Robert Oppenheimer was in the starring role and playing it brilliantly, if with perhaps a shade too much self-satisfaction. Someone quoted a bit of poetry to point up an objection, and Oppenheimer, in reply, completed the quotation. A physiologist sitting behind me sucked in his breath as if Oppenheimer had just made a record pole vault. It is the kind of brilliance which does not really support a scientific position and may on the contrary provide fraudulent support [as mathematics confers prestige on psychologists without really helping them solve their problems].

I CONTINUED TO HEAR from animal trainers. A falconer wrote that he had used positive reinforcement to solve an old problem. If the falconer does not get to the falcon "before she has eaten a full meal, she is lost forever." He had succeeded in training his falcon to bring captured prey to him without eating it—in other words, to retrieve.

Bloodhounds had long been used to find criminals and lost children, and I thought their extraordinary olfactory sensitivity could be put to other uses. Could they not detect byproducts of cancer or of other illnesses in saliva, sweat, or urine? Og Lindsley tried to find out. He arranged contingencies under which dogs successfully distinguished between the urines of pregnant and nonpregnant women, but the apparatus became contaminated with odors he himself could not detect, and he abandoned the project. Dogs were soon in use, however, spotting heroin and other drugs at airports and piers.

Thom Verhave, a student of Fred Keller's, was one of the first to set up an operant laboratory in the pharmaceutical industry. He not only screened new compounds for the Eli Lilly Company, he tackled a personnel problem. Inspecting millions of capsules was a job no one wanted, and the company had tried unsuccessfully to mechanize it. Thom solved the problem with a system in which a pigeon pecked a key to discard a defective capsule as it passed on a belt. Pigeons were actually more accurate than people, but the Board of Directors decided, 12 to 1, that it should not be used; the quality of Eli Lilly products was not to be controlled by pigeons. Another student of Fred's, William Cumming, designed a similar system to spot defective parts for Western Electric. Labor protested.

When it came to making the first dangerous flight into space, everyone was happy to leave it to animals. The Russians, good Pavlovians, used dogs. The first American passengers were chimpanzees. One was conditioned on a multiple schedule with positive and negative reinforcers (the positive being banana-flavored pellets), another manipulated two levers to keep a small cross within a circle on a panel, and still another looked at a number flashed on a screen and pressed a lever a corresponding number of times.

The Moscow circus came to Boston, and a trainer named Filatov who worked with the Russian bears asked to talk with me. Eve and I invited him and a translator to dinner on their day off. The translator had a date with the Master of Ceremonies, and we invited him too. We offered them a choice of drinks and they chose whiskey—before, during, and after dinner—but caution was not destroyed. Filatov refused to discuss animal training until I had agreed (with no qualifications whatsoever) that it was all a matter of Pavlovian conditioned reflexes.

As it turned out, my retirement arrangements would not be substantial; I had started to teach late and was stopping early. My mother's finances had been well managed by old friends in Scranton, and when I took over my share of her estate, Owen Aldis, an economist who was spending some time in my laboratory, gave me helpful financial advice about growth stocks, which were then the thing. But I did not become rich, and so I went again to John Gardner of the Carnegie Corporation, who had supported our Center for Programmed Instruction. Would he also support me as a scholar for five or perhaps ten years, during which I would finish *The Technology of Teaching* and write a book on the evolution and design of cultural practices ("Some of the humanities people keep sniping at me on [the freedom of the individual] and I want a chance to clear things up")? I would also look at scientific methodology ("I have been examining the whole formal approach to the analysis of behavior, including mathematical models of decision-making, game theory, information theory, and so on") and at the intellectual implications of an experimental analysis of behavior ("Psychology has failed to make its case with intellectuals—with the single exception of psychoanalysis, to which what I have in mind would be an antidote").

It turned out that help from the Carnegie Corporation was not needed. The government had begun to give Career Awards to people in the behavioral sciences. Harvard was not happy about them because they took scholars off the teaching rolls, but since I would otherwise retire, I was permitted to apply, with "A Behavioral Analysis of Cultural Practices" as my project.

The Site Committee for the award came to our house, and I offered them coffee in the living room. As I later noted, "that was a mistake. Down to my study and business. They asked the necessary questions: what would I do if I didn't get the grant? What would I work on? Would I concentrate on the behavior of the individual in every case? . . . It was a mistake to bring them out here, though honest. The scene was too luxurious. I don't *need* them. . . . My prediction: my application will be denied." The following day I added: "I have marked the whole thing off." And two days later: "completely." But I was wrong. I received a Career Award for five years, renewable for another five.

A different future suddenly presented itself, however. Seymour Harris, a distinguished Harvard economist, had retired to California, and he called to ask if I would be interested in setting up a department of psychology in a new branch of the University of California at La Jolla. I could bring in two other full professors, an associate professor, and two assistant professors of my choice. Since one of the others could be Chairman, I would have almost as much freedom as with a Career Award. The department could be concerned almost exclusively with the experimental analysis of behavior. Though I had never done any empire building, it was a tempting offer. As I said in a note:

It would fit my intellectual plans perfectly. But— 1) I love Cambridge. In spite of its weather, which is by no means all objectionable, it is an exciting place to live. 2) I like Harvard. 3) I have always loathed California. 4) I have always feared lotus-blossoms. I am not a λωτοφάγος.

On the other hand, there are reasons to consider a change: 1) I am convinced Harvard is going soft under Pusey's weak leadership. 2) I feel that I am *persona non grata* here. Pusey has never shown it, but I believe he would be happy to see me leave if he were not blamed for my departure. 3) I am unhappy about psychology at Harvard.

In December, I went to La Jolla and saw the Chancellor. I had lunch with Harris and Leo Szilard, and they urged me to come. Three months later I went out again with Eve and Deborah. We looked at houses and talked with Carl Rogers, who had moved to La Jolla and liked it. The University would give me several months to decide, but by March I was writing to Julie that "I have more or less made up my mind not to go." I had grown up among the green (or snow-covered) hills of Pennsylvania and simply did not feel at home among the brown hills of California. Eve was in tears at the thought of leaving our friends in Cambridge.

I took the Career Award. I would remain Professor of Psychology, but would no longer attend department meetings. I would not teach, with the possible exception of an occasional noncredit course for graduate students. I would keep my office, but I would cut down on my schedule there by working part of the time at home. I had a study built into the basement of our house, where I began to spend two or three hours every morning before walking to my office. I also converted part of the basement into a machine shop and installed benches, a floor-model drill press, a band saw, and other tools. I bought plasteline and armature wire and began to do a bit of sculpting.

IN 1958 I had thought of revising *Science and Human Behavior* to make it more of an introductory text. I would omit the more difficult sections, add a few figures, tables, graphs, and pictures, describe a few demonstrations, and give more examples from daily life. In an ecumenical move I would add something about traits and attitudes and spend more time on Freud. A second book, an advanced analysis, could contain the material removed from the first, with more attention to technical issues such as perception, decision-making, and value judgments. It could be a book to which economists, political scientists, linguists, and educators might turn. Later I saw that the last three chapters could be part of the published version of the Mead-Swing Lectures.

When Dick Herrnstein began to help in Natural Sciences 114, he and I considered a more sweeping revision. It would be even closer to a standard introductory text, with some coverage of all the conventional fields. I was interested in it primarily as a potboiler. Retirement would be costly, but good introductory texts were making their authors hundreds of thousands of dollars. When we sent an outline of a revision to Macmillan, they reported that *Science and Human Behavior* was enjoying the biggest sales in its history. Herrnstein and I were really planning a different book, which they would be happy to publish, and they sent us a contract and a small advance.

By 1961 I began to have doubts:

> I don't need the money as much as I need the time; and it would be a bad bargain. What else is to be said for writing it? (1) Most other introductory texts in psychology are bad, and we see the effect in the graduate students we are teaching as the psychologists of the future. (2) An experimental analysis of behavior would be more freely extended to human affairs in general if the analysis were better known and understood, but I see no chance that another text will do this in the near future.
>
> And can I collaborate with Dick? Can we agree on subject matter? Can we agree on the analysis? Can we write the prose? I have some doubt about all of these.

By 1962 I was talking about a sabbatical which would put such a book far in the future, and we soon abandoned it. In 1967 A *Chronology of the Western World* listed *Science and Human Behavior* as one of two outstanding books in psychology published in 1953, but I was not too happy about the other one, Rhine's *The New World of the Mind*.

In 1961 the Office of Special International Programs of the National Science Foundation told me that NATO was interested in a Summer Institute in the United States the following year, and that the Foundation had suggested operant behavior as a field. Would I organize it? I talked it over with the Pigeon Staff, who felt that a meeting would be more useful if it were closer to European sources. I wrote to H. M. B. Hurwitz at Birkbeck College, the University of London, and he submitted a proposal. Members from the United States would include Nate Azrin, Charlie Ferster, Norman Guttman, Dick Herrnstein, Roger

Kelleher, and Murray Sidman. Seventeen people would come from Britain and about the same number from Canada and seven European countries.

The proposal was warmly received by NATO and their Senior Advisory Committee, and Sir Solly Zuckermann, the United Kingdom representative, strongly supported it. But I was told that an Advisory Committee on Human Factors turned it down, and when the Royal Society was asked for its opinion, the society consulted Niko Tinbergen and Oliver Zangwill, who also turned it down. I wrote to Hurwitz:

> *I am surprised by Zangwill's reaction, particularly since I have just been invited to speak to the Royal Society, an invitation about which he would, I suppose, have been consulted. Tinbergen I can understand. We have the same problem with the ethologists in this country. They seem to get their primary motivation out of attacking operant conditioners on the vague ground that we are neglecting something. It is true that we don't study a very wide range of species, but neither do they, when you stop to think that there are millions of species waiting to be studied. Just what they would like to have us do escapes me.*

In 1960 Joe Brady, at the Walter Reed Hospital Institute of Research, founded the Institute for Behavioral Research (IBR) in Silver Spring, Maryland. David Rioch, a physiologist, was Chairman of the board and in 1962 Charlie Ferster took over as Director. Charlie had completed important work on the behavior of autistic children at the Indiana University Medical Center and had published a successful book in collaboration with J. I. Nurnberger and J. P. Brady. He had visited Czechoslovakia where he had talked with groups of Czechs, East Germans, and Russians. With a Career Development Award he continued to do basic research. Fred Keller and I served as Directors of IBR and eventually received honorary degrees from its Experimental College. An experiment on the rehabilitation of juvenile delinquents at the National Training School in Washington was carried out under the direction of Harold Cohen, who was at the time Director.

* * *

In 1961, Fred Keller went to Brazil to teach and promote the experimental analysis of behavior. In January 1962 he wrote:

> I have a nice well-manned operant conditioning lab in the Univ. of S. Paulo, another in a branch faculty at Rio Claro, and the beginnings of a third in Sao José at Rio Preto. At S.P. we have an experimental program going steadily and a project on self-teaching which includes a translation of the Holland-Skinner program (which will be used in the 1st year course at the University next March), a verbal-behavior dissertation of my assistente, Rodolfo Azzi, and other features. Azzi was a great find: A pupil of the French logician, Granger, Rodolfo came from Sao Jose de Rio Preto to work with me. He is now established at Sao Paulo; and he is perhaps the most brilliant pupil I have ever had. He's the guiding spirit for a new group of about 6 very able kids who found a new reason for living in Reinforcement Theory our style.

When I told Clyde Kluckhohn, the anthropologist, that I was embarking upon an analysis of cultures, he said, "Have you got your hunting license?" He meant, "Do you know any anthropology?" The fact was, I knew very little, but from what I knew, I thought a different approach to culture was possible and, indeed, necessary. Anthropologists had borrowed theories of behavior from many sources, most recently from psychoanalysis. Kluckhohn, and Harry Murray had not gone beyond defining a culture as a system of values and ideas. I thought I could do better, but I would have to begin to read the literature.

Ivor Richards took up my disagreement with Chomsky. He sent me a poem (more than three pages long when it was eventually published in his So Much Nearer) in which he compared two passages. One was from Verbal Behavior:

> Hundreds of puzzling questions and obscure propositions about verbal behavior may be dismissed while the new questions and propositions which arise to take their place are susceptible to experimental check as part of a more unified pattern.

The other was from Chomsky:

> The questions to which Skinner has addressed his speculations are hopelessly premature. It is futile to inquire into the causation of verbal behavior until much more is known about the specific character of this behavior; and there is little point in speculating about the process of acquisition without much better understanding of what is acquired.

Ivor's poem began:

> Confidence with confidence oppose:
> Knowledge ducks under in between two No's
> So firmly uttered. Look again. You'll see
> Uncertainty beside uncertainty.

A few weeks later he sent me another poem, beginning:

> No sense in fretting to be off the ground,
> There's never hurry whither we are bound,
> Where all's behavior—and the rest is naught,
> Not even rest, but void beyond all thought.

and summarizing my position:

> So, though Psychologists disdainfully
> Tear off our wings, crying, to set us free:
> "These gleaming sails are but the flattering means
> (Theologic gear, Pythagorean beans!)
> Whereby grubs flit and feed and lay their eggs,
> By metaphor, beyond the reach of legs.
> No Psyche more! Homunculus-theory, out!
> Verbal behavior's all it's all about."

I thought this had gone far enough, and I sent Ivor a poem of my own:

> Yes, "all's behavior—and the rest is naught."
> And thus compressed
> Into "the rest
> Of all,"
> A thought
> Is surely neither bad nor wrong.

Or right or good?
No, no.
Define
And thus expunge
The *Ought*,
The *Should!*
Nothing is *So*
(See History).

Let not the strong
Be cozened
By *Is* and *Isn't*,
Was and*Wasn't*.
Truth's to be sought
In *Does* and *Doesn't*.

Decline
To be.

And call
Him neither best
Nor blessed
Who wrought
That silly jest,
The Fall.
(It was a Plunge.)

Ivor suggested that we publish the poems, and he submitted them
to the *Atlantic*. The executive editor felt that "the joke may turn out
to be somewhat too private for most of our readers," and so Ivor sent
them to Stephen Spender, and they appeared in the November 1962
issue of *Encounter*.

*   *   *

IN FEBRUARY, Debbie broke her leg while skiing in the Deux Alpes and
was taken to a hospital. After two or three days of unsatisfactory phone
calls, I decided to go to France. I flew to Geneva, planning to drive to
Grenoble. Road conditions in the Alps were bad and no agency would
rent me a car, but someone offered me a VW with front-wheel drive.
Though it was a bad break, Debs was recovering well. It appeared that

she could not continue at the University. Because of a fuel shortage, the elevator in Madame Guillot's building was not in use, and her apartment was on the eighth floor. I could not stay until Debs was ready to travel, but I arranged for ground transportation to Paris and a flight to Boston, and she soon came home.

She spent the rest of the academic year in Cambridge, unhappy and rather difficult. I recorded some instances:

> Debs has been quite unreasonable about the loss of several articles in the move back from Grenoble. She stayed in her nightclothes all of yesterday, sleeping a good deal, and when I encouraged her to practice going up and down stairs with her crutches, she was emotional and uncooperative. This morning a note was tucked into the bowl of cereal waiting for me on the breakfast table:
>
> Dear Pop,
>> How are things? This is just a note to tell you I love you.
>> Love, Debs.
> P. S. & that I apologize for my poor behavior of yesterday (today, as I write this).
>
> Dining at Hartwell Farm, she began a characteristic pet when she could not get her cast arranged comfortably under the table, and I expected a black meal, but she got herself out of it very quickly and was soon quite gay. Progress.
>
> It is certainly not fair to say I have never used punishment with Debs. The Puritanism of my father and mother has been extended to the third generation in many subtle ways. But a successful compulsiveness in me is only episodic in Debs. She has, however, her full share of guilt.

We were slow in finding a college for her. During my sabbatical term in Europe, with Debs at Grenoble, communications were difficult, and we failed to send important documents to several colleges. When she came back it was too late, but fortunately, through an agency which listed available openings, we discovered Western College in Oxford, Ohio, and she was admitted.

Near the end of the summer I wrote:

> I think my plan for Debs is paying off. In Grenoble she met interesting people and learned some French, but the skiing accident

ended that. It was an emotional strain and was followed by wasted and not very happy months at home. The college situation remained uncertain. Then, when she was mobile again, things began to clear up. She is not too happy in anticipation of Western College, but she is pleased that they seem to want her. She is doing good work (B+) in French at the Harvard Summer School. Though she has not spent much time on them, her piano lessons have interested her and had some effect. She is exhibiting 30 pictures at Club 47.

She is beginning to act like a college freshman. She drives our car skillfully and safely. She chooses friends wisely. She converses well with our friends. I am sure she is on her way. What a pity she could not have been a year older all the way along!

A few days later, I wrote her a letter:

Dearest Debs,

I was swinging along at top speed this morning, working on a paper I am to give at Los Angeles in two weeks, when I suddenly thought: "I should give some of this clearheadedness to Debs." I think our discussion last night was profitable, in spite of the wet Kleenexes which strewed the floor afterwards. We badly need to communicate. *(Example: last Wednesday when you and Martha went to the Beatles, I assumed you had forgotten or were neglecting your drawing class. I damn near sealed my lips with adhesive tape to keep from bringing this up. "Why make Debs feel any guiltier?" I said. Now I know the course was finished.)*

You are wrong on the following points:

1) If you don't really want a college degree, I don't want you to work for one.

2) I'm not embarrassed by any supposed shortcomings of yours or afraid you will prove to the world that I am a bad psychologist. Live your own life, not mine. Be yourself. I like your Self.

3) When I offer to help you, or try to give advice about how to study or take tests, etc., it isn't criticism. *You are still developing, learning about life. I'm an old-timer. Men have emerged as the dominant species of animal because they can store and pass along their experiences. Let's not start devolution by breaking that useful habit.*

4) You are intelligent and there is some point in trying. Don't fail before you try.

I am wrong on the following:

1.

2.   *(to be filled in*

3.   *by addressee)*

4.

∞ ← *infinity*

Love,
Daddy

WHILE ERNIE was completing work for his Ph.D. in sociology, Julie became a teacher in a suburb of Pittsburgh. She was in contact with a class of thirty-one students from eight in the morning until three in the afternoon and then worked for two or more hours at her desk. Since she had to commute ten miles in each direction, it was a long day. I wrote to Robert Glaser, who had a large project in education at the American Institute of Research, and the following year he hired her. She began to take courses at the University of Pittsburgh toward a Ph.D. in educational psychology. When she told me, with amusement, that she had come around to my field, I insisted that I had never intended any such thing. "The most I ever wanted was to hear you sing with the Boston Symphony," I said.

She had problems but they were small ones:

> Somehow Julie's call last night was typical. A surprise party was arranged, and she had planned to use her Polaroid camera, but the flash was not working. Where could she get a new battery? And the party was to start in 20 minutes!
>
> Why typical? Surely a thing like that often goes wrong. But—
>
> 1) Julie does too much, too many things. Picture-taking comes up at the last minute. If it were a common part of a smaller repertoire, there would have been no trouble.
>
> 2) She is persistent. Another person would have dropped the plan, but not Julie. It is part of never-making-a-mistake. The idea must be carried out. I can visualize—and I hope incorrectly—a last-minute dash to a camera store.

In writing to a friend who asked about our experience with Debs at Woodstock as a school, I said: "While at times I envy parents of children who come from disciplined school environments, in the long run I am very happy about the originality and continuing growth of my daughters."

EARLY IN 1960, I had examined my relation with Rheem. I had resolved to "a) reserve the right to get out at any time, b) remain free to cooperate scientifically with anyone regardless of Rheem's interests, c) agree to do only those things which I do as a scientist." I would stop asking "Have I botched the matter, either scientifically or commercially?" in favor of "Is this what I should do to maximize the acceptance and success of the teaching-machine principle?"

By March 1962 I was in the hands of still another officer of the company, to whom I wrote: "We differ on: 1) the diligence with which Rheem has carried out the terms of our agreement, 2) the direction and scope of further activity, 3) the value of my services." Eventually Rheem proposed that they develop Didak 501 and pay me royalties, but that our original agreement be terminated. No satisfactory licensing arrangement was worked out, and in March 1963, almost four years after our first discussions, our association came to an end.

I was once again on my own. Teaching machines had a commercial future, but I was not the man to promote it. I had been altogether too innocent. I should have seen that Rheem was simply "waiting to see how the ball bounced"—an officer once admitted as much to Hal Robson, at IBM. Those trips to California had nothing to do with business; they were to keep me quiet while the company waited.

FOR A SYMPOSIUM ON BEHAVIORISM and Phenomenology at Rice University, I wrote a paper called "Behaviorism at Fifty." I had given an earlier version in London, and again as the R. M. Elliott Lecture at the University of Minnesota. The symposium was unbalanced; Sig Koch had presumably been chosen as one of three behaviorists but, instead, delivered a long, vitriolic attack. Norman Malcolm was the other "behaviorist," from a Wittgensteinian point of view. The three phenomenologists were Carl Rogers, Michael Scriven, and R. B. MacLeod.

In my paper, I distinguished between methodological and radical behaviorism and discussed privacy, self-knowledge, and conscious content. I spent some time on the copy theory of perception. If we saw the world by constructing a copy in our head, how did we see the copy? "Operant psychophysics" was a better solution. We saw the world itself —because of the discriminative contingencies to which we were exposed.

Koch and Rogers argued that current trends in scientific theory were on their side—away with Newton, down with determinism and causality, up with uncertainty and the subjective experience of the scientist. I recorded my answer later in a note:

> Scientists know very little about human behavior, even that of the practicing scientist. Hadamard on mathematical thinking is elementary. Bronowski on the concept of penny in Science & Human Values is 17th century. Niels Bohr ditto. Physical theory is in trouble at the edges. If I were a younger man, I would press the analysis in Verbal Behavior in that direction. The first thing I would go after is Gödel's theorem.

I gave a copy of "Behaviorism at Fifty" to Békésy, who was a rather untheoretical person. His first report: very interesting. Later he came into my office, rather shaken. "Some very interesting ideas," he kept saying. He was going to study the paper. He wanted it angled for physicists. He was particularly interested in the relevance of discriminative contingencies to an understanding of what it meant to see. It was quite unlike Stevens's "operational" argument that the processes of discrimination were, for all practical purposes, what we meant by sensations.

I sent a copy to Julian Huxley, in return for papers he had sent me. In a note I asked myself, "Do I hope to change him? Not much. But if he is now at least aware of a *reasonable* alternative view, he may be less outspoken. His unquestioning assumption of conscious experience gives support to biologists who might otherwise be inclined to question it." With the article I sent a none-too-tactful letter. "I am always disturbed," I said, "when I find a distinguished scientist accepting a dualistic view of the universe. This seems to be commoner in England than in the United States." That was *lèse majesté*, and I soon had his answer:

> *Thanks for your letter and interesting article. I too am disturbed by distinguished scientists taking dualistic views of the universe. I have always striven to reach a truly monistic or unified view, in which "mind"*

and "body," both "subjective" and "objective," should find a place. I am equally disturbed when I find scientists taking a reductionist point of view and arriving at a spurious monism by disregarding one of the two aspects of reality.

I was not *reducing* mind to behavior; but I despaired of making that clear.

The Unity of Sciences group in Boston arranged for me to debate Jerome Lettwin on the subject of Mind, and he and I met to discuss procedures. At one point he crumpled an empty cigarette package and threw it on the table. "A physical description of that is next to impossible," he said. He did not mean that the stuff of which it was composed was not physical or could not be analyzed as such; he was talking about the package as a stimulus. It had meaning, he said, and hence the eye and the optic nerve had to "talk to the brain" rather than "merely report stimuli."

I could not, of course, reconstruct the long history of contingencies of reinforcement which led Lettwin to see the object as a crumpled cigarette package, but his behavior, like the package, was still a matter of physics, as physiology would eventually show. Meanwhile, we should have to be content with the contingencies of reinforcement in explaining what such a stimulus "meant."

A COMMON DEFENSE of mentalism was convenience. Behavioristic paraphrases are awkward and forced. There must be something in mentalism if it is so natural. Only out of sheer stubbornness can behaviorists continue to look for an alternative.

In the thirties, certainly, the future of behaviorism was more important to Fred Keller and me than convenience, and hence stubborn we may have been, but things were changing and in 1963 I could write in a note:

It is gratifying to see the progress that has been made in 30 years in working out behavioral equivalents of traditional psychological terms. I remember the great cardboard sheets fastened together with rings in my room in Winthrop House on which I classified "verbal reflexes." I tried to identify *S*'s and *R*'s in reading, repeating, responding to speech, and so on. It was certainly crude. I could continue only because of a stubborn faith that this was the only thing to do. In the *Behavior of Organisms* I avoided the problem: "Let him extrapolate who will." But in *Science and Human Behavior*, and the course it was written for, I came back to paraphrase, translate, and reinterpret mentalistic expressions. One of Macmillan's readers of *Science and Human Behavior* complained of my obvious efforts to avoid traditional expressions. *Verbal Behavior* in its final form went more easily, and the programming of instructional materials had helped by forcing a behavioral translation of educational goals.

The empirical facts were enough. I had no taste for dialectic. In 1963 in a paper in *Philosophy of Science*, Rochelle J. Johnson replied to Michael Scriven's attack on me in "A Study of Radical Behaviorism" (1956). What interested me was the reflection that I had never read Scriven's article myself and had never thought of answering it, and I wrote a note:

> . . . What has become of the *Philosophy of Science*? Has anything been settled? Has science been given a leg up, comparable in extent to the top dozen advances of the 30 years during which the Journal has been published? [I had canceled my charter subscription after a year or two.] I doubt it. My "theoretical" writing has addressed two questions: 1) What is the nature of the behavior of the scientist? 2) How can he avoid unproductive forms of that behavior? I have never expected the philosophy of science to contribute to science. Johnson's first sentence reads: "B. F. Skinner is perhaps even more widely known for his views on science than for his experimental work," but I should be sorry if that were, or were to prove to be, the case.

I HAD MAINTAINED CONTACT with Pei Sung Tang, and on August 3, 1959, he wrote:

> *Do you remember, in* Walden Two, *you mentioned the obligation of a scientist to his society? Do you really and wholeheartedly mean it? If so, that is the thing which we are practicing here. We work on specialized problems, theoretical! But always with the aim in view—directly or indirectly—for the welfare of the country and the people. Of course in certain fields (as in math., and even in plant physiology, such as CO_2-*

fixation) where relations to practical affairs are not immediate, we do not stick to this restriction.

In 1961, Pei Sung reported that he had not received the latest volume of the *Annual Review of Plant Physiology*. Relations with China were becoming rather strained; perhaps it had been intercepted. I decided to stop sending books from America, and set up an account at Foyle's in London. They were to send the *Review* every year and accept orders for other books from Pei Sung. Two or three years later, someone at Foyle's placed the order with the publishers in Palo Alto to be sent directly from there, and the embargo was thus lifted. At one time I was considering a visit to Malaysia, and Pei Sung gave my name to the President of the Chinese Psychological Society, who was working on machine teaching, hoping that I could be invited to speak there. Pei Sung reported that "we do not see any obstacle standing in the way of obtaining an invitation from this end, but I have been reminded to use caution in this matter in view of the present world situation: the possible consequences of your visit to us on your return to the U.S." At the time I was amused, but later I discovered that the San Francisco office of the FBI had been following the correspondence "between T'ang and Professor B. F. Skinner, a.k.a. 'Fred.' "

In 1963, an article in *Life* magazine began with the scene in which Frazier compares himself with God. When Burris suggests that Frazier must have "considerably less control," Frazier replies, "Not at all, it's rather the other way around. You may remember that God's children are always disappointing Him. . . . I don't say I'm never disappointed, but I imagine I'm rather less frequently so than God." Was this science fiction, the writer asked, "the always-good-for-one-more thrill," the story of the Eccentric Scientist who has discovered the Secret of Controlling People? No, ". . . the author believes the plot and moreover he insists on it. He believes that human behavior *can* be and *ought* to be controlled by scientists such as Frazier, mastermind of the social utopia for which *Walden Two* is an honest-to-goodness working blueprint." But Frazier bears a "striking intellectual likeness to the author," who does indeed maintain that "man merely has illusions that he possesses free will and that actually all human behavior is caused by material events. . . . What is extraordinary is that so many scientists do agree with this basic premise: that man is to a large degree controllable, that science can and will know enough about him to manipulate his behavior in many ways and with a great deal of precision."

I had discussed the issue with the authors three years earlier, before they were taken off the article and reassigned to the Kennedy campaign. It was now clear that they were writing from cold notes. The article was called "Chemical Mind Changers," a phrase borrowed from Aldous Huxley, and most of it was about marijuana, mescaline, and LSD. It quoted the prediction I had long since abandoned that "in the not-too-distant future the motivational and emotional conditions of normal daily life will probably be maintained in any desired state through the use of drugs." It then turned to George Orwell's 1984, "a society in which behavior engineering has finally made possible almost complete control of human behavior." But the practices Orwell described were well known in the history of political and religious tyranny, and they were far from what I would have described as behavioral engineering. Two years later *Esquire* made a more useful point in an article on "The Control of the Mind." "From the point of view of behaviorist psychology, whether Pavlovian or as promulgated by Harvard's . . . B. F. Skinner, brainwashing goes on all the time. All the classic conditions are fulfilled many times during the day of the average citizen."

Many years later in a televised round-table discussion, Margaret Mead responded to something I said by shouting, "I don't want to play God! I don't want to control people." The studio audience roundly applauded, but I could point out that God did not control people. If He did, He would be responsible for the mess in the world today. Instead, according to Christian theology, He put people on the earth and left them to behave as they would. Frazier had designed a *world* which controlled people, but he himself was no longer in control. Given this reservation, he could exclaim, "I like to play God! Who wouldn't, under the circumstances? After all, man, even Jesus Christ thought he was God!" In another television conversation, when Charles Hampden Turner characterized me as a power-mad scientist, I said, "I do not want to control or to be in position to control. I merely want to improve the culture that controls."

* * *

JOHN KENNEDY HAD TAKEN many Harvard people to Washington with him, and when Lyndon Johnson took over, many of them came back. The mood in Cambridge was caught in a short musical by Felicia Lamport (Kaplan) called *Waiting for Bobby*. Eve and I had seen a good deal of the Kaplans, and when the musical was staged in a small theater near Harvard Square, Felicia asked me to play a part. I had never been able to sing on key, nor was I able to "talk it" in the style of Rex Harrison in *My Fair Lady*, but I agreed. I was one of those who were waiting and I sang (to the music of *Jenny Made Her Mind Up*):

> Ah, life was lovely on the pinnacle.
> Our status there was priestly—or rabbinical.
> But now if we must sink into a den of Ph.D.'s
> The torture will inevitably kill us—by degrees.

The Boston papers were generous.

In much the same mood another friend, Molly (Mrs. Mark) Howe, staged the bitterly satirical attack on President and Lady Bird Johnson called *MacBird*. I played Lord MacNamara, who is forced to confess to MacBird that

> ... touching on our war in Viet Land,
> The pacifying program we embarked on
> Did not compel surrender, as we hoped.

NEAR THE END of 1963, I wrote:

In less than four months I shall be sixty. What does one do to make the best of the tag end of a life? Mostly what has been reinforced in the past, but much of it is on a lengthening ratio schedule. One tries harder and harder (as in sex—see my note on de Sade) to get the old familiar reinforcements. Aversive consequences pile up: the gourmet must cope with impaired digestion, the athlete with arthritis and sprains, the lover of literature, the arts, the theatre, and music with failing vision and hearing. It is too late to undertake long courses of action. Fatigue comes more quickly, and lingers when one rests.

My plan for the next five to ten years is, I think, realistic and should be productive. I am still alive intellectually and I am still improving my intellectual efficiency. I have not been wholly successful in cutting out unproductive work. My correspondence could, in part, be turned over to a secretary. "Visiting firemen" are presumably inevitable so long as I am geographically within range. Frequently they surprise me by being worthwhile, but I think only with respect to my past interests.

Early in 1963, I reported progress:

There is no doubt of my fine working conditions these days. I am getting important things done. Three deadlines ("Operant Behavior," "Behaviorism at Fifty," "Reflections on a Decade of Teaching Machines") do not worry me. I am reconciled to further delay on *The Technology of Teaching*. Possible improvements:

1) Further reduction of office and departmental work. No lecturing. Minimal correspondence.

2) Organizing, filing, clarifying materials, getting a better over-all view of what is to be done, being able to relate a current interest or idea to a project.

3) Minimal social stimulation (Eve has been away a week; I stay alone in the house for days at a time).

4) Unguilty relaxation. Light reading. TV. Music seems too disturbing; I listen much less than usual (it is listen or nothing, no "background") and play not at all (the piano is out of tune, but I have just ordered an electric organ).

5) Better contact with psychology as a field (through initially forced reading and consequent clarification of my position).

THROUGHOUT THE FIFTIES, I had asked myself whether I should not write a novel. I did not say "another novel," because *Walden Two* was closer to a Platonic dialogue. I occasionally made notes about verbal traits which "reveal character," collected themes that seemed worth developing, made trial runs by describing people I saw in airports or bits of nature from a car window.

Eve and I began to see more of Harry and Elena Levin and some of their literary friends. In February 1961, Arthur Koestler came to see me and, lunching at the Faculty Club, we talked science and literature.

In 1962, Ripon College gave me an honorary Doctor of Literature degree. *Walden Two* was beginning to sell again, and more and more readers wrote to me about it. It had been written in seven weeks; if I could write a novel in a term or even a year, my professional career would not be seriously interrupted.

Could I write a behavioristic novel without referring to feelings or states of mind? After all, dramatists did not refer to them, stage directions apart, nor did the conversation in a novel. If readers felt emotions, it was because they were responding as the characters responded.

> The novelist who says, "She was sad," communicates a fact but does little or nothing to make the reader feel sad. To say, "She felt as if . . ." and then describe a sad occasion may do so. Henry James used "as if" for this purpose, but George Eliot cautioned against it. Nevertheless, it is one of the ways in which the verbal community circumvents privacy. (A point now occurs to me: use my four methods [in my 1945 paper] not in teaching A about his private world, but in telling B about A's!)

The French novel of the nineteenth century was possibly close to what I wanted, and I reread Stendhal and Balzac. I was caught up in a renewal of interest in George Eliot and tried rewriting parts of *Middlemarch* and *Daniel Deronda*, replacing references to feelings with references to the actions from which the feelings were inferred. It did not work. Mentalistic terms were like the "abbreviations" of John Horne Tooke; they served as rough summaries of the contingencies of which they were the products. Accurate reports of the same contingencies ran to much greater length.

I considered themes:

> I see no great theme welling up in me. The control of human behavior, yes. The ethics—the new ethics—of control could be dramatized but I have my doubts about its value. Is it true that novelists have been the avant-garde? Or is this simply part of the propaganda of the humanities people? I suspect one could find an earlier nonfictional statement of any point made by a great novelist—even by the same man (e.g. Voltaire). If novelists (Cervantes, Fielding) were the first to record social change, perhaps it was only because there were then no social scientists.

> Yet *Walden Two* was written quickly, pleasantly, and it was ahead

of its time *in my own chronology.* Can I not tap similar verbal reserves, which will be a revelation to me?

Why not *self*-control—a new *Pilgrim's Progress*—the hero gradually discovering how to control himself by controlling the world in which he lives, adapting techniques for controlling others to control oneself? That was close to the theme I had found most moving in literature —a readiness to sacrifice a career for love, like Plantagenet Palliser's in *Can You Forgive Her?* or Mosca's in *La Chartreuse de Parme*—not as a trait of character but as the expression of a better understanding of one's own behavior. I was skeptical of inner struggle. Was Luther wrestling with the Devil or with his hypothalamus—or, better, with another part of his genetic and environmental history?

MY ANALYSIS OF religious practices was often viewed as an exposé, but *Walden Two* and *Science and Human Behavior* received favorable reviews in religious journals, and my debate with Carl Rogers was reprinted in *Pastoral Psychology.* I declined invitations to conferences on religion, but many Protestant churches in Cambridge held Sunday evening meetings for young people, mostly students, and I often spoke at them. For many years I contented myself with saying that science could help religion promote the ultimate good of the species, but later I pointed to scientific applications with which, I thought, men of good will would advance religious goals, with or without the help of religion. When Cardinal Cushing wrote a pastoral letter along standard lines ("The world is immoral, and our salvation lies in a return to Christian morals") I wrote in a note: "One may agree that a world which abided by a Christian code would be a better place, but the test of a code is not the behavior *it would produce if followed* but whether it is followed. Why have Christian principles not done a better job? How can they be improved?"

I thought I could lay claim to a reasonable amount of good will, if that term had any meaning, but I was frequently shaken by signs of a different image:

Last night Debbie and I went to the Gardner Coxes' for some music in their garden. A group of young people, mostly current or former

Harvard and Radcliffe students I suppose, sang a Mass by William Byrd. It was *a capella* and, for most of the singers, sight reading. Very well done. The night was pleasant. Ragged clouds moved across the sky, one of them dropping briefly a fine misty rain. The garden is a circular lawn surrounded by shrubs and a few old trees. Half a dozen lights burned among the green branches. Several kittens played on the grass. We sat in small groups, in folding chairs. Except for a few jet planes, the night was quiet and the music delightful. *Kyrie eleison*—I thought of *Walden Two* and the B-minor Mass scene. And of the fact that this kind of harmless, beautiful, sensitive pleasure was probably nearing the end of its run. This was Watermusic, floating down the Thames and out to sea. And why?

Phyllis Cox may have answered the question. As I said goodnight, she motioned toward the young man who had conducted the music and said, "You know, he thinks you are a horrible man. Teaching machines, a Fascist . . ."

As one of the conditions of my Career Award, I could no longer be a paid consultant, and my relationship with what had become the Merck Institute for Therapeutic Research came to an end. John Boren had gone back to the Walter Reed Laboratories, leaving the research at West Point to Harley Hanson. I attended one last meeting in November 1963—a symposium on "Recent Developments in the Laboratory Analysis of Behavior." In a morning session Robert Galambos, Roy John, Ross Adey, and Murray Jarvik discussed physiological issues, in which I had little interest, but in the afternoon Philip Teitelbaum talked about the use of operant techniques in the study of experimentally induced obesity, Nate Azrin about aggression, Frank Beach about sex, and I about the field in general.

Although I had lost my enthusiasm for the psychotropic drugs, my prediction that we were entering the age of the chemical control of behavior continued to haunt me. Aldous Huxley had set the pattern in *Brave New World* with his "soma." That was satire, but in a later utopia, *Island*, he seriously proposed the use of drugs as a social measure. I had discussed nineteenth-century communities in America with Huxley at a meeting of the Fund for the Republic, and when he came to speak at MIT, Timothy Leary tried to bring us together again, but we got no further than a telephone conversation.

In 1956 I bought the twenty-two-volume set of the Goncourt *Journals* (published in Monaco because of the strict French censorship) and I liked many of its observations about human behavior. The Goncourt brothers had anticipated Huxley's faith in drugs by a century. The café, they wrote, was in its infancy. Someday there would be better ones, *débits de consolation* (a pun on *débit de consommation*, a bar), where one would find happiness by inhaling a gas rather than drinking wine, and where waiters would "serve Paradise by the cup." Young people were now constructing their own *débits de consolation*: on a Sunday afternoon on the Cambridge Common, cannabis was in the air.

The Harvard Medical School abolished its Department of Pharmacology, and Bill Morse and Peter Dews moved on to broader fields. Bill began working on what would eventually be called "behavioral medicine," and in a search for something between commitments to pure neurology and pure mental process, the Medical School made Peter the Stanley Cobb Professor of Psychiatry. (A psychiatrist told me that the psychoanalysts in Boston regarded his appointment as a "catastrophic defeat.")

IN JANUARY 1963 I wrote:

END OF AN ERA
I have given my last lecture, held my last class. I said I would do it—and I did. I have no regrets. I had a relatively short life as a teacher—27 years—but I had good students and it was worthwhile. I am sure that my plans for the next 5–10 years will be justified. I will be more effective if I never teach again.

A year later, my Career Award went into effect. William James Hall, the new building for the behavioral sciences, was nearing completion, and a few of us began to move in. I chose a suite of moderate size on the seventh floor, leaving the larger corner suites for those who would be more active in the affairs of the department.

* * *

"THEORETICALLY, you can answer for animals, by tests of discrimination or by observation of conditioned reflexes, any of the questions of sensory or perceptual capacities that have been answered for human beings by the use of the introspective method," but the procedure "is terribly laborious and no added precision is gained for the added pains." That was Garry Boring, writing in 1931. But procedures had become much less laborious, and the advantages were not to be overlooked. At the Merck Institute, Harley Hanson was studying color vision in pigeons with a modification of the Blough technique. He was destroying red-green vision with a drug called Catron. Important pigments in the retina could also be washed out with a diet free of carotinoids. Nothing of the sort, of course, was possible with human subjects.

I pointed this out to Edwin Land in 1960. I had seen his extraordinary demonstration in which, looking through a green filter, you saw a full spectrum of colors. It would not be difficult to find out whether pigeons also saw the colors, and the part played by retinal pigments could then be discovered. Another friend, George Wald, was a pioneer in research on the substances in the retina responsible for color vision, and I suggested that the pigeon technique would make *in vivo* tests possible. Unfortunately I could not persuade either Land or Wald to take advantage of the pigeon as a psychophysical subject.

IN 1957, John Gray organized the Aircrib Corporation and began to produce as many "boxes" as he could with limited funds. *Newsweek* reported that the crib would cost $335, but should save $100 in layette items. Gray also supplied plans, thermostats, plastic sheeting, and other parts to those who preferred to make their own. He exhibited a deluxe model at several meetings and arranged some local advertising, but, largely because of the patent issued to another "inventor," he could not raise capital.

Papers invariably ran articles about local users, and a sale to a Miami couple was carried on the UP wires. In August 1962, *This Week* reported additional statistics which Gray had collected with a questionnaire. Almost 98 percent of parents using the Aircrib felt that freedom of movement made their babies "muscularly precocious." Half said that their babies had fewer colds than might have been expected.

The babies cried less, "getting their 'lung exercise' from shouts and gurgles as they expend their energy exercising freely." Jim and Audrey Holland had an eighteen-week-old son in an Aircrib at the time, and answered a complaint of undue confinement by saying that "the real prison is the crib. What can be more prison-like than spending your first years on earth looking out through bars?" An obstetrician-gynecologist at New York University School of Medicine disagreed with "those who think the box fosters neglect on the mother's part. I think temperature control is a terrific idea. Our babies nowadays are overclothed—not quite as bad as the Russians' constricting swaddling clothes, but almost." A few months later, *Time* picked up the story, adding that more than four hundred babies had been raised in boxes. When *Cumulative Record* began to be used in classes, it brought my article to the attention of a new generation of potential users.

Joe Brady bought an Aircrib, and it was hotly discussed in the Walter Reed Hospital community. An early promoter of teaching machines in England, Graham Franklin, imported one which was featured in two television shows. Graham wrote that French Television had made a film and that the Germans were planning to do so. "Interviews have been given to Dutch, French, Swedish, Swiss, Italian, and Australian newspapers and, although I don't understand why, many American newspapers are making enquiries and we have had to hand this thing over to a public-relations man."

There was still little professional interest. Kimball Young, a sociologist, was one of a very few scientists who asked for technical data. Owen Aldis, the economist, was interested in ethology and had, as I wrote to a friend, "filled a crib with all kinds of gadgets and two television screens which smile at the baby," but I knew of no other research. Psychologists were even among those who continued to misunderstand. In the *American Psychologist*, in 1962, a report said that the "Skinner Baby Box" was germ-proof.

Lloyd Homme's company, Teaching Machines Incorporated, produced a model in which most of the cabinet work was replaced with a great plastic bubble. Gray agreed to license the name "Aircrib" if the model had our approval. It seemed safe enough, but I did not like the resonating acoustics of a bubble or the radiant heat loss through clear plastic. A revised model, attractively designed, had fewer of these faults. I also told Lloyd about the musical toilet-training seat I had designed for Deborah, and he thought they might add it to their line. But his company was soon taken over by the Westinghouse Corporation, which was interested only in teaching machines.

In 1967, John Gray died and so did his company.

INVITATIONS TO SPEAK were becoming a problem. I refused to give a lecture I had published, although I was often asked to do so ("Very few in the audience will have read it"), but I had no time to prepare new ones. I could always improvise something about programmed instruction and teaching machines, but I had given more than fifty lectures on those themes and was thoroughly sick of them. I could talk about new work in operant conditioning, but my audiences now tended to be "all-university" rather than departmental, and even nonacademic. I solved the problem with a lecture called "Utopia Now?" which I planned not to publish until I had grown tired of giving it.

The utopian dreaming in my sabbatical term at Putney had been short-lived. To a young woman who asked whether I would start a Walden Two, I replied, "Unfortunately—and I say it with real regret— my life is full of so many interesting things that I could not possibly bring myself to break with it and wager the rest of my life on such a venture." But some of my students were more venturesome. Matthew Israel had taken Natural Sciences 114 and had been converted to Walden Two. For several years in the late fifties, he and other graduate students met regularly to discuss the practical problems of an experimental community. Conferences were held, one of them at one of Joel Wolfson's camps on Cape Cod. Another, organized by William Shepherd, was held at Waldenwoods, Michigan, and I wrote a greeting to be read there.

The Russian safari renewed my interest. As I reported to Alexander Luria, "As one result of my trip and the many reflections it generated, I am now seriously considering an experimental community something along the lines of Walden Two" and, to Pei Sung Tang, "I am seriously thinking of starting a Walden Two. I still believe in non-political action and there is so much we need to know which can only be discovered from experimentation." Soon after returning from Russia, Eve and I spent a few days in another kind of utopia on Martha's Vineyard, visiting Harry and Elena Levin, and I wrote notes about a community. Among them were answers to some standard objections: it has never worked before; you can't change human nature; and you won't be let alone. As to the last: "We are at least to be allowed to start."

I was encouraged by the sales of *Walden Two*. Only 9,000 copies had been sold between 1948 and 1960, but in 1961 alone another 8,000 were sold; in 1962, 10,000; in 1963, 25,000; and in 1964, 40,000. More and more readers wrote to me, and to one I replied, "I am more convinced than ever that something along these lines ought to be done." Halleck Hoffman wrote, "Rumors fly around here that you have determined to start a Walden II, that somebody has given you the money to do it, and that you are actually under way. Is there anything to the rumors? How does one get in?" But to a young correspondent who asked, "What are you doing that is more important than this?" I replied, "I can only plead my own environmental control which, at the moment, dictates finishing a book on the technology of teaching, plus miscellaneous activities on comparable problems taken one at a time, rather than in a package in the manner of utopian thinking." But then, when a cabinetmaker wrote that he and his wife would join, I noted that "somehow a practicing non-intellectual encourages me." To a friend who was now marketing materials to teach reading, I wrote:

My plans for retirement are still contingent upon small details, such as finances, but I am quite serious in pushing an experimental community. Sometime before I leave for England next fall I'm going to get out a brochure. It may be published in Science, and in any case will be circulated among the faithful. Then we'll see what happens.

Some suggestions about the design of a successful community I dismissed as likely to be unhelpful. Timothy Leary urged me to try psilocibin, mescaline, or LSD to guarantee brotherly love. Henry S. Huntington, Jr., came to see me to recommend nudism. He had noted that I had received the Howard Crosby Warren Medal. Had I known Warren? Huntington had met him in Germany in the thirties, and both had become converts to nudism. Huntington, a former Presbyterian minister, came back to the States and founded a nudist colony in the Berkshires.

I read the *Rule of St. Benedict* and the *Rules of the Society of*

Jesus. Rules were necessary when the prescribed behavior was not conspicuous enough to be acquired through imitation or maintained by face-to-face sanctions. Reinforcing consequences were offered: members who followed the rules would enjoy a peaceful life and would resemble Jesus, who would then love them. I tried to translate terms like "penances," "corporal austerities," and "spiritual development" from Latin to English to Behavior, and to reformulate rules. "It is better to undertake repugnant duties first" was an easy one; "Abhor all that the world loves and embraces" was harder—but did "love and embrace" make a distinction between feeling and the action appropriate to the feeling?

I received some unexpected help from the Central Intelligence Agency. The Russians had designed communities called microrayons— small urban units containing apartments, schools, hospitals, factories, stores, in short, everything needed during a standard lifetime—with vehicular traffic only between microrayons. Two officers from the CIA came to see me with an apparently quite serious proposal: A microrayon sounded pretty much like Walden Two, and they could gauge its feasibility more accurately by watching an American experiment than by spying on the Russians, and they sent me Russian publications on microrayons. I was not impressed by the behavioral engineering. For example, the apartments were deliberately made small so that families would more readily send their children to boarding schools, where the state could take over family functions.

I wrote a note about another visitor quite unlike the men from the CIA:

> What is one to say to a man like James Pinney—this intense, gaunt, patient figure going about the country like some Johnny Appleseed of the soul? He came in yesterday—on a general mission. He is a champion of lost causes. He had spent two weeks in Washington trying to sell disarmament. Next year he will be at Pendle Hill. (Has the Society of Friends always sheltered such people?) A British friend of his is now making a second tour of China, and Pinney feels that the Chinese are bringing off the greatest social revolution in history. He has no difficulty in welcoming the change from the point of view of an early Christian.
>
> What I try to say to him is that we need a workable conception of man, and that we must not permit our affection for unworkable ones to stop us in our search. . . . I tried to argue for the no-man-is-an-island kind

of interested charity. He is for it, but immediately mystifies. "The Self is here (pointing to himself) and there (pointing to me). It is the same Self. Self-interest is therefore charity, love . . ." I found myself making a quick translation: *man*, as a species, works for his own survival—via his culture as well as his body. This is all that is essentially man. If some crucial part of it fails, man fails. Pinney's Self is the evolutionary essence of man as a species.

I discussed the physical setting of a Walden Two with an architect, Raymond Studer, who spent some time at Harvard and at the Rhode Island School of Design. In a note I credited him with a "monolithic conception of architecture as behavior-contingent space." He was conducting a seminar on environmental programming and was in contact with a "D. C. Walden II Committee" in College Park, Maryland. I also spoke with Martin Meyerson, who had written a paper on "The Future Metropolis" in an issue of *Daedalus* on utopias, and who liked *Walden Two*. Ivor Richards was interested in utopias and I gave him copies of all my relevant notes. Harry Levin and Harry Murray were still giving their seminar on utopia and occasionally asked me to speak.

Owen Aldis had made a lot of money in the stock market and I thought he might back a Walden Two venture. He thought a community could profitably provide quarters for scholars on sabbatical leave, and he hired the Arthur D. Little Company to find out how many people went on sabbatical and how much they spent. One day he told me of a different plan. The same end could be achieved by paying members wages and charging them for rooms, food, medical care, old-age insurance, and so on. And I should abandon an "antidemocratic" political structure and use at least token elections in the manner of labor unions. Members should live in families and make their own decisions about child care, dining arrangements, and so on. Such a capitalistic frame would avoid unnecessary and possibly fatal criticism. The proposal depressed and discouraged me, and I returned to planning my future as an individual. To an inquiry from London I replied:

After long consideration I have decided that it would not be well for me personally to undertake an experimental community. I have a great many things planned for the next five years of an intellectual nature all of which bear, I think, on the eventual success of a radical reform of our way of life, and I do not feel that I should jeopardize those plans on the chance that something of a much more practical nature could be put through.

I had not, however, lost my "faith in human nature." A note written in 1964 reads:

I was in the front line as the Waverley car pulled into loading position in the Harvard subway. The motorman was facing away from the door talking to another motorman. The door did not open. I thought it might be stuck and pulled at the rubber bumper. The door snapped closed with a bang. The motorman turned in a rage, opened the door, and cried, "All right, all right, you'll get on." I was instantly furious and said, "The doors often stick." I sat down, boiling, and fantasied revenge. Should I ask him for his number and report him? What could you do with people like that in a Walden Two?

Then I began to wonder about his behavior. He was tired, the weather was bad, traffic was tied up by snow. It also occurred to me that he had thought I had rapped loudly on the door. When it came time to get off I went forward and said quietly, "Next stop, please." He turned with a sheepish grin and apologized. He had not been sure which route he was to take and hadn't opened the doors until he had found out. He now realized I had not been knocking on the door. In a burst of warm feeling I said I had supposed he might have misunderstood, and could hardly blame him, having to drive such old equipment. We all but embraced in a spasm of good will. I walked home glowing in optimism for the human race.

WHEN MY COLLEAGUES complained that operant conditioners neglected them and their work, I wrote a defensive note:

Though I would make a more effective contact with current psychology if I read the literature and talked about it, I do not believe I am missing anything of value. At the moment I am neglecting a host of writers in the field of learning and I feel some guilt, but what would the *Behavior of Organisms* look like today if I had not neglected my contemporaries then? It would be full of temporal mazes, "centrifugal swing," "insight," Lashley jumping stands, latent learning, and God knows what. What I neglected then, a science of behavior is forgetting now.

Certainly there was neglect in the other direction, with practical results. By the early sixties, the experimental analysis of behavior had not yet found a secure place in academic psychology. Young operant conditioners had taken jobs in medical schools, drug companies, and government laboratories and were out of touch with departments of psychology. Introductory textbooks had begun to mention rats and pigeons in boxes, but learning theory was still in the S-R mode or about the memorizing and forgetting of nonsense syllables.

Walden Two was being read in courses on utopias and, with *Science and Human Behavior*, in sociology and political science, and when I lectured at other universities I often found myself playing a part in a stock comedy. Before the lecture the chairman of the Department of Psychology would warn me not to expect a large crowd; students were busy with examinations, a popular speaker was scheduled at the same time in another building, the publicity had come out too late. We would then go to the lecture hall and find it overflowing. My obviously astonished host would make frantic phone calls in search of a larger auditorium. One episode of that sort occurred during the Kennedy campaign for President, when a small crowd at Princeton was predicted because Kennedy was speaking in Trenton. The pattern prevailed into the seventies.

THE WORK OF Jerrold Zacharias of MIT on teaching high-school physics was probably the best (certainly the best supported) product of the post-Sputnik boom in American education. When I met Zacharias at a conference at Woods Hole (later reported in Jerome Bruner's *The Process of Education*), he was surprisingly aggressive. When I demonstrated a machine to teach children subtle color and form discriminations, he said, "Why do you want to teach children *that?*" As I was going through a short program for the disk machine on incandescence, he stopped me and said, "You've already made four mistakes in your physics!" Fortunately, I had taken the material from his MIT project. At the White House conference he had been equally critical.

In a conference on "The Dimensions of Education" at the Johns Hopkins University, in which I also participated, Zacharias taught two classes about the velocity of light, one a fifth-grade class in a local school, the other a graduate seminar in the Physics Department at the University. He was a brilliant teacher, but I was not sure that he knew why or how to teach others to teach as well. And before long he was blaming the failure of much of the material from his project on the fact that "the teachers were no good." On New Year's Day, 1964, I reported another exchange:

> I went to a party last night at [Paul and Helga] Doty's knowing that Zacharias would be there, and I promised myself not to lose my temper. I saw Z. and approached him in a friendly way and he responded similarly. But as we talked, the same old issues came up. The net effect was of peace-making but I nevertheless, against my resolution, told him that his project needed a different psychologist and that, unless he recognized the possibility of a scientific analysis of behavior, he would probably not be able to use (did I mean "understand"?) my book.

In trying to keep my schedule within bounds, I particularly refused invitations to speak about programmed instruction and teaching machines. I was sick of them and had nothing new to say. I made one regrettable exception. In 1964 the Canadian Council for Programmed Instruction sponsored a first national convention, and when the Director strongly urged me to come, I agreed. I was writing a paper on the first decade of programmed instruction and could use that. I suggested "How Can We Improve Education?" as a title. To my acute embarrassment, the Director sent a news release to all prominent magazines, newspapers, and other media throughout the United States and Canada, reading:

> Dr. B. F. Skinner, World Famous Harvard Psychologist who has been acclaimed as "Father of Teaching Machines," has chosen the First Annual Convention of the Canadian Council for Programmed Learning as a platform from which to introduce new findings of world significance. . . .
> It is believed that this report, based on recent research findings at the Harvard Psychological Laboratories, may eventually affect every life to an even greater degree than Dr. Skinner's first paper in 1954 on "The Art of Teaching and the Science of Learning."

I wrote to the Director that I had not promised anything of the sort, and asked him to send out a correction.

When I reached Toronto, it was clear that the first release was still in control. Great things were expected. Fortunately the date was April 1, and I began by reminding my audience of the tricks I had played as a child on April Fool's Day and said I sympathized with those who might think that I was now playing another. I had no new findings of world significance to report. When reporters later complained, I told them that I had not been responsible for the publicity, and they made stories of that. The President of the Council wrote:

> *I must apologize for the hyperbolic announcements preceding your main speech. You can be assured this is not characteristic of Canadian groups. In fact we are often too reluctant to announce things adequately. Our hope is that you will accept our apology and forgive us for not being more aware of the situation.*

The Director's enthusiasm was not allayed. Without consulting me he sent a transcript of part of my talk to the editor of the *Journal of the Association of Programmed Learning* in Britain and promised him a second part later. Fortunately the editor checked with me, and I was able to keep the transcript out of circulation.

SIDNEY PRESSEY HAD CALLED our breakfast at the meeting of the American Psychological Association "the most stimulating episode of the meeting." When Horace English, a colleague of Pressey's, wrote to Garry Boring to protest his reference to me as the inventor of the teaching machine, he added that Pressey thought "it was just fine to have Skinner stirring things up," and when my paper appeared in *Science*, Pressey wrote, "Your generous recognition of my early efforts towards teaching machines . . . is very much appreciated. Would that more scientists were as gracious in recognition of others' work. And I am delighted that your program seems moving toward a substantial fruition, which my less adequate efforts failed to attain." The following year he sent me one of his punchboards and several "chemo-cards" which could be used rather like his machine, a model of which he had previously sent me, and he added, "I plan no more work in the field, myself, but continue convinced that there are great opportunities here and much hope you can carry through to their realization."

As the movement accelerated, however, certain differences became clear. He wrote a paper in which he called his own proposal "adjunct" auto-instruction. The student "read a chapter in the textbook, went down a mimeographed sheet of multiple-choice questions on the major points of that chapter and selected his answers. A machine or a 'chemo-card' reported whether his response was correct, and if incorrect he made another choice." Pressey contrasted this with "initial" instruction in which the student "may have *instead* of the textbook, some 2,000 questions on long rolls of paper." He described my machine but did not mention my name. He insisted that only after "contact with a complex structured topic should a student turn to auto-instruction for review," and he cited experiments said to show that multiple-choice questions were no less effective than constructed responses. He thought it was unfortunate that new multiple-choice machines remained "largely in an experimental stage because of the current preoccupation with constructed responses and problems with initial programming." He sent me a copy of the paper saying that he knew I would not like it but thought he had to write it.

Of another paper he said he was ashamed of "the petulance, especially the slaps at animal laboratory work." More important was the fact that he was missing the point of the experimental analysis of behavior. He said that "much current theory is based upon rote or animal learning," although there was no rote learning whatsoever in our experiments or in our programs. Nor were we "applying concepts derived from a rat's maze running." We were not "shaping the student's responses so that, without his quite knowing what is happening, he is cued, reinforced, and faded into his learning." Like many educators, Pressey used expressions like "enlarging understanding," "grasping the larger structure" of an idea or subject matter, and "giving the student a lively challenge." All of these I deplored.

According to an article in the German publication *Lehrmaschinen* (as reported in a bulletin of the British Association for Programmed Learning), my lectures in Moscow and Kiev in 1961 were followed by the publication of "a few articles in the Soviet educational press in 1962. The idea of individual tuition as superior to class tuition did not appeal to Soviet teachers at first, the emphasis having always been on collective instruction. However, the fact that mass tuition will be available by employing a highly qualified specialist as programmer was very attractive to the Soviet pedagogues. They argued that *in principle* one person will teach an unlimited number of students. . . . Although two years ago the Soviet Union hardly had a single teaching machine, a fantastically fast development has taken place." Two articles on programmed instruction appeared in *Soviet Pedagogy* in August and September 1963, and in the same year a bulletin from Minsk College of Radio Engineering reported that programs for "teaching and counseling machines have been developed for nine engineering studies and for foreign languages."

In my exchange with Joseph Wood Krutch, I had not resolved the issue of freedom and dignity. Behavior for which people traditionally took credit was attributed to other sources by an advancing science. That was a kind of theft and vigorously resisted. The issue came up repeatedly as I read history and political science, but I found it hard to follow through with an analysis. Satisfactory restatements seemed almost out of reach. I thought of taking a book like *The Measure of Man* or C. S. Lewis's *The Abolition of Man* and translating all the issues into such behavioral terms as might be understood by the kinds of readers for whom these books were intended.

Krutch returned to the attack. In the *Saturday Review* for April 21, 1962, he quoted from *Science and Human Behavior*: "The free man who is held responsible for the behavior of the external biological organism is only a pre-scientific substitute for the kinds of causes which are discovered in the course of a scientific analysis, all of which lie outside the individual." That, he said, was "the dead end of the tendency represented by Darwin and Marx." The following year he went back to that *conversazione* in the *American Scholar* in which I had agreed that I would accept a healthy and enduring society in which, as Krutch put it, people were "so automatically perfect that consciousness was no longer necessary and would disappear." A year later, he was pleased to note that Professor Bridgman, though "expressing great admiration for that extreme behaviorist, his one-time colleague, was compelled to add 'I do not think that Skinner's solution is the only possible one or that it is a solution which takes into account all we can see that is significant.' Bridgman, said Krutch, was opting "pragmatically for the open universe of William James as opposed to the closed universe of Laplace, Skinner, and other behaviorists." And still another year or two later, he wrote a paper called "Danger: Utopia Ahead," in which he accused me of dehumanizing people by "conditioning them into perfect virtue."

I discussed some of these issues in a televised interview with Richard Heffner on Channel 13 in New York City. The program was called *Open Mind*, and our announced topic was the control of human behavior. I arrived at the studio and was made up and taken to the set. Heffner came in very late and sat down without makeup just as we went on the air. He began by saying that it would be the last of the series and that there was something rather appropriate in my being the last guest. The next morning I learned from the *Times* that he had come back to the studio from a meeting at which he had been fired.

The interview was nevertheless productive, and I made many of the same points in a lecture at a meeting of the American Psychological Association in Los Angeles in 1964. I had been invited to give it by the Division of Personality and Social Psychology. Jerry Bruner told me that he would preside, and since we seldom read each other's papers, I said, "Good, then I shall have you as a captive audience," but he nearly escaped. When the hour came, I found myself alone on the platform. Minutes passed. Finally I went to the lectern and said, "I appear here in the title role of a play by Pirandello entitled, *One Speaker in Search of a Master of Ceremonies*." At that moment Jerry entered the back of the hall. He had been held up by a parade; Barry Goldwater was campaigning for President.

The title of my lecture, "A Science of Behavior and Human Dignity," alluded to the inevitable conflict between a science that traces human behavior to genetic and environmental histories and a tradition which traces the same behavior to an initiating self.

IN THE *Annual Review of Psychology* for 1959, Howard Kendler called the experimental analysis of behavior "a playing-by-ear type of research generating a mass of data difficult to analyze systematically." Neverthe-

A MATTER

less, "Skinnerians have been able to generate an enthusiasm and conviction among themselves resembling a quaint mixture of . . . a
revolutionary party, a revival meeting, and homecoming football
gathering." Could the enthusiasm and conviction maintain itself on
such a skimpy diet of theoretical notions? Kendler thought not, if for no
other reason than that its extreme methodological position would "dis-
integrate in the face of additional facts and more complicated experimental situations." Rumblings, he said, were being heard.

It was true that not everyone who made important contributions to
the experimental analysis of behavior stayed in the field. Bill Estes never
recovered from his "service-connected disability," and went on to a
distinguished career in mathematical psychology. Norman Guttman and
his students had opened a new era in the study of stimulus generalization, but Norman often drifted back into philosophy. Ralph Hefferline,
who had taken stenographic notes of my course on verbal behavior at
Columbia in 1947 and had published a classic experiment in which a
movement of the thumb too slight to be noticed by the subject (and
hence unconscious) was effectively conditioned as an operant, was now
looking at the psychotherapies of Fritz Perls and Wilhelm Reich. Nat
Schoenfeld was becoming less and less active in the operant field and
found the behaviorism of J. R. Kantor more congenial. When Dick
Herrnstein returned to Harvard, I sensed a change in him and wrote
several notes about it. I remained friends with all of them. And within
the operant field the friendship was extraordinary. Meetings of the editors of the *Journal of the Experimental Analysis of Behavior* were full
of good will. There was no reason to quarrel; the experimental analysis
of behavior was flourishing, and there was something in it for everyone.

In 1956, our Conferences on the Experimental Analysis of Behavior began to be held as part of the annual meeting of the APA. More
and more people were attending, and we had trouble finding space. By
1960 we needed three or four half-day sessions, but we were dependent
upon the largesse of the Division of Experimental Psychology and often
found ourselves crowded into small, poorly ventilated—and in those
days smoke-filled—rooms. We often looked for larger, unscheduled
rooms and moved our meetings, but that was inconvenient and wasted
time.

Something had to be done, and the editors of the *Journal of the
Experimental Analysis of Behavior* appointed a committee to explore

the possibility of a separate division of the Association. Late in 1963 a petition in the form of a Memorandum to the Council of the APA was sent to subscribers of *JEAB*, who easily supplied enough signatures, and it was presented at the 1964 meeting.

When Joe Brady proposed that I be the first President, I wrote:

I am very anxious that this organization not be dubbed Skinnerian. You have all suffered from that, and you have my sympathy. I think it would be best for everyone if the new Division were drawn up and set on the road without my being involved in it. There are many reasons why [the President] ought to be you. You have done a lot of work and supported a lot more, and you are not a student of either Keller or Skinner. Moreover, you are an amiable chap who can spread good will as needed. The President would, of course, be serving on the Council during his term of office. I don't know of anyone who would be a better liaison man.

Joe attended the meeting of the Council. As I wrote in a note,

I forgot about the meeting and was reminded by Charlie Ferster after the vote had been taken. Joe said later it was just as well, since it carried out our plan to associate the Division with me as little as possible. It was well for another reason. I am sure that if I had been called on to explain why Division 3 would not serve, I should have gone into our grievances. Joe, as he reported later, did not mention the real reasons, "of course." Why could *I* not have seen the importance of that strategy? Expressing our resentment at the pitifully small space assigned to us last year would have got several backs up, a discussion would have followed, and the Division could well have been tabled for a year. I have done this several times. I can control jealousy, for example, reasonably well. A grievance still controls me.

Anticipating the creation of a new Division, I gave a paper explaining how the experimental analysis of behavior differed from other fields. It studied one organism at one time and place and treated its behavior as such rather than as the sign or symptom of an inner process. It did not regard the organism as initiating exchanges with the environment, as terms like "detect," "receive," and "judge" suggested. It did not look at what people said they would do under a given set of contingencies, because that was usually not what they actually did. It seldom planned research in the manner expounded by statisticians or scientific methodologists. A cumulative record was much closer to the actual behavior of the organism than an old-style learning curve showing, for example, how the time required to complete a task changed during a series of trials.

I could have said more. Psychologists like James and Freud drew their principles from happy accidents in their own experience and applied them to facts having the same order of complexity. The experimental analysis of behavior used the controlled conditions of the laboratory to guarantee the validity of its principles. Where mental or cognitive analyses seldom pointed to conditions that could be changed, an experimental analysis necessarily did so and therefore led directly to a technology. James's *Talks to Teachers*, for example, was little more than common sense. Psychoanalysis began as a technology, but the unconscious causes to which it pointed could be changed, if at all, only very slowly.

After the meeting I wrote a note:

> I was, I suppose, crowing a little. Things are going well and I enjoyed the luxury of pointing that out. I am also beginning to strike out at my critics, playing now from a position of strength. This is to some extent personal and petty, but I am not inclined to bury the paper or moderate its character. There *is* an extraordinary neglect of our position. Students still go on in the old tradition.
>
> Am I suffering delusions of grandeur or is there really an extraordinary advantage in my position? The arguments in "Behaviorism at Fifty," "Operant Behavior," and "What Is the Experimental Analysis of Behavior?" are beginning to jell. I want to get at a paper by [Herbert] Simon and [Allen] Newell on "computer simulation of thought." The new division is off to a great start. I'm sure I have the measure of the psycholinguists. Etc., etc. It could be a very exciting decade.

Another note, in October 1964, is perhaps more revealing:

> Last night at the Playreaders I played Sir Isaac Newton in Dürrenmatt's *The Physicists*. I wore a wig, square spectacles, and a magnificent red and gold robe close to the traditional garb of the magician. "I am Newton. Sir Isaac Newton. President of the Royal Society. . . ." (One month from today I am to lecture before the Royal Society.) This morning, in spite of a slight cold, I feel a general euphoria. Going over my notes for the lecture I can easily adopt an appropriate stance—confident,

relaxed, with a touch of humor. I was way inside the part. But the final speech, quite spontaneously and possibly not as the author intended, I read with a loss of confidence. Newton is not sure of his position; he tries to reassure himself, reviewing his achievements, some of which now seem pitifully trivial. (Charles Walther tells me this is not the way Hugh Cronin played the scene in New York. He was proud, boasting, ready to serve.) For an hour I *was* Newton. Or was I, as the author suggests, simply mad? Or am I now, in my euphoria, mad?

I had written a note about the "cryptic boasting" in MacArthur's speech before Congress; could I protect myself against that sort of thing—"except by dying young?" I consulted Jonathan Swift's "When I Come to Be Old."

"Not to boast . . ." was not quite explicit enough to cover the cryptic case. "Not to talk much, nor of myself . . ." was possibly the only safeguard. But did that mean no autobiography, no notebooks, no reminiscences?

Other notes written at the time offer some evidence of my reaction to success:

March 31, 1963
The articles in *Time* and *Life*, the profile in *Harper's*, and my "successes" in Texas, Arizona, and Washington have plunged me into a sustained depression. Feelings I can vaguely describe as guilt and anxiety overwhelm me. . . . Much of this is the result of losing control. Flushed with success I go too far. It was once a more devastating flaw; it could still destroy me. Writing a paper in the silence of my study—that is the only verbal behavior I can really trust.

THE EXPERIMENTAL ANALYSIS of behavior was furthered by several bootstrap operations. The first college course ever taught by machine was the material Jim and I published as *The Analysis of Behavior*, and when Fred Keller, consulting at universities in Brazil, invented Personalized System Instruction—"PSI"—he used it first in a course on the experimental analysis of behavior. Fred was leaving Columbia and moving to Arizona State University, where he would also teach an introductory course in psychology in this new way. He and Nat Schoenfeld had let their students work with real rats in lever boxes, and by 1956 their example was being followed in at least five other universities. Harold Schlosberg, at Brown, wrote to me that "our freshmen and sophomores are getting a big kick out of their rats." Kathy Safford and I had never finished our classroom manual, but Ellen Reese, at Mount Holyoke, carried it on, and a final version appeared in 1964. A small experimental manual by Lloyd Homme and David Klaus was published in 1957 by the Lever Press (a touch of Lloyd's whimsy), and in 1963 Jack Michael brought out *Laboratory Studies in Operant Behavior*.

A useful literature was in the making. In 1960, Murray Sidman published *Tactics of Scientific Research*. I sent him a telegram— BRILLIANT JOB. SURE TO HAVE LASTING EFFECT ON PSYCHOLOGY. CONGRATU- LATIONS—and I wrote: "You have written a remarkably good book, and one which is going to be useful to all of us. I hope it gets the attention it deserves from scientific methodologists, but knowing these people from of old, I hope you are prepared for neglect for some time. What is more important is that young people in the field will now have a chance to consider quietly and thoughtfully the many practices which have become a standard part of our own behavior." The book became a kind of Bible among operant conditioners.

It had been suggested that the Society for the Experimental Analysis of Behavior compile a book of readings, but in 1959 Werner Honig, of Dalhousie University in Halifax, showed me the prospectus of a much more ambitious project—a book written by selected authors on basic concepts, techniques, and data, together with applications to physiological psychology, psychopharmacology, psychophysics, motivation, space technology, the behavior of psychotic and retarded people, teaching by machine, and programmed instruction. There would even be sections on theoretical and philosophical issues. The Society's volume was abandoned and Honig's appeared under the title *Operant Behavior* in 1966.

My reaction was curious:

Last week I got my copy of Honig's *Operant Behavior*—twenty-eight years after my first copy of *The Behavior of Organisms*. What a productive twenty-eight years they have been! An astonishing contrast. It should have been a great moment in my life, but I was perfectly cold. Someday I may get a thrill, but not now.

The experimental analysis of behavior was entering the public domain, though not without difficulty. In a new edition of *Webster's New International Dictionary*, the word *operant* was defined in part as "2. of, relating to, or emphasizing the overt, observable, or measurable (—— behavior) (—— responses)"—a definition obviously written by someone who thought that behaviorists were distinguished by the fact that they confined themselves to observables. When I suggested an alternative version, the editor wrote that he thought I would find "the complicated sequence of mischances that brought the definition in question into being . . . as amusing as we find it embarrassing." Later someone called my attention to a reference under *skinner box* in which "operational" was used instead of "operant."

In 1962, an advisor for the U.S. Science Exhibit at the Seattle World's Fair wanted a demonstration of operant conditioning. Behavioral research was to be emphasized, with displays of homing in salmon, imprinting in chicks, mother-child affection in monkeys, and hereditary determiners of behavior in mice. I referred him to the Grason-Stadler Company, and they built an exhibit in which the behavior of a pigeon was recorded as it discriminated between various colors and patterns. When the exhibit was moved to the Time-Life Exhibition Center in New York City, it was billed as "COLLEGE EDUCATED PIGEONS! See these feathery geniuses match colors and perform other astounding mental [sic] feats."

TRACES OF WATSON and Pavlov persisted. The *Columbia Jester* once published a cartoon showing two rats in a box, one with its paw on a lever saying, "Boy, have I got this guy conditioned. Every time I press the bar down he drops in a piece of food." I used it in "A Case History in Scientific Method" to make a valid point: my behavior was shaped and maintained by my subjects as much as theirs by me. But in 1962 the *Boston Globe* printed the story this way: "Bit of conversation between two guinea pigs in a laboratory. Said one: 'I've got the professor well trained. Every time I ring the bell he brings me the grub.'" The guinea pig of laboratory science had replaced the rat, and Pavlov's bell the lever.

A writer in the *Washington Post* said, correctly, that I "seriously expounded the desirability of conditioned virtue" (people should be-have well not because they were good but because they lived in a good environment), but then he went on: "just as Pavlov's dogs salivate to the sound of a bell." Arthur Koestler, writing in the *Listener*, may have been right in saying that I "symbolized an extreme form of the trend toward the dehumanizing of man" (if dehumanizing meant, as I thought it should, dehomunculizing), but he then went on: "be-haviorism is based on the crudely mechanistic conception of the nineteenth century," in which behavior is regarded as a series of S-R units. I had not been a stimulus-response psychologist for more than thirty years.

JULIE HAD ALWAYS FOUND mathematics congenial and her doctoral dissertation concerned item analyses in testing, but she began to write programs for the American Institute of Research, and in the fall of 1963 a letter from her restored my faith in programmed instruction:

> I tried out my present-participle program on the Goldstons, who live below us. It was truly heartwarming to see. Mrs. Goldston especially. She would read a frame aloud, comment to herself, "Well, let me see," then read the frame again, this time with the response verbally included, and comment, "I think 'Present participle' should go there. What do you think, Julie?" I would smile, or sometimes break down and say, "What-ever you think goes there." Finally, after rereading the whole thing aloud, this time with the now-written answer, she would survey her work, hand it to me with the comment, "You look, I'm not sure it's right." I wouldn't take it so she would slowly turn the page. Then all Hell would break loose: "Look, Julie! Look, Max! It has 'Present participle!' That's what I wrote. Look, here's where I wrote it. See, it says 'Present participle.' Now look here, it says the same thing, 'Present participle.' " This was followed, and accompanied, by laughter, upon occasion so hard that she had to go get a handkerchief to wipe her eyes. Then, "Oh, Julie, I'm going to get a gold star. You'll make us educated yet. You know we don't get much learning at the store, but I always said to Max, 'Max, we should take some courses' and now, Look!, I'm learning all about present participles."

*　　*　　*

WHEN I READ that Lawrance Thompson had published *Selected Letters of Robert Frost*, I thought he might be interested in Frost's letter to me and sent him a copy. In return he sent a copy of the book, which contained my letter. He had made a transcript of a copy, with no further identification, in the Jones Library at Amherst many years before. The library no longer had the copy and there were no Mr. Skinners among the Amherst alumni at the time the letter was written. In the copy he sent he added "Burrhus Frederic" to the salutation, and emended "Mr. Skinner seems to have been one of the students" in a course in creative writing that Frost taught at the University of Michigan during the summer term of 1926 to read: "But he was not. He had met RF at Bread Loaf during the summer of 1925, while BFS was taking a course with Sidney Cox, and RF had asked to see some of BFS's work." Thompson had also used the last sentence of the letter in his introduction.

MY LECTURE BEFORE the Royal Society was called "The Technology of Teaching: Its Nature and Some Problems Encountered in Its Use." It was given in the "Society's apartments" at Burlington House, Piccadilly. Although it was the most prestigious audience I had ever faced, I was quite relaxed, and the lecture went well. I could report a good deal of interesting work. Montrose Wolf, Hayden Mees, and Todd Risley had used reinforcement with food to induce a severely autistic boy to wear the eyeglasses without which he would soon become blind. Murray Sidman and colleagues had taught a microcephalic idiot to select circles from among ellipses which became progressively more like circles. Herbert Terrace had devised a system for teaching pigeons complex pattern discriminations without errors. I described machines designed to teach a sense of rhythm and pitch and a "magic ink" technique for teaching handwriting. At the university level, I described the program in crystallography by Bruce Chalmers and Jim Holland and the one in neuroanatomy by Murray and Philip Sidman.

Sir Howard Florey was President of the Royal Society at the time. Two other American psychologists had given review lectures, and Sir Howard's comments were said to have been rather caustic. He liked my lecture, however, and after the lecture Eve and I were shown the mace of the Society and I took snuff from the diamond-encrusted snuffbox given by Charles II.

Then Sir Howard and I walked to the Athenaeum for sherry and dinner with a few members. Lord Adrian was there, and we talked about some of our friends at the Harvard Medical School. At dinner, after suitable toasts (to the Queen, standing), Sir Howard asked me to say something about teaching machines, but I was sick of the subject and talked instead about the wartime uses of animals and later, for some reason, about the possibly harmful contingencies of reinforcement in scientific prizes. When it was over, one of the guests drove me to his home for a drink, and his wife took me back to my hotel. It had been, I thought, a successful day.

The next morning, I underwent a slow and painful change. My lecture had indeed gone well, but I began to see that in the elation which followed I had behaved badly. I had taken only one glass of sherry and very little wine at dinner, but, as I now slowly realized, I had made one mistake after another. I had rudely dismissed Sir Howard's request to talk about teaching machines, and it was scarcely tactful of me to criticize scientific prizes when both Florey and Adrian were Nobel laureates. I recalled a growing coldness in Florey's comments during the dinner, and afterwards, when I looked for him to say good-bye, I saw him with another member, and it was clear that they had been talking about me—unfavorably. The fact was, the evening had been a disaster. For months I felt a twinge of shame upon hearing any reference to London, seeing anything I had bought in London, seeing an English movie, hearing an English accent, or even seeing people sitting around a large table.

By 1965, I found myself "drifting away from good italic." It was too slow a hand, and my rapid italic was even less legible than my rapid cursive. Moreover, ballpoint pens were now the thing, and italic needed a chisel point. A handwriting program taught cursive, and I found that I could produce a pleasing page if I did not hurry. Although I still enjoyed the appearance of carefully written notes, I abandoned italic and was soon writing execrable cursive again.

*   *   *

I CONTINUED TO BE SURPRISED by the size and enthusiastic reactions of my audiences, and by how widely my work was known. In a single week, for example, a lecture at MIT filled a large auditorium, and I continued to run into people who had gone out of their way to be there. A dinner meeting of an association of pediatricians at which I spoke was the largest in many years and the discussion was sympathetic, to the evident surprise of the officers. When I met a group of John Hays Fellows, I found that one of them had used "Freedom and the Control of Men" and *Walden Two* with a select class of high-school students and many of the others had read *Walden Two*. I no longer needed to begin at the beginning.

The danger was the temptation to relax and enjoy. It would be a mistake simply to give people what they expected to hear. I resolved to present more and more technical material and to "get over my embarrassment in using terms like 'operant' and 'schedules of reinforcement.'" I would follow the same pattern in writing *The Technology of Teaching*. If I wrote it *down*, it would have a wider sale, because it would be closer to a teacher's manual, but if, instead, it expounded the experimental analysis of behavior, more and more people would look into the basic science, and in the long run it would do more for educational practice. It would also reassure laboratory workers of the importance of their work, helping to give them the status they deserved.

IN 1966, I wrote a note called "Operant Behavior in the Design of a Real Culture":

The history runs like this: John Throne, working for the Joseph P. Kennedy, Jr., Foundation [for Research on Retardation], gives Eunice Shriver instruction in operant behavior, *Walden Two*, and *Science and Human Behavior*. [Several years later Mrs. Shriver introduced me to her mother as "my personal psychologist."] An effort to get me to meet her husband at dinner at their home aborts. A second effort gets me as far as a committee meeting of the Foundation in New York, delaying my departure for Europe by two days, but because of a schedule mixup I have to leave before saying anything. In Washington Ferster, [Israel] Goldiamond, and Brady are invited to meet the Shrivers. They are advised by Throne to stick to mental retardation, but Shriver himself turns to the Anti-Poverty Campaign. Then in August of last year Eve and I are invited to Hyannisport. We swim with Eunice Shriver, meet Bobby and Teddy and their wives, Pat Lawford, the Smiths, et al. [Charles Addams, the cartoonist, Mary McGrory, the columnist, and Senator Birch Bayh were other guests.] After dinner Shriver takes me into the library and asks what I think can be done. Responds electrically to my definition of contingencies of reinforcement; "That's what I want!" he says. I agree to explore the possibilities.

[I visited a Job Corps Camp on the Cape. It was near the excellent summer camps which Joel Wolfson and his wife were running on behavioral principles, and I tried, but failed, to draw Joel away from the idyllic life he had built for himself in order to take part in the Job Corps program.] I call a meeting of applied operant conditioners at the APA meeting in Chicago, ask for suggestions. A conference in Washington is to be held next week. Nothing may come of it.

The conference was held, I filed a report, and, indeed, heard nothing. A year later someone looked for the report in Washington, could not find it, and asked for a copy. A year later one of Shriver's aides came to see me about motivating the peasants of Venezuela.

In 1968, the Society for the Experimental Analysis of Behavior began to publish the *Journal of Applied Behavior Analysis*. It would contain "reports of experimental research involving applications of the experimental analysis of behavior to problems of social importance." Many applications were obvious. As early as 1953, I had sent an article on schedules of reinforcement to the *Scientific American*, and the editor had immediately asked me to give more space to industry, education, and psychotherapy, although little or nothing had yet been published in those fields.

As to industry—piece-rate pay was a fixed-ratio schedule, salary and commission a mixture of fixed-ratio and fixed-interval, and all gambling systems variable-ratio. What would industry not give for workers as preoccupied with what they were doing as bingo players? But fixed- or variable-ratio wage systems were prohibited by unions or governments; they were so powerful they were dangerous. Less threatening uses were usually acceptable. For example, a free lottery ticket received each day upon arrival at work, with a weekly or monthly drawing, reduced absenteeism.

That same year, 1953, I refused to write an article about incentives for *Dun's Review*; "our work on schedules . . . has important implications for increasing productivity and improving interest, morale, and enthusiasm [but] it might be misused to increase productivity without enough concern for the welfare of the worker." Several years later, Owen Aldis published a paper called "Of Pigeons and Men" in the *Harvard Business Review* in which he considered wage schedules which could "make jobs so interesting that aversive threats can be held to a minimum. . . . The promise of newer methods of wage payments lies not only in the increase in productivity that might follow but in happier workers as well."

A few years later, *Business Week* reported that the Emery Air Freight Company had saved millions of dollars by "improving employee performance" through the use of positive reinforcement. The employees showed greater contentment as well as improved efficiency. When I mentioned the Emery Air Freight example in a filmed interview with Elizabeth Hall of *Psychology Today*, my remarks were used (without my permission) as the introduction to a separate film in which the employees were shown getting nothing more than commendation as their share of the gains. The fact was, they had held their jobs and had been given raises when other companies were laying off workers. When I protested, I was told that it was too late to change the film.

A year or two later, someone sent me the "Positive Reinforcement Skill Guide" which American Airlines gave its supervisors. It listed opportunities for reinforcing employees' behavior and even suggested a schedule: "First week thru 4th week—twice a week; 5th week and after—once a week; after goal reached—random." Former students wrote to me about the incentive systems to which they were exposed or which they were using as managers. Insurance companies, for example, paid their agents in many different ways, and "the company which comes up with a plan which is only five percent more efficient than the competition will have a tremendous advantage."

An undergraduate once told me that he was going to spend the summer in a village in Brazil with a group of anthropologists who were studying the lack of entrepreneurship among its inhabitants. Fantasies would be studied in evaluating initiative, but the student saw a chance to try operant reinforcement as well. Together we designed a portable nonelectrical apparatus to be used with children, in which making small toys would be reinforced on a slowly stretched variable-ratio schedule. The project was rejected as too ambitious, however, and a less mechanized version failed when the boys' fathers stood around and supplied the aversive control which it was designed to supplant.

INCENTIVES WERE NOT ALWAYS economic. Schedules of reinforcement were at work in unlikely places. I described an example at a conference celebrating the first twenty-five years of the RCA Laboratories in Princeton, New Jersey. Most of the other speakers (physicists or engineers) had contributed something to the industry, and I tried to do as much. People watched television, turning it on or off or switching channels, because of the reinforcing consequences. Producers knew how to contrive amusing, exciting, or attractively violent episodes, but they overlooked scheduling. The programs that really held their audiences were sports, and they did so because the exciting events occurred on a variable-ratio schedule. Watching a football game was like playing a slot machine: a five-yard gain was two cherries; a first down, three; a long run, three bells; and the touchdown pass that wins the game, the jackpot. The dedication shown by the football aficionado was puzzling only to those who were unaware of the power of a variable-ratio schedule. The same schedule would keep viewers watching other kinds of programs. With a group of editors meeting in Cincinnati, I proposed a similar solution to the problem of keeping their readers reading.

In 1963, I discussed still another problem of incentives with Frederick Ordway III of the Science and Technology Information Center: What were space travelers to do with their time? Admiral Byrd had experienced severe psychological difficulties during a winter spent alone in the Antarctic, and experiments on sensory deprivation were revealing problems of the same sort. What could voyagers do that would not require much space? I thought programmed instruction might be the answer: the voyager could leave Earth ignorant of mathematics or history, and return an authority.

GEORGE LEONARD, a senior editor of *Look* magazine, wrote a particularly good article on teaching machines, and we became friends. His wife, Lillie, liked my books. George knew Michael Murphy of the Esalen Foundation in Big Sur, California, and I was invited there for a weekend to give a lecture and two seminars. George assured me that I would enjoy myself, and that "Utopia Now?" would be a suitable topic. But Esalen specialized in theories and practices in which I had little faith, and I was uneasy about the prospect. As I said in a note,

> Certainly I shall be a maverick. Topics to be dealt with before my visit include 1) Man in Confrontation with Nature (to be held out of doors, including an all-night vigil). 2) Movement (the dance) as a non-verbal experience of feeling. 3) Zen—the flow of life. 4) The therapeutics of self-disclosure, risk-taking, and intimacy. 5) Phenomenology and deeper levels of consciousness.
>
> What will I be doing there? I too am a body-worshipper, a self-searcher, an explorer in self-control. I too am concerned with awareness, experience, the "meaning of life." It is only the methods which differ. But what a difference!

I drove down from San Francisco with George and Lillie and learned that a massage had been reserved for me. Big Sur was known for its hot springs, and massage was one of the practices through which visitors came to know themselves. I went to a cement-block building with a porch reaching out over the surf and was soaking in a tub of very hot water when a masseuse came in and prepared a table. It was my first massage and when it was over an hour later I sat up, shook my head, and said, "It will take me a long time to get back to the real world." She pointed to the table. "This is the real world," she said. The rest of the weekend was similarly exotic according to my standards, and when I walked into my office on Monday morning my secretary looked at me and exclaimed, "*What* has happened to *you?*"

When someone at Esalen with a Polaroid camera took a picture of me with Mike Murphy, there seemed to be a misty halo around my head and, Esalen being what it was, another picture was immediately taken. Alas, the aura had gone. I went back to Esalen a year later, when, according to the catalog, I would describe the use of operant conditioning "in gaining self-knowledge and self-control and show how understanding societal and family contingencies of reinforcement could help explain the behavior of such geniuses as Ramakrishna and Mozart" —which was not exactly what I had planned to say. Esalen was moving further toward mystical forces and experiences, and though I told myself that I gained by "stretching my interest," I concluded that further visits would not be worthwhile. I did go back for a rather different meeting in San Francisco, and gained at least another example of the application of a principle of scheduling.

Allan Sherman was appearing at a nightclub called the "hungry i," and came to see me before my lecture. His psychiatrist, Andrew Salter, had told him about schedules of reinforcement, particularly "the schedule that made pigeons behave like people at Las Vegas." Sherman had applied it to a personal problem: He wanted to introduce a new style of humor, but his followers came to hear the old. He solved the problem by spacing the old stuff on a variable-ratio schedule, which he then "stretched." "It worked like magic," he said.

AT THE ANNUAL MEETING of the American Psychological Association, the new Division 25 arranged for me to debate Professor Brand Blanshard, the Yale philosopher, on the subject of consciousness. My paper was straightforward behaviorism. Where Blanshard said that "the experience of pain . . . is self-evidently not the same thing as a physical movement" because physical movement is not "dull" or "excruciating," I pointed out that pains are private events inaccessible to those who teach us to talk about them and that as a result we use words borrowed from their public causes. A sharp pain is a pain caused by a sharp object, a dull pain by a dull one; excruciating is related to crucifixion. Where Blanshard said that behaviorists were forced into the absurd position of asserting that "Hitler's hatred of the Jews contributed nothing to his orders to have them exterminated," I said there was nothing absurd about it. Hitler's persecution of the Jews *and* the private conditions he felt as hatred were the joint results of a well-documented anti-

Semitic history. If Shakespeare had represented Othello as moved to action only by feelings of jealousy, we should justly complain that he had not motivated his character. I was not questioning the existence of private events but rather their nature and their place in a behavioral account. Radical behaviorism, unlike methodological behaviorism and logical positivism, did not confine itself to public observables.

A year or two later two Norwegian philosophers, Steinar Kvale and Carl Erik Grenness, published a paper called "Skinner and Sartre: Towards a Radical Phenomenology of Behavior?" which drew more or less the same conclusions. Sartre and Merleau-Ponty rejected dualism and stressed behavior as the fundamental subject matter of psychology.

SHORTLY AFTER MY LECTURE at the Royal Society, Sir Lawrence Bragg asked me to speak at the Royal Institution. According to a plaque in the building on Albemarle Street, "In the year 1812 a ticket for the last four lectures delivered here by Sir Humphry Davy was given by a member, Mr. Dance, to an apprentice named Michael Faraday," and Faraday became the Institution's best-known lecturer.

I decided to demonstrate operant behavior. Ralph Gerbrands made some photogenic equipment, including a cumulative recorder that projected a sharp red line on a screen, and I sent it to England early enough to be used in preparing the pigeons. Leslie Reid, who had taken my graduate seminar in 1948 and was now professor of psychology at the University of Exeter, conditioned a beautiful multiple-schedule performance, and Eve Segal, who was spending the year at the Royal College of Physicians and Surgeons, prepared demonstrations of shaping and superstition. On the day before the lecture she and I set up the apparatus on Faraday's demonstration desk.

The routine at the Institution was strict. Speakers wore white tie and tails (which I rented at the famous Moss Brothers); the lecture began precisely at nine o'clock and ended precisely at ten; and the speaker went into his first sentence without being introduced and without saying "Ladies and gentlemen."

Eve and I dined with Sir Lawrence and Lady Bragg in their flat above the Institution, and at an early hour Sir Lawrence took me to

Faraday's study, where I was locked in for thirty minutes—a precaution taken since a day in the nineteenth century when a speaker disappeared before giving his lecture. I was to read some passages written by Faraday on how to give a lecture. On a shelf were a large crystal and a jar of preserved barnacles, and I asked if the latter were by any chance Darwin's. They were not; they and the crystal were to remind me to "stick to my subject like a barnacle and be crystal clear."

While I was locked in, Eve met officers of the Institution in the library, where copies of my books were on display, and then she and Lord Fleck of Saltcoats, the President, led a small procession into the amphitheater. Just before nine o'clock Sir Lawrence unlocked the study, put me in charge of two beadles who stood with me at the entrance to the hall, and went in and sat down. One beadle watched the clock through a crack in the door and, as the hour struck, threw the door open. I walked in and began my lecture.

In white tie and tails and surrounded by performing animals, I resembled the ringmaster in a circus. Fortunately the animals performed well. I put a pigeon in a space in which food was discharged every twenty seconds and then concealed it from the audience. When I uncovered it near the end of the hour, a marked superstition had developed: the pigeon was "making food come" by striking one wall of the space with its wing. In another pigeon I shaped lifting the head and pacing a figure eight. Meanwhile a beautiful cumulative curve under the multiple schedule was appearing on the screen as the hour passed.

I had prepared some terminal remarks which could be adjusted to any remaining time, and my last sentence ended immediately after the stroke of ten. Lord Fleck then came up to congratulate me, and Sir Lawrence took me back to Faraday's study and gave me a whiskey. A reception was held in the library afterward.

In *Verbal Behavior*, I had cited John Horne Tooke and his disciple, John Barclay, for their behavioristic analyses of mental and spiritual terms. I went much farther back in history when I read Dodd's *The Greeks and the Irrational* and, later, Onians's *The Origins of Western Thought*. To the early Greeks human behavior was due either to inner forces of an uncertain nature, often imparted by the gods, or to organs, particularly the heart and the lungs because of their conspicuous involvement in emotion and speech, respectively. Centuries later, improved physiological knowledge gave the brain its due recognition, and philosophers and cognitive psychologists used it in the same way. These were the mental and physiological theories I opposed. But I did not oppose them because they appealed to unobservables. Private events had to be taken into account in any successful analysis of human behavior, but they were mediators or by-products, not initiators of behavior.

Psychologists like James and Freud observed events within their own bodies called feelings or states of mind which often occurred at just the right time to seem like initiating causes. That kind of misleading information was lacking in the psychophysics of rats and pigeons. I had said much the same thing almost thirty years earlier in my "Sketch for an Epistemology." And now Garry Boring had almost come around. In an unpublished manuscript he wrote:

> In 1931 [Skinner] argued that a reflex should be regarded as a functional relation in which response is dependent upon stimulus and is nothing more. It is not a neural mechanism because no one really knows anything about the physiology of it. It is an "empty correlation" in an "empty organism" as someone, not Skinner, has said. [It was Garry who said it.] ... He is perfectly clear that in observing behavior he is observing also the sort of phenomena that others have called consciousness. "I contend that my toothache is just as physical as my typewriter, though not public, and I see no reason why an objective and operational science cannot consider the processes through which a vocabulary descriptive of a toothache is acquired and maintained." Perhaps we may leave consciousness right there, safe in the arms of Skinner, the vacuous stuffing for an empty correlation, but nevertheless all that consciousness ever was except the part that was pseudo. That is a way of preserving consciousness, not of casting it out.

I was not happy with the last sentence. I had heard it said that my 1945 paper on how we learn to talk about private events had brought sensations back into behaviorism, but I was not preserving consciousness in any form.

When I sent Percy Bridgman the first three hundred pages of the mimeographed manuscript of Science and Human Behavior, the chapter on private events in a natural science had not yet been written, and I was not surprised when he said that, although I had "got rid of the excess intellectual baggage usual in talking about behavior, . . . you never peep about how your own behavior appears to you. . . . As I have said somewhere myself in print I am not at all convinced that the private cannot be expressed without residue in terms of the public, but it at present seems clumsy in certain contexts. On the other hand, I am not sure either whether there is not an unresolvable residue. For instance, you say that statements about behavior are probability statements. Is not here a possible distinction between public and private, in that I do not recognize any haze of probability about the statements that I make about my own behavior?" But unless I had missed some way in which the verbal community can teach us to report, and hence to know, private events, our statements about them should be hazier.

Bridgman was shaken by the Adelbert Ames demonstrations. (In a typical example, a slowly rotating trapezoid is seen as flipping back and forth rather than turning around.) "They force you to see something you know is not true," he said. I wrote:

> There is nothing new about the Ames demonstrations except their rather considerable ingenuity, nor is there anything in them which helps to clarify the problems which they raise. The common experience of the after-image of movement raises the very point you mentioned last Sunday. After looking out the window of a rapidly speeding train, we find that when the train comes to a stop the landscape seems to be moving backward. No matter how much we can convince ourselves logically that it is standing still (it certainly is not getting anywhere), we cannot keep from seeing it as moving. Not only must the physiologist and psychologist eventually explain the after-image of movement, they must explain the perception of movement which is "really" there. In the long run, we shall have an account of the physical world, including moving objects and observers of moving objects, and we shall give a plausible explanation of the whole system.

When Bridgman published *The Way Things Are,* he sent me a copy with a note: "Here it is. Now do your damnedest."

Soon afterward, he began to fail, and in my last public discussion with him he forgot words, lost the thread of his remarks, and was deeply distressed. In a note I said, "He has lived too long." Later I added:

He has now remedied that defect. Yesterday, at Randolph, N.H., he shot himself. . . . The morning paper says he was found in bed, and I said to Eve that it was a shame the thing had to be so messy for those who survived. The afternoon paper said he did it in a pumphouse, as his wife was working in a garden nearby. Did he leave any comment? Did he debate it for minutes, days, months? Had he taken any special leave of his wife, to whom he was especially close? Of one thing I am sure. No matter how desperate it may have been, there was no muttered prayer, no commending himself to his maker.

A month or two later, at "a meeting of the friends of Percy Bridgman" in Memorial Church in the Harvard Yard, Gerald Holton told the story. He had left two short notes, one saying that it was too bad society insisted it be done that way and the other that it was the last day upon which he thought he would be able to do it. Later I wrote: "I failed Bridgman in his old age. It was the dilemma of the individual. He found himself shrinking—not only in submission to the state but to the more remote issues affecting the evolution of a culture—a culture which necessarily transcended *him*, what was important to him, and what he could hope to live to see."

As THE WAR in Vietnam was escalated, ambushes became a serious problem, and Dick Herrnstein taught pigeons to fly along jungle trails and stop when they found a person, their behavior reported by tiny transmitters. (The Army later asked for bids on a similar project, and returning from a meeting in Washington, Keller Breland, then only fifty, had a fatal heart attack.) In 1966 the National Aeronautics Administration asked for bids on a "preliminary design study" for an Orbiting Primate Spacecraft, in which two monkeys would remain in space for as long as one year. They would press levers to obtain food and water. A decade later, in Israel, pigeons were trained to locate military targets, and in 1979 the Coast Guard used pigeons carried beneath a helicopter to spot objects at sea. According to a technical report, "The Sea Hunt System demonstrated not only a superior [probability of detection] on the first approach of each trial; it detected the target before the flight crews."

A report in the *New York Times* in April 1966 that the Navy was training porpoises to guide torpedoes to enemy submarines drew a letter of protest from an anthropologist, Ashley Montagu, which I answered. It was admittedly a dirty trick on the porpoises, but were we not also playing dirty tricks on human animals in Vietnam? "The best way to get rid of porpoise-guided torpedoes is to get rid of submarines." The porpoises died instantly, a far less painful death than was suffered by the 35,000 porpoises we allowed to drown in nets every year in order that we could enjoy tuna fish.

On a visit to a horse farm in Lexington, Kentucky, in 1960, I said I thought horses could be induced to run faster. The roar of the grandstand as the horses came down the stretch could be used as a discriminative stimulus. With a recorded roar in the background, keeping just ahead of a simulated horse mounted on a car could be differentially reinforced. When I visited the farm five years later, I was told that a law had been passed (I am not sure whether by the state or a racing association) banning the use of anything but "conventional training practices." As I said in a note: "Almost like education."

I WAS STILL UNHAPPY about "the humanities":

> I am astonished by the superficial "scholarship" in current writing. It is almost as if people in the humanities were protecting themselves against being persuaded by the facts. E.g.—

>> Jacques Barzun: "Dr. Skinner is said to have remarked . . ." (Why did he not find out what I have remarked?)
>> Paul Goodman: "Power of operant conditioning is overestimated . . . " (a wholly inaccurate account then follows).
>> Joseph Wood Krutch: "The conditioned reflex short-circuits thought."
>> Arthur Koestler: A few fragmentary sentences about problem-solving from *Science and Human Behavior* and then, "The organisms referred to are presumably rats in Skinner Boxes and pigeons trained by selective reinforcement to perform figures of eights."
>> Thouless: Whipping a horse until it runs would be the "method of training in a world created in accordance with the principles of Professor Skinner."

Relaxed standards of scholarship were perhaps necessary if people in the humanities were to hold their readers. They attracted them in the first place by not overwhelming them with strange terms, masses of detail, and intricate analyses. A responsible attack on a scientific position needed scientific terms, and readers would be quickly lost.

A DIFFERENT ISSUE was taking the center of the cognitive stage, and I heard a good deal about it from our graduate students. Behavior was not always shaped and maintained by contingencies of reinforcement; it could be rule-governed. Cognitive psychologists were arguing that even the behavior of the rat in the box was rule-governed: The rat pressed a lever, received food, and was then more likely to press again when hungry, not because it had been conditioned, but because "it had learned (and now knew) that pressing the lever produces food." The phrase "pressing the lever produces food" was a description of the contingencies in the apparatus; somehow or other it was said to move into the head of the rat in the form of knowledge.

Human subjects did not need to be exposed to contingencies of reinforcement; they could be told what to do and thus "given the necessary knowledge." I had dealt with that issue, but not too clearly. In *Science and Human Behavior*, I called a law a "statement of a contingency of reinforcement," its effect being mediated "by complex verbal devices which cannot be fully analyzed here." I am not sure I could have analyzed them fully anywhere at the time. In "Freedom and the Control of Men," I cited three examples of "verbal mediating devices" which "emphasize or support 'contingencies of reinforcement'" and "strengthen behavior we wish to set up," but, again, I did not say how they worked, although I noted that the contingencies alone could set up the behavior without help and that they eventually took control. I went further in the analysis of priming and prompting and the programming of instruction, as well as in my treatment of instruction in *Verbal Behavior*. My paper "Operant Behavior," published in 1963, contained a fairly complete analysis.

I extended the analysis in a paper at a symposium on problem-solving at the Carnegie Institute of Technology in April 1965. Israel Goldiamond and I represented the experimental analysis of behavior, and the other speakers were specialists in information-processing and computers. I brought the issue I wanted to talk about under the rubric of problem-solving by defining a problem as a set of contingencies for which there is no immediately effective response. It can be solved either by emitting available behavior until a response appears which satisfies the contingencies (trial and error) or by analyzing the contingencies. In the second case, the problem is solved by manipulating rules. The solution is a rule constructed on the spot. Individuals also profit from rules constructed by others—for example, by taking advice, heeding warnings, observing maxims, and obeying governmental and religious laws and the laws of science. New rules derived from old describe contingencies which have never been directly experienced.

When I published the paper in *Contingencies of Reinforcement*, I added sixteen "classical distinctions" between rule-governed and contingency-shaped behavior—ranging as far as reason versus faith and truth versus belief. The evolution of verbal behavior had made possible the formulation of rules and hence the emergence of man as a rational animal. It explained, for example, why "only man knows that he will die," an event that is scarcely part of a contingency of reinforcement.

(I could also have added the distinction between causes and reasons. One behaved "for cause" after being exposed to contingencies of reinforcement and "for a reason" when the contingencies had been described. As a specialist in contingencies I found myself on the side of Erasmus, who pointed out in *The Praise of Folly* that rational behavior was all very well but that there would be nothing to be rational about if it were not for "folly." (His examples make it clear that by folly he meant behavior shaped and maintained by various positive reinforcers.) I began to translate Erasmus, but, as with La Rochefoucauld, it proved to be a perfunctory exercise and I soon stopped. I also abandoned a projected essay called "In Praise of Positive Reinforcement.")

The distinction was an old one: one could "know by acquaintance" (through direct exposure to contingencies of reinforcement) or "by description" (from having been told about the contingencies.) Polanyi and Bridgman had made the mistake of putting the bulk of science in the wrong class. Scientific behavior resulted either from direct exposure to the world as a set of contingencies of reinforcement or from descriptions of that world in the form of laws specifying what one should do to produce a given effect or what happened when one did so. The descriptions were quite impersonal. Solving a problem in mathematics intuitively—that is, without taking certain intermediate steps—was presumably contingency-shaped rather than rule-governed behavior, but the solver would then be asked for proof—that is, for rules indicating the explicit steps which would bring others to the same solution. I liked Polya's *Induction and Analogy in Mathematics,* especially because Polya, like Wittgenstein, agreed that research on animal behavior was needed to answer some of the central questions.

In 1965 the Washington School of Psychiatry asked me to give a lecture at the Walter Reed Army Medical Center. I spoke about the different ways in which cultures solved a genetic problem. At one time in the history of the species strong susceptibilities to reinforcement by sugar, salt, and other foodstuffs, sexual contact, and signs of damage to others must have had great survival value, but they were now leading to obesity and ill-health, overpopulation, and war, respectively. There were two classical solutions: the voluptuary (enjoy and so far as possible prevent unwanted consequences) and the puritanical (punish the behavior). Two other solutions were now possible. One was physiological: reduce susceptibilities with appetite and sex depressants and tranquilizers. The other was behavioral: create a world in which the harmful contingencies of reinforcement were lacking.

Critics of an operant analysis had pounced upon the Breland paper with delight. There was defection in the ranks! I did not think the issue deserved comment, but in 1965 I reviewed my position in a paper called "The Phylogeny and Ontogeny of Behavior" at a Conference on the Biological Sciences at the University of Kentucky. Contrary to the popular image of the behaviorist, I was sure that some behavior was inherited. It had been shaped through natural selection in a manner which, except for time scale, resembled the selection of behavior in the individual by operant reinforcement. Natural selection and operant conditioning raised many similar questions. How did the first instance of a bit of behavior arise? What were the sources of variations? Through what stages could complex behavior be shaped before the present consequences would follow? Social behavior presented a special problem. What would have been the survival value of the dance executed by a bee returning from a supply of food before other bees responded to it, and how could other bees have learned to respond until dances were being executed? I used the behavior of the African honey guide to show how an apparent example of innate communication could be acquired in the lifetime of the individuals.

My NOTEBOOK REPORTED my growing alienation from the department:

"Meanwhile, back at the ranch—"
I attend staff meetings in a standard mood: I must watch tradition playing itself out. A preliminary examination in Learning and Motivation is approved (with my consent) even though it raises almost no important current issue. We agree to offer an assistant professorship to a young psycholinguist (who is "really a psychologist, not a linguist"), and I quietly imagine how he and I might discuss verbal behavior—to no effect whatsoever. A training grant is in prospect which will permit the cognitive psychologists to influence the research choices of a large fraction of our graduate students.

A science of behavior moves forward in spite of all this, and I succeed in keeping out of the local picture in order to move with it (or, as I like to think, ahead of it) as effectively as possible. The energy I save from not fighting my colleagues is better spent elsewhere, but my pretending to be part of the *status quo ante* is rather absurd.

When I RECEIVED the annual request to allow my name to stand for President of the American Psychological Association, I replied:

I still feel it would be a great honor to be President . . . but so far as I know, it is still also a lot of work. It happens to be a kind of work in which I am not particularly effective, and in which I am not particularly interested. You may very well say that I am shirking a duty, but I think it ought to be left to me to decide how I can most effectively contribute to psychology in my remaining years. I don't think it would be fair to accept the honor and then refuse to contribute my share of the work of the Council.

I had discussed the matter with Kenneth Spence and Neal Miller, who were also disturbed by the way in which the elections were conducted, and Ken joined me in deciding not to run. In 1964, however, his name was on the ballot and in late July he wrote to explain why he had changed his mind: he had wanted to prove that an experimental psychologist could not be elected. I replied that I hated to disillusion him, but I was sure he would win. "My own reason for not running has always been that I was afraid I would also. I am interested in not more than five percent of the activities of the Association, and I have no inclination to become familiar with the other ninety-five." Ken proved his point; he was not elected.

I BECAME PRESIDENT of another society more or less as a matter of course. Horsley Gantt and Howard Liddell, two Americans who had worked with Pavlov, founded the Pavlovian Society, and I was invited to join. At one meeting Gantt said, "You should be President," and before long I found myself in that office, apparently appointed by the board of directors. I presided at a meeting in Princeton, and gave my Presidential Address, called "Some Responses to the Stimulus 'Pavlov,'" at another at Harvard.

In my address I recalled how Bugsy Morrill, my biology teacher at Hamilton, had shown me Pavlov's *Conditioned Reflexes*, of which I immediately bought a copy, and how I had obtained Pavlov's autograph when he spoke at the Harvard Medical School as President of the International Congress of Physiology in 1929. I retold some of Professor Cannon's amusing stories about Pavlov, who had stayed with the Cannons in a house an easy stone's throw from the William James Hall in which we were meeting. I learned from Pavlov a respect for controlled experimental conditions and for simple facts: "On December 15, 1911, at exactly 1:55 in the afternoon a dog secreted nine drops of saliva." I expressed my respect for him in a way I was sure he would have approved by listing some differences. He had really studied behavior rather than, as he supposed, the nervous system, and he had never taken the consequences of behavior into account.

At one meeting of the Society, I met John Dos Passos. He had seen Pavlov's work in Leningrad in the early twenties and had met Gantt. I had assigned his *Nineteen Nineteen* in a course on the psychology of literature at Minnesota nearly a third of a century earlier.

MY RELATION TO the field of psychology was changing. At a meeting of the American Psychological Association in New York in 1966 I wrote a note:

Last year was the first when I have not been depressed by these meetings. When I was young, it was a sort of resentment that so little attention was being paid to things I felt were important. Later, I suppose, it was resentment that so little attention was paid to *me*. Then there was my decision not to stand for president and my not-quite-successful repression of envy. That is all over. Division 25 flourishes and there are excellent papers, symposia, and sessions on operant behavior.

Earlier that year, I had confessed that I could learn something from nonoperant people:

Several times this year I have been forced to listen to lectures and papers that I would otherwise have avoided. As president of the Pavlovian Society I sat through two days of papers in which I had no real interest. It is not time wasted. I discover interests, formulations, theories I would otherwise neglect (and not always to my advantage). I have promised myself, as part of my Career Award Project, to maintain a more intimate contact with current psychology for practical reasons (to make my position felt) as well as theoretical (to be sure I am not missing anything because of a provincial position).

IBM WAS ONE of the companies exploring computer-aided instruction. Seven years before, they had terminated an agreement to develop my teaching machine. Had I a claim against them? My lawyer reviewed my files and reported that a claim "would probably be worth a bit of risk capital." I told him to go ahead, but that night, as I wrote in a note, "I woke up thinking about what it would mean. I recalled the nights of silent rage over the perfidy of Harcourt-Brace and Rheem—the endless dark monologues, the scheming, the planning—and the next morning I called it off. 'You are not paranoid enough for that kind of thing,' my lawyer said."

WILLIAM PARKER, a graduate student at MIT, occasionally dropped in to talk political science and the experimental analysis of behavior. He knew Karen Pryor, who directed Sea Life Park in Hawaii, and through Parker I invited her to come and show us some of her films, in which porpoises displayed their talents thanks to operant conditioning. Karen was looking for someone to work at the Park during the summer, and she hired Debs. During the summer Debs taught four porpoises to respond in unison in two different ways: at one underwater signal, they came out of the water in back flips; at another, they swam while slapping the water with their tails.

That September I lectured to incoming freshmen at the University of Hawaii (they had supposedly read *Walden Two* during the summer) and when I visited Sea Life Park, Debs was allowed to put all the porpoises through their acts. I swam with the porpoises, let them pull me about a bit, and with a pail of small fish and a whistle shaped a bit of behavior, just to be sure I could do it. (In a nearby marine laboratory, under contract to the Navy, porpoises were being trained to retrieve objects from the sea floor.)

FOR THE *International Encyclopedia of the Social Sciences* I wrote a piece on "The Design of Experimental Communities." I had come upon traces of an earlier design when I spent a week at Omaha Municipal University. In my lecture ("Utopia Now?") I mentioned Étienne Cabet's *Voyage en Icarie*. Cabet had brought a group of enthusiastic Frenchmen to America to set up an Icarian community on the Red River in Texas. He had died on the way, in St. Louis, but members of his group had organized several communities. After my lecture the University librarian told me that some of Cabet's books were in the basement of the library, still uncatalogued. One of the Icarian communities had founded a small college, and when it was closed, the

University had bought its library. I had hoped to find a volume or two of Diderot's *Encyclopédie*, but alas, there were only a few practical formularies and handbooks.

My own Icaria was still aborning. In 1967 the Johnson Foundation financed a fairly large conference on planning a Walden Two. It was held, appropriately, in Wingspread, a building designed by Frank Lloyd Wright in Racine, Wisconsin.

IN 1964 Julie and I met in Binghamton, New York, rented a car, and drove south along the Susquehanna River. In the small town of Halstead, we called on a cousin of my father's, a retired banker, and his wife. We went on to Susquehanna, where Julie took pictures of the house I was born in and the houses my grandparents lived in. I saw a few old friends and we went on to Windsor, New York, beyond which we found a motel where we could stay for the night. The next morning Julie told me her secret: she was pregnant. Unfortunately she miscarried, but by 1966 she was happily pregnant again. She and Ernie were still living in Pittsburgh, and Eve and I saw them when I lectured at Chatham College. Their baby would be born less than a month later. We saw our granddaughter, Lisa, for the first time through the window of an Aircrib.

At Chatham College I learned from Julie that Debs had recently come through Pittsburgh on her way to visit friends at Western College in Ohio, and that she had taken some marijuana to a friend. That night, lying in bed, I imagined a scenario: Student writes to parents, "Pot has come to Western." Shocked parents call president of college. President contacts federal authorities. Debs's apartment in Cambridge is raided. Marijuana is found, and she is charged with transporting drugs across state lines. Headline reads: PSYCHOLOGIST'S DAUGHTER CAUGHT TRAFFICKING IN DRUGS. It was two o'clock in the morning, but I called Debs. "Do you have any marijuana in your apartment?" She said she had. "If you love me," I begged, "flush it down the toilet." She did so.

Later Eve and I came into possession of one or two joints, and we tried them. I thought I detected some of its supposed effects, at least a sharpening of sensory acuity, but Eve smoked doggedly, burning her fingers with the "roaches" to no effect. A year or so later, it was a different story. We had already had a late afternoon drink when Tom Lehrer phoned to ask us to a steak cookout. He served us some rather large bowls of "grasspacho" (his own term and recipe) before moving to a table in the garden where the steaks were being grilled. I began to feel strange and told Eve that I thought we should go home. She agreed instantly and we managed to make our way back through the house to the car at the curb. I said I did not think I could drive; could she? She was not sure, but she would try. It was a new car, and she drove the eight or ten blocks to our house at less than ten miles an hour.

THE ORIGINAL PRINTING of *The Behavior of Organisms* consisted of eight hundred copies. Some were not bound until after World War II and the demand barely justified reprinting. By 1966, however, a seventh printing was needed and I wrote a special preface, in which I placed the book historically with respect to Tolman's *Purposive Behavior in Animals and Men* and Hull's *Principles of Behavior.* I could point to progress. Twenty-eight years had seen a great improvement in the control of experimental conditions and hence in the grain of the cumulative records. Much more complex arrangements of variables were being studied. I had dismissed applications to daily life by writing "Let him extrapolate who will," but applications were now underway.

None of this reached the critics. Arthur Koestler, in *The Ghost in the Machine,* summarized the current status of the experimental analysis of behavior in this way: "The record of fifty years of ratomorphic psychology is comparable in its sterile pedantry to that of scholasticism in its period of decline, when it had fallen to counting angels on pinheads—although this sounds a more attractive pastime than counting the number of bar-pressings in the box."

IN 1966 Scribner's asked me to contribute to a series of scientific memoirs. I had just written a short sketch of my life for the fifth volume of *A History of Psychology in Autobiography,* and several of my papers, particularly "A Case History in Scientific Method" and "Pigeons in a Pelican," were autobiographical. A short memoir should not take much time, and I signed a contract. The following year a psychiatrist, Dr. Robert Butler, asked me to participate in a study of creativity, and under the guidance of a clinical psychologist, Dr. Marian Sanders, I recorded ten hours of reminiscences and self-analysis. I had also written many autobiographical notes, particularly about incidents which bore upon my life as a scientist and philosopher. I began to look more closely at my life as a whole. Was I not duty-bound to give a behavioristic account of myself as a behaving organism? A year or so later I returned Scribner's advance against royalties and began to plan a larger work.

DURING World War I, at an impressionable age, I was exposed to anti-German propaganda: the Germans were Huns. During the thirties and early forties, Hitler supplied better reasons for being anti-German. In 1962 in Minnesota, a pro-German history professor challenged something I said: Had I been to Germany since the war? I said I had not and would never go. I had refused several invitations to lecture there with all expenses paid. He insisted the Nazi movement could have happened in the United States.

A German psychologist, Werner Correll, who spent a year in Boston, was interested in programmed instruction and began to translate some of my papers. When he returned to the University of Giessen he invited me to speak there, and I agreed to give my lecture "Teaching Thinking Through Programmed Instruction." Eve and I stopped off on our way from Italy to England. We spent our first night in a rather luxurious hotel in Frankfurt, and I recorded a certain amount of culture shock in a note:

> This is no doubt a culture very close to the Protestant American with which I have been identified. Strong "internalized" ethical control, great mechanical ingenuity and skill, cleanliness, etc. The awful by-product is the ease with which a centralized control can grow up and function, as under Hitler, who used every gram of German "self-control." Could the culture be changed to preserve the efficiency and prevent the misuse?
> I hate the obsequiousness of the doorman. I hate the fact that when I asked the floor maid where Room 200A was, she insisted on hurrying ahead of me to unlock the door. But I like a room cleaned as soon as we

leave it. I like fresh soap in the bathroom (versus no soap in Italy). What must I pay?

In America a comparable "internalized" ethic seems to be going under—and its demise is defended in the name of freedom. The beatnik is the symbol. He has discovered that he does not *have* to do things—and he stops doing them. What does he really gain? Temporarily, sponging on the rest of the culture, he gets along. Other people build the phonographs he listens and dances to, the motorcycles he rides; they raise the food he eats; they warm and cool the buildings he lives in. . . .

Discipline leads to order, to the production of enjoyable goods, to beauty, cleanliness, and health. How can one make sure it does not lead to 1) contempt for the undisciplined, 2) fear of those equally well disciplined in other ways (the Jews) and 3) war? I wish I knew.

I think it is possible to find out. I must spend more time clarifying the difference between intellectual speculation (of which the above is an example) and a scientific analysis. And I must press as fast as possible (time grows short) for a workable formulation based on such an analysis.

There is something good here. It should be preserved. It may lead to the future. But what future?

Correll prepared a translation of my lecture to be read simultaneously, but we agreed that I might as well read the translation myself. I was not sure I was being understood until I reached an amusing quotation from Winston Churchill and the laughter reassured me.

In 1966 Garry Boring developed myeloma. A new drug failed to save him and he became very frail. To cough was to risk cracking a rib. He was soon bedridden in the Stillman Infirmary, where I occasionally went to see him. He had lost weight, and I often found him sprawled awkwardly in tangled sheets. (He retained his sense of humor. On one occasion I told him I had just been asked to wait so that my doctor could see President Pusey first. "Let's hope it's nothing serious," he said, and winked.) Later a stroke made him slightly aphasic, and when a wrong word came out, he would cry, "Oh, why can't I speak *English!*"

I saw him for the last time in the spring of 1968. On the way to the infirmary, I resolved to deal carefully with his aphasia. I would not show the slightest sign of impatience when he blocked and above all I would not finish a sentence for him. To my great surprise he soon began to speak fluently. Evidently, he had been suffering from the self-punishment of his mistakes, exacerbated by thoughtless reactions of his listeners. He apparently knew that I had done something to help him because he called to me as I was leaving. "Fred," he said, "you are a good listener." Those were his last words to me.

I was asked to write his obituary for the necrology of the American Philosophical Society.

I MADE ONE MORE EFFORT to work with a company on teaching machines and programmed instruction. The essentials of programming, as I understood them, had emerged from my analysis of verbal behavior, which Appleton-Century-Crofts had published, and an officer of the company, Charles Walther, asked me to work with them on a "verbal arts" program that would cover handwriting, spelling, and reading. My early notes show a comprehensive plan. If children first learned to discriminate speech sounds and written patterns, good automatic reinforcement would follow as they learned to speak and write. (I thought good discrimination could be taught on the preverbal panel-pushing machine, and when Rheem decided not to produce it, Walther turned it over to a small company for development. Practical problems soon arose, and I lost interest, but Walther pressed forward, and a student of Sue Meyer Markel's, Larry Mace, developed a much more elaborate version. It taught pattern discrimination but not verbal behavior, as it was not intended to do.)

I designed a system in which acceptable behavior was reinforced by a magic-ink treatment of worksheets (a process registered as "Write and See"). For example, in the handwriting program, a properly formed letter appeared in one color but deviant parts in another. At first the students completed only parts of letters, with generous tolerances in the "Write and See." Then they moved on to whole letters.

I soon ran into problems. Teachers were not trained for, and had little time for, many of the things I thought they should do, and standard practices could not be disturbed. For example, it would be helpful if students first copied simple forms and drew strings of loops across the page while staying between parallel lines which became visible when touched, but that was dismissed as "drill." Drill was out of fashion because it had been taught punitively, but the "Write and See" technique could have provided abundant positive reinforcement and made it fun. Nevertheless, it would be misjudged and would not sell. There were also technical problems. The magic ink must be harmless and must remain invisible during a long shelf life.

A young woman, Sue Ann Friedman (later Krakower), came to Cambridge to work on the handwriting program, and early versions were tested in Cambridge and Arlington schools. A complete program was eventually sold to schools by Lyons and Carnahan, a subsidiary of the company which had purchased Appleton-Century-Crofts. It was expensive to produce and after a very short but successful trial was discontinued.

The "Write and See" process was more successful in teaching reading. For a number of years, I worked with a changing roster of people in New York and Cambridge. Appleton-Century-Crofts was eventually sold, and the "verbal arts" program was taken over by the New Century Education Corporation under Charles Walther's direction. It installed several hundred Learning Centers in schools throughout the United States, some of which I visited. Each center contained thirty or forty carrels, in which children listened to instructions from cassette recorders and wrote on worksheets treated with Write and See. The material reached from first grade through junior high. The students learned to read, almost without exception, even when they came from non-English-speaking or illiterate homes. The centers were the only practical evidence I could cite of my effect on instruction in public schools.

The Committee on Programmed Instruction was disbanded when I took up my Career Award, but the School of Education maintained an office of Programmed Instruction for a number of years. It contained a library of instructional materials, and Doug Porter was in charge.

THE PAGE-BARBOUR LECTURES were usually published by the University of Virginia, but the field was changing rapidly and I made so many changes in the manuscript that it slowly disintegrated. I signed a contract with Appleton-Century-Crofts for a different kind of book. I was tempted to call it *The New Émile,* because I greatly admired Rousseau's treatise on education, but having written *Walden Two* I was afraid it might appear that I was planning to rewrite all the classics. Instead, I called it *The Technology of Teaching.*

My notes reported slow progress. Early in 1961: "What I have to say is becoming clear, and this is especially valuable against the welter of confusion in the teaching machine field." Later that year: "This morning, nearing the end of a busy week but with a luncheon this noon with a French educator, an explanation of programming to Harvard's new committee [on instruction] this afternoon, and a weekend at the American Academy on 'freedom' still to come, I look at the manuscript and long for time and energy to work on it as I should." A year later, to Fred: "I have put in 700 clocked hours but the manuscript is still a long way from finished." A year and a half later I was still at work.

The book was to be a systematic analysis of the whole field of teaching, with thirty-three chapters. I began to draw material from it for other purposes. In 1964 "The Technology of Teaching" was the title of my lecture to the Royal Society in London. In 1965 I spoke on "Why Teachers Fail" before the Philosophy of Education Society in New York, and wrote "Reflections on a Decade of Teaching Machines" for a volume published by the National Education Association. In 1966 I spoke on "Teaching Thinking" at the Harvard Graduate School of Education, on "The Motivation of the Student" in accepting the Thorndike Award at a meeting of the American Psychological Association, on "The Creative Student" at the dedication of a new psychology and education building at Mount Holyoke College, and on "Teaching Thinking Through Programmed Instruction," first at chapters of Sigma Xi in several Rocky Mountain states, and then, in German, at Giessen.

As I became immersed in other fields, I abandoned my plan and put together a book consisting of seven of those previously published papers and four chapters on some of the other material. In April 1967 I began a note: "Yesterday I finished the *Technology of Teaching.* I felt numb. It has dominated me for years, and with increasing ferocity." When it appeared, a reviewer said that it was evidently a book thrown together quickly for the benefit of Appleton-Century-Crofts.

* * *

In May I was one of a rather large number of people who received honorary degrees in a special ceremony at the University of Chicago. Julie came, bringing Lisa, who could be left with her grandmother during the ceremonies. At breakfast Noam Chomsky came to our table to say a friendly hello, and after he left, Julie said, "You *speak* to Noam Chomsky?" A brass choir played as we marched in a procession toward the cathedral, and as we entered I saw Eve and a very proud Julie in the audience. As I later reported it:

> There were 15 or 20 recipients, from all over the world. Each recipient stood up, went forward, and stood before the president as the citation was read. I could see Julie; I knew she was bursting with pride. How in God's name could I keep from crying? I could even imagine bawling like a baby. I decided that while the citation was read, I would count the holes in the carved-wood grill back of the president. My name was near the end of the list and when my turn came I was calm enough, but tears flowed as I passed Julie on the way out. And I'm proud of it!!!

Deborah liked Western College, but she did not like a small town, and in the fall of 1965 she transferred to Boston University, sharing an apartment with a friend who was working with retarded children at the Fernald School in Waltham. Then she spent one term in Florence and graduated in 1967 with a B.A. Like many young people in the sixties, she was not sure what she wanted to do. She tried behavioral science for a year, working with Barbara Ray and Murray Sidman at Massachusetts General Hospital, and liked the work, but she was not a scientist, and in the fall of 1967 she sailed for Florence to study art.

Rather than find another summer place after leaving Monhegan, we improved our garden, put in a swimming pool, and air-conditioned the house. Although not all our friends remained in town, we had pleasant poolside parties. Episodically, at other times of the year, we spent some time away from Cambridge. In 1964 we went to Egypt, going up the Nile as far as Abu Simbel. The dam at Aswan was nearing completion, and equipment was already being assembled to move the temple to save it from the rising waters of Lake Nasser. Later that year we went to Portugal and Spain. We began to spend a few days in Vermont every October when the foliage was most beautiful.

In 1966 Eve went around the world on a guided tour and that summer we spent two weeks in the Caribbean, in Barbados and Grenada. The following year Eve took a bus tour of Ireland, interrupted when she stepped into a haw-haw and broke her foot, and in 1968 we took the first of several Swan Cruises to the Greek islands.

On the first of these I was miserably unhappy. A few weeks before, a writer named Rice had come to see me. He said that the *New York Times Magazine* had asked him to do an article on behaviorism. He knew nothing about the field, but that was editorial policy; in learning about it, he would be in the best position to present it to readers of the *Times*. I had several meetings with him, lent him books, and gave him papers to read. I arranged for him to see a baby-tender in use (at the Kellehers'), and pictures were taken. Eve and I were in Paris attending a meeting of the International Brain Research Organization when the issue, airmailed, was pushed under the door of our room on a Sunday morning. The baby-tender was on the cover.

The text was a shock. Rice had not been an apt pupil. The baby-tender was said to be "air conditioned, germ-free, and sound-proof." Direct quotations were fabricated; I was said to have complained that my daughter's school was "ruining minds." Much more painful was his portrait of me as a conceited ass. He called the article "Skinner Agrees He Is the Most Important Influence in Psychology." (He had raised the question of whether behaviorism still led the field among different kinds of psychology, and to answer him I had shown him a report in which eighty-nine department chairmen had ranked contemporary psychologists and had put me first and Neal Miller third.) He said that I regarded myself "as an event in the history of man." (He had visited my seminar in verbal behavior on a day when I was talking about individuality, and I had made the point that *everyone* was a unique event in the history of the species.) He said that when I saw how Deborah was being taught, I had asserted, "I can do better than that."

Eve and I went on to spend a week in Amalfi. We saw Herculaneum and Pompeii again and then embarked at Naples on the two-week cruise of the Greek islands with Harry and Elena Levin. Not a day passed when I did not cringe at the thought of Rice's article. What would my colleagues think of me upon hearing that I considered myself a unique event in history? When I returned to Cambridge, I wrote a not-to-be-published letter to the editors. They agreed that I had been misrepresented and offered to publish a correction if I wrote one, but a month had passed, and I thought it was too late for a letter to be of any use.

A year or two later, the *Times Magazine* published an article called "Walden Two: Three? Many More?" by Richard Todd, who reviewed the history of the book (it had then sold about 600,000 copies), summarized its arguments, and reported on a trip to Twin Oaks.

A YOUNG WRITER for the Dick Cavett Show told me that they were going to show some experiments in which teachers screamed at children to teach them to read. Would I appear on the show and comment? I said I would not, but why did they not show some good research? I put her on to Mont Wolf, Sid Bijou, and Roger Ulrich, and she made an arrangement with Roger. Would I also appear? I said that I was going to be in New York and could videotape a brief comment. When she then outlined a presentation in which I would participate throughout, I said no, but in the end we agreed on five minutes.

I reached the studio at six, walking a mile in very cold weather because there were no taxis. My name was on a billboard in front of the theatre below Ella Fitzgerald's. Backstage was bedlam. Lots of props for a Bob and Ray skit (very good). We sat in a small room watching a monitor. Ella Fitzgerald heard us called "doctor" and she said she had just met Christiaan Barnard. Walter Kerr was waiting his turn.

We did not talk with Cavett before the show, and I had not seen the set before I walked on. Cavett shook hands and got our names straight; but he had not done his homework, and the script was forgotten. He brought up Freud, and someone asked if we could prevent murder. Suddenly a piano started playing, and we disappeared from the monitor. The show had lost eight minutes and there would be only one minute left.

After the show a lone figure came out of the audience to ask about

Walden Two. I went with Roger and his two young children to Schrafft's for supper. The children were well-behaved but outgoing, too, and they took over Schrafft's.

EXCEPT FOR A SEMINAR on self-control at Indiana, based on a suggestion made in Walden Two and yielding material later used in Science and Human Behavior, I was never successful in teaching seminars. I was not skillful in getting students to talk, either with me or with each other. I talked too much myself. For my seminars at Harvard on the "advanced analysis of behavior" I usually chose fields in which I was at work—verbal behavior, the Mead-Swing lectures, teaching machines and programmed instruction. Dick Herrnstein would later report that my seminar on verbal behavior had been exciting, but in 1968 the topic was verbal behavior again, and it was a different story. Among the students were one or two linguists, a few cognitive psychologists, and a hippie who came late and whose presence in my office could be detected for some time after he left. Only one or two students did any serious work or showed any interest. I refused to threaten, and we all wasted our time.

As EARLY AS 1962 I was planning another book on "the experimental analysis of behavior and related issues," and in 1967 I published a collection of nine papers with a number of relevant notes. I thought of writing several chapters especially for the book, but changed my mind. As to something on physiology "I had had my say," on verbal behavior "I was not ready to answer Chomsky—and may never have to do it if I wait," and I was "not nearly ready for a behavioral epistemology." I called the book Contingencies of Reinforcement. More than a dozen other papers I had recently written remained uncollected, and later I added them, together with an old paper on a paradoxical color effect and two papers with Bill Morse, to a third edition of Cumulative Record, published in 1972.

*   *   *

I SPENT THE SPRING TERM of 1969 as an Overseas Fellow in Churchill College, Cambridge. We were given an attractive flat, and the college community was cordial. (So was the city. Deborah drove us up from Florence and after she returned, a traffic ticket came for her. I called at city hall and paid ten shillings. A month later the city council voted that "Professor Skinner should not be asked to pay a fine," and the ten shillings was returned.)

Two notes describe bits of our life during the term. W. H. Thorpe, the zoologist, invited me to dine in hall:

Jesus College is beautiful at any time of year but particularly so now. I was early and walked about the cloisters and gardens for fifteen minutes. Thorpe's room is reached by badly worn oak steps. The room has windows at both ends. An electric fire, and an assortment of ancient furniture, including a mechanical phonograph with the biggest horn I have ever seen. We had sherry until a bell rang. Thorpe slipped on his gown and we went to the Common Room, where I met the Master. There was another guest but Thorpe had seniority over the other host so I followed the Master into the dining room and stood by the seat at his right. A bell was rung and the students all rose from their benches. One of them took a wooden paddle and read grace from it—rather long, and of course in Latin.

We sat down to an excellent meal, the Master referring to "their chef." So far as I could see, the students ate much inferior food.

Thorpe sat on my right. We talked about animal behavior among other things, the Master joining in. Back in the Common Room, there was the usual punctilious seating of everyone in their proper places. I was still on the Master's right. I skipped coffee but had port (the only one to take it). Thorpe and I left early, and to my surprise everyone rose.

Leslie Reid asked me to speak at Exeter. Eve and I stayed with him and his wife, Dorothy, in a charming "listed" house. I reported one day of our visit:

My lecture was to be at 5:15 and I asked to have the day alone. I borrowed an FM radio and went to our third-floor room. I had intended to make a new set of notes for the lecture but Brahms's *Violin Concerto* was playing on the Third Programme and I listened instead. Then a Haydn Symphony, some Ravel, and then Strauss's *Don Juan*. During the *Don Juan* I began to meditate on the theme of my lecture, uplifted. It was now lunch time, and after lunch I took a nap, bathed, and dressed for the lecture. Went over my *old* notes and decided they would serve. At 4:15 I left with Leslie for a tea before the lecture. It was held in the hall serving as a foyer to the lecture hall, where another lecture was in progress. A crowd began to build up for mine. At 5:10 the earlier audience left and mine streamed in. The hall was filled while a long queue, mostly of students, still extended a block from the building. Hasty phone call. A change to a larger theatre. We all scrambled up a grassy slope. The lecture began a half-hour late, students sitting in the aisles and on both sides of the speaker. Words came slowly. I forced myself through the opening paragraph, then warmed up. A very responsive audience. At the end, as agreed, the chairman and I left during the applause. Greedily I listened as they applauded for several seconds after the door had closed and I was no longer there to hear it. We went almost next door to a lovely new theatre, where we had beer and snacks and, beginning at 7:30, watched a ballet. One by an Israeli composer, Ben Haim, one based on Mahler's *Kindertotenlieder*, one electronic ("Embrace Tiger and Return to Mountain"). Surprisingly, I enjoyed it all. Home for a glass of Drambuie before bed. Music had almost taken over my day. Although it was the biggest audience ever to attend a University lecture and very well received, I was not happy about it and am resolved to spend a good part of tomorrow to work up better notes before giving it again at the Royal Institute of Philosophy.

(In July I flew back to England and went again to Exeter to receive an honorary degree. The Reids were teaching summer school at Harvard that summer, and we often saw them and their delightful daughters around our swimming pool.)

I gave a lecture at Churchill College on "Behavior and Psychotherapy," which Adrian came to hear. I had given several lectures on related themes (one at the Massachusetts Mental Health Center on "Do Psychiatrists Treat Feelings?") and I should have been able to achieve some kind of closure, but I was simply not working well and, going over the manuscript eight months later, I wrote:

I am shocked at how badly written it is. I must have been very tired or wholly disorganized. There are paragraphs of the greatest confusion, usually because of a false articulation of ideas. Phony sequiturs and transitions. Great lacunae or ellipses. Sentences recast until all flow is blocked. It will take a lot of work to rescue it. I came within an ace of turning it over to Heffer's [a publisher]. It would have been a disaster.

In short, it was not a productive term. I had received invitations to speak at other universities and associations, and I thoughtlessly accepted too many of them. Looking back, I wrote:

What have I accomplished in five months? Not a line of publishable text, except for my paper on "Contingency Management in the Classroom." Perhaps fifty of these notes. Forty talks or lectures, to perhaps a total of eight or ten thousand people—students, psychologists, social scientists, a fair number of biologists, chemists, and physicists, philosophers, linguists, and a smattering of laymen. Personal contact with, say, a hundred individuals in those fields—but often only a polite exchange. A vacation from serious work. And that is about it.

And in another note:

I want to get back *into* things. I have been living superficially for almost five months. What I have said has been what I have already said, because that is what people have wanted to hear. I have changed it a bit, as audiences have altered my behavior, and that is good, but I have not dug in. I have had very few of those moments, so common in my study under my old routine, when I felt I was reaching into new territory, having ideas no one had ever had before. (And that *is* possible. English thinkers are hemmed in by intellectual hedges over which they cannot peek. They drive along familiar roads unaware of the green fields all around them. And the hedges?—logical, cognitive ways of thinking. I really *believe* it is possible to do something *essentially* different and better.) That parenthesis is a taste of what I have been missing. I long for enthusiasm, for dedication, for high seriousness.

DRIVING WITH DEBS from Florence through Switzerland and France and on to Cambridge, we had been incommunicado, and as soon as we reached Churchill College I learned that the U.S. Embassy had been trying to get in touch with me. I had received a National Science Award and would have to return to Washington to receive it. Eve would come too, at National Science Foundation expense. Had we any children they might invite? I told them about Julie and Ernie. To my surprise, Debs wanted to go too, and an invitation was negotiated. First-class tickets arrived from the American Embassy (Debs went tourist at her own expense) and we were taken to and from airports by couriers. It was only four days before Nixon's inaugural, Washington was crowded, and space was found for us at one of the less prestigious hotels.

On the morning of the ceremony, with a babysitter in charge of Lisa, we went by taxi to a White House gate and walked up a long drive between rows of guards. Eve, Debs, Julie, and Ernie went directly to the East Room, and I joined the other recipients. Vice-President Humphrey and Mrs. Johnson were there, along with former recipients of the medal. In the East Room the President made a little speech, and as each citation was read, the recipient went up, toed a marker on the carpet, turned so that the cameras could see his face, took the medal, and shook hands. Johnson fixed me with a steady eye as the citation was read. We agreed afterward that he was much more impressive than on television.

At lunch in the State Department's Franklin Room, I found a small gold lapel medal at my place. We couldn't get a taxi and walked back to the hotel. Eve and I left almost immediately for the airport. We were on American soil twenty-six hours.

A MONTH LATER I came back to the United States to give a lecture at the Guggenheim Museum. I had accepted the invitation only because Deborah urged me to do so, and I rather enjoyed my role as a presumed philistine and chose a provocative title, "Creating the Creative Artist." "Creativity" was one of the shabbiest of explanatory fictions, and it tended to be used by the least creative of people. It was said to be out of reach of the behaviorists, and would, indeed, have been so if behavior were simply a response to stimuli. But, as Darwin had shown, selection as a causal mode dispensed with a creator, and that was true of operant conditioning. Just as contingencies of survival replaced an explicit act of creation in the origin of species, so contingencies of reinforcement replaced the supposed creative acts of artist, composer, writer, or scientist. Artists could be taught to increase the likelihood that new forms of behavior would occur by generating variations which would be selected when they proved to have reinforcing consequences.

To make artists more productive, we needed a technology that would do for the visual arts what the high-fidelity phonograph had done for music. Fidelitous copies of masterpieces were no more spurious than a good recording of a symphony, and it should be as easy to put a new picture on the wall as to put new disks on a phonograph.

MANY WELL-KNOWN ETHOLOGISTS, European and American, attended a week-long Conference on Biopsychology at the American Museum of Natural History. Margaret Mead, Daniel Lehrman, and I spoke at an evening session open to the public. My paper, "A Behavioral Analysis of Value Judgments," summarized some of the points of my forthcoming *Beyond Freedom and Dignity* and had little to do with ethology (nor had a small piece of the moon which had just been put on display). Mead and Lehrman asked me to speak first, and then spent much of their time criticizing me. Since they were on the staff of the Museum and I was a guest, it was a curious move, and a British member of the Conference later expressed his surprise. At dinner before the meeting Mead and I had talked about feminism, and when I pointed out that *Walden Two* was an early feminist tract, she said, "Yes, and that's why you killed the book in the last scene. You killed the whole book in the last scene."

I DREW FARTHER AND FARTHER away from the department. No longer teaching, I had little contact with our graduate students. In 1969 a few students suggested a kind of informal seminar with no assignments or grades, and a sandwich luncheon was arranged. At other universities I usually found students excited and exciting, but at Harvard, within a month, I was writing, "It is not going well. They are not following me," and at the beginning of the spring term none of us wanted to go on.

HALFWAY THROUGH THE PERIOD of my Career Award, I wrote a note with a title borrowed from Jonathan Swift:

"WHEN I COME TO BE OLD"

Late afternoon. Physically tired from cleaning my shop. Listening to Bruckner's *Fifth*. Thinking about getting old. Yesterday I read a book in which people in their fifties were worn out, through. Some of my classmates have retired! Yet I have never worked more efficiently—if for shorter hours. Or, I *believe*, thinking more clearly. I keep saying, as I have said for five years, that I probably have five good years left. How much can I really do? [The book on freedom and dignity] is going well. The autobiography should be fun and relaxing. I have half a dozen papers lined up but none really necessary "to make my point." If I try the novel (but nothing is taking hold yet), I will need a change of scene. I am quite serious about leaving psychology to get a change, but am I ready (and able?) to take such a definite step?

MANY OF MY NOTES in the late sixties were about a novel:

The Theme: the control of human behavior and its justification. Not simply the portrayal of human bondage or tyranny; the fact of control is clear enough. It must be deliberate control, and to what end? That is the question.

Certainly the theme must be the death of the liberal—the Don Quixote of the 20th century. The personal relations arising from a knowledge of human behavior, the standards governing the use of that knowledge, the sources of those standards ("values") in the ultimate good of the individual and the species.

But what sphere of life do I know well? I have no parliament like Maurice Edelman, or theatre like Margaret Drabble, or medical profession like John Rowan Wilson [three British novelists I had recently read]. The academy has been done to death, but it is my world and it will suit. Political control? No, I loathe the politics of academe. Personal, uxorial or parental—that seems to be it.

But could I again write fiction? In 1967, disturbed by a reference to the seeming usurpation of literature by the social sciences and psychology, the British psychologist T. H. Pear had asked colleagues and friends for the names of novels written in English by fully trained psychologists during the past thirty years. In most of their replies, *Walden Two* was the only one mentioned. When he asked why, a cynical colleague said, "Scientists are traditionally detached, objective and dispassionate men. In psychology, this is often curiously interpreted to mean that what we must be detached from is life." (How curious, then, that I who was so often accused of dehumanizing man should be the only one to have written a novel.)

Whether I could still write one was in part a practical question, and I considered a rather mechanical answer. In the days when I "wanted to be a writer," I had bought a device called Plotto, with which one created a character by spinning a dial to select a profession, a field of interest, and a few traits of character.

Something of the sort could be used to create consistent and convincing characters and themes, if it were complex enough (computerized, say— and I shall not be surprised when the first computer-written story is published), and it could be defended if it supplied probes and prompts to make what an author had to say more readily available. Shakespeare had no Plotto, but he had Hollingshed, Plautus, Saxo Grammaticus, and the Ur-Hamlet—a large body of material *from which he selected themes and characters to which parts of his own behavior were relevant.*

DURING THE SIXTIES many young people were living in communes of a sort, and they were often said to be responsible for the increasing sales of *Walden Two.* They responded to Vietnam with a famous slogan: "Make love, not war," and Frazier had asked, "What is love, except another name for the use of positive reinforcement?" In my paper at the RCA laboratories I had pointed out that we were "pouring enormous quantities of positive and negative reinforcers into Vietnam, [but] no one has really identified the behavior on the part of both North and South Vietnamese that we want to change. Certainly the contingencies are about as bad as they could be." And I had contributed a few dollars to help pay for full-page advertisements in the *New York Times* in which I joined hundreds of other scholars in protesting the war and urging that it be ended.

I was never one of the gurus of the sixties, however. It was Norman O. Brown, preaching a kind of Freudian permissiveness, and Herbert Marcuse, mixing Freud and Marx, who were the apostles of the new freedom. True, an old friend later told me that his daughter had gone "off with the raggle-taggle gypsies" to live in Haight-Ashbury but after reading *Walden Two* came home and became a successful businesswoman. I would eventually be contending that *Beyond Freedom and Dignity* was a kind of watershed between the individualism of the sixties and a concern for the culture as a whole.

I was not unwilling to take credit if *Walden Two* had made a contribution. In a note written at Churchill College I said:

> In the thirties I seemed to have taken up rat-psychology just as it was dying, when social psychology was aborning. I developed a rationale: wait for fashions to change. Now I find serious writers taking Lorenz, Koestler, and their ilk seriously, as if in the forefront of knowledge, and myself paraphrased as if I *were* a coelacanth accidentally surviving from an earlier geological epoch.
>
> As a result I have been slow to recognize that I may now be the immediate future. Things have changed. I have waited. Fashions have died. Back of the student revolt I see the philosophy of *Walden Two*. The student I talked with in a pub near the University of London last week might have been Rogers. "We don't want to spend our lives working for money. We want to build a new way of life."
>
> After the destruction of the current order must come rebuilding. But the thing missing in these young people is a plan to build. They will discover it. Possibly in *Walden Two*.

Soon after giving my paper "A Science of Behavior and Human Dignity," I began to write what I called "the freedom and dignity book." The theme was central to the field of my Career Award and to behaviorism. Dignity and freedom, as personal possessions, stood in the way of a scientific treatment of the very behavior that was said to demonstrate their possession. Traditionally, freedom meant freedom from punitive control, and evidence that the environment exerted a different kind of control was resisted. So was the view that greater achievements would follow from improving the environment rather than from promoting dignity and worth as personal possessions.

I was not too sure of myself:

> It seems to me that I have arrived at new ideas in a natural sequence beginning with the inevitably awkward formulation of certain traditional matters in terms of operant behavior. The argument rests solidly on an

experimental foundation, but I am haunted by the possibility that others may have reached a similar position by a shortcut. It could have happened, but—(1) Where are these others? My critics do not seem to have found them. Whoever they are, they have had precious little effect on philosophy and social science today. (2) Even if someone else has been "right"—from my point of view, naturally!—it would be right for the wrong or irrelevant reasons. At least I have put the foundation under the house, and with this effect—that it is now possible to go on with the building.

Between 1965 and 1970 I spent nearly three thousand hours on a manuscript that eventually contained only eighty thousand words. That was more than the two minutes per word I had calculated for *The Behavior of Organisms* and *Verbal Behavior*. Passages in my notebook trace the last stages of gestation:

> The birth of *Freedom and Dignity* is drawing to a close. It has been labor in the most aversive sense. Only now am I beginning to be able to "think" it as a whole. I do not have the energy to try to reconstruct the process, although three boxes of discarded sheets are available.
> I have a dull stomachache most of the time. I do not easily digest a meal and take an anti-acid tablet after almost every one. I often wonder whether I *can* finish it. Going through it for what I hoped was the last time, I found many things that needed to be changed. Things I once emphasized have been pushed out of place. I console myself by saying that it is (a) a unique book, there is nothing now remotely like it, and (b) an *important* book, though it could be better. I find myself groaning aloud. I cannot stop but I am in some kind of physical pain.

The book was essentially complete when Eve and I went on a cruise to the Mayan ruins with Harry and Elena Levin. Rather unexpectedly, I found myself writing summaries of the chapters. I brought them back and added them to the manuscript without checking to see how accurate they were. Later I could write:

> I finished *Freedom and Dignity* two days ago. For a day I was numb, unable to think of much of anything. I began to look at notes—for the autobiography and for a possible notebook—but without getting in very deep. This morning (and I was up yesterday before five as usual) I began to see stirring within me some of the behaviors I have suppressed in order

to finish the manuscript. I am slowly discovering that I begin to think again without being punished by the delay in finishing *Freedom and Dignity*.

I resist looking at the manuscript. Just now I wanted to check something I had written about the process of selection. I looked in *Contingencies of Reinforcement* but then realized that what I wanted was in *Freedom and Dignity*. I wrote this note instead of looking for it. Am I afraid it is badly written or that I will discover mistakes or passages I could still improve? (I have just reassured myself. I have read the section, and I like it.)

And still later:

I am getting anxious. I want the book to appear. It is becoming *my* book. What will people say? There is no chance at all that it will be understood and liked by everyone. What percentage can I count on?

John Hutchens had suggested Athenaeum as a publisher. I knew Tom Wilson, who had joined the company after leaving the Harvard University Press, and sent him an abstract. He came to see me, and negotiations were under way when Murray Curtin, a Hamilton College graduate who was working for Random House and Alfred A. Knopf, dropped into my office. When I told him about *Freedom and Dignity*, he called people at Knopf and I immediately received another offer. Offers and counteroffers followed—a new experience for me. I chose Knopf not so much because of the offer but because forty-five years earlier, when I was still hoping to be a writer, Alfred A. Knopf had published the most prestigious books.

Robert Gottlieb, my editor at Knopf, was responsible for what seemed at the time to be a minor change. I was calling the book *Freedom and Dignity*, but he pointed out that there was not much left of the traditional concepts when I had finished. Was it really an appropriate title? I immediately suggested *Beyond Freedom and Dignity*, aware that I was borrowing from Nietzsche's *Beyond Good and Evil* and Freud's *Beyond the Pleasure Principle*. It seemed right, Gottlieb liked it, and we let it stand. It was probably responsible for much of the controversy about the book and quite possibly for its success. It was, however, misleading. As a scientist I did not think of people as free initiating agents to be credited with their achievements, but I was proposing changes in social practices which should make them *feel* freer than ever before and *accomplish* more.

By 1963 the hastily contrived paperback edition of *Walden Two*, though not listed in *Paperback Books in Print*, was selling well, and Macmillan added the book, reset, to its Free Press list. It began to be used as a text and when I visited other campuses students asked me about it. Some of the teachers collected statistics. About a third of the students at San Diego State College who were given their choice of books to read, "within the broad limits of psychology," chose *Walden Two*. (The runner-up was C. H. Hall's *Primer of Freudian Psychology*.) Their reports of my book ranged all the way from "When can I join?" to "an infuriating, frightening novel." At the University of Toledo, one-third of a class said that they would like to live in Walden Two.

George Kateb discussed the book in his *Utopia and Its Enemies*, a title that recalled Karl Popper's *Open Society and Its Enemies*. (I had often said that psychoanalysis had not produced a *Utopia*, but Kateb included Freud's *Civilization and Its Discontents* and Marcuse's *Eros and Civilization* among his examples.) Robert L. Stillwell used *Walden Two* to ask whether in a perfectly happy society there would be any "necessity for literature, except perhaps as some sort of idyllic diversion? If behavioral engineering makes all individuals carefree and good, a frightening number of the well-springs of literature . . . would run dry." Frazier's reassurance that "we shall never produce so satisfying a world that there will be no place for art" was vague. But if there remained a need, "would it not become possible . . . to create at will a novelist as great as, say, Cervantes or Tolstoy or Proust, a poet as great as Blake or Emily Dickinson or Rilke? . . . Literature, one feels, would be somehow cheapened and vulgarized if its creators could simply be turned out mechanically and at will. . . . Yet by what ultimate standards should the test-tube Blake or Cervantes . . . have to be inferior to the historical Blake and the historical Cervantes, who became what they were, and thus able to make their art, simply through haphazard processes? (Which is to ask: Is Frazier's 'There's no virtue in accident' a valid proposition?)"

To Chad Walsh, in *From Utopia to Nightmare*, *Walden Two* depicted "a world so repulsive that I should like to think it was intended as a dystopia. But I know it isn't. Professor Skinner is plainly out to present an ideal world from his point of view." Behaviorism was more favorable to utopian thinking than Freud, but, said Walsh, "the practical triumph of behaviorism is in selling cars and conducting propaganda."

Karl Popper (in *Of Clouds and Clocks*) called *Walden Two* a "charming and benevolent but utterly naive utopian dream of omnipotence." Several critics pointed to a common theme in *Walden Two* and the "Grand Inquisitor" chapter in Dostoevsky's *Brothers Karamazov*: Man was to be saved but at a fearful cost, the loss of his freedom. In Dostoevsky, men lost their freedom in the torture chambers of the Inquisitor; a subsequent eternity of bliss was adequate compensation for the rack. Frazier did not need to destroy freedom, because the citizens of Walden Two were not free to begin with, but by replacing punitive methods with positive reinforcement he created a blissful world in which they *felt* freer than ever before. Both the Grand Inquisitor and Frazier played God, but as wrathful and loving Gods, respectively.

Someone suggested a musical play with Walden Two as a background, but I was not sure it could be done fairly. It would be too easy to point up the failures, as in Shaw's *You Never Can Tell*, where love destroys the plan. But I could think of possible themes: a pessimist (Joseph Wood Krutch?), like the optimist in *Candide*, made ridiculous; boy loses girl and finds another who does just as well; a philosopher sings of his freedom, though obviously controlled by his past; the strength of the community tested with negative propaganda—"but I love it just the same." I decided "it would never make Broadway."

Time magazine, in an essay on "A Voyage to Utopia in the Year 1971," referred to Walden Two as a "briskly efficient community," but called Frazier a master manipulator and picked up on his comment: "I like to play God. Who wouldn't under the circumstances? After all, even Jesus Christ thought he was God!" But Frazier, like God, was not currently in control. Vacationing on St. John in the Virgin Islands where Julie and Ernie had bought a house, I wrote a note:

NON SUB HOMINE

The alternative to *sub homine* is not *sub deo* or *sub lege*. A culture is "under" the contingencies of reinforcement *it* has arranged. *Walden*

Two is, I think, unique among utopias in having no leader. Plato had his philosopher-king, St. Augustine his God, Bacon and More their legislators, and Marx and Bellamy their commissars. Rousseau's South Sea Idyll, in which the natural goodness of man needs no government, is no exception because it is *sub nihilo*.

Walden Two is a designed culture in which the designer has arranged his own demise as leader. There is no hero, no philosopher-king, no Führer, Duce, or Caudillo. That is the answer to the inevitable question—who is to control? No one. [*Beyond*] *Freedom and Dignity* explains why: Control is a form of 19th century causality, but cultures are *selected* by their consequences.

ON MARCH 4, 1970, I wrote a note:

Julie is running true to form. Her baby is due tomorrow. Last night she played viola in a performance of Beethoven's *Ninth*, and she is spending the day on her book about behavioral objectives.

Her second daughter, Justine, was born on March 7 and went into the Aircrib a few days later. The book, *Writing Worthwhile Behavioral Objectives*, was born the following year.

Later, another note:

I am listening to Brahms's *Fourth*. Julie played in it last week and came home so "turned on" that she called me. Today I got the program from her with a note. She had almost burst into tears when playing. I know how that is. Call it mawkish sentimentality, maudlin, or what you will, I'm for it. I weep at movies, when listening to music, or just thinking about someone I love. And I'm not ashamed.

FOR SOME TIME I had noticed that many of the papers in the *Journal for the Experimental Analysis of Behavior* were marked "Dedicated to B. F. Skinner in his 65th year." In November 1969 Eve and I, with Julie and Ernie, were invited to a dinner at the Harvard Club in Boston. A Festschrift was to be published early in 1970. It would contain thirty-three of these experimental papers and two articles especially written for it. In one of them Fred Keller recalled our days together in the Department of Psychology at Harvard, and in the other Charlie Ferster our work on *Schedules of Reinforcement*.

AMONG MY MOTHER'S POSSESSIONS was a hearing aid built into a temple piece of her eyeglasses. I had the temple pieces put on my own glasses and made something of a show of wearing them. My father had resisted help for his deafness; I would use an aid before I really needed one. But fiddling with the control was a nuisance and I soon gave it up. A year or so later I was writing:

> I have recalled a dream or two in which someone speaks to me without making any sound I can hear. There is nothing of the nightmare in it, although it is memorable. Recently Debbie pantomimed speaking to me as a joke, and I replied in kind. Obviously this has something to do with my growing deafness. But in general I seem to get along better than a year or two ago. Perhaps I *look* as if I am not hearing well, so that people speak up.

It was not long before I bought a cheap pocket aid with a cord going to one ear, which, again, I used rather ostentatiously. Somewhat earlier I had built my "prosthetic ears"—small flaps of plastic mounted on a stiff wire frame which I clipped on my head when listening to television or phonograph. By 1970 it was clear that I needed professional help, and I began to use a proper behind-the-ear appliance.

COGNITIVE SCIENCE, neglecting the reasons why people acted upon the information they were said to process, was a form of structuralism: behavior occurred because of the way in which it was organized. Powerful movements in anthropology and linguistics were lending support. In psychology, the commonest form was developmentalism—structure as a function of age. Structuralism was especially strong in Britain. I had discussed it with Edmund Leach, a leading exponent, when I dined in

hall at King's College, Cambridge. I thought it was politically dangerous. Some students I talked with in the King's College Bar defended
protest as a political measure. "We want to change the structure of
society," they said. And when I returned to our flat, I found some
literature from Harvard sent by a Student Committee for Structural
Change. They would destroy and rebuild.

I was appalled by the news from Harvard. As I put it in a note:

> Vietnam was a just issue, but Harvard professors were protesting
> that, too. Harvard was moving to abolish the ROTC, she was doing some-
> thing about the problem of black students, she had many liberals on her
> faculty. It was inexcusable to manhandle a gentle person like Dean Frank-
> lin Ford [who had been one of my sophomores at Minnesota]. One does
> not pilfer private papers and publish copies. It is ridiculous to call that
> the mark of a democratic society. How do I explain it? I have been asked
> that question a dozen times recently. My answer must be clear in [Be-
> yond] *Freedom and Dignity*.

I suggested an explanation in another note:

> In Green Park yesterday morning a girl sat alone picking tentatively
> at a guitar. In a subway at the eastern tip of Hyde Park a bearded youth
> stood playing a flute beautifully, a few coins in a cup at his feet. In the
> streets, especially at night, young couples move about, with their ruck-
> sacks. Otherwise they do nothing. They sit in groups in odd corners by
> monuments, or alone in doorways, or stand about in the squares. They
> have nothing to do.
>
> Is it any wonder they turn to drugs or violence? Any excuse for a
> protest or riot will suffice; there are no standard issues. They wait. But
> what *is* waiting? And what is wrong? Why is there no world to *engage*
> these people? What must be done to build such a world?
>
> I chose this theme *as a mere example* for my BBC talk; it is one I
> should carefully expand.

The BBC program was not very good. The filming was unusually
time-consuming and cumbersome. Background shots were taken in my
office at Harvard as I dictated, as I looked at apparatus (in someone
else's laboratory), as I walked away from William James Hall, as I sat
reading in our garden, as I worked in my study. At the Royal Institution
in London, at an afternoon rehearsal and again in the evening, there

were great power trucks in Albemarle Street and in the building room-fuls of equipment. Men with headphones gave cues, and films were cued in with a blue-background technique. The five people who commented on my talk had not been told what I was going to say and did not ask relevant questions.

What I said was published in the *Listener*:

> Young people stay aloof from their families or leave home altogether. They neglect the social amenities: they are poorly dressed, dirty, and rude. They take time off from school or the university, or drop out completely. They work, if at all, irregularly and indifferently, and many are content to beg for the things they need. They steal and condone stealing, call the police "pigs" and attack them when they enforce the law, desecrate flags, refuse to serve in the armed services, and sometimes defect to other countries.

But they were not misbehaving because they had disturbed personalities, were alienated or rootless, lacked purpose, or were suffering from misperceptions of the world. They were suffering from a lack of positive reinforcement. One had only to look at what happened when they went home or stayed at home, went to school or stayed in school, went to work or stayed at work. The consequences, mostly punitive, bred the escape and defection we were seeing.

THE EXPERIMENTAL ANALYSIS of behavior was criticized in many ways. It was called oversimplified. I agreed that it was simplified: all sciences start with events which can be brought under control and move on when order has been demonstrated. Those who said "oversimplified" were often not aware of what was actually being done or what lay behind behavioristic interpretations of the world at large. What we learned under experimental control might not cover all behavior, but neither did a cultured bacterium tell us everything we might want to know about the bacterium in the bloodstream. It was more than we could learn in any other way. I could only agree with an editor of the *Boston Globe* that a demonstration of superstition in the pigeon did not explain the Twenty-third Psalm.

The behavior chosen for study in the operant laboratory was said to be "so mechanical that even rats had no chance to show their higher faculties," but rats and pigeons had, in fact, done things during the past thirty years which they had never done before in the history of the species, simply because the necessary contingencies had never before arisen.

Many operant conditioners were not interested in the implications of their work and were, in that sense, narrow. The very success of the experimental method tended to select graduate students who preferred discovering new facts to formulating theories about old ones. It was also true that experimental analysts tended to cut themselves off from the rest of psychology and the other social sciences. In 1971 David L. Krantz reported that the papers in the *Journal of the Experimental Analysis of Behavior* showed a strong tendency to refer to other papers in the same journal. Murray Sidman had given one explanation of that apparent narcissism in his *Tactics*; rate of responding, taken as a measure of probability, was a special kind of fact. The time required to run through a maze or the number of errors made in learning a discrimination was a quite different kind. One could also say that, since the experimental analysis of behavior was a new field, it was not surprising that relevant papers were found in only a few journals.

GEORGE HARRIS, the enterprising editor of *Psychology Today*, bought the serial rights of *Beyond Freedom and Dignity* and published a substantial condensation in the August issue of 1971. When he asked if I would appear on the David Frost Show, I suggested William Buckley instead. He had known Buckley at Yale and would speak to him. He also talked with people at *Time* magazine, and it was not long before I was at work with their editors on a cover story. It was written in New York with material obtained in interviews with their Boston correspondent, Ruth Galvin. Just before the issue was put to bed, Galvin called to check a fact: Was I still doing isometric exercises? I said I was not, but where had they heard about that? To her great regret, she said, they were using material from the Rice article in the *New York Times Sunday Magazine*. I said I hoped they were not using the what-a-big-boy-am-I motif. "They aren't making you out exactly modest," she said. The next morning I wrote a note: "So the story persists, as I was sure it would. I shall suffer. But this morning at six at my desk I have *never* been clearer-headed. I have *never* 'thought bigger thoughts.' What a productive life I should have had if I had been like this steadily for fifty years!"

The cover story was scheduled for September 6, to be on the stands during the convention of the American Psychological Association, but labor's reaction to Nixon was suddenly news, and George Meany bumped me off the cover for that week. The issue of September 13 went to Edmund Muskie, who was beginning a thirty-state tour, evidently with help from *Time*. That left September 20 for me. But on Saturday, September 18, Khrushchev died. *Time* went ahead with my story, closing the issue around midnight, but all day Sunday the possibility of a change was explored. It would be too late to take me off the cover in the advertisement in the *New York Times* on Monday, but could Khrushchev be on the issue itself? At 10:30 Sunday evening the decision was made: No change was possible; I was left in possession. Above my picture were the ominous words: "B. F. Skinner says we can't afford freedom."

The first reviews of *Beyond Freedom and Dignity* were mixed, but on September 22, as I was leaving a hotel in Pittsburgh for the airport, I was called to the phone. It was Eve, who wanted to read me a review in the *New York Times* by Christopher Lehmann-Haupt. It included a sentence of which the Knopf advertising people made great use: "If you plan to read only one book this year, this is probably the one you should choose." But Lehmann-Haupt had reservations, one being my failure to mention Chomsky.

Other reviews were openly hostile and it seemed as if, when reviewers read each other, they became more aggressive. One review was illustrated by a picture of a rat bearing my face. (It was some consolation that in an issue of the Sunday *Times* with my head on a pigeon, Darwin's head also appeared on a monkey.)

One wrote that my "approach . . . may strike many of my own generation as quite familiar and sensible. To our children, now of college age or just beyond, it may seem . . . like a voice from another age, as bygone in its way as Vitalism or the Divine Right of Kings. Something new, they will say, is still needed." But young people flocked to hear me and were almost always enthusiastic. When I spoke at Brandeis

University the hall was jammed, and afterward the professor who introduced me expressed his surprise that the questions were not hostile. "I thought they'd go after you," he said. But the only mildly hostile comments came from him and one or two other older people. I recorded a few other instances of my young audiences. At the University of Maryland Baltimore County, "the auditorium was so jammed that two university guards were needed to get me onto the platform." At another lecture there was "a huge crowd, many coming long distances by bus and several hundred unable to get in. Violent applause when I came on the stage. Prolonged applause at the end. I had to take bows, which I do with embarrassment."

Jane Friedman, the promotion director at Knopf, asked me whether I would go on other shows, and shortly after saying yes I found myself with a schedule of nearly forty radio and television commitments. Some were entertainment—David Frost, Dick Cavett, Mike Douglas—but others were serious—not only William Buckley but Martin Agronsky and Edwin Newman. (Buckley's show rather fizzled. He had asked Donald MacKay, a physicist whom I had met at Keele University in England in 1969, to appear with me. MacKay was a devout Christian—a Presbyterian, I gathered—and spent much of the hour explaining God's plan for the world.)

Beyond Freedom and Dignity soon appeared on the *New York Times* best-seller list and stayed there for twenty weeks. I became for the moment an embarrassed VIP. I recorded a few instances:

> At the Fantasia with Julie, the headwaitress came to our table. "Are you Professor Skinner?" she said. "One of the girls recognized you." At Anthony's Pier Four restaurant in Boston, Anthony himself came to our table and told me to be sure to ask for him when I came again so that he could give us a good table. Someone stopped me on the street. "I saw you on television," he said, and walked on. At the bank a very old man came up to me. "Professor Skinner?" he said. "I want to congratulate you." In the Dreyfus [Restaurant], as I was waiting for a table, a girl asked if I were Professor Skinner and then turned to three young girls who were with her and exclaimed: "Now you have met a celebrity!"

In London for Christmas I read four of the five reviews of *Beyond Freedom and Dignity* in the London papers and wrote a comment:

They are all quite negative. They uniformly ignore the basic analysis of behavior and its current technological uses. They call me naive, quaint, hollow, etc., because of the "simplicity" of my discussion. They do not get the point of what will eventually lead to better cultural design, asking instead, "Who is to control?" They all miss the nature of control by the environment.

I am unhappy about this, as I am unhappy when a gadget I make or repair doesn't work. I have not been successful. But I am by no means any the less convinced that I am right. "Disheartened" might be close, because if the relatively elementary arguments in *Beyond Freedom and Dignity* are not understood, how long will it be before I can make clear the kinds of points which turn up these days in my notebooks?

I considered some objective evidence of my reaction.

When we first reached London I slept well. After two or three days I decided to look at the criticisms I had brought along and that night I slept badly. I worked again the next day and slept badly, then I put it all aside until after Christmas and slept well. Tonight will be the test: I learned today that Chomsky has reviewed my book for the *New York Review*, as I knew he would. How shall I sleep tonight?

The next day I wrote "Well," but I could not dismiss Chomsky's attack. In a review in the Paris *Herald Tribune*, reprinted from the *New York Times*, Lehmann-Haupt had recanted. Possibly my book was the one you should choose if you planned to read only one book this year, but Chomsky's was the review you should read. When I returned to America, Chomsky's "Case Against B. F. Skinner" was being widely discussed. It opened with a characteristic gambit: A century ago anthropologists made racist statements about the Chinese; the reader was now asked to consider a generalized version of that pseudo-science. I listed some samples of misreadings:

"When Skinner tells us that a fascinating hobby is 'reinforcing,' he is surely not claiming that the behavior that leads to indulging in this hobby will be increased in probability." That is precisely what I did claim. "Rather he means that we enjoy the hobby." That is precisely what I did not mean; the bodily condition felt as enjoyment was at best a by-product of positive reinforcement.

When I pointed out that "a state which converts all its citizens into spies" or a religion which alludes to an "all-seeing God" makes escape from the punisher practically impossible "because there is no visible supervision," Chomsky had me advocating such a state and hence unable to avoid the conclusion that a concentration camp "with the gas ovens smoking in the distance" would be "an almost perfect world."

When I noted that in large groups "the control of the population as a whole must be delegated to specialists—to police, priests, owners, teachers, therapists," Chomsky had me approving such an arrangement, although I said I preferred small groups where face-to-face censure and commendation could take over the same functions. (Richard Sennett, in reviewing my book for the New York Times Sunday Book Review, made the same mistake, and when I complained in a letter to the editor, he replied simply by citing the page reference.)

Chomsky portrayed me as a man who wants to control people—a dictator, a fascist, a totalitarian ruler. That was a misunderstanding of all my work as well as of Beyond Freedom and Dignity. People were controlled by their physical and social environments, but that did not mean that any person should control them. The task of the designer of a culture was to create a controlling environment. That environment would include people, but as friends, acquaintances, or strangers, not as would-be controllers. The designer of a better social environment was no more in control of the possibly millions of people who would live in it than the man who designs a governor for a steam engine is henceforth in control of the millions of steam engines built with governors.

The New York Review of Books put what it called "Chomsky's devastating review" at the top of a list to show nonsubscribers what they had missed, and Chomsky included it in his For Reasons of State, published two years later. An article called "America's Great Intellectual Prizefight," in the London Times in February 1972, began with a reasonable appraisal of Chomsky's review of Verbal Behavior and called the difference between us on other issues "fundamental and incapable of resolution."

I DEVELOPED AN EXAMPLE of the central argument of Beyond Freedom and Dignity in a lecture at the Poetry Center in New York. I had accepted the invitation, as at the Guggenheim Museum, as a presumed philistine, and when the lecture was published in the *Saturday Review of Literature*, that role was confirmed by many of the letters the editor received. *Why* had he published it?

I began with the story of Chomsky's criticism of *Verbal Behavior* and added a postscript. *Newsweek* had carried our disagreement back to the seventeenth century. I was said to be a modern disciple of John Locke, for whom the mind began as a *tabula rasa*, while Chomsky was said to represent Descartes. When *Newsweek* suggested that the battle was going my way, the reaction of the generative grammarians was so violent that four pro-Chomsky letters were published, all of them showing standard misunderstandings: I was a stimulus-response psychologist, I thought people were very much like pigeons, and so on. One at least had a touch of wit: *Newsweek* was advised to "lock up Skinner and give Chomsky *Descartes blanche*." But I pointed out that Chomsky could not use a *carte blanche*, it was too much like a *tabula rasa*.

I presented my limited credentials by reading the poem I had published in *Encounter*, together with a parodied exegesis, and then argued that "having" a poem was like having a baby. We say it is the mother's baby, but she was not responsible for any of its genetic features. She gave it some of its genes, but she got those from her own parents. Similarly, poets receive what they put into their poems from their verbal and nonverbal histories. Samuel Butler had said that a hen was only an egg's way of making another egg, and modern evolutionary and genetic theory seemed to bear him out. As a geneticist later put it, "An organism is the servant of the gene." Similarly, a poet is only a literary tradition's way of making more of a literary tradition. The individual is a locus, not a creative agent.

BECAUSE I OBJECTED so violently to the war in Vietnam, I asked myself:

Is it inconsistent of me to take money from a government with which I disagree? Thoreau would have chucked it. But I do not disagree with all the things the government is doing, and I think it is good that it will continue to finance a dissenter. (Even if, no doubt, because no one knows it is doing so. When will some administration bloodhound begin to look into the government's grants to its critics?)

Shortly after the publication of *Beyond Freedom and Dignity* I had my answer. Congressman Cornelius E. Gallagher, speaking on the floor of the House, questioned the propriety of my NIMH Career Award. Should the government subsidize a person who is "advancing ideas which threaten the future of our system of government by denigrating the American traditions of individualism, human dignity and self-reliance?" Gallagher was proposing that Congress create a "Committee on Privacy, Human Values and Democratic Institutions." The Committee would be "designed to deal specifically with the type of threats to our Congress and our Constituents which are contained in the thoughts of B. F. Skinner." In particular it would limit the use of wiretapping by government investigators, an issue in which, it soon appeared, Gallagher had a personal stake: his name came up in a tap on the phone of a gangster named Joe Vicarelli, and within a year he was serving a jail sentence for nonpayment of income taxes. Gallagher also had read into the *Congressional Record* an attack on brain surgery by a psychiatrist, Dr. Peter Breggin, in which I came under fire as representing "the greatest future threat that we are going to face for our traditional American values."

Another critic of *Beyond Freedom and Dignity*, higher in the government, was also only briefly there. At a meeting of the Illinois Agricultural Association, Vice-President Spiro Agnew said that my book advocated " 'conditioning' people to conform to a bizarre view of what society should be like—a utopia to be achieved through what the author calls a 'technology of behavior.' . . . Dr. Skinner holds, in effect, that man has neither soul nor intellect and is completely a creature of his environment. If you can control man's environment, he theorizes, you can control his actions and his thoughts. . . . Skinner attacks the very precepts on which our society is based, saying that 'Life, Liberty and the pursuit of happiness' were once valid goals but have no place in 20th Century America or in the creation of a new culture such as he proposes." Agnew quoted Herbert Hoover on individualism in American life.

My notebook records other reactions:

> Listening to the last part of *Das Rheingold* I read a few pages of *Beyond Freedom and Dignity* and for the very first time felt resentment at my critics. It is a good book—a great book, I believe. Every sentence is as clear and honest as I could make it. There are no appeals to emotion.

No rhetoric. No padding. No false support, such as mathematizing, model-building, physiologizing, or brain analogies. I found myself weeping slightly, not in anger at the vicious criticism but in gratitude for having been able to write the book. That is something granted to very few men. (But why the metaphor of "granted"? By whom? Something only a few men succeed in doing—to be reinforced by the result. I have held a winning ticket.)

On another occasion:

I am overwhelmed by one ruthless fact: *I can't stop now*. My dream of a more relaxed intellectual life, of exploring my own history in an autobiography, of writing a novel, is quite shattered. Too much remains to be done. The extraordinary misunderstanding shown by the critics of *Beyond Freedom and Dignity* demands rectification—not by rewriting the book (it is not the book they misunderstand) but by presenting the operant position at a more popular level. And, alas, I mean popular. The quality of writing in criticisms of *Beyond Freedom and Dignity* is shockingly low. Scholarship is dead (was it ever really much alive?).

I WAS ONE OF A NUMBER of people who received awards from the Joseph P. Kennedy, Jr., Foundation for Mental Retardation at a meeting in the new Kennedy Center in Washington. (It was the first time the acoustic properties of the auditorium could be tested with the seats filled, and the engineers asked the audience to be quiet while they fired a cannon on the stage.) David Frost was master of ceremonies, Edward Kennedy spoke, Jean Kennedy played something of Debussy's, and, rather unfairly I thought, Loren Hollander, a concert pianist, had also been asked to play. Ethel Kennedy gave me my trophy—a crystal vase, etched with an angel holding a baby, mounted on a very heavy silver base.

It appeared that, with *Beyond Freedom and Dignity* under attack, the Foundation had had second thoughts. My citation or "tribute," written by Norman Cousins, given to me afterwards replete with italics, read in part:

. . . he must be feeling these days like a man who goes for a quiet stroll down a country lane, and ends up stepping into a wasp's nest. But arguments about theory to one side, the happy fact is that Dr. Skinner has developed, *on the purely practical level,* teaching and therapeutic methods that have proved extraordinarily effective in work with mentally retarded persons. It is for these admirable *practical* accomplishments in the fight against mental retardation that we today honor Dr. B. F. Skinner.

The heavy silver base of the trophy was obviously expensive, and it was said that Mother Teresa, who also received one, immediately sold it to support her hospitals in India. After I had gone to bed, I recalled that there was an envelope in the vase and got up to open it. It contained a check for $15,000.

The next day I gave a paper called "Compassion and Ethics in the Care of Retarded Persons." It was a theme I had developed at the dedication of the Eunice Kennedy Shriver Center at the Fernald School in Waltham, Massachusetts. We did not care for others because we had compassion; we cared (and felt the condition of our bodies that we called compassion) because of the genetic history of our species and a personal history characteristic of our culture. We might do for others what we ourselves had found reinforcing, but more often we helped in order to avoid the aversive consequences of not helping. It was significant that the five kinds of people for whom "compassion" was most often lacking—small children, the chronically ill, the aged, the psychotic and retarded, and prisoners—were powerless to retaliate when mistreated. Treatment could be made more compassionate and no more costly if we recognized the fortunate by-products of positive reinforcement.

IN FEBRUARY 1970 I wrote one of my "stock-taking" notes:

Sunday morning. Eve is in London and I sit here listening to the last part of *Götterdämmerung.* A mood of some sublimity.

What am I to do with my next five years? (Every year I tell myself I have five good years left.) I am in excellent health. No aches or pains. A slight retinitis in my left eye has threatened but seems to be responding to a form of cortisone. Stocks are down but my royalties go up. I do not need money. Eve, Julie, Debs, and Lisa will be well provided for. My influence spreads. *Walden Two* is among the ten best sellers in campus bookstores. There is a growing high-level recognition of my position. I am working on an important, but terribly difficult, book [it was *Beyond Freedom and Dignity*].

What is there left to do?

1) The *Autobiography*. At the moment I prefer to keep it a scientific memoir. Only as much of my private life as seems to bear on my work. This will free me for a more personal "Confession" later, possibly in fictional form.

2) A novel. I really want to do it. Experiment with recollections à la Proust. With themes related to my work. A behavioral tour-de-force—a non-mentalistic technique?

(Visiting a friend on the coast near New Bedford, I had gone for an early-morning walk along the shore, come back, and written a note:

An occasional cry of a seagull marks the silence of this morning. (And just now a distant car as it was started and driven off beyond earshot.) Nothing remains but my tinnitus with its rhythmic pulse at sixty-eight beats per minute. I feel a nonscientific repertoire stirring. I think I could—in 1974—close up shop as a psychologist and turn (at long last, my work done, *return*) to literature. Yesterday, sorting autobiographical materials, I looked at my early fiction. Frost was not entirely wrong. But was T. H. Pear right? Has objectivity—horrid word—destroyed, not my imagination or creativity, but my capacity to look at things in ways which induce me to act and feel?)

My "stock-taking" continued:

3) A critique of current mentalists, showing the trouble they get into —and cause.

4) Specific analyses. Philosophers and "intentions." Linguists and "rules." It is all there in my books right now. This would be propaganda —spreading the faith.

5) Something new: social science, epistemology?

When the manuscript of *Beyond Freedom and Dignity* went off to the publisher, I had another look at the notes in the open file beside my desk. What was to be done with them? Some could go into the autobiography; others into a book on intellectual self management called *How to Think*. Still others could go into a *Notebook* ("if for psychologists, it can be technical"). I also needed to write a defense of the experimental analysis of behavior ("sharp criticism of much current stuff"), and there would be a book I called *The Revolution* ("clarifying the death of the man in the middle, free of the other issues in *Beyond Freedom and Dignity*").

Within the year emphasis had changed, and I was writing three books in troika style. The autobiography was an easy assignment, and I permitted myself only one hour a day on it. Discovering how little the critics understood of my current position, I was writing a *Primer of Behaviorism*.

For forty years I have been arguing behaviorism, the possibility of a scientific analysis of behavior, and the implications of such a science. I have made my contribution to a small group of "true believers," but I have not got through to a large segment of psychologists, to biologists, to social scientists, including economists and political scientists, or to linguists and philosophers. Further exposition is needed.

And a new issue had emerged: why was so little being done about the dangers threatening the human species? Through what behavioral processes could we take the future into account? But as criticism of *Beyond Freedom and Dignity* continued to reveal how badly the behavioristic position was misunderstood, I decided to finish the *Primer* first:

It is turning out to be an intellectual adventure, far from saying over again what I have already said. [A sentence by Jorge Luís Borges had obsessed me: "What can I do at seventy but plagiarize myself?"] It is an important step in the direction set by *Beyond Freedom and Dignity*. Fantastic misunderstandings to be corrected if we are to get on with solving our problems. It therefore ranks ahead of the other three projects. I now wonder whether I shall ever feel that I can afford the time to do the autobiography.

ON MONHEGAN, Eve and I had seen a good deal of Zero and Kate Mostel. Zero was at heart an artist. He had an extensive collection of pre-Columbian art, and throughout his career as a nightclub entertainer and then on the stage and in the movies he kept a studio in New York. I sat for an oil portrait which, alas, he never finished. In June 1971 he called to say that he was taking over the Dick Cavett show for two nights and wanted me to be a guest. I remembered our good discussions and said yes.

Eve and I watched the show the first night, and it was clear that Zero had had a very different kind of show in mind. He mugged incessantly, referred to Cavett as a "little pipsqueak," made fun of the cameramen, the director, and the commercials, and pawed his guests. (In a discussion of *Portnoy's Complaint*, the word "masturbation" was blipped out.) At the end it was announced that the "famous psychologist B. F. Skinner" would be a guest the following night.

What was I to do? I could not go on the program, but if I called Zero and told him why, he would have no explanation to give the producers or the audience. We decided that Eve should call the show the next morning and say that I was down with the flu. After the second show had been videotaped, Zero called to ask how I was, and I said I still had a slight fever. We were both playing a game. He said that young people in the gallery had cheered the announcement that I would be a guest and he still wanted to do a show with me. "A serious one," he said.

In 1970 a small lesion in the retina of my left eye pulled the macula slightly out of place. I could no longer read with that eye, and I covered part of the lens in my glasses with a surface which fogged the image. A year later I found that I had developed glaucoma in my right eye and had lost the use of a large part of the field. The doctor was not sure it could be arrested. I could probably finish my *Primer of Behaviorism*, but beyond that he was not sure. I might have to dictate the autobiography. I wrote a note:

> I look across the room at all the books I shall never read again. I suppose I have never been a great reader, but I shall never be one now. What is one to do? Hire a reader? But how does one know in advance when one wants to be read to? Have a reader tape a book? The recordings for the blind are almost certainly not the books I want to have read to me.

No, the trick is to change my style of life. I am driven back upon *myself*.

I planned to return to the study of music, and I bought about 150 monaural records: the complete keyboard music of Bach, the organ works of Bach, the piano quartets of Beethoven and Mozart, the symphonies of Haydn, and so on. Fortunately, the glaucoma was brought under control. For a time I found the large-type books in the Cambridge Public Library helpful, and I bought a large lens mounted on an arm which could be held in front of a page, but slowly I learned to use my remaining vision efficiently.

With only one good eye, I misjudged stairs, curbs, and piles of snow, and I bought a cane. I had always liked the feel of a cane, and now I had a good excuse for carrying one. A less fortunate consequence was that I could no longer play the piano. I had never been able to memorize music or read music without looking at my hands, and with only part of one eye I performed wretchedly. I had also never been able to improvise, but I found to my surprise that, if I adopted just the right stage of relaxation, my hands would move pleasantly from chord to chord, as they had moved during more than fifty years of reading music; Eve said it sounded like cocktail-lounge music. But there was little variety, and I found myself always in the key of E-flat Major. We had the piano refurbished and sent it to Julie. Later I gave my electric organ to a country day school. I kept the clavichord, by now almost a true antique.

AT THE HEIGHT of the promotion of *Beyond Freedom and Dignity*, I developed symptoms of a more serious sort—a pain in my chest brought on by even light exercise. As I reported in a note:

> I am quite possibly risking my life by meeting certain obligations between now and next Sunday. I have developed symptoms of coronary trouble—anginal pain. Yet I must—(a) fly tonight to Dayton for a morning TV show (Jane: "It's a big show; they are counting on you"), (b) fly to New York on Wednesday for a TV show in the afternoon and my lecture at the Poetry Center in the evening (Sold out—800 tickets at $3 each), (c) record two shows on Thursday, (d) speak to 600 high-school

students in Washington on Friday, (e) take part in the Kennedy Foundation ceremony on Saturday. It is too much. Will my sense of responsibility, my Protestant Ethic, kill me?

A week later, another note:

Well, it is official. I took an exercise EKG today with Dr. Gorlin and, as he put it, I definitely have "rusty pipes." I asked him to be frank. One third of the people in my condition will be dead in five years, he said. I must lead a less active life. I must let it be known, since I cannot otherwise explain my inactivity. I will check with him in a month to see how the thing is changing.

I almost broke down when I discussed telling Julie and Deborah, but I recovered. I shall miss seeing what becomes of Lisa and Justine. But I shall probably have time to finish my work—with careful planning—unless, of course, things get worse quickly. At least I shall not have to solve the problem of a deteriorating old age.

On the following day, another note:

With Eve away [she was on a safari in Africa] I am feeling very much alone with this thing. Last night, after debating with myself for an hour, I called Julie and told her. She was wonderful, as I knew she would be, and is coming here Saturday. I want to explain about a lot of things—the stuff in the basement, the material in my office, and so on.

It is strange how easily one can forget such an important thing. Not once during two hours of recording at WBZ-TV did I remember that I have angina. Just now I was watching television. Then I went into the living room and only then, after more than an hour, as I looked out upon our garden, did I suddenly reflect that I might not see many more leaf-strewn autumn lawns.

Julie came and we went through my files and various things in the basement—a dozen assorted teaching machines, the nose of the Pelican missile, a box of awards and medals. We labeled some of them and tape-recorded descriptions and histories.

Julie refused to accept the doctor's opinion. I should simply stop eating fats ("But the doctor says it is too late") and reduce my weight by ten percent. When Eve returned, she put a very strict routine into effect. I walked more slowly to my office and avoided all strenuous exercise. I reduced my weight from 160 to 144 pounds and kept it there. It was not long before my commitments on the book came to an end, and with them the symptoms of angina.

I WAS BECOMING less and less a psychologist, and I began to wonder whether meetings of the American Psychological Association were worthwhile:

> I see friends I have not seen for a long time and whom I should otherwise not see at all. I see books and apparatus—but scarcely any of which I shall ever read or use. People come up and speak to me. (And I hear people whispering and see them pointing at me. The young woman who gave me my registration badge seemed amazed to see me in the flesh. "The Box?" she said.) I listen to a few papers which I would otherwise not read. And that is about all. I am bored. Travel is itself boring. Accommodations are bad. I must remember all this. It is too easy to recall the few satisfying moments.

The Association itself was changing. Psychology as a profession, particularly clinical psychology, was taking over. The Psychonomic Society, founded in protest, had weakened the scientific sessions. Psychologists were turning more and more to social problems. George Miller had proposed that we solve them by "giving psychology away," but I did not think that cognitive psychology had much to give. Other solutions were a kind of laymanship, garnished with a few technical terms but otherwise without benefit of science. The only exception was the experimental analysis of behavior.

In spite of all this, I continued to go to meetings and was happy to accept the Gold Medal of the American Psychological Foundation.

AN OLD GHOST walked again, as I recorded in a note:

> A book called *The Hundred Most Important People Today* has an article on me. It begins on the theme of the Rice article in the *New York Times*: My modesty is underwhelming. I suppose that article will be in

all the files—the "morgues"—from now on. I can see my obituary in the *Times*, and I shall not be able to correct it. But would I be in this book if the article had not been written? Its title—"Skinner Agrees He Is the Most Influential Psychologist"—would certainly have brought me to the attention of anyone writing such a book.

When the author, Donald Robinson, came to see me, I told him about Rice. He could not stop apologizing, although I kept telling him it was not his fault.

IN SPITE OF THE PROTESTS of many people, among them friends, I continued to speak of the control of human behavior. To say "influence" instead of "control" was to avoid the problem by concealing it. Nothing was gained by calling for "a better utilization of human resources" unless one was willing to specify how they were to be utilized. Another softer word was "modify," and "behavior modification" became the popular expression, although strictly speaking it did not cover the shaping of new behavior or its maintenance in strength.

The "control of behavior" was often misunderstood because it immediately suggested punishment, which had long been the measure of choice. A newspaper article citing my experiment on superstition replaced the intermittent delivery of food with intermittent threats. A speaker with whom I shared the platform at the Kennedy symposium on mental retardation described a particularly punitive state of affairs and then turned to me and said, "I suppose that is the kind of thing Professor Skinner would like to see." One of our graduate students, John Schneider, was hoping to work in a home for the blind in Boston. Blind children were often treated as feebleminded just because their teachers found it hard to work with them, and John hoped to devise better instructional programs. The institution applied for a grant from the Department of Health, Education, and Welfare, and all went well until it was discovered that John had worked with me. The application was then turned down with the comment, "We don't want him putting babies in boxes and shocking them."

In 1971 the Superintendent of Schools in Dallas, Texas, invited me to see some classroom experiments and to talk to his school board and principals. When he asked, "What about punishment?" I said I was against it, but that we could not abandon it until something was ready to be put in its place. "That's what we think!" he said, with satisfaction. Later I learned that he had meant corporal punishment. Dallas teachers were spanking their students, and spanking was a political issue. Late one night I received a phone call from a tearful woman who said that some of the children had been spanked so viciously that they were hospitalized. How could I possibly approve? And when the father of a boy who had been spanked sued the school and the Superintendent testified that "the Board's policy is consistent with that of Dr. B. F. Skinner of Harvard," I sent a correction to the Dallas papers. I also wrote to the editor of *Educational Leadership*, which had reported that the Board had arrived at their policy "after personal consultation with Dr. Skinner, who believes that corporal punishment is helpful to some children." Still later I offered to testify when the Supreme Court agreed to hear arguments of parents in Dade County, Florida, who complained that their children had needed medical treatment after being paddled.

And now Pavlovian conditioning was making punishment scientific. The child-molester who was shocked or made nauseous when looking at pictures of attractive children was essentially being punished for doing so. The practice worked, as it had worked throughout the ages, but positive reinforcement could work as well, with fewer unhappy side effects. For example, where most students still studied to avoid the consequences of not studying, programmed instruction could maximize the positively reinforcing consequences of good work. Where most employees worked, not for the weekly paycheck, but to avoid losing it when discharged, positive incentive systems could work better for both employees and employers. Where government was still defined as the power to punish, and the Jewish and Christian God was a god of wrath as well as love, the behavior needed to maintain a community like Walden Two could be positively reinforced. Operant techniques were also examples of the move away from punishment in psychotherapy. (It was not much help when the superintendent of a hospital for the retarded alluded to more humane practices by saying that the profoundly retarded functioned "below what we might call an animal level," but that we were on the way to taming "their unpredictable behavior with the techniques of the Roman circus: the trainer with his operant conditioning techniques.")

Pavlovian conditioning and extinction were more appropriately used to correct the by-products of punishment. As Rousseau had pointed out in *Émile* more than two hundred years before, a baby will not cry when plunged into cold water if one begins with warm water and reduces the temperature one degree a day, nor will a child be frightened by a grotesque mask if one begins with a pleasant mask and changes it slightly from day to day until it becomes grotesque. The children in Walden Two were freed from envy and other destructive emotions in much the same way, and I had argued in Natural Sciences 114 that the patient in psychoanalysis undergoes a similar change in discovering that it is possible to talk about tabooed subjects without being punished.

Ironically, applications of operant conditioning were attacked precisely because they replaced punishment. That was a major point in *Beyond Freedom and Dignity*, and no critic seemed to disagree. When a culture suppresses bad behavior by punishing it, any surviving good behavior can be credited to an inner goodness; when, instead, the culture shapes and maintains good behavior with positive contingencies, the goodness must be credited to the culture. The attack on automatic goodness, in the defense of freedom and dignity, perpetuated social measures under which people felt least free and were least achieving.

Behavior modification became more threatening when advances in neurology suggested that behavior could be "modified" by implanting electrodes or infusing drugs into the brain, or by cutting away parts of the brain. (I appeared before Senator Edward Kennedy in one hearing on brain surgery.) The public was frightened, and all forms of behavior modification began to be proscribed. When an article on these more violent forms of behavior modification appeared in a Netherlands newspaper, someone wrote ". . . if you are the same doctor as the one who uses the so-called Skinner boxes, which is of the utmost criminality, you must reckon that your life will be made impossible to live after today."

A brilliant film, A Clockwork Orange, travestied the use of aversion therapy in the rehabilitation of criminals. I was in London when it reached the theaters there, and a magazine attributed the technique to me. Though it was not my kind of conditioning, there was a connection. Anthony Burgess, the author of the book from which the film was made, said that he was arguing that "it is preferable to have a world of violence undertaken in full awareness—violence chosen as an act of will—than a world conditioned to be good or harmless . . . B. F. Skinner, with his ability to believe that there is something *beyond* freedom and dignity, wants to see the death of autonomous man. He may or may not be right, but in terms of the Judaeo-Christian ethic that *A Clockwork Orange* tries to express, he is perpetrating a gross heresy." Krutch had, of course, criticized *Walden Two* as a world in which "no one would *have* to be good," and I had defended my position (that we needed good environments, not good people) in "Freedom and the Control of Men."

To exemplify an act of will, Burgess (and Kubrick, the producer) had chosen particularly offensive behavior. An aging drunk is viciously beaten, and a wife raped in view of her husband. They had also chosen what I should have called an absurd way to teach people to be good, and it was easier to believe that they were making a different point—that violence and sex are preferable to anything else in writing a successful novel or making a successful movie.

A year or so later, Arthur Koestler travestied behavioral engineering in a novel called *The Call Girls*. A reviewer in *Time* magazine listed his characters as "an MIT answer man, with his cool dream of computerizing the future, a biologist with the notion of dropping 'anti-hostility agents' into the world's drinking water, a social engineer fitting the future into a box by B. F. Skinner, and a neurosurgeon preaching the implantation of pacifying electrodes in the brain."

The *Guardian* ran a full-page special on behavior modification, reporting the number of volts in the electric cattle prods used to bring mentally handicapped children and adults into line. A boxed quotation in large type read: "While Skinner dreams of putting the world into a big black laboratory for its own good . . . there have been some appalling illustrations of what can happen when the behaviour shapers themselves have not first been conditioned into using their tools with circumspection and science. . . . Behavior modification programs are going on in the United States in schools, hospitals, and prisons with electric shock as well as candy for their tools. Are Professor Skinner's ideas for our chaotic society a blueprint of hell or a program for salvation?"

Of all forms of control, self-control was the least threatening. Social environments (or cultures) turned to it to make constant supervision unnecessary, but one needed to look further to explain the controlling self. *Science and Human Behavior* was said to be the first textbook in psychology with a chapter on self-control, albeit in quotation marks. People controlled themselves as they controlled other people—by changing their environments—but only when taught to do so by their cultures.

I WAS OFTEN SAID to associate Pavlovian conditioning with the autonomic nervous system and operant conditioning with the skeletal, but as early as 1935 Edward Delabarre, Jr., and I found that the blood vessels in the forearm contracted slightly when contraction had reinforcing consequences. In the 1960s operant conditioning of autonomic responses became known as "biofeedback," and important medical consequences were claimed. It would be helpful, for example, if one could lower one's blood pressure "at will." I discussed the issue at the Harvard Medical School. Possibly such a change was the indirect effect of skeletal behavior. One could increase one's blood pressure simply by running up and down a flight of stairs. Less conspicuous forms of action or inaction might produce some of the changes in biofeedback.

THE PUBLIC WAS UNAWARE of other applications of the experimental analysis of behavior and hence not alarmed. Operant equipment was becoming a familiar feature of pharmacological, neurological, and biochemical laboratories. Among the books on biochemistry and biomedicine most often cited between 1961 and 1972, according to *Current Contents*, in 1974, *Schedules of Reinforcement* held a respectable fifteenth place.

IN JANUARY 1972 the Center for the Study of Democratic Institutions in Santa Barbara, California, sponsored a week-long conference on *Beyond Freedom and Dignity*. Robert Hutchins, who had founded the Center, was not well and did not take part in the discussions. Eve had been a junior at the University of Chicago when he had taken over as its president and, like all the other students, had been in love with the handsome twenty-nine-year-old genius. When she found herself sitting beside him at dinner at the Center, she could only exclaim, "It is forty years too late!"

The Fellows of the Center who participated included Harvey Wheeler, Elizabeth Mann Borgese, Alexander Comfort (whose *Joy of Sex* would later help support the Center with a share of its royalties), and Lord Ritchie-Calder. Scholars invited for the occasion included, more or less for the defense, John Platt, Dennis C. Pirages, Arthur Jensen, and Joseph Schwab and, for the prosecution, Michael Novak and, in absentia, Arnold Toynbee, Chaim Perelman, Karl Pribram, and Max Black.

Recordings of the discussions were distributed to radio stations, and nineteen of the papers, including my "Answers for My Critics," were published in a volume called *The Non-Punitive Society*. The title was Harvey Wheeler's. As a political scientist he was impressed by my contention that the punitive practices often used to define government could be replaced by positive reinforcement. The point was relevant to the theme of my book, but only to the extent that the struggle for freedom had left nonpunitive measures, unseen or misunderstood, in control.

An issue of the *Center Magazine*, which went to press while the conference was in session, contained three of the papers. One by John Platt was a strong defense of my position:

> B. F. Skinner's book, *Beyond Freedom and Dignity*, is a revolutionary manifesto. It proposes the design of a new society using new methods for improving the behavior and the interactions of human beings. It has been roundly condemned, as all Skinner's earlier books have been, by humanist critics who at other times call for improved human interactions. In fact, Skinner may have had the worst press of any scientist since Darwin.

Another paper was by Arnold Toynbee, who felt that living creatures could be "only partially conditioned" and that human behavior was therefore only partially determined by heredity and environment. "Try to 'condition' a goat, mule, camel, or horse," said Toynbee, "and you will find that the exercise is counterproductive." It was a tempting challenge, but the only animals at the Center were Elizabeth Mann

Borgese's dogs. The third paper, by Max Black, was an example of the extraordinary violence shown by some of my critics. It was etymologically appropriate—a denigration, a blackening. *Beyond Freedom and Dignity* was said to be a "melange of amateurish metaphysics, self-advertising technology, and illiberal social policy . . . a disservice to scientists, technologists, and all who are seriously trying to improve the human condition." Black supported those claims with an unusually extensive list of misunderstandings, of which the following are a small sample:

It was "unintentionally amusing" that I should speak of the control exerted by an experimental subject upon the experimenter. (But it would amuse only those who were unaware of the variables of which their behavior was a function.)

I used the term "environment" in a "vacuously inflated sense" to include persons. (I had spent a great deal of time in analyzing the origin and function of social environments.)

I was said to misuse the word "control." "In its familiar and proper use [it] implies a controller or controllers." (I used it as an astronomer might do in speaking of the control exercised by one planet upon another.) Chomsky had made the same mistake.

I was wrong in saying that feelings made no difference. "The anger felt by a father whose child has been killed by a reckless motorist may move him to commit murder." (As I might have said in my debate with Blanshard: The father murders the motorist because he has killed his child; as he does so he may feel a condition of his body, caused by the same event, which is called anger.)

I was said to belittle "the literature of freedom and dignity." (I recognized its great accomplishments in reducing the extent of punitive control and expanding human achievement, but an exclusive preoccupation with individual freedom and dignity could mean the end of life on earth.)

Having misunderstood my book to such an extent, it was not surprising that Black found it "marked by incoherence," "endemic ambiguity," "lurking fallacies," and "habitual equivocation" and that it was "disingenuous" and "conveniently vague." But why the misunderstanding? Was Black simply an intellectual Luddite bent on smashing a science of behavior to save his job as a philosopher?

I was given a weekend to prepare a general reply. Eve spent the time with Martha Smith, the old friend through whom she and I had met and who was living on the Coast, and I was alone. I found myself unusually indolent. Early on Monday morning I wrote:

> How am I to explain my lack of interest in what I am going to say? I had assumed that I would really get down to work on Saturday and Sunday, but in fact I did almost nothing. I have not read the reports carefully. In part it is the distasteful character of the negative ones. I cannot really *read* them. They are so far off the mark, and many of them unfriendly.
>
> In part it is a lack of confidence in the method of the Center [a continuation of the Great Conversation which began with Plato] or of any hope that much will come of these meetings. To make matters worse, I have agreed to cooperate in "getting a book out of them."

After breakfast I sat down and wrote what seemed to me suitable comments, but when I saw the transcript a month later I wrote:

> I am shocked at how bad they are. The worst kind of meandering thought, wrong words followed by other words twisted in an effort to set them right. Near the end of the second day the stuff becomes almost gibberish. I dredged up old verbal behavior—as from the Kennedy Symposium, for example. There are few acceptable sentences in the last three or four pages.

The Center was housed in a grove of eucalyptus trees—aromatic and as poisonous as hemlock. In my closing remarks I said that I had received a strange message reading, "Will you join me in a cup of eucalyptus?" signed, "Socrates."

Harvey Wheeler told me that the Fellows thought that the conference was the best the Center had held in something over ten years, and they would be pleased to have me join them at any time for any length of time. I could even write a novel as my contribution. Looking back, I agreed that the conference had been worthwhile, and I was inclined to let the public record stand as my reaction to the criticism of my book. If I wrote anything else as a response to criticism, it would be the primer of behaviorism.

✳   ✳   ✳

A TWO-DAY CONFERENCE on *Beyond Freedom and Dignity* held at Yale University in April was stacked even more heavily against me. Of the fourteen speakers, only Professor Kenneth Clark of CCNY could have been said to be on my side. At each session I found myself on the platform with three or four critics, listening as they explained what was wrong with my book. One of them, Alain Enthoven, was a former Assistant Secretary of Defense and another, Zbigniew Brzezinski, would move into a similarly combative position. I reported one episode in an Op-Ed piece in the *New York Times*:

> On the second evening, several students brought in a large banner reading "Remember the Air War," which they hung from the balcony. It could not be seen by everyone in the audience, but it confronted the five panelists on the platform throughout the evening. It had a predictable effect: Every one of us mentioned the war in Vietnam at some point in his discussion and the last speaker, Sir Dennis Brogan, put aside his manuscript and spoke only of the war.
> That was good behavioral engineering. We should learn to live with it.

I stayed comfortably and pleasantly with the Elting Morisons. One of their other guests, Stephen Spender, told me when the conference was over that if he had known me better he would have written a different paper. It was a comfort, but it came rather late.

ON GOOD FRIDAY, I reviewed some of the effects of the success of *Beyond Freedom and Dignity*:

> I have just finished listening to *Parsifal*. . . . At the moment I feel as if I had betrayed some sacred trust during the past year. I have been unduly affected by my book and all the publicity. The first six months after finishing it I relaxed, then caught up on lectures and manuscripts I had postponed in order to finish it. The second six months have been almost wholly promotional—unless I exclude the Los Angeles and Venezuelan lectures and the Center and Yale conferences.
> I want to get back to work, but the "purity" of my motives is suspect. I am defending my position. I must hold to my plans for the future if I

am to save myself. To "offset a sense of failure, discouragement"? No, to offset extinction.

IN THE LATE SIXTIES I received several inquiries about a movie based on *Walden Two*—one from a story editor at Columbia Pictures, who could not, as it turned out, interest any of their directors, and one from Universal Studios. Several agents also wrote to me. I made inquiries about agents and was soon talking with one, but in 1970 I gave the movie rights in the book to Julie and Deborah, in a trust administered by a local bank and my lawyer. During the next four years a great deal of correspondence passed between bank, lawyer, agent, and three or four people interested in taking an option on the book. There were endless discussions of rights, including those of the Macmillan Company, and in the end, nothing was done.

EDWARD TOLMAN, the purposive behavorist, was often said to have initiated the cognitive movement. His most distinguished disciple was David Krech. In a review of Arthur Koestler's *Ghost in the Machine*, Krech referred to "behaviorism (the paleo-form of Watson or the neo-form of Skinner) [as] one of the greatest of catastrophes that has befallen [psychology]." We should turn instead to "psycholinguistics, personality research, brain and behavior research, the modern and very much refurbished research in verbal learning, cognitive psychology, [and] social psychology." The Tolman I knew would not have been pleased. Explanatory fictions of the kind Robert Kantor liked to call ghosts were haunting the world again.

And beginning to haunt William James Hall. I wrote a note about the first meeting of the new Department of Psychology and Social Relations. It was

a distressing experience. There was a great deal of nervous laughter, some of it raucous, in which I could not join, resulting in part from the administrative imposition of social proximity on a group of intellectual strangers. We approved four or five Ph.D. theses which seemed to show nothing more than a layman's way of dealing with their subjects—backed up, I am sure, by "data" and "statistics" but with no concern for basic dimensions.

MEMBERS OF THE "D.C. Walden Two Committee," of which I began to hear in the middle sixties, soon went on to found Twin Oaks, a community near Louisa, Virginia. It was too small to be very much like Walden Two, but the point of my book had been experimentation and change, and I was encouraged.

In 1972 Kathleen Kinkade, one of the founders of Twin Oaks, published *A Walden Two Experiment: The First Five Years of Twin Oaks Community*. In a preface I noted her "disarming candor"; the community had made mistakes but had muddled through. The same thing was happening in the world at large. "While Kat and her friends seek solutions to their problems, the rest of the world must do something about *its* food supplies, *its* educational systems, *its* sanitation and health, *its* 'interpersonal' relations, *its* cultural activities, and *its* Olympic Games."

Kat left Twin Oaks and tried to start a community in western Massachusetts (while there, she typed the manuscript of *About Behaviorism*) and helped found another community in Missouri, called East Wind, like Twin Oaks except that new members were accepted rather more freely. Both supported themselves by manufacturing rope hammocks, a labor-intensive product which did not appeal to big business.

A rather different community in Mexico, Los Horcones, was founded a few years later. It ran a school for retarded children and prided itself on its strict adherence to behavioral principles in its own self-management. Members of Los Horcones attended meetings of operant conditioners in the United States and at conferences on behavior modification in Mexico and gave interesting reports.

NAMED "HUMANIST OF THE YEAR" by the American Humanist Association, I discussed "Humanism and Behaviorism" at its annual meeting in 1972. Where existentialism, phenomenology, and structuralism seek to discover what a person *is*, I thought we should more effectively "actualize the human potential" if we examined what people do and why they do it. Behaviorism was simply effective Humanism.

Many people objected to my nomination. Must a Humanist not believe in free will and freedom of thought? Would a Skinnerian world not mean "the destruction of all that we who are Humanists know ourselves to be?" On other grounds I myself had had doubts. I had been a contributing member of the American Humanist Association for many years, and I was an honorary member of the Rationalist Press in Britain, which published the *New Humanist*, a journal more militantly anticlerical and anti-big-state than the American *Humanist*, but I was bothered by the aggrandizement of the individual in much Humanist writing. With the publication of *Beyond Freedom and Dignity* my position became awkward. If Humanism meant nothing more than the maximizing of personal freedom and dignity, then I was not a Humanist. If it meant trying to save the human species, then I was.

In 1972, I participated in a confrontation between humanists and Catholics at the LaFarge Center in New York City. Sidney Hook and Charles Frankel were the spokesmen for humanism, and I was so unhappy about the case they presented that I left the meeting on the second day—and not without telling the Catholic co-chairman that I thought he had won every round.

My fellow Playreader, Amos Wilder, and I occasionally discussed Christian practices. A famous passage in Matthew 5:40 advises one, when sued for one's coat, to give one's cloak as well. It seemed to me a way of saving face; one can then claim to have given the coat, rather than to have yielded to superior force. The grace of God raised the question of the noncontingent reinforcer. There are those who have been selected by God's mercy, "but if it is by His mercy," according to the Goodspeed translation, "it is not for anything they have done. Otherwise His mercy would not be mercy at all." Carl Rogers had advised psychotherapists to imitate God in that sense; the reinforcers under their control were not to be made in any way contingent upon the behavior of the client.

I questioned the curious contingencies of reinforcement in Romans 12:20, which St. Paul borrowed from Proverbs 25:21–22: Give your enemy bread when he is hungry and water when he is thirsty and "you will heap coals of fire on his head and the Lord will reward you." It seemed a very uncharitable principle. A Dead Sea scroll had confirmed the punitive nature of the argument, but Amos Wilder thought the point was that punishment should be left to God, who had much more powerful means.

Tom Sebeok, who had audited my course in verbal behavior at a University of Chicago summer school decades before, was writing on "zoosemiotics." As in an earlier book by Grace de Laguna, human verbal behavior was said to be an extension of innate modes of communication. I thought there was a clear difference between behavior shaped by natural selection and behavior shaped by operant conditioning. How a community which maintained the contingencies responsible for verbal behavior could have come into existence was the old question of the origin of language, about which I had hazarded a few guesses in an epilogue in *Verbal Behavior*. The same question could be asked about nonverbal behavior acquired in a social environment.

I started a file of articles and notes labeled "paleobehavior." How could early man have invented the digging stick, the spear, the snare? How could more remote consequences, as in learning to bank a fire or carry a club, have come into play? No artifacts survived, but current knowledge of behavior helped. Some paleolithic art could be explained, for example, if coloring or changing the shape of a boss on a wall improved the resemblance to an animal and was thus reinforced.

When the first trip to the moon was scheduled, Jane Friedman at Knopf asked if I would go on an NBC show on the moon landing with John Chancellor. I said no. She tried again and I said yes. Then I regretted it and wrote to say that I had discovered a previous engagement. Bridget Potter of NBC called, apparently almost in tears. They had announced my participation, they had been so happy about it, could I not get out of my previous engagement? Eventually I said yes, but, as I added in a note, it would be "David dancing before the people. I have little if anything to say and it is small consolation that no one else will have either. . . . What am I doing on the program? Am I mad?"

I went to New York and waited in my hotel room. The landing was delayed, and Bridget Potter eventually called to say that the program had been scratched. What a shame that I had canceled my Harvard appointment. Better luck on the next moon shot. I grabbed a taxi to LaGuardia and was home for dinner.

The next day NBC had a panel discussion, with General Gavin, Peter Ustinov, Alan Shepard, and Marshall McLuhan. McLuhan played the part I was to have played the preceding day, and he did not have anything to say about moon walks either. Instead, he asked a question: "Did the world seem right side up to astronauts in *zero-g?*" He mentioned the Stratton glasses, said no psychologist had any explanation, and showed his own ignorance by supposing that the absence of gravitation would reverse the visual field. He looked as unhappy as I should have been.

THE SUCCESS OF *Beyond Freedom and Dignity* attracted the attention of editors. I was asked to write a regular feature for *World,* a new magazine founded by Norman Cousins. The Op-Ed editor of the *Times* liked my piece on "Freedom and Dignity Revisited" and suggested that I write others. Newspaper and magazine writers began to call, hoping for a useful quote. What would I say about a young man who takes a rifle into a tower and starts shooting at people in the street? How would I explain Patty Hearst? I took my cue from politicians and said "No comment."

Some interest was shown by people in government. Senator John Glenn asked me to appear, with Buckminster Fuller and others, at a hearing on what could be done about America's future. (I was not always happy about political or economic references. According to a paragraph in the *New York Times* for Tuesday, May 2, 1972: "Low Fook Poey, president of the Pork Merchants Association, is to ban lean pork from slaughter until the fat ones are sold. 'If other kinds of pork are also available in the market, housewives will not buy the fatty pork,' he said. The proposed solution is somewhat authoritarian, but Singapore, under Prime Minister Lee Kuan Yew, has for some years been practicing what B. F. Skinner, the Harvard psychologist, recently preached about the need to subjugate individual freedoms for the collective good.")

* * *

FRED KELLER AND I made a documentary called *Together*. We were filmed as we sat in my study reminiscing about our lives as psychologists and behaviorists. For a full hour we relaxed and enjoyed ourselves, joking about our contemporaries, discussing theoretical issues, and expressing our concern for the future. Fred and I had known each other for nearly forty-five years. When I said that, in all that time, I could not remember an unkind word, Fred capped it nicely with, "I cannot remember an unkind thought."

I GAVE ONE OF A SERIES of Herbert Spencer lectures at Oxford University on "Obstacles to Scientific Progress." Fresh from criticism of *Beyond Freedom and Dignity*, I called it "The Steep and Thorny Way to a Science of Behavior." The science was fighting its way through thickets of history, and I pointed to a parallel in the history of medicine:

> Until the present century very little was known about bodily processes in health and disease . . . yet it should have been worthwhile to call in a physician. Physicians saw many ill people and should have acquired a kind of wisdom, unanalyzed perhaps but still of value in prescribing simple treatments. The history of medicine, however, is largely the history of barbaric practices—bloodlettings, cuppings, poultices, purgations, violent emetics—which much of the time must have been harmful. My point is that these measures were not suggested by the intuitive wisdom acquired from familiarity with illness; they were suggested by *theories*, theories about what was going on inside an ill person. Theories of the mind have had a similar effect, less dramatic, perhaps, but quite possibly far more damaging.

VACATIONING WITH EVE in Bequia in the Caribbean, and recovering from an attack of influenza, I wrote:

> I am in an expansive mood. I think I know what is wrong with the thousands of efforts people make each year to say something helpful

about human affairs. They cannot find the right things to talk about! I should go over the magazines read by intellectuals and try to analyze them. What are the facts? What is to be done about them? How much sheer mentalism? How much simple historical narration? How much analogical thinking?

Why am I expansive? Because I think I am beginning to see the scope of a behavioral—or behavioristic—analysis. It *does* talk about the important things; it *does* point to conditions which can be changed; it *does* show what is wrong with other ways of talking about things.

IN A PICTURE of "Harmey" Warner's ten-piece orchestra taken in Susquehanna in 1896, a young man with a trombone stands beside another with a cornet. The cornetist would become my father, and the trombonist the father of Reuben Brower, Professor of English Literature, also at Harvard. In 1973 Ben Brower was the senior editor of a collection of essays in honor of I. A. Richards. (Another editor was John Hollander, who had written that poem on *Science and Human Behavior.*) As an old friend of Ivor Richards, I was asked to contribute.

I was unhappy about an article Ivor had published in the *Times Literary Supplement,* in which he expressed his admiration for a structural analysis of a Shakespeare sonnet by Roman Jakobson. Jakobson's structuralism had spawned both Chomsky and Claude Lévi-Strauss, whose work I deplored, and now Ivor had come under its spell. Moreover, the poem was one I had analyzed, functionally rather than structurally, in *Verbal Behavior.* Jakobson once told me that he had read my book, but evidently with no great effect.

For my paper I went back to my analysis of alliteration and to some unpublished statistics about the density of thematic material in the lines of a Shakespeare sonnet. (I used a graph that had been in my files for thirty years.) I was the only contributor who made any effort to approach literature scientifically, as Ivor Richards had tried to do, and that point was made by a reviewer for the *New York Times,* who made fun of my "comma counting." I was said to be in the "wrong category."

Perhaps it was because psychologists made such a point of being scientific that they were so often put in the wrong category and taken to be philistines. When Zero Mostel gave a lecture on humor at Harvard's Loeb Theater, Eve and I, together with the Leon Kirchners, drove him back to the airport. The Kirchners came back to our house. As Professor of Music at Harvard, Leon naturally went straight to the piano. He saw a book of Schumann's songs and said "A strange volume to find on a psychologist's piano." A week later at a garden party, someone started to talk about suicide. Mrs. Jacob Rosenberg, the wife of the distinguished historian of art, brought up the problem of Ophelia's burial. "Oh, that the Almighty had not set His hand against self-slaughter," I said, none too accurately. "Oh, you know it better than I," said Mrs. Rosenberg, "and you are a *psychologist!*"

As LATE AS 1972, I was still planning a paper to be called "Behavior and Psychotherapy," based upon my Churchill College lecture, but references under "behavior therapy" in the *Psychological Abstracts Annual Index* began to outnumber those under "psychoanalysis," and it did not seem that anything more needed to be said. Progress was being made in other ways. For many years there had been something close to open warfare between clinical psychology and psychiatry, but the behavioral approach had helped. In 1973 a task force of the American Psychiatric Association concluded that "behavior therapy and behavioral principles . . . have reached a stage of development where they now unquestionably have much to offer informed clinicians in the service of modern clinical and social psychiatry."

Behavior therapy was still primarily respondent conditioning, in part because the contingencies could be more easily arranged in the clinic or consulting room. Operant therapy usually meant changing the daily life of the client, which verged on designing a culture and offered more promise as preventive therapy. By replacing punitive practices, however, it reduced the need for respondent therapy, which was largely concerned with alleviating the effects of punishment.

DEBORAH HAD FOUND Florence a good place to study art history, but not drawing and painting. She did some work in mosaics, but then moved on to London, where she became a student at the City and Guild Art School. She found a good instructor in etching, and one of her etchings was shown in a group show at the Royal Society of Painter-Etchers in 1972. For a year or two she shared a flat with several other young women, but in 1971 she met Barry Buzan, who was completing a doctoral program at the London School of Economics, and they took a flat at Highgate. Eve and I spent a merry Christmas there with them and Barry's father and mother. Deborah and Barry were married in the spring of 1973. All four parents participated in the ceremony. I recited "Let us not to the marriage of true minds admit impediments" and Eve read a poem written by Richard Wilbur for the wedding of his son. Deborah and Barry spent two years in Vancouver, where Barry was working on a book on seabed politics. Deborah showed etchings at several group shows, had solo shows in the Vancouver Art Club and the Studio Gallery, and was awarded the *Event Magazine* Graphic Prize.

Although an article in the *Boston Herald American* said that "whatever its virtues or vices," the Aircrib was "now a sentimental artifact from the past," second-hand models were bringing high prices, and prospective parents were building new ones. It was still, however, beyond the reach of American business. Market research could not give a reliable estimate of potential users, and boards of directors would not authorize spending the money for the mass production needed to assure a reasonable price.

Misunderstandings were still common. I was said to believe that "babies should not be raised by people." An English newspaper, reporting the use of one of these "electronic cocoons," quoted a psychiatrist as saying that "the machine seemed deliberately to foster infantile apartheid in an age of diminishing family togetherness," and a Harvard pediatrician was said to have urged the American Academy of Pediatrics to outlaw them as no substitute for "warm parent-child give-and-take." But as many users reported, Aircribs made it easy to be affectionate. More and more often after I had given a lecture, a former Aircrib occupant would come up to say hello. The sample was no doubt biased, but they all seemed to be remarkably fine young people.

In 1973, according to *Time* magazine, a German psychologist found that thirty-eight infants raised in "plexiglas cribs," evidently much like the Aircrib, showed a much faster "mental development" than the control group. At eighteen months of age they were "measurably more intelligent than two-year-olds who had been confined to traditional cribs."

*   *   *

THE SUCCESS OF *Beyond Freedom and Dignity* induced a number of people to take another look at behaviorism. Many of those who reviewed the book or participated in the conferences at Santa Barbara and Yale read it carefully and may even have looked at some of my other work. Not all philosophers took the virulent line of many of my critics. In a sympathetic paper Max Hocutt, a philosopher at the University of Alabama, argued that I had satisfactorily answered G. E. Moore's criticism of a naturalistic ethic. Willard Day, a psychologist at the University of Nevada, enlisted a distinguished international board of editors for the journal *Behaviorism*, which began to publish interesting papers.

I tested the manuscript of what I began to call *About Behaviorism* in an advanced seminar in the experimental analysis of behavior, and the book was published in 1974. It began with a list of twenty common misunderstandings, which were reviewed (and, I hoped, corrected) at the end. It was used as a text and continued to sell well.

IN 1974 I became Professor of Psychology and Social Relations Emeritus. The department gave me a retirement party in the court of the Fogg Museum. Van Quine and George Homans told stories about me, and Brendan Maher, Chairman of the department, presented a first edition of Thoreau's *Walden*. My daily life continued unchanged. No one said anything about vacating my office in William James Hall, though I would have to pay my secretary's salary and other expenses. A former secretary agreed to come in once or twice a week to pick up work to do at home, and I began to answer most of my correspondence with a card reading:

> *In order to devote myself to work in progress, I have had to curtail many activities. I can no longer answer letters as I should like to do, and I am unable to take on other commitments. I hope you will forgive me for replying to your recent communication in this way.*

I found myself dropping farther and farther behind, and after a year or two went back to a full-time secretary.

AN ORGANIZATION CALLING itself the National Caucus of Labor Committees (the committees not being further identified) began to harass me. I was a "leading light of fascist behaviorism," somehow connected with Nelson Rockefeller, their chief target. They picketed a meeting at the New York University School of Education in 1971, where I gave a paper called "The Free and Happy Student" and two nights later a dinner at which I received an award. They began to attend my public lectures. There were only three or four of them, but they would sit in different places and ask questions. The questions were always the same and about issues in which I was never particularly interested: Why did I not protest the use of my theories in the New York City welfare system, and why was I in favor of zero growth? When I spoke at an evening meeting in a Unitarian church in Cambridge they were there, and during the question period someone fired a blank cartridge in the back of the room. On the campus of Indiana University the NCLC hanged me in effigy. In their magazine *Solidarity* they reported "breaking up" a meeting of mine at the Cambridge Union in England; "members of the European Labor Committee in the audience had little trouble pointing out to the assemblage that the real purpose of Skinner's research is to aid the capitalist class in imposing human recycling and zero growth austerity on the world's working class." What actually happened was that during the question period someone stood up, called me a fraud, and sat down; the moderator asked if I wished to comment, and when I said no, the audience applauded.

After I had accepted an invitation to speak at the Fernald State School in Waltham, I suggested that no public announcement be made: the Caucus would not know about the meeting and we could avoid trouble. But extensive publicity was planned. The Waltham Police would be asked to stand by. At the meeting a member of the Caucus was told that he could speak for five minutes if he would agree that there would be no further disruption. He spoke for fifteen minutes, asking the audience to join the Caucus, and alluded to mysterious connections with underground groups in Eastern Europe. Not surprisingly, the agreement was broken: as I began to speak a young woman stood up and began to shout, and the police led her screaming from the hall. Someone sent me a copy of the Caucus's report of the event: "The NCLC delivered a Nuremberg indictment for Crimes Against Humanity against the panel's featured speaker, the nation's number one populizer [sic] of Nazi medicine, B. F. Skinner. The indictment was delivered from the floor despite the heavy-handedness of the moderator."

Two members called on Norman Zinberg, a psychiatrist friend of mine, and asked him to testify that I was using operant techniques from a distance to force them to do unspeakable things. The group moved farther to the left and even began to break up meetings of Communists. People attending their own meetings were subjected to a full body search. They disrupted the classes of Israel Goldiamond at the University of Chicago, who needed police protection for some weeks, and ten members of the Caucus were arrested when they invaded the office of Eugene Galanter at Columbia University and injured a student researcher. At the Fernald meeting, a friend of mine heard one of them say, "We've got to get Skinner," and for a time I walked to my office by different routes.

It was only to be expected that behavior modification would play a part in paranoid fantasies. Someone signing himself "Little Albert II" wrote to ask my help in removing the stimulator that someone had implanted in his brain, and someone who said he had read *Beyond Freedom and Dignity* asked my help in taking legal steps against "being used against my will as a guinea pig for mind control and biomedical and behavioral research." Inevitably, I myself was accused of harassing people. One letter began: "You will have to pay for the damage you have done to me psychologically and physically with your electronic controls." A man complained to the president of Harvard that I was employing as many as a hundred operatives to modify his behavior.

IN AN ARTICLE in the Columbia *Forum* in the spring of 1974, James R. Mellow quoted Gertrude Stein's comments about the analysis of her work I had published in the *Atlantic*, and the editor asked me to reply. I wrote a short letter, saying that I thought Gertrude Stein had admitted that my interpretation of her work as automatic writing was not far from the truth. I also reported what Alfred North Whitehead had told me about her references to him in the *Autobiography of Alice B. Toklas*. She had been invited to spend a weekend at the Whiteheads' country house near Salisbury Plain and had stayed on when the outbreak of the war tied up her money in Paris. As Whitehead said to me, "She said she stayed six weeks, but she *stayed three months!*" She had also said that "Gertrude Stein and Dr. Whitehead walked endlessly around the country. They talked of philosophy and history." When I asked him about those intellectual exchanges he said, "Of course she made a fool of me, but I suppose she couldn't help that."

I COPIED A FEW of Mr. Pusey's sentences about college and university instruction into my notebook:

> Education must "penetrate into the very marrow of the learner and set up there a process of desiring that will not be stilled. When the impact of the thing learned, bursting into the self and filling it with excited awareness of the far-reaching implications in the thing studied, engenders a thrilling realization that the self really matters . . ."

Had that sort of thing ever told anyone how to teach more effectively? Would it "inspire" better teaching or simply discourage those who stopped to ask themselves whether they knew how to set up a process of "desiring" or "engender a realization?" I thought Ernie Vargas and his colleagues at West Virginia were doing more for college teaching, though it did not sound as exalted, and, of course, Fred Keller had been the pioneer. I reported briefly on Fred's Personalized System Instruction in a paper called "Designing Higher Education" at a symposium at the American Academy of Arts and Sciences in 1974, published in *Daedalus*. Fred had devised the system when consulting for the Brazilian government, and more and more "PSI" courses were now being taught. Many of the advantages of programmed instruction could be realized without solving the hardware problem of teaching machines. Students moved at their own pace, took no punitive examinations, and saved a great deal of everyone's time. By 1970 more than a thousand courses were being taught by the Keller method in the United States alone.

* * *

IN 1974 the Law Enforcement Assistance Administration (LEAA), which had spent about $1.5 million on programs involving behavior modification in prisons, suddenly banned further grants. The principal targets were psychosurgery and aversion therapy, but positive reinforcement was included, possibly just because it meant control (a psychiatrist once spoke of "sadists cowering behind the apron of operant conditioning"). A different issue concerned rights. Prisoners were not to be deprived of goods or privileges to be used as reinforcers. When two officers of the Prison Project of the American Civil Liberties Union came to see me, I argued that it was foolish to quibble about rights of that kind when the government was depriving them of the right of freedom. What would be wrong if prisoners earned their own living in an institutional setting? If that was "forced labor," it was still better than forced idleness.

But what about psychotic and retarded people? Were they not entitled to goods and privileges? I discussed that issue in a symposium titled "The Control of Behavior: Legal, Scientific, and Moral Dilemmas," at Reed College in March 1975. People who could not help themselves had rights in the sense that a strong culture would help them. Those who could help themselves also had rights, and one was the right to an interesting life, which was denied them when the goods and privileges they received were not contingent upon what they did. As Ayllon and others had shown, psychotic patients were much better off when performing useful work in return for goods and privileges previously supplied gratis.

The noncontingent reinforcer was a problem for both the wealthy and the welfare recipient, and a solution was not within range of the doctrine of rights. The deinstitutionalization of psychotic and retarded people and, to a certain extent, prisoners was not a solution so long as psychotic or retarded people needed care and the public needed protection. Institutions should be redesigned.

I had first realized that the problem of leisure was the basic problem of institutionalized people at a Grand Rounds at the Boston University Medical School in 1968. I had just said that an effective physical environment was possible in a psychiatric hospital, and a psychiatrist asked what I meant. I could think of only a few examples: harmless tools used to produce countable items on a fixed-ratio or variable-ratio schedule, possibly with a bonus; some kind of assembly-line work with quality-controlled contingencies; or gambling, which would at least consume time though not productively.

A highly successful experiment at the National Training School in Washington, D.C., conducted by the Institute for Behavioral Research had shown what could be done. When young offenders were exposed to daily contingencies under which they rapidly acquired useful skills, a reduced recidivism during the first year after release more than paid for the program. Unfortunately, the saving was the kind of deferred consequence to which administrators were not always sensitive, and when the school was moved to Morgantown, West Virginia (where Julie was briefly a consultant), it slowly returned to standard practice.

A Harvard colleague in the field of criminology was reported to have said that he had never seen a rehabilitated prisoner. I had, and I had had encouraging letters from them. A prisoner in Philadelphia wrote that he was teaching his fellow prisoners techniques of self-management which they could use in coping with problems not only in prison but presumably in their daily lives when released. When I sent a prisoner on Death Row in San Quentin a book of mine that he had asked for, he organized discussions with other prisoners and wrote a paper which, several years later, I called "a remarkable achievement. I was alerted by the first paragraph, which mentioned 'supplementing' personal histories instead of changing them. [You can't change a history; it has passed beyond reach.] It is a beautiful summary of my position—almost uncanny in its anticipation of *Beyond Freedom and Dignity*." The prisoner was eventually released and later worked as a volunteer for the editor of the *Journal of Behaviorists for Social Action*.

WHEN A MEMBER OF the Shop Club discussed Wegener's theory of continental drift, he pointed to the relevance of the fact that both American and European eels breed near the Sargasso Sea, the larvae eventually returning to their respective shores. Presumably the distances were once much shorter. It occurred to me that the slow separation of the continents could have shaped the extraordinarily complex, protracted behavior with which the mature eels found their way back to the breeding place. Ernst Mayr, a member of the Club and one of the most distinguished evolutionary theorists, did not agree, but I began to collect other evidence of the possible role of plate tectonics and wrote a paper called "The Shaping of Phylogenic Behavior." It appeared in a volume of *Acta Neurobiologiae Experimentalis* honoring Jerzy Konorski.

In 1975 the annual meeting of the American Psychological Association was held in Chicago. I left a meeting at one hotel and took a cab to another. The young driver said, "Get in. I know all about you. I've read your books. What is it—a convention of humanists?" "No," I said, "but there are some humanist psychologists here." "Have you read this?" he said, holding up a paperback of Castañeda's *Journey to Ixtlan*. "No," I said, "but I should. Somebody was mentioning it to me recently." "It's yours!" he said, holding it toward me. "Go on. Take it. I can get another copy." He said he was a student at a small college. "Probably inferior faculty. But there's a sociologist there who teaches all your stuff. He got me to read your books." When we reached my hotel, we discovered he had forgotten to start his meter. "Forget it," he said, but I gave him the fare I had paid going the other way.

I HAD ALWAYS believed in progress. My father believed in it for good reason: he had come a long way beyond his father, and he had seen me go a long way beyond him. Most of the parents of my boyhood friends had had at best a high school education, but many of my friends went on to college (and I was surprised when some of them did not). Behaviorism appealed to me because I believed, with Watson, that a better knowledge of human behavior would help solve our problems. *Walden Two* was written in the perfectionist spirit of nineteenth-century America, and I had not been joking when I said that even a small contribution to a science of human behavior could eventually help *billions* of people. My decision to devote the period of my Career Award to the design of cultural practices was a natural next step.

At the level of personal self-management, the problem was central to morals and ethics: how to forego a current reinforcer in order to avoid a future aversive consequence or accept a current aversive consequence for the sake of a future reinforcer. The evolution of a culture involved a different kind of selective consequence.

On one of our excursions from Cambridge in 1969, we visited Tintern Abbey. I reread Wordsworth's poem and wrote a note called "Making a Break":

The story I wrote during my last year in college—"Elsa"—developed a theme which has remained with me ever since. An unsuccessful marriage told from the girl's point of view. A powerful but rather foolishly idealistic husband who in the most subtle way forces her to live *his* kind of life. The crucial point: no one day is bad enough to make a break. The aversive consequences of saying "I am leaving you" are immediate and overwhelming; she accepts less aversive conditions, presumably for a lifetime, although in sum they will far outweigh the trouble of making a break.

Tintern Abbey has revived that theme on another scale. The life we lead displeases us, but no day is bad enough to induce us to act. We are whirling toward our doom, but we keep on patching up our way of life and avoiding the drastic change which alone can save us. *Walden Two* was a proposal to make a *big* change rather than take small remedial steps here and there, but the problems it would raise are so big that we go right on doing nothing.

In 1969, working on an early stage of *Freedom and Dignity*, I had written: "The whole point may be the need to bring remote consequences into play in determining conduct." In 1971 the word "beyond," although added to my title as an afterthought, made the same point. Something, possibly the very future of the species, lay beyond freedom and dignity. To put it more generally, too great a concern for the present meant a neglect of the future. I began to write a book on the future. Through what behavioral processes could people be induced to take it into account? A culture might evolve in such a way that it made a future more likely, but only its own future and only in a world much like the past. Could we design cultural practices which would be more likely to solve that problem?

I used some of the material from an early version of the manuscript in a lecture at Syracuse University at the opening of the academic year in September 1972. It was a name lecture and the sponsor wanted something about freedom, so I called it "The Freedom to Have a Future." It made an interesting extra point, which I developed further at a Walgreen Conference at the University of Michigan in April 1973 in a paper called "Are We Free to Have a Future?" The title could mean two things: "Put commas around 'free' and the question is this: We who call ourselves free, are we to have a future? We value practices in government, religion, economics, education, and psychotherapy to the extent that they promote feelings of freedom, but do practices *chosen for that reason* have survival value?

"Remove the commas, and my title is more to the point: Are we sufficiently free of the present to have a future? Our extraordinary commitment to immediate gratification has served the species well . . . but we [must now] design a world in which our [outmoded] susceptibilities to reinforcement will be less troublesome and in which we shall be more likely to behave in ways which promise a future."

By 1975 I had completed a draft of a book on "taking the future into account" but was unhappy about it and put it aside for revision.

A FIRST LATIN AMERICAN CONGRESS on the Analysis of Behavior was held in Xalapa, Mexico, in 1971. I had planned to attend and give a paper at the end of our cruise of the Mayan ruins, but bad water taken on at Guatemala wrought havoc with passengers and crew alike (a New York paper reported it as "A Cruise to the Ruins; the Ruin of a Cruise.") Eve and I were among the few who escaped, but when we returned to Jamaica I came down with pneumonia and could not go to the meeting. I spoke at a third Congress held in Mexico City in 1975, however, attended by behaviorists from Brazil, Venezuela, Peru, the Dominican Republic, Panama, and Mexico. Julie and Ernie came and brought our charming granddaughters. I spoke on the application of a behavioral analysis to everyday life.

SALES OF *Walden Two* were rising. By 1970 nearly a million copies had been sold, and a new hardcover edition was a Literary Guild selection.

In 1976 I wrote a preface to still another edition. An entirely different set of issues had become relevant. A community like Walden Two was minimally consuming, minimally polluting, and maximally productive of good personal relations. It had no need for a nuclear stockpile.

When I wrote *Walden Two*, the experimental analysis of behavior had not yet been applied to the world at large; thirty years later some parts could be said to have come true. I was often asked whether I would now write it in a different way. I had mistakenly assumed, along with Karl Marx, that a person would simply give a certain amount of work in exchange for the privilege of living in such a culture, provided everyone else did the same. I would now describe better incentives. I would also find a place for retarded, mildly psychotic, or otherwise handicapped members, and I would change educational practices from John Dewey to programmed instruction.

Rather similar issues were raised by Meredith W. Watts in a paper called "B. F. Skinner and the Technological Control of Social Behavior," published in the *American Political Science Review*. I was asked to comment. With respect to the use of laboratory data in the interpretation of daily life, I drew a parallel between the experimental analysis of behavior and modern astronomy. Astronomers

> observe events occurring in outer space, under conditions beyond any hope of experimental control, and mostly unreproducible on the earth. They have available, however, facts about gravity, radiation, pressure, temperature, and so on, obtained under the controlled conditions of the laboratory. They assume that both terrestrial and celestial events are of the same kind and interpret their observations of outer space in the light of the laboratory results. In other words, they use what is learned under favorable conditions to talk about facts about which they know very little. There is room for disagreement, of course, but no serious person complains that the facts in outer space are being *reduced* to facts of a different kind. . . . No other information about the facts in space is available.

As to my supposedly illiberal social position, I said:

> I am not antidemocratic. I am ultra-democratic. Most political practices, including democracy, arise from the opposition of controlling and

countercontrolling forces. I do not believe that is the only, or necessarily the best, source of cultural practices. What we call democracy, particularly as observed in contemporary America, is certainly not the last word in government. The evolutionary process continues. I do not believe it is pointing in the direction of totalitarianism; the evidence is all too clear that *that* is a lethal mutation.

The question I had asked about the ethics of helping people could be asked about the world as a whole, and I tried to answer it in a paper called "Human Behavior and Democracy" delivered at the annual meeting of the American Psychological Association in 1976, the year of the Bicentennial. I paraphrased Lincoln's concern "that control of the people, by the people, and for the people, shall not perish from the earth." Lincoln had said "government," not "control," but was that an important difference? In a small group people controlled each other through face-to-face commendation and censure. In larger groups, the control was delegated to governments, religions, and industries, but these delegated authorities could be as troublesome as tyrants. In small groups reinforcers would be more often natural rather than contrived, behavior would be shaped by contingencies of reinforcement rather than directed by rules, and that would be an improvement. It would be better if practices promoted the use of positive reinforcement rather than aversive control and in particular avoided the noncontingent reinforcers of leisure and the welfare state.

Through a historical process not unlike that which I discussed in *Beyond Freedom and Dignity*, Western culture had freed itself from much pain and discomfort and from extreme states of deprivation. In one sense, these could be counted as gains but in another as a serious threat. Western culture had reached the point at which wages were no longer exchanged for the bare necessities of life but rather for expendable goods. Incentives were weakened by unemployment insurance, welfare, health insurance, and social security. Families were no longer held together by making sexual behavior contingent upon marriage. Military service was no longer maintained by a threat of death for defection nor was heroism beyond the line of duty encouraged by strong reinforcers. Face-to-face commendation and censure were less effective the larger the group, and supernatural sanctions were eroded as science made the underlying myth less credible. The punitive contingencies of government had grown weak and in most states the death penalty had been abolished. Most of this followed as people acted to escape from extreme states of deprivation or aversive stimulation or, through "compassion," to help others escape. The loss of reinforcing power could not be denied.

MARX CONTENDED THAT the economic theory of his time was the ideology of the industrial and commercial bourgeoisie, but I did not think that anything of the sort could be said of interpretations of economic practices in the light of laboratory research. For thousands of years employers had used various schedules of reinforcement, but that fact could scarcely have affected the analysis of schedules in the laboratory, where the rat or pigeon (free of ideology) told the story rather than the scientist. Not only could we reach an understanding of human behavior free of ideology, we should be able to design practices which were also free of it. In general people taught as they had been taught, governed as they had been governed, and arranged the kinds of incentive conditions under which they had themselves been employed. Accidents might lead to new practices, but better practices could be designed, and a laboratory analysis of teaching, governing, and employing could free a culture from many historical restrictions.

ANNUAL CONFERENCES on the Unity of the Sciences, not to be confused with the Unity of Science meetings sponsored by members of the Vienna Circle, were chaired by Sir John Eccles. I had refused to participate because they were supported by Sun Myung Moon, whose name appeared prominently in all the conference publications. When Eccles invited me to the fifth conference in 1976, he sent a summary of several position papers. One of them contended that "the absence of crime is not a good in itself if produced by social controllers à la Skinner." That was the pseudo-argument of A Clockwork Orange, and I wrote to Eccles that it "closed the door on what could be one of the most productive approaches to harmony among the sciences in the field of human behavior."

*   *   *

IN MY PAPER for the Honig book I complained of research designed to show that behavior maximized or minimized principles. How could consequences which have an effect only after fairly long periods of time play any role in natural selection? I thought the data described by Dick Herrnstein's matching law and by classical theories of utility could be explained in other ways. A "principle" seemed more comprehensive, and hence more impressive, than a simple process, but the process was all that could have figured in evolution. One could say that certain biological processes "maximized health," for example, but they were selected by much more specific effects on the body.

Because of an interest in steady states, especially on the part of those concerned with mathematical formulations, most of the cumulative records published in the *Journal of the Experimental Analysis of Behavior* were simply straight lines, offering no useful information beyond that of a rate. I wrote a short paper called "Farewell, My Lovely," a title taken from an article by E. B. White eulogizing the old Ford car, in which I expressed a similarly nostalgic longing for curves that were curved. (I told my secretary to "capitalize 'lovely' " and she misunderstood and put it all in caps. I thought the editor would change it and sent it off, but it was published still all in caps, displaying a little more affection than I had intended.)

I sensed an uneasiness on the part of current workers when an experimental subject was not responding. They tended to choose schedules which kept their subjects busy, but I had had a greater faith that when a rat wandered around a box for two or three minutes and then pressed the lever just once, a possibly significant process was being shown.

WHEN *About Behaviorism* was finished, I reviewed my agenda. The masses of notes filed under "How to Think" were pretty much limited to my own style of thinking, and I began to use a different title: "How to Discover What You Have to Say." Many other notes were too technical for the general reader, but I was not moved to collect them in a technical book. At one point I reflected that "I may have come to the end of my days of clear, scientific thinking. It is time to fall back upon art." I would turn to the autobiography.

As it turned out, research was needed. I learned that a nephew and niece of my teacher Miss Graves were living in New York, and they sent me her notebooks. Annetta Kane, now Sr. St. Francis, did not remember where she had read the passage from Chesterton that had figured in my decision to abandon literature, but I learned that a G. K. Chesterton Society had been founded, and when I asked the editor of its newsletter to insert a query, he himself gave me the answer. Frank Lorenz, in the Hamilton College Library, ran down the article in the *New York Times* in which H. G. Wells had compared Pavlov favorably with Bernard Shaw.

By 1975 I had reached the year 1928—the point at which I abandoned life as a writer and went off to Harvard to become a psychologist. That seemed a good stopping place, and I sent the manuscript off to Robert Gottlieb at Knopf. A title was needed, and under "life" in the Harvard Shakespeare Concordance I came upon the line from *Henry IV Part I*, "Do thou stand for my father and examine me upon the particulars of my life." Possibly because my father's opinion had always been important to me, it seemed just right. *Psychology Today* was offered the serial rights, but I turned down their proposal to publish the parts about my sexual behavior under the title "The Early Sex Life of a Behaviorist." In general the critics liked *Particulars of My Life*. Because it challenged no doctrine, it drew no fire.

IN 1975 an advertising agency sent me copy for a full-page advertisement showing photographs of six people—Vladimir Horowitz, Sir Georg Solti, George C. Scott, Rudolph Nureyev, Pearl Bailey, and me—who were said to watch television's *Great Performances*. Would I permit them to use my name and picture? I would be paid a thousand dollars. At the bottom of the page in small letters was "Exxon." I was concerned about professional ethics and talked it over with Dick Herrnstein, who saw no reason why I should not accept the money: if the government was not going to support good television directly, why not permit it to do so indirectly through tax-deductible contributions from large corporations?

But I was still not sure. In the end I agreed that they could use my picture, but they were to send the thousand dollars to Channel 2, the Public Broadcasting Station in Boston.

Another proposal was easier to refuse. As I reported it in a note:

A man from the Ziff-Davis Company phoned me yesterday. The company publishes *Psychology Today* and six other "leisure magazines," as he called them. He was preparing a film to show to potential advertisers. Would I consent to be filmed? They would pay, of course. They expected to have Margaret Mead in the film (they had "used" her in the past). When I asked what they would want me to say, he read the script: "Listen to Dr. B. F. Skinner, foremost, etc. . . . . 'People who do outstanding things in the world are the kind of people who do outstanding things in private. A dedicated scientist is probably a dedicated skier.' Etc."

I said I had never said anything like that, and could think of many examples to the contrary.

"Okay," he said. "So I tried."

IN JANUARY 1972 I gave several lectures in the Los Angeles area. An informal discussion with several psychiatrists in the Department of Psychology at the University of California was filmed by Phillip R. Blake, Associate Professor and Media Unit Coordinator. He was producing an educational film on behavioral self-management, and I agreed to let him film some introductory and concluding remarks the following May in Cambridge. He then began to talk about a full-length TV documentary on prime time with 35 to 40 million viewers, but I could not believe that such a film was feasible. More than a year later he told me that he had collected about three hundred pages of material about me, including letters from people throughout the world, and was hoping to go ahead with the documentary. I still would not agree. Later he came to Cambridge to ask me again, and he had gone so far that I felt I could no longer refuse. The Department of Psychiatry at UCLA would help support the film and so would Research Press of Champaign, Illinois.

The shooting took place in late September 1974. Fred Keller came to Cambridge and he and I were filmed walking along the shore of Walden Pond. Gerald Paterson came from Washington and we were filmed talking in our living room. Charlie Ferster came from Washing-

364

ton, Sid Bijou from Illinois, Deborah from London, and Julie, Ernie, and their children from Morgantown. I was filmed talking with Van Quine in Emerson Hall, with the liberal theologian Joseph Fletcher at his home in Belmont, and with Dick Herrnstein in his office. I was filmed lecturing to a class at Boston College, while walking and talking with Deborah on Crane's Beach, and with Julie along the Charles River (the Harvard crew rowing past in the background under radioed instructions). A family birthday party was filmed in our dining room with Lisa blowing out the candles on my cake. Lisa and Justine and I were filmed exploring the Children's Museum in Boston, and I was shown at my electric organ playing and reciting *The Three Trees* to Justine.

Eve and I were filmed reading a play. Gardner and Phyllis Cox offered their house, and a few members of the Playreaders came as an audience. I chose a scene from Tom Stoppard's *Jumpers*, in which I played a moral philosopher closely resembling G. E. Moore, with Eve as my secretary. According to the *New York Times*, Stoppard said that he sympathized emotionally with the character, "but intellectually I can shoot him full of holes. As much as anything this is an anti-Skinner play. Skinner is a highly provocative, fascinating, intelligent, brilliant, wrong-headed oaf." (A year or two later the *Times* published a dispatch from London in which *Jumpers* was said to be "concerned with the possibility of believing in moral absolutes in the age of Noam Chomsky and B. F. Skinner.") I read a short passage (omitted from one published version) about the apparently intelligent person who would admit that the Bristol train left Paddington Station "only on the understanding that all the observable phenomena associated with the train leaving Paddington could equally well be accounted for by Paddington leaving the train." When Eve and I went to Grafton, Vermont, for the autumn foliage, Blake took his crew there and photographed me walking up an old logging road.

In December I flew to Los Angeles to see a rough version and in April 1975 a still very rough version was sent to Cambridge. Laurence Olivier, Blake reported, had agreed to do the narration *gratis* because he had been a friend of Bertrand Russell and Russell had been responsible for my becoming a behaviorist. Unfortunately, Olivier was ill, and the narration had not yet been written. In late February 1976 I was sent a final version. It lasted twenty-four minutes, only nine of which were actually filmed during those thirteen days. Another editor produced a half-hour instructional film for Research Press which was fairly widely distributed.

In July 1976 Queen Elizabeth and Prince Philip came to Boston to help in celebrating the Bicentennial. Eve and I were invited to a reception on board the Royal Yacht *Britannia*. We went through the reception line (Eve not curtseying) and then had cocktails with the other guests and "members of H. M. Household." Later someone spoke to me: "The Queen would like to have a word with you." Eve said, "Does that mean me?" I said, "It does," and led her through the crowd. I was wholly unprepared and neglected some of the amenities. According to the Boston *Globe* I said, "It's just wonderful to have you here!" and the Queen replied, "It's been wonderful to help celebrate your bicentenary!" The Queen had had a long day and retired after talking with us.

When computer models of human behavior began to turn up in economics, political science, artificial intelligence, and elsewhere, cognitive psychology became cognitive science. It remained close to the input-output, stimulus-response pattern, but with "feedback" added as a substitute for reinforcement. In a paper called "On Skinner and Hull" in the *American Psychologist* for May 1977, Norman Guttman subscribed to the crucial mistake: "What people acquire through experience consists of more than respondents and operants. They learn concepts, rules, schemata, attitudes, and roles. . . ." Dick Herrnstein also talked about concepts. In his research on ambush-spotting pigeons, he had discovered how quickly a pigeon can learn to identify a particular feature—say, the presence of a person—in hundreds of colored slides. But where Dick said that the pigeon "had formed the concept of a person," I insisted that he, Dick, had formed it when he connected the slides showing a person with the reinforcing mechanism. We did not need to suppose that some copy of those connections moved into the pigeon's head. Rules were more elaborate descriptions of contingencies, and cognitive science was continuing to overlook the difference between the behavior they governed and behavior directly shaped by the contingencies.

I published a paper called "Why I Am Not a Cognitive Psychologist" in *Behaviorism*. One paragraph:

> Having moved the environment inside the head in the form of conscious experience, and behavior in the form of intention, will, and choice, and having stored the effects of contingencies of reinforcement as knowledge and rules, cognitive psychologists put them all together to compose an internal simulacrum of the organism, a kind of doppelgänger, not unlike the classical homunculus, whose behavior is the subject of what Piaget and others have called "subjective behaviorism."

To escape the charge of dualism, cognitive scientists leaned heavily on "brain research." They used "brain" and "mind" almost interchangeably. Lashley and Boring had done the same; sensations and other mental processes were states of the nervous system. From Jacques Loeb, who was said to "resent the nervous system," and W. J. Crozier, with his rejection of the "organ physiology" of our Medical School colleagues, I had learned to analyze behavior in its own right. (There were no doubt personal reasons. Whenever I spoke in the Department of Biology or at the Medical School, I sensed a slight contempt for psychology, except on the part of Walter Cannon, who was too gentle to be contemptuous of anything, and I no doubt responded by more stoutly defending the independence of my own field.)

It was not true, however, that I was opposed to physiological research. (In 1981 a writer in the *Economist* would say that I was "no longer opposed," which was at least an improvement.) I had, of course, criticized the conceptual nervous systems of Sherrington, Pavlov, and Hull and the use of merely inferred neural entities to explain the behavior from which they were inferred. Direct observation of the nervous system called for special techniques, and I was content to leave it to the physiologists. Meanwhile an experimental analysis of behavior would give them a correct assignment, whereas cognitive science sent them looking for things they would never find.

I felt about cognitive science very much as I felt about extrasensory perception. Rather than spend time spotting its flaws, I was inclined to ask why anyone believed in it. I felt the same way about the religions of the world; the question was not whether they were true but why people believed. In a book called *The Roots of Coincidence,* published in 1972, Arthur Koestler argued that there was a kind of order in the world which science had not recognized. In a paper called "The Force of Coincidence," written for a Festschrift in honor of Sidney Bijou, I pointed out that people could readily give examples of strange coincidences, not because there were so many of them, but because they were hard to forget. When operant conditioning had evolved to the point at which a single instance of response and consequence worked a change, organisms became vulnerable to coincidences, and superstitious behavior followed.

Mentalists were superstitious in the sense that, having observed various states of their bodies just as they were about to behave, they concluded that the states caused the behavior.

In 1966 Werner Honig's *Operant Behavior: Areas of Research and Application* had been a stabilizing force, but a second edition, edited jointly by Honig and J. E. R. Staddon in 1977, was a disappointment. As George Reynolds put it in a review in the *American Scientist,* "Many will relish the invasion of Skinner's box by the tired troika of encephalization, S-R connectionism, and species-specific behavior. But it is yet moot whether such theories of learning are really necessary; operant conditioners can still hope that the headlong rush backward toward Lashley, Hull, and Lorenz can be halted and reversed by a renaissance of . . . radical behaviorism. . . ." Two of the contributors had sent me their manuscripts, which I did not like, and when the book was published I put my copy on the shelf unopened, and there it remained. Dick Herrnstein said, "You must be immensely pleased," but I was not.

I was, however, pleased that the operant journals were expanding. By 1977 the number of subscribers to the *Journal of the Experimental Analysis of Behavior* had risen from 333 to 4,092. After a period half that long, subscribers to the *Journal of Applied Behavior Analysis* numbered 7,097. An analysis of the 1975 Science Citation Index, made to discover the "impact on science of 80 psychology journals," showed *JEAB* in 8th place (the 431st of 2,630 journals in all the sciences), with *JABA* in 42nd place. A subsequent slight decline in subscription did not, I thought, show a loss of interest; other journals were competing for the same contributors and readers, in part because operant research was becoming better known.

Membership in Division 25 of the American Psychological Association continued to rise, and in 1977 a separate association was founded. For a number of years the Midwestern Association for Behavior Analysis, organized by Neil Kent, Richard Malott, and Margaret Peterson (Vaughan), from Western Michigan University, and Gerald Mertens, from St. Cloud University (Minnesota), had attracted more and more people on both coasts and from abroad, and in 1978 it was converted into an international Association for Behavior Analysis. Its membership rose steadily. For several years Fred Keller and I were after-dinner speakers at the annual banquet and in 1979 the Association invited Albury Castell, so that he and I could play Castle and Frazier in an extemporaneous sequel to *Walden Two*.

In London I talked with Duncan Dallas, a producer for Yorkshire Television, the branch of ITV that made science documentaries. He wanted to do a program on *Particulars of My Life*. I told him of my unhappiness with the Blake film, but he reassured me; they would cover the Susquehanna years only and would keep close to the spirit of my book.

In January 1977 I spent a week in Susquehanna with a crew of ten people. There was no longer a hotel in the town, and we stayed at a motel in Halstead, a small town ten miles away. (I was invited to dinner by some relatives on my father's side and rediscovered the excellence of the native cuisine of rural Pennsylvania).

Reviews of *Particulars* had reached Susquehanna before the book itself, and a reference to the fact that I called the town "dirty and unkempt" inspired letters to the *Transcript*, one of them so long that it was run in three issues. When the book began to be read, it was seen that I had reported my life there warmly enough, and I was forgiven. My return with a television crew from Britain was an event. A large sign on Main Street read, "Welcome B. F. Skinner and British Television."

I had warned Dallas that it could be very cold and that the countryside would be more photogenic if we waited until spring, but he wanted to proceed at once. There was heavy snow on the ground, and fresh falls kept it white.

I was filmed looking across the river at the town, walking into the town past a sign reading "Welcome to Susquehanna," ringing the door-bell of an old friend, Alice Moore French, who had been valedictorian in my high school class, and greeting her as she appeared. I was filmed visiting with another old friend, Pinky Schmidt, whom I had not seen for more than fifty-five years. She and her husband lived on the outskirts of the town, and her children and grandchildren had snowmobiles, which were soon being driven with abandon by the Yorkshire camera crew.

We filmed set pieces. A passing freight train revealed me standing in front of the once-handsome hotel station, whereupon I said two or three sentences to be used in the opening of the film. The crew carried heavy equipment a quarter of a mile through waist-deep snow to shoot me talking about my contact with nature while standing in front of a frozen waterfall. I talked about my early life in the house in which I was born and had lived for eighteen years, I talked about Francis Bacon and scientific method in the bedroom where I had last seen my teacher, Miss Graves, who was responsible for my interest in Bacon; I was shown helping the editor of the *Transcript* feed sheets of paper into his small press—much smaller than the press at the *Transcript* when I worked for it; I talked about programmed instruction in the building in which I attended school for twelve years, and about utopias and perfectionism in front of the monument three miles down the river that marked the spot where Joseph Smith dictated the Book of Mormon.

In all these settings I was interviewed by a Yorkshireman who had been an unsuccessful candidate for Parliament (he ran successfully after returning to Britain), and somehow we always got around to free will, which I could have discussed as well in a studio. Eve and I saw the film when we were next in London. There was very little autobiography left in it, and when it appeared on ITV the critics thought someone should have been given a chance to answer me.

WGBH (Channel 2) in Boston had contributed to the Yorkshire venture in exchange for some of the film to be used in a documentary in the *Nova* series. Veronica Young, the director, was not happy with it and produced a different program, with newsreel footage of the baby-tender taken in Bloomington, Indiana, and a bit of the Blake film showing my birthday party. Most of the program covered a visit to Twin Oaks with Eve and Deborah, during which I discussed some of the problems of a Walden Two community with its members.

I WAS NO STRANGER to variable-ratio schedules. They had once kept me playing Parcheesi with my brother and dominos and Pedro with my Grandmother Burrhus. They had sustained my interest in literature, art, and music, and they explained my dedication to my laboratory and the desk at which I wrote papers and books. But I resented the gambling enterprises which used them to take money away from people. State lotteries angered me. Legislators were afraid to raise taxes, but could turn to lotteries because people were said to be free to buy or not to buy tickets. I wrote a satirical piece for the Op-Ed section of the *New York Times* in which I explained how states could use the school system to make all their citizens into pathological gamblers. The lotteries would then pay for everything. My piece was called "Freedom, at Last, from the Burden of Taxation."

AT MEETINGS OF the American Psychological Association I frequently saw my former student, Sister Annette Walters, S.S.C.C. Upon one occasion, when she had just returned from a year in Belgium, I showed her a copy of a Simenon *roman policier* which I had in my pocket, and she asked if I would send it to her when I had finished. I sent instead two or three which were rather less spicy. When she wrote that she and her friend Sister Rita Mary Bradley had thoroughly enjoyed them and would appreciate others, I sent a few less carefully selected and received no acknowledgment. Sister Annette was a leader in a women's liberation movement within the Catholic hierarchy, and when *Time* magazine ran a story about it and printed her picture, I wrote: "Since I know you are above the sin of pride, I can tell you that you are as beautiful as ever."

Later she wrote that she and Sister Rita Mary would be driving to Boston and would love to drop in and see us. She warned me that I might not recognize her because she was out of habit. I was, indeed, surprised.

She arrived in a knee-length green dress, her hair attractively styled. She was teaching at St. Ambrose College in Davenport, Iowa, and hoped that I would come to lecture there whenever I was in the Midwest. When a date was finally arranged, she hired the Masonic Temple and charged admission in order to offer me an appropriate fee. I said no fee was necessary, but she insisted, and we eventually split the proceeds.

In 1978 I heard that she was dying of cancer in a Minneapolis hospital and tried to phone her. She was too weak to talk, and so I wrote. My letter was read to her just as she was entering the operating room from which she would not return alive. In it I said, "it is at times like these that one wishes one could pray."

WHETHER THE HUMAN SPECIES would have a future was really a question of whether we could solve our problems, and on several occasions (one of them when giving a Phi Beta Kappa Oration at Harvard in 1976), I asked the question, "Why are the behavioral sciences not more effective?" I thought mentalism was the answer. As an example I used the lack of confidence which was blamed for many of our troubles. What was lacking was behavior, and the lack was due to the very contingencies said to be responsible for the lack of confidence.

I appealed, against my better judgment, to history. China had invented the compass, gunpowder, and movable type but had never taken advantage of them because of inhibiting cultural practices. The West had used them to conquer the world and spread Western thought. Would China, never having suffered from the Greek bifurcation of nature, now reverse the process and use our behavioral technology more effectively than we could do because of *our* inhibiting cultural practices?

I could have used a policy decision at Harvard as an example of the survival of mentalism. When clinical psychology was ruled a profession and hence not to be taught in the Graduate School of Arts and Sciences, a program in "Clinical Psychology and Public Practice" was set up in the Graduate School of Education. It would accept students in five fields—education, religion, government, economics, and psychotherapy. These were the five "agencies" I had analyzed in *Science and Human Behavior*, but they were treated in a very different way. In education, for example, it was said that "attitudes expressed in the structure of school systems affect the cognitive and creative potential of virtually every child, as do the feelings and personalities of teachers and their supervisors." But was the "cognitive and creative potential" of students to be changed, or their behavior? Were the feelings and personalities of teachers and supervisors to be improved, or the contingencies of reinforcement they maintained for students? In the long run, a change was needed in the contingencies under which teachers and supervisors worked.

FOR SOME TIME I had planned a new collection of papers, of which by 1977 there were eighteen, including two Op-Ed pieces for the *New York Times*. Robert Epstein, one of Charlie Catania's graduate students at the University of Maryland, Baltimore County, had published a carefully edited listing of my books. During the summer of 1977 he came to work for me as a volunteer, and before the summer was out had arranged to stay on as a graduate student. He reduced the references in my papers to a single style and made other editorial changes, and *Reflections on Behaviorism and Society* appeared in 1978.

I had dedicated *The Behavior of Organisms* "to Yvonne," a name that Eve had abandoned when we moved from Minnesota to Indiana. I dedicated *Reflections* "to Eve renée," suggesting that she had been not only renamed but reborn. For many years she had made tape recordings for the blind. Her voice recorded well, and some of her tapes were copied for national distribution, but she also read for local students. (When a book was about psychology, she would first look at what it said about me, and if it was critical, she would leave it for another reader.) In 1972 she found a much more absorbing role as a volunteer at the Museum of Fine Arts. She began to go into the Greater Boston schools with a slide projector and talk to students about the pictures they would see when they visited the Museum. She was surprised to discover how well she held the attention of young people and was soon taking courses to qualify as a Gallery Instructor. She began to lecture to special groups and to give courses to new volunteers. Everyone who knew her commented on the reborn Eve.

M. Brewster Smith reviewed *Reflections on Behaviorism and Society* in *Political Psychology*. Much of what he said was sympathetic; nevertheless, his review illustrated the kinds of misunderstandings that still persisted. He said that I was a positivist of the Vienna Circle school, that I rejected "self-correction, self-investment, and self-development," that my views were mechanistic (though granting that "strictly mechanistic" might be unfair), that I ascribed to people the same unthinking blindness that was a good fit for pigeons, and so on. I felt that none of this was true.

THE BANDWAGON OF behavior modification soon attracted cognitive psychologists, with slightly improved versions of traditional ways of "changing minds." Although there was something contradictory in the expression "cognitive behavior modification," there was at least a recognition that advice, argument, and persuasion were effective only if behavior changed. One could pretend that one first modified a mind which then modified behavior, but in practice it was a matter of working with descriptions of contingencies rather than the contingencies themselves. No one would have recommended shaping the behavior of a person who could instead be shown or told what to do, but people did not respond to descriptions of contingencies as they responded to the contingencies themselves. The reasons why they took advice and obeyed laws needed to be considered.

ALTHOUGH DICK HERRNSTEIN and I occupied adjacent offices in William James Hall, we seldom discussed our work. I had written notes about his occasional use of mentalistic terms, but I was unprepared for a manuscript called "Post-Skinnerian Behaviorism" which he handed me in 1977. When I returned it, I told him that I thought he would be sorry if he published it. Nevertheless it appeared in the *American Psychologist* in December 1977, slightly revised and retitled "The Evolution of Behaviorism."

It began with a paradox: Skinnerianism was simultaneously waxing and waning. On the one hand, I was gaining public recognition (Dick cited a curious poll taken to discover the one hundred most important people who had ever lived, according to which Jesus Christ was first and I was about fortieth, not far from Luther and Calvin), but on the other hand, many people were "finding holes in the fabric of Skinnerianism."

Dick thought the paradox could be resolved. The success of the operant movement was due to certain "tacit assumptions," which should be more closely examined. I did not remember ever having made any of them and could cite explicit statements to the contrary. For example, according to Dick I believed that there were only a few drives, but in the thirties, when I was still using the term, I had said that there must be a drive for every reinforcer. He thought that my criticism of the "botanizing of reflexes" meant a rejection of ethology, but I had never denied that some behavior was due to contingencies of survival in natural selection, and my first experiments had been ethological. Dick thought that I had failed to acknowledge that behavior due to contingencies of survival was emitted because it was automatically reinforcing, but since it often occurred only once, I could not see that it needed to be reinforced at all. Naturally I did not agree that the success of the experimental analysis of behavior was due to the concealment of flaws and wrote an answer, and Dick a rejoinder. It could not be said that we reached agreement.

Fortunately, we remained friends. I attributed much of the tone of his paper to his own position at the time. He had published an article in the *Atlantic Monthly* on the IQ and was under rather violent attack. A group who called themselves "Students for a Democratic Society" disrupted his classes, and for some time the doors on the seventh floor of William James Hall were kept locked. When a writer in the *Boston Globe* implied that Dick was a racist, I wrote a denial which the *Globe* published.

IN 1978 I received a newspaper clipping from Africa about a wild boy whom soldiers were said to have seen climbing trees with a band of monkeys. Harlan Lane, Chairman of the Department of Psychology at Northeastern University, who had taken his degree with me in 1961, had published an excellent book on the wild boy of Aveyron, and I sent the clipping on to him. He and a psychiatrist friend, Richard Pillard, raised funds, went to Burundi, and tracked the boy down. The story had, of course, been much exaggerated. The boy had presumably suffered from an illness when very young and his parents had abandoned him. When Lane and Pillard found him, he was living with some nuns, and it seemed that nothing better could be done for him.

WILLIAM JAMES HAD OPENED his laboratory in 1878, and in 1978, when the American Psychological Association celebrated the hundredth anniversary of psychology in America, I was asked to give a paper on my part in its history. I could cite some amusing numerology. It was the fiftieth anniversary of my entrance into the field, the fortieth of the publication of *The Behavior of Organisms*, and the thirtieth of *Walden Two*. I had been a year early with *Verbal Behavior* and *Schedules of Reinforcement* in 1957, but on the mark again in 1968 with *The Technology of Teaching*. It was hard to believe that I had been an experimental psychologist for one-half the life of the science itself. For that matter it was hard to believe—it was the sort of reflection that comes with age—that my birth reached one-fifth of the way back to Shakespeare or about one-thirtieth to Plato.

IN 1977 Julie published *Behavioral Psychology for Teachers*, a book which she had carefully tested on her own classes and in which Lisa and Justine, to whom it was dedicated, appeared among the illustrations. One chapter was contributed by Ernie, who with Lawrence Fraley was running a learning laboratory at West Virginia University. Julie's first book had been dedicated "To my husband and my father," but there was no further identification, and there was no reference to me on the jacket or in the advertisement of either book. They were excellent and needed no help. In 1978 Julie became a full professor of educational psychology. She began to give workshops in many parts of the country and became a consultant for Charles Walther's New Century Education Corporation. A learning center was set up in a school in Morgantown, and Julie began to write a program called "Something to Think About."

* * *

FOR SEVERAL YEARS, M. J. Willard, a clinical psychologist, had occasionally worked for me as a volunteer. One day she came in greatly excited: Why not teach chimpanzees to help the severely handicapped —say, quadriplegics? I reminded her that chimps were dangerous and suggested that she try monkeys. She bought a capuchin (organ grinder's) monkey and set to work. She found she could train it most efficiently by first building an imitative repertoire, with which she could then "show it what to do." The quadriplegic directed the monkey's behavior with verbal or other stimuli and delivered pellets of food as reinforcers by operating a switch with his head or mouth. The first monkeys M. J. used were hyperactive and often troublesome, but she solved that problem genetically: she found a much quieter strain.

In a report of her project on the television show *Sixty Minutes*, a monkey fed the quadriplegic with a spoon, took a bottle from the refrigerator, opened it, and put in a straw, put a cassette on a player, and cleaned a table with a cloth and the room with a small vacuum. A fairly extensive research program followed.

In 1979 Eve and I went to Japan at the invitation of the Japanese Psychological Society and Keio University. Our quarters were luxurious, and sightseeing was skillfully arranged. Keio gave me an honorary degree, and I enjoyed discussions with Professor Sato and Dr. Watanabe. Young scientists at the Kyoto University Primate Center in Inuyama took us to see an early example of the practical use of animal behavior: cormorant fishing.

In our hotel we found, in place of a Gideon Bible, a book on Buddha's teachings, and I could not resist a behavioristic note:

Compassion, tenderness, gladness, and equanimity are the "Four Unlimited States of Mind." Greed is removed by cherishing compassion, anger by cherishing tenderness, suffering by cherishing gladness, and discrimination against one's enemies and in favor of one's friends by cherishing an equitable mind.

But how does one "cherish" a state of mind? Is this saying anything more than that one is not greedy when generous, not angry when tender, not unhappy when glad, not unfair when being equitable? To those who turn first to their bodies, the states they feel appear to act upon each other, but one is then unlikely to look at (1) the environment responsible for the behavior called greedy, generous, etc., (2) the techniques of self-management which could be said to change these states, and (3)—of greater importance—what one *does* to others when one is said to be greedy, generous, angry, and unfair.

I gave a lecture on "The Nonpunitive Society," of the relevance of which to Japanese culture I was not sure. Daily life in Japan was less violent than in America, but the social behavior seemed to me so "meticulous" in the etymological sense of fearful that I suspected concealed punitive sources.

Whether punishment was always expendable was still an unanswered question. Autistic children were sometimes so severely self-destructive that they had to be kept in straitjackets, but Ivor Lovass, at UCLA, had found that an electric shock would suppress self-destruction and make it possible to use positive reinforcement. Matt Israel had organized a center for the care of autistic people who were often so violent that punishment seemed necessary. To minimize its use he ranked acceptable forms in order of severity; no form was to be used until less severe forms had failed. When the list reached the newspapers, he was in trouble. New York State removed a number of people who had been placed in his care (they were returned when no one else would take them). Julie served briefly on a committee which inspected Matt's center and in general gave it her approval.

One reached the heart of the issue of punishment in a sequence rather like a syllogism. Students should not be punished when they have failed to learn; their teachers have failed to teach. But the teachers should not be punished; the culture has not properly trained them or given them good material. But the culture cannot be punished. (It could be said to be automatically punished when it grows weak, in part because of faulty education, but it is not then, as a result, improved. When a better culture is designed, teachers will be more effective, and young people will learn more.)

A similar sequence was implied by a maxim that guided my early research: "The rat is always right." If my experimental subjects did not behave as I had predicted, my predictions were at fault. But was I then at fault? No, my science had not yet evolved to the point, nor had I reached the point myself, at which I could predict the behavior of my experimental subjects accurately.

READERS HAD LIKED *Particulars of My Life,* and I began to spend most of my time on a second volume. The urge to write a novel had been attenuated, and other issues could wait. Where I had limited myself to one hour a day on the autobiography, I now spent an hour on the "book about the future" and the rest of the day on what was eventually published as *The Shaping of a Behaviorist.*

Ken Galbraith was writing an autobiography, too, and his secretary sent me a page marked "Check with Skinner." It reported an incident which I not only could not remember but thought quite unlikely to have happened, and I asked him not to use it. In return I sent him a short account of something he had told me when we were living in Winthrop House in the early thirties. He, too, could not remember it and asked me not to use it.

Early reviews of *The Shaping of a Behaviorist* were not kind. The *New York Times* said that I asked my readers to slog their way through my scientific life. It is true that the research leading up to the publication of *The Behavior of Organisms* in 1938 was of interest mainly to psychologists, and my life during that period was not particularly eventful (though not many people brand their arms with the initials of someone they have loved and lost). Interest should have picked up with the story of the pigeon-guided missile and the baby-tender. My William James Lectures on verbal behavior, the publication of *Walden Two,* and my return to Harvard as a full professor in 1948 had seemed an appropriate denouement for that part of the story. *Psychology Today* published an excerpt about my naive efforts to promote the production of the baby-tender.

ALTHOUGH I WAS STILL TRIMMING my schedule, I could not refuse an invitation to speak at the Concord School of Philosophy on July 18,

1979, almost one hundred years to the day after Bronson Alcott founded it. One of the speakers during its first year was William James. The building was still standing on the grounds of Orchard House, which figured in Louisa May Alcott's *Little Women*. Eve and I were invited to dine in the house beforehand and, out of deference to Alcott's views, the dinner was vegetarian. The school building held about eighty people, watched over by plaster or marble busts of several philosophers. I discussed the Good Life as it was thought of then and might be thought of now.

JOHN B. WATSON HAD ATTENDED Furman College in Greenville, South Carolina, and in April 1979 the college (now a university) opened the John B. Watson Laboratory. Watson's son attended the ceremony and Fred Keller and I were among the speakers. Half a century had passed since Fred and I defended Watson against the psychology of Titchener and Boring, and a great deal had happened to support our position. The current science was not exactly the science Watson had projected, but his central theme, "Study behavior not mind," had survived.

IN 1975 Barry and Deborah returned to London and bought a flat in Hampstead. Barry began to teach in the Department of International Studies at the University of Warwick, commuting from London. Deborah continued to have solo shows in the Studio Gallery in Vancouver and at the Harvard Cooperative Society in Cambridge and at several galleries in London. Her etchings began to be shown in the summer exhibitions of the Royal Academy.

I HAD STARTED DATING and titling my notes in 1955. As early as 1962 I thought I "had enough for a daybook," especially if I included bits of the Natural Sciences 114 lectures. By 1973 I was considering several separate collections. One would be "light on psychology, for the general public," to be called *Things I Have Said to Myself*. Notes suitable "for psychologists only" could be added to another collection of papers, as in

Contingencies of Reinforcement. Others were finding a place in the autobiography, and there might even be enough on verbal behavior for a separate volume. In 1977 Robert Epstein began to read my notes and offered to edit a collection. About seven hundred of them were published as *Notebooks: B. F. Skinner* in 1980.

A SWELLING IN FRONT of my right ear was diagnosed as an enlarged lymph gland and removed. The swelling returned and proved to be a tumor of the parotid gland. When removed it was found to be malignant, and every weekday for six weeks I was clamped into a machine and one side of my face was intensely irradiated. For a time I lost all sense of taste. My other salivary glands dried up, and I could not swallow solid foods. I lived for several weeks on a liquid diet. When I canceled a commitment to speak at the annual meeting of the American Psychological Association, the reason was exaggerated. It was rumored, among other things, that I had had a brain tumor.

TWENTY YEARS HAD PASSED since I had first given myself five more years to finish my work. The angina and the malignant tumor had reminded me that I could not continue to do so forever. I needed to accelerate my program, and I needed help. I had met Dr. Margaret Peterson at meetings of the Association for Behavior Analysis, of which she was an officer and a prime mover. She had taken her degree from Western Michigan University, under Jack Michael and Howard Farris, and was teaching at Kalamazoo College. In April 1981 she came to work with me on the autobiography. Together we went through the last thirty years of my correspondence, notes, and clippings. (In August, in our garden, she was married to Will Vaughan, one of our former graduate students who was working with Dick Herrnstein.)

IN AUGUST 1967 Grant Kenyon, a student of Robert Kantor's, called me from the Boston airport. What did I think would happen if a deaf-mute couple using sign language were to adopt a baby chimpanzee?

Would the chimp learn the language? I said I would be surprised if it did. Later I was surprised that I should have said so. Efforts to get chimpanzees to talk had failed because their vocal apparatus was not under good operant control, but there was no reason why they could not behave verbally, although not vocally, with a different part of the body. As it turned out, B. T. and R. A. Gardner were conducting their rather similar experiment at the time. It led to others and to a great deal of controversy.

When an article appeared in *Science* reporting an experiment in which two chimpanzees engaged in "symbolic communication," with a suggestion of mental processes to be found only in the higher primates, I thought the behavior could be better formulated along the lines of *Verbal Behavior* and suggested to Robert Epstein that we shape a similar performance in pigeons. Budgetless, I made the apparatus in my basement workshop, cutting plastic keys from boxes once used to hold tape cassettes and hammering contacts from silver wire which Deborah had left in a box of jewelry-making tools. Robert wired the controlling circuits, and Robert Lanza, a student on leave from the University of Pennsylvania Medical School, helped maintain the rather complex instructional contingencies.

We called our pigeons Jack and Jill. Jack could get food only by pecking that one of three keys which matched a sample color, but the sample was hidden behind a curtain on Jill's side of the apparatus. Jack "asked for Jill's help" by pecking and thus illuminating a key reading "WHAT COLOR?" Jill looked behind the curtain and then illuminated a key bearing a black-on-white letter—R if the sample was red, Y if it was yellow, and G if it was green. By pecking a key marked "THANK YOU," Jack then operated a food dispenser which reinforced Jill's behavior, thus "assuring that she would continue to help." He then looked at the illuminated symbol, pecked the corresponding color, and received food. All of the contingencies responsible for the behavior of both speaker and listener could be found in the early verbal histories of children. A report was published in *Science*.

We embarked upon a more ambitious series of experiments on other "cognitive processes" and I suggested that we call the project "Columban simulation"—the simulation of human behavior in pigeons rather than computers. One experiment was on the "concept of self." In an article in the *American Scientist* a chimpanzee was said to have demonstrated such a concept by touching a spot on its forehead which it could see only in a mirror. Within twenty-four hours after reading the article I had thrown together an apparatus of heavy cardboard cut from packing cases, which could be operated mechanically by pulling strings. Robert and I, with the help of student volunteers, shaped a repertoire of pecking spots in real space to mirrored stimuli. A spot was then put on the pigeon's breast. A small bib hanging from the pigeon's neck dropped to cover the spot when the pigeon looked down. The spot could be seen only in the mirror. When no mirror was present, the pigeon walked idly about. When a mirror was uncovered, it looked in the mirror and almost immediately tried to peck a corresponding point on its body.

Robert and I also simulated the spontaneous use of memoranda and, with Lanza's help, the insight said to have been shown by Köhler's ape when it reached a suspended banana by moving a box underneath. Robert Lanza and I also found that a pigeon would lie. When Jill was more generously rewarded for reporting red, she began to call yellow red.

In *Science and Human Behavior* I had said that an inherent reflex mechanism by which "a pattern of behavior in another organism elicits a series of responses having the same pattern . . . does not seem to exist." I had been misled by an early experiment at Indiana University. When I conditioned one pigeon to peck a Ping-Pong ball fastened to the wall, a second pigeon in an adjacent space did not peck a similar ball. Robert Epstein and I thought we could at least *train* a pigeon to imitate, and I built a similar apparatus consisting of two compartments separated by a clear plastic sheet with Ping-Pong balls fastened on adjacent walls. With the pigeon on the left pecking the ball rapidly under a suitable schedule of reinforcement, we asked a student to watch a pigeon on the right for a few hours to make sure that there was no innate imitation. She soon rushed into my office to tell us that the pigeon was pecking. In subsequent work Robert found that the imitator would even peck a ball that was made available only after the other pigeon had been removed. An innate imitative repertoire was obvious. At Indiana I had also crudely measured a pigeon's reaction time. Robert and I used our computer to make more accurate measurements and found that, with the proper contingencies, they came within range of the value for human subjects.

Although Columban simulation was different from my early research, I had not given up my dedication to the cumulative record and to rate of responding as a basic datum. I was pleased to see that the 1980–81 Guide to Scientific Instruments published in *Science* listed five companies manufacturing cumulative recorders.

In an article in *Psychology Today*, February 1978, two well-known writers on ethology, Lionel Tiger and Robin Fox, wrote, "Skinner brings it all to its miserable conclusion by flogging a dead rat (or at least a highly selected, hungry, imprisoned one) to prove that suitably bribed organisms are malleable." I entered a comment in my notebook: "When will they grow up and become scientists? How can they expect people in the experimental analysis of behavior to take them seriously when they say things like that?" They were not the only ethologists who were refusing to acknowledge the importance of environmental conditions and, at the same time, accusing operant conditioners of neglecting genetic endowment.

The new field of sociobiology was also raising the question of genetics, but issues were confused because the field was being attacked as racist. E. O. Wilson, a friend and colleague, said he was learning what I must have gone through after the publication of *Beyond Freedom and Dignity*. I sympathized with him, although we did not agree on the role of genes. All behavior was genetically determined, since we were nothing more than products of natural selection, but that did not mean that there were separate genes for everything we did. The genes responsible for the behavioral process of operant conditioning could explain many of the kinds of behavior that Wilson attributed to separate genes. Altruistic behavior, for example, could be genetic (perhaps due to kin selection) or it could be due to operant contingencies arranged by a culture. In many cases it could be due to both.

I thought I had treated the relation between innate and acquired behavior well enough in my paper on phylogeny and ontogeny, but it appeared that more was needed, and I spent a good deal of time on a paper called "Selection by Consequences," published in *Science* in 1981. Selection was a causal mode, discovered very late in the history of science and not yet well understood. Some aspects of natural selection were still debated, operant conditioning was still viewed skeptically by many psychologists, and many anthropologists did not agree about, or were not interested in, the evolution of cultures. The special nature of selection as a causal mode was responsible for issues common to all three levels—in particular, a prior act of creation, purpose or intention, certain essences (Life, Mind, and Zeitgeist, respectively), and values. It was hard to dispense with a supposed initiating agent, especially at the level of human operant conditioning, where we seemed to have inside information and more at stake personally.

A BIOGRAPHY REACHES a natural end when the subject dies; an auto-biography must be brought to an end. Like those novelists who once told their readers what eventually happened to all their characters, I shall end by summing up.

Julie was only a few months old when I taught summer school at Harvard in 1938. I had resolved not to talk about her with my colleagues, but near the end of the summer I discovered how poorly I had succeeded when the wife of one of them said to me, "I like a man who talks about his children." (Many years later Julie reciprocated by writing a paper called "B. F. Skinner: Father, Grandfather, and Behavior Modifier," published in the first issue of a new journal, *Human Behavior*.) Eve and I have continued to talk about our daughters, perhaps excessively. For one thing, a psychologist's children are always under inspection: Are the shoemaker's children poorly shod? Julie and Deborah were never serious problems, but they were not well disciplined. I used to say that I was not trying to produce a well-behaved ten-year-old; I wanted a happy twenty-year-old. In that way I could avoid the use of punishment.

By 1982 Julie and Ernie had both become professors at West Virginia University, where they were actively promoting the experimental analysis of behavior in education. Their older daughter, who now called herself Kris, was a senior at Choate-Rosemary, and Justine was in junior high. They spent their summers in their house on St. John, in the Virgin Islands, and for that reason we saw less of them than we liked. Julie's books were selling well, and she was on the Council of the Association for Behavior Analysis.

Deborah had survived the rumors about her. When a distinguished

English critic told Harry Levin that he was sorry to hear that she had committed suicide, Harry replied, "Well, when did she do that? I was swimming with her yesterday." A well-known psychiatrist told Eunice Shriver that the child we "raised in the box" became psychotic; he apologized abjectly when I wrote to ask where he had heard the story. Later it was said that Deborah was suing me. These rumors were sometimes fostered by clinical psychologists who found it useful in criticizing behavior therapy. One night, just as I was falling asleep, the phone rang and a young man said, "Professor Skinner, is it true that you kept one of your children in a cage?"

Possibly because of the baby-tender and the rumors about it I had been too solicitous. When Deborah was quite young I once took her to the dentist and asked if I could be with her as he worked on her. He wisely refused and made me stay in the waiting room. Deborah's school reports complained of lack of motivation, but I should have said lack of reinforcement and, indeed, when she found something that she did well, the problem was solved. Of one of her shows in a London gallery, a reviewer in *Arts Review* wrote:

> She is, first, a composer of considerable subtlety, selecting colours and shapes from her subject to produce maximum impact. Further, she has a number of "artistic" ways of treating the simple landscape which turns the image into a complex and profound statement for the eye. In some for example she focuses the main theme by framing it in a contrasting fragment of landscape seen in a different light. In others, and among them to my view the best in this extremely worthwhile exhibition, she as it were projects the landscape on to a folding screen, with panels lightened or darkened as they face towards or away from the supposed light source.

Deborah gave us a print of one of the etchings that she had shown at the Royal Academy, and we hung it above the clavichord. She appeared in public in a less serious way on a television program called "To Tell the Truth."

Deborah and Barry had moved to a garden flat in Belsize Park, London, and often traveled on the Continent. In April 1982 Eve and I took them on a cruise of the Greek islands, and Barry and I made it something of a busman's holiday by discussing the role of an analysis of behavior in political science, in part in relation to his book, *People*,

States, and Fear: The National Security Problem in International Relations, which was then in press.

At the Museum of Fine Arts, Eve was giving courses to those who, like herself ten years earlier, were fresh volunteers. I heard two of her lectures—one, called "Fun and Games on Greek Pots," on the collection of erotic Greek vases in the Museum, and another titled "The Origin of the Greek Theatre in the Rites of Dionysus." They were both delightful.

MORE THAN HALF A CENTURY had passed since I had brashly written to Percy Saunders, "I have almost gone over to physiology, which I find fascinating, but my fundamental interests lie in the field of psychology, and I shall probably continue therein, even, if necessary, by making over the entire field to suit myself." Alas, I had not made it over. It was, in fact, in disarray. For inexorable economic reasons professional psychologists had taken control of the Association, and a conspicuous relaxation in the use of scientific terms and principles had followed. More and more psychologists found everyday English adequate for their purposes and were impatient with technical terms. Psychology was becoming more and more like psychiatry, which had never had a basic science. The exigencies of the profession were giving mentalism another chance. When a writer in Contemporary Psychology said that "behavioral theorizing reads more and more like a demonstration of how many concepts can be made to dance on the pin of reinforcement," I commented in a note:

Try a parallel in another science:

... on the pin of relativity
... on the pin of plate tectonics
... on the pin of genes and chromosomes

Psychologists want a changing scene. Something new every half-generation. The possibility that a science may be built on a substantial substrate, that early concepts may be refined but need not be discarded, is seldom considered because the history of psychology has not made it plausible.

Psychology Today celebrated a birthday by asking eleven psychologists to review progress during the fifteen years of its existence. I professed ignorance of other fields than my own and reviewed progress only in the experimental analysis of behavior. When the issue appeared, an editorial comment in the *New York Times* reviewed it scathingly: the eleven psychologists had failed to agree upon a single advance. A few weeks later, at a meeting of the Association for Behavior Analysis, I took much the same line. Nothing of importance was happening in psychology. In divorcing itself from behaviorism (or rather in asking that behaviorism be declared legally dead), it was relinquishing its claim to being a science. Psychologists who had not fled to physiology had fled to computerized versions of traditional explanations of human behavior. Humanistic psychologists still called behaviorism reductionistic and destructive of valuable traits of character: a world so designed that people behaved mercifully and compassionately toward each other was defective if the behavior was not due to traits of mercy and compassion.

Behaviorism was on its own, and its task was formidable. As I wrote in a note:

> It will be a sweeping change when it comes. There is so much to be changed in so many fields. I read *TLS*, the *New York Review*, and books and articles, and *in almost every field* there looms the prospect of a great clarification. The ice dam holding back the flood is the stubborn unwillingness of those raised in the humanities to look at behaviorism, even when the behavioristic account comes close to their own and their own shows no growth in decades. The whole thing will burst—as behaviorism displaces the egocentric emphasis on feelings and states of mind.

At a special symposium organized by the International Center for Epistemology as a birthday celebration for Willard Van Orman Quine, I reviewed a minor problem:

> In every field of science there are two languages. The astronomer speaks one when he tells his children that after the sun has gone down the stars will come out. He speaks another to his colleagues. Many years ago Sir Arthur Eddington called attention to the two tables of the physicist—the table on which he wrote and another that was mostly empty space. Behaviorists must also speak two languages and are much

more likely to be misunderstood when they do so. Everyday English is suffused with terms which have come down to us from ancient ways of talking about human behavior. It is impossible to speak English without calling up spirits and invoking gods. Young behaviorists are often embarrassed when they speak English to an older colleague, but often nothing else will serve. Their older colleagues have resigned themselves to the necessities.

OPERANT RESEARCH CONTINUED to flourish. I had not kept up with it and could not always understand the papers which appeared in the *Journal for the Experimental Analysis of Behavior*, now in its twenty-fifth year. I continued to think of new experiments, and I enjoyed building simple apparatus in my basement workshop—in part because it showed that research could still be done without a grant. With Will and Maggie Vaughan I checked a point concerning the relation between the number of responses and the number of reinforcements in a single key setting, and I hoped to join them in the systematic coverage of long-term memory that I had proposed and abandoned nearly thirty years earlier. But active research did not seem to be part of my future.

In 1982 Research Press published a text, *Skinner for the Classroom*, containing fifteen of the papers most often assigned in courses on my work, to which Robert Epstein and I added editorial notes.

IN A SURVEY conducted in 1968, I had found myself among the first fifty "great teachers" of all time, and third among the five on the list who were still alive, with Hutchins and Conant ahead of me, both of whom were soon dead. I noted:

> That is just absurd. I have never felt that I was much of a teacher. It is true that a lot of my students have gone on to do good work but mainly because, having learned from my own experience, I left them alone. Probably what is meant is people who have influenced education. Even so, I am amazed that the three hundred deans of education who made the list should have put me that high.

Two decades had passed since three companies had looked at my teaching machines, "waited to see how the ball would bounce," and dropped them. Had they been right? Certainly my machines were cumbersome, but the calculating machines of the time were cumbersome, too, and nonetheless useful. Teaching machines could now be as simple as pocket calculators. What had kept them from coming into wider use? Current philosophies of education seemed to be the answer. Schools of education, state and federal departments, administrators, teachers— none of these seemed to believe that better teaching was possible. The Spring 1982 issue of the *New York Times Educational Supplement* contained fourteen articles on familiar topics—the cost of education, the problems of private schools, coaching for college entrance tests, and so on, and four articles on teaching students to use computers, but there was only one reference to a teaching machine and it was in quotation marks. The question raised was whether machines would replace teachers. There was nothing about the improvement of teaching.

In 1981 my colleague Fred Mosteller was president of the American Association for the Advancement of Science, and in his Presidential Address, published in *Science*, he urged the Association to promote innovation in science education. In a letter to the editor I summarized the experiment in Roanoke, Virginia, in which an eighth-grade class, using a simple teaching machine, covered all of ninth-grade algebra in one term. That had happened twenty-one years ago and was now forgotten. "What is needed in education," I wrote, "is not innovation but a change in the establishment that will permit efficient teaching methods to be used."

A few weeks later I happened to see Mosteller and asked if he had read my letter "about teaching machines." He was puzzled. Then he said, "Oh, you mean computers. Teaching machines to *you!*" It was an apt remark. Teaching by machine had long since become "computer-aided instruction." The computer I had seen at RCA in 1967 which had laboriously typed, "Hello, Fred. We have been waiting for you," would now have displayed its greeting and added a smile. Computers were much smaller and much less expensive, and video tapes could be used to present other kinds of instructional material. The hardware problem had been solved, but there was still a tendency to make the computer act like a teacher; the basic principles of programming were not often followed. Television could now be made "reactive," but as a mass medium it could not adjust to the speed of the individual student.

For a number of years Julie had involved herself in the use of computers in education. She was still working for the New Century Learning Centers and would be putting the old program on reading and her own program called "Something to Think About" on computers.

By 1982 *Walden Two* had sold more than two million copies in English alone, and I was still willing to accept it as a fair statement of my position with respect to behavioral engineering. According to a writer in the *Intellectual Digest*, the Golden Age of modern utopian writers was "just another and more surreptitious way of smuggling the idea of heaven—which medieval philosophy and theology openly imported— back into the mundane context of man's world. In a thinker like B. F. Skinner, it is more than a tendency; it is an assertion that his science can accomplish all that religion and humanism and ethics ever sought to accomplish, and much more." I would not have said "can accomplish"; a science could only "seek to accomplish." But it could do so, I thought, with greater promise than religion or ethics. The Eisenhower years had been marked by a maudlin show of religion—patrons of Howard Johnson restaurants were invited to send their compliments to the Great Chef by reading a grace printed on their menus. Religion became less conspicuous during the sixties, but returned in the seventies when revivalist television programs proved highly profitable. In October 1980 I joined sixty prominent scholars and writers in issuing a "Secular Humanist Declaration II," calling for an emphasis on science and reason rather than religion in solving our problems.

Sir Karl Popper refused to sign it because I had done so. As he explained in a letter to Paul Kurtz,

Skinner is an enemy of freedom and of democracy. He has explained his contempt for freedom quite openly in his book *Beyond Freedom and Dignity.* He has expounded it many years before in a book *Walden Two*, which is the dream of a very kind but megalomaniac behaviorist who defends a behaviorist dictatorship. . . . I regard these two books—especially *Beyond Freedom and Dignity*—as worse and more dangerous than the most fundamentalist religious tract: there is a mixture of naiveté, sheer ignorance, arrogation of omniscience, and Caesarean megalomania in these books, which is, in my opinion, far more urgent to combat than the churches.

Kurtz published the letter in his journal, *Free Inquiry*, and in an answer I said I thought Popper was angry for reasons he had not mentioned. He had taken his degree in psychology under Karl Bühler in Vienna, and I had committed *lèse majesté* by criticizing Popper upon several occasions. He had said things like "What we want is to understand how such nonphysical things as *purposes, deliberations, plans, decisions, theories, tensions,* and *values* can play a part in bringing about physical changes in the physical world, and "*It is impossible to derive a sentence stating a norm or decision from a sentence stating a fact.*" I did not think my alternative treatments of these issues showed naiveté or ignorance, and I could add that "certainly nothing has followed [from my work] which encourages any delusion of omniscience or power!"

My views on freedom, scientific or philosophical, were far from contempt, and there was no dictator in Walden Two. Nevertheless, I was sure that "Those who call themselves humanists are likely to be more comfortable with Popper's 'open society' than with a behaviorist's version of a better world. I have had doubts about my position as a humanist for the same reasons. The central issue is not the actualization or aggrandizement of the individual (no matter how strong that theme may have been in Western political philosophy) but the construction of a social environment or culture in which individuals will enjoy the greatest sense of freedom and make their greatest contributions."

Verbal Behavior was coming into its own. Kenneth MacCorquodale had long ago published two articles about it, one of them answering Chomsky, and they were sold for classroom use by the *Journal of the Experimental Analysis of Behavior*. In 1976 one of MacCorquodale's students, Steven Winokur, published *A Primer of Verbal Behavior: An Operant Analysis*. I spoke with a philosopher at Brandeis who was exploring some of the philosophical implications of *Verbal Behavior*, and in a note I reported that "we talked about epistemology, intentionality, Wittgenstein, and Chomsky—all in perfect agreement." In 1981 an old friend, Ilona Lappo, wrote her doctoral thesis in philosophy at Boston University on my book.

Chomsky's influence was still strong; in 1975 the reviewer of a book on second-language learning in the *Times Literary Supplement* noted that "The Skinner/Chomsky conflict runs predictably enough through most papers." (One of the editors of the book was Paul Pimsleur, who had been best man at Ernie and Julie's wedding.) A review in the *Times Literary Supplement* of a debate between Chomsky and Piaget alleged again that Chomsky had "demolished" the behavioristic position, but in a letter to the editor, which was published, I pointed out

how badly both Chomsky and Piaget need a behavioral account of the role of the environment in shaping and maintaining verbal behaviour. Piaget's horticultural metaphor of development is as much an appeal to genetic endowment as Chomsky's innate rules of grammar. Language does not "just grow." What develops in the life of a child is a more and more demanding verbal environment. The universals which lead Chomsky to imagine that rules of grammar are innate are simply the uses of language: in all languages people make requests, give orders, ask questions, describe objects, and report events. Sentences are generated, not by speakers who apply rules, but by the contingencies of reinforcement maintained by verbal communities—contingencies which I surveyed in *Verbal Behavior*.

An operant analysis of verbal behavior differed from structuralism in the rapidity with which one advanced to practical applications. Programmed instruction was one example; another was verbal self-management. In 1981 I published a paper called "How to Discover What You Have to Say," in which I reviewed the practices with which for many years I had improved the efficiency of my work at my desk. The techniques grew more relevant as I grew older and in 1978, at a Conference on Aging sponsored by Nova University, I talked about "Intellectual Self-Management in Old Age." Under what conditions could one avoid the ravages of old age and continue to work effectively? When I gave essentially the same paper at the annual meeting of the American Psychological Association in 1982 it made all the papers and newsweeklies. Particularly newsworthy seemed to be my suggestion that in practicing eutrapelia, or the productive use of leisure, the aging scholar could freely admit to his younger colleagues that he watched Archie Bunker on television.

A dozen publishers were soon suggesting that I write a book on old age, and when I discovered that Maggie Vaughan had once taught a course in gerontology and would be willing to help, she and I signed a contract. We called the book *Enjoy Old Age*. We met a self-imposed deadline and finished it in three months, thereby violating, for me, one of its basic principles: avoid fatigue. I was scarcely enjoying old age when we finished the book, but I soon recovered. I was still keeping to my early-morning schedule, writing from 5:00 to 7:00 every day of the year and spending weekday mornings in my office. A Spanish linguist, Père Julià, who had taken his degree with Stanley Sapon at the University of Rochester, came to the department as a visiting scholar. He had written an excellent book, *Explanatory Models in Linguistics: A Behavioral Perspective*, based upon my *Verbal Behavior*, and then in production at the Princeton University Press. Gerald Zuriff, one of our former Ph.D.'s who was now Professor of Psychology at Wheaton College, was another visiting scholar. Both Will and Maggie Vaughan were interested in many extensions of an experimental analysis of behavior, and with these four people I began to meet once a week to discuss issues. We often invited another person to join us for the day—Willard Van Orman Quine, Murray Sidman, Dick Herrnstein, Lars Gustafson (a Swedish linguist and poet), Richard Held, and Herbert Terrace, among others. We recorded our discussions.

IN EACH OF THE Tom Swift books I read as a boy, the last paragraph mentioned a sequel. Two which are appropriate here are well characterized in a passage by Bertrand Russell, who played a role in my early professional life and will serve as well at the end. "The serious part of my life . . . ," he wrote, "has been devoted to two different objects . . . to find out whether anything could be known and . . . to do whatever might be possible towards creating a happier world." I have devoted myself to the same objects, but in different ways. Whether anything can be known is not to be discovered by speculation but by empirical research, and a happier world is not to be created by talking about what is right but by analyzing and arranging environments in which people behave in happier ways. I would go further: a merely happy world is not enough; it must be a world which has some chance of surviving. How we know the world and how we can save it are the subjects of two books on which I am now at work.

I OFTEN CALLED EPISTEMOLOGY my first love. A few references to the problem of knowledge by Russell were the original enticement, and my early "Sketch for an Epistemology" was my first approach. The paper I wrote for the Symposium on Operationism in 1945 (taken from the manuscript on verbal behavior) was a further step, and two notes written in the middle seventies showed my continuing affection:

I have been watching a television program, Bronowski's The Ascent of Man, about Einstein and Newton. Bronowski spoke of the problem of light as the problem of communication between two people, and I suddenly had a glimpse of the future, when we shall have an adequate theory of knowledge and can talk about these things sensibly. But I also felt that I shall never return to my first love and resolve these difficulties. An article about nonstandard mathematics asks whether certain properties are matters of how we think or really properties of nature, as if we could ever tell the difference. I still believe that physicists could get out of a lot of their traps with even a crude theory of knowledge based on my Verbal Behavior. And a refined theory? It could make all the difference.

Almost every day I run across something to which I could give a year of my life. Just now, reading Clark's Life of Bertrand Russell, I was reminded by Russell's first contact with Peano of my old project—a behavioral analysis of logical concepts closely related to my analysis of autoclitics: If, then; Either, or; All, some; Is contained in; There exists (assertion as autoclitic!). We need to examine the contingencies from which the rules governing these expressions are "extracted." (Dangerous word!) [Van Quine's Elementary Logic came close to what I wanted.]

395

Père Julià knew my *Verbal Behavior* better than I remembered it myself and, with his book in press, was turning to epistemology. He was trained in the experimental analysis of behavior and knew modern philosophy better than I. Together we began to write a behavioristic analysis of intention, belief, knowledge, causes and reasons, thinking, and some features of scientific method. I hoped that before we finished we should have "done something about Gödel," as I had long hoped to do.

We designed a method of collaboration suggested by my paper "How to Discover What You Have to Say." We met once a week and recorded an hour's discussion of some part of the book. Julià then extracted useful parts from the record and put them, together with material from our reading, into place in a decimally indexed outline. The manuscript slowly came into being.

I WROTE A SECOND VERSION of "the future book," but did not like it. At one point I wrote, "I am ready to give it up—call it a mistake—reduce it to one paper—forget it completely," but I marked the manuscript only "TEMPORARILY ABANDONED." After finishing *The Shaping of a Behaviorist* I turned to it again and resolved that it would be "the main work for the rest of the year." Nevertheless, I was soon spending most of my time on the last volume of the autobiography.

In 1981 I was asked to participate as a "philosopher-psychologist" in a third "Conference on the Environmental Future" to which people from several disciplines would contribute. A first conference had been held in Helsinki, a second in Reykjavik. I wrote a paper called "A Matter of Consequence," in which I argued that the process of selection responsible for our present existence had a subtle flaw: It could prepare a species, an individual, or a culture only for a future which resembled the past. Cultural institutions promoted their own futures, but they were often in conflict with the future which threatened the species. Who, then, would induce 4,500,000,000 people to have fewer children, minimize consumption and pollution, and reduce the threat of a nuclear holocaust?

In my paper on the environmental future, I had looked at a "fourth estate," composed of scientists, scholars, teachers, and writers.

Physical and biological scientists could give us the most accurate prediction of the future, behavioral scientists could design contingencies under which people behaved in ways which made a viable future more probable, and teachers and writers could make it all as widely known as possible. But they could not go directly to 4,500,000,000 people; they would have to change governments, religions, and the possessors of capital— and there they would meet all the same problems. My paper was much more pessimistic than anything I had written before.

Maggie Vaughan was interested in ecological issues, and together we began to write a much-improved book about the future. Unfortunately, too much of the future turned out to be in fields in which we were not specialists, and we gave up the book. I would deal with the behavioral issues in a revised version of my paper for the conference. I have not yet justified the optimism I expressed in *Beyond Freedom and Dignity*. I believe the world will be saved only if we begin to understand ourselves well enough to take effective action, but I am no longer sure that an experimental analysis of behavior has evolved in time.

EPILOGUE

Time hath, my lord, a wallet at his back,
Wherein he puts alms for oblivion.
—*Troilus and Cressida*

I HAVE TRIED to report my life *as it was lived*. That does not mean as I now remember it. I have seen how badly memory fades when, after recalling some episode, I have come upon contemporary evidence. Fortunately I have been able to turn from reminiscences to more durable things. In writing *Particulars of My Life* I had my mother's scrapbooks, my letters home, a diary, my college themes, my stories and notes, and a few publications; in *The Shaping of a Behaviorist* I had my letters, particularly those to Fred Keller, my notes, and my papers and books; in *A Matter of Consequences* I have had a much wider correspondence, many more clippings, my publications, and a mass of notes. My autobiography is, in a special sense, a documentary.

I have tried to recount my life *as it was lived* in other ways. I have seldom mentioned later significances. When I first bent a wire in the shape of a lever to be pressed by a rat, I was making the prototype of many thousands of levers, but I did not know it then, and it would have been a mistake to mention it. (Occasionally I have slipped. When I described the accident which led me, in eighth grade, to read some of the works of Francis Bacon, I could not resist adding, "Francis Bacon was to serve me in more serious pursuits later on.") For the same reason I have avoided comparing my life with other lives, except in those rare instances when I made the comparison at the time.

There are several reasons why I have not often reported my feelings. Occasionally I have said how I felt (or, more accurately, how my body felt to me) either literally ("I was angry, happy") or metaphorically ("I was stunned, shaken"), but I have not tried to "convey my feelings" in other ways—as by describing other situations which evoke the same feelings. (I did not say that upon looking into Pavlov's great work, I felt "like some watcher of the skies when a new planet swims into his ken.") Paleontology is a science of bones, teeth, and shells because the softer parts of organisms have disappeared, and feelings are softer parts too. Only when I recorded how I felt at the time have I accepted it as part of the story.

I also do not think feelings are important. Freud is probably responsible for the current extent to which they are taken seriously. Lytton Strachey made a comparable point about a period in French literature: The eighteenth century was supposed to be unemotional, but "if anyone had asked Voltaire to analyze his feelings accurately he would have replied that he had other things to think about. The notion of paying careful attention to mere feelings would have seemed ridiculous."

Rather than tell my readers how I felt, I have left them to respond as I myself may have responded. It is the reader who must be judged warm or cold. When Nedda rejected me, I said that I suffered an almost physical pain, but I gave my readers better evidence by telling them how I branded my arm with her initial. (The brand still survives as a rare kind of evidence—not of a feeling, but of behavior from which the reader may infer a feeling.) When I learned of the death of my friend Raphael Miller, I was playing something of Scriabin's, and I said that "I have never heard it or played it since then without reliving that moment." That broke the rule against mentioning the future, but it pointed to a kind of lasting evidence.

I have also tried not to select episodes which show me as I now want my readers to see me. I have reported my failures as well as my successes. It is not easy to deal in the same way with others. I have not "honored my father and my mother"; I have described them as accurately as possible. Closer to the present, honesty about oneself is often gossip about others.

Scientists face a special problem when they have anticipated the work of others but have not published. I studied the Sidman avoidance arrangement in 1937 and what came to be called "autoshaping" in 1948, but, as George Sarton pointed out in connection with Cavendish's anticipations of Faraday, one cannot take credit if one has not been willing to submit one's work to the review of one's colleagues. Nevertheless, what happened was part of the story, and I can now report my regret at not having published.

If, when I entered Harvard as a graduate student, I could have seen my present position, I think I should have accepted it as a satisfactory *terminus ad quem*, but of course I did not see it, nor is it evidence of a plan operating throughout my professional life. My life was scarcely planned at all. It is true that I began to "take stock" two or three times a year, but mainly to discover where I had arrived, not where I was going. The main course of my life was set by a series of accidents. (An unplanned life has advantages. Pasteur said that chance favors the prepared mind, but it also favors the uncommitted. I have been free to follow a principle enunciated in my "Case History in Scientific Method": "When you run onto something interesting, stop everything else and study it.")

To some extent I have written the story as if I were writing a novel, not by inventing incidents but by including trivial facts. I do not think that all the things I have recorded here are important, but they are the kinds of things which novelists are free to mention without explaining why and which portray a life a little more clearly as it was lived. It was easier to do that during the early years; later the story becomes more and more one of ideas and hence less and less suitable as the theme of a novel. But I have not tried to hold the reader's attention in spurious ways. Just as I never constructed a theory after finishing an experiment which the experiment could then be said to have proved, so I have not contrived suspense to be resolved in a moment of triumph when there was actually neither suspense nor triumph.

I am sometimes asked, "Do you think of yourself as you think of the organisms you study?" The answer is yes. So far as I know, my behavior at any given moment has been nothing more than the product of my genetic endowment, my personal history, and the current setting. That does not mean that I can explain everything I do or have done. I know more about myself than about anyone else, but it is still far from enough. Nevertheless, I have tried to *interpret* my life in the light of what I have learned from my research. I have done so increasingly as the experimental analysis has advanced, and some of my efforts are part of this story. Something more may now be called for. An autobiography is a case history, and as a behaviorist I may be expected to say something about it.

I DO NOT BELIEVE that my life shows a type of personality à la Freud, an archetypal pattern à la Jung, or a schedule of development à la Erikson. There have been a few abiding themes, but they can be traced to environmental sources rather than to traits of character. They became part of my life as I lived it; they were not there at the beginning to determine its course.

I was born to healthy, long-lived parents, who were important to me in other ways. I fell in love with two or three women who looked as my mother must have looked when I was a child, and I think breasts are beautiful, but so far as I am concerned, Darwin and Pavlov offer a better explanation than Sophocles and Freud. My mother and, to a lesser extent, my father were always ready to correct me, but they rarely punished me, and I cannot identify the sanctions which kept me from hurting them. The theme of "Elsa," the story I wrote during my senior year at Hamilton, is probably relevant. No single day was bad enough to justify the trouble of a break. My parents' control was so well sustained that I had no chance to learn to revolt; I never tasted the fruits of little revolts which would have led me on to bigger ones. I was never quite free. I would not have published *Particulars of My Life* while they were alive. But I grew away from them in ways they accepted while I was still in grade and high school; it was my brother who teased me about my cultural eccentricities. The Saunders family at Hamilton College showed me a very different way of life, and with my later friends and acquaintances I found my father and mother rather an embarrassment. I grew to feel sorry for my father as I recognized my mother's dominant role.

I HAVE NOT HAD MANY close male friends. Raphael Miller and I shared very few interests. Cuthbert Daniel was mainly my scientific superego. When we were graduate students, Fred Keller and I spent a good deal of time together. In addition to our research and our joint defense of behaviorism, we ate lunch together and went to movies, made home-brewed beer, and listened to Marlene Dietrich and Instructional French on my phonograph. It was fun to be with Fred no matter what we were doing. Only with Eve have I shared so many interests and pleasures. My other male friendships have been limited to special fields of interest.

I LEARNED TO READ and write and do arithmetic without any trouble—and so did everyone else in my class. Under Miss Graves, to whom I dedicated The Technology of Teaching, I read Washington Irving, James Fenimore Cooper, Sir Walter Scott, George Eliot, Tennyson's Idylls of the King, and Shakespeare—works not chosen because they were rele-vant to life in Susquehanna. Miss Werle was not a Latin scholar, but she taught me to translate, if not to read, Virgil. Mr. Bowles knew mathe-matics and believed in discipline, and he took me through algebra, plane and solid geometry, and trigonometry. At Hamilton College only one of my professors was known for his scholarship, but most of them taught well. No educational counselor would have recommended my program of courses, but at some time or other I have used something from every one of them. In graduate school I had the advantage of scarcely being taught at all.

MY EARLY RELIGIOUS EXPERIENCE was important. In 1969 I read Leavis's The Great Tradition, and a chance remark at a cocktail party led me to read Middlemarch and reread the other novels of George Eliot. I wrote: "Just now, finishing Silas Marner and Leavis's Notes, I see that the point of [Beyond Freedom and Dignity] could be summarized as a scien-tific defense of the radical dissenting Protestantism of early 19th century England." In another note, after reading Gilbert Seldes's The Stam-mering Century, I translated some of Seldes's comments about Jonathan Edwards:

"[Edwards] reconciled predestination with man's moral responsi-bility [BFS: he formulated 'responsibility' within a determined system of behavior]. He said that consciousness was a delusion implanted in man to give him a sense of responsibility [BFS: awareness is of social origin possibly designed for the good of others] . . . Freedom consists not in making a choice but in pursuing an inclination [BFS: operant strength is to be studied not in comparing the strengths of alternative responses but in measuring the probability of a single response] . . . The acts of the human will are caused otherwise than by mere power of willing [BFS: the relevant variables are external; an inner will as a causal force is a fiction]. [It is] plausible that men, who cannot be converted except by God's will, should attempt to force that will. [BFS: though not free to act, men nevertheless behave as if they were]."

These seem like a remarkable set of similarities. If *a*. God is all powerful; *b*. nature is an orderly determined system, then man's freedom, responsibility, awareness, achievements, and worth must be interpreted in new ways. Much of my scientific position seems to have begun as Presbyterian theology, not too far removed from the Congregational of Jonathan Edwards.

I HAVE SAID THAT "I was taught to fear God, the police, and what people will think," and traces of that childhood survive. I have never cared much about clothing, but I would never appear at a scientific meeting in an informal jacket or sweater. Thoreau said of Emerson that he would rather have walked down the street with a broken leg than a broken pantleg, and I am afraid I am rather like that. I worry about whether I am tipping too much or not enough, and I say "please" and "thank you" excessively. (I am rarely deferent, however. I find it hard to say "sir" in addressing senators at hearings, and when I talked with Queen Elizabeth on the *Britannia* I forgot to address her as "Your Majesty.")

When I played the saxophone in dance orchestras, I read the notes; I could never break free as jazz required. I found it almost impossible to paint nonrepresentationally. William Sewell, the sculptor who made the satirical ceramic statue of me, once told me I would "have to be psychoanalyzed" if I were ever to paint well. I hope that unedited pages of my writing will never be published.

I have reacted to punitive contingencies in other ways. I have escaped from the punishers. I concealed unacceptable behavior from my parents, I stay away from the kinds of people who complain of my behavior, and I do not often read my critics. (When I was very young, hellfire was the great punishment, and I escaped to agnosticism.) I have also counterattacked the punishers. I have been aggressive (and have almost always regretted it). In a note written in 1955 I confessed that my 1930 review of a paper by E. M. Vicari "was not written to clear up the facts but to make a fool of the author." I made a list of the aggressive phrases in my William James Lectures. I noted that I was less aggressive "in those fields in which I feel secure, but I must watch it elsewhere. It is childish and damaging." Six years later, as I reported in another note, I was not always "watching it" effectively:

> After my talk at the Academy on Wednesday evening President Mather called for one last question. Someone with a heavy English accent rose, told a story about an Oxford questionnaire ("Do you expect to live to the age of thirty?" "No, but we should like to."), referred to his connection with atomic research, and reported his observation that the children of parents who plan the lives of their children usually go unplanned ways. There was laughter. Mather turned and nodded to me. I went to the lectern and said:
>
> "I can only say that that is the kind of social thinking we have learned to expect from atomic scientists." Mather quickly adjourned the meeting.
>
> It was a successful remark (Walter Rosenblith even told Van Quine he suspected the question was a plant); it fitted my current anti-physical-science tack. Yet I felt very guilty. The man had made me mad with his assumption that physicists would have the last word about behavior. How to spot that rising gorge and keep my mouth shut?

To free myself from these emotional effects of punishment, I have practiced a kind of self-management. Frazier taught me (read: "In writing about Frazier in *Walden Two* I discovered") how to offset the punishing effects of the more rapid rise of my colleagues by telling myself that they had made real contributions.

It was not only to suppress wrongdoing that I was taught to fear God, the police, and what people will think; it was to strengthen right behavior. I have adjusted reasonably well. I usually do what I have to do without a struggle. I have studied when I did not feel like studying, taught when I did not want to teach. I have taken care of animals and run experiments as the animals dictated. (Some of my first cumulative records were stamped "December 25" and "January 1.") A large number of my papers were written for occasions and would not have been written without the occasions. (It was not always coercion. An invitation set a deadline to be met, but it also offered an audience interested in something I was ready to talk about, whether or not I yet knew it.)

I have written many notes about the strengthening effect of negative reinforcers. Here are two:

Yesterday I did not work well. I told myself it was fatigue. Then late yesterday afternoon I read the first chapter of Teilhard de Chardin's *The Future of Man*. This morning I am "motivated" again. I am attacking philosophy, theology, cheap poetry, nonsense, and mentalism (glorified as the end-all of the evolution of man). My reading has given me an audience, an adversary to be answered or shown up. Not a pretty thought but a useful one.

I am working on "Teaching Thinking Through Programmed Instruction," which I am to give in two weeks. A colleague gave the first of the series last Thursday. Lowell Lecture Hall was full, but a student told me the audience walked out in droves before the lecture was over. Last night, lying awake, I recast my opening paragraphs, and I wrote an alternative version this morning. Evidently I have gained something from the challenge. An audience and a competitive motive have made a difference in the availability of my verbal behavior and, as an indirect result of the added strength, in the clarity of my thinking.

Fortunately, positive reinforcers have played a much more important role in my life. Like most people I have enjoyed many things— food, sex, music, literature, art, games. Some of them I have had to learn to enjoy, but most can be traced readily enough to genetic predispositions. The reinforcers in my professional life are not so easily identified. I think my scientific behavior has been reinforced primarily by its results. As I have said many times, my rats and pigeons have taught me much more than I have taught them; I have simply continued to do the things which most clearly revealed order in their behavior. At my desk the obvious reinforcers consist of getting things said in acceptable ways, resolving puzzlement, creating sentences which please me when I read them. That my publications have been commended and my practices adopted has no doubt been important, but it is hard to identify the behavior upon which they were contingent.

ONE OF THE HAPPIEST ACCIDENTS of my life was that remark of my father's about the authorship of Shakespeare, which led me to become for a number of years an ardent Baconian. I read much more of Bacon than I could have understood at the time, as well as much that was said about him. When I recently read Peter Gay's account of Voltaire, Diderot, Adam Smith, Gibbon, and others in the Enlightenment, I was puzzled by how much I agreed with them until I realized that Bacon was the source of us all. A note suggests that his effect on me was emotional as well as intellectual:

> Before leaving for the airport I looked for a book to take with me. I picked up Farrington's *Philosophy of Francis Bacon*, which I had read several years before. I sensed an immediate change. In the taxi to the airport I was relaxed, looking forward to the day, hard as it would be. Before boarding I wrote two or three notes—one about my high-school days, the others about plans for the future. I was quite expansive. There was a delay before take-off, and the plane was bitter cold because the door remained open, but it did not seem to matter. I noted with admiration our quiet and beautifully cushioned take-off, the steep angle at which we climbed. Thirty-five minutes to New York.
>
> I cannot say that the book revived early dreams of science and human betterment or the hope of improving the condition of humankind, because I do not remember having dreams of that sort when I first read Bacon. I wanted to be a writer, not a scientist. All the more remarkable that I should now be so thoroughly Baconian. The link through Diderot pleases me particularly, though it does not seem to be related to any influence Diderot has had on me.

Three Baconian principles have characterized my professional life. I do not mean that they have governed it. The facts of my life have confirmed them, and my early acquaintance with Bacon may have improved the chances that they would do so.

I have studied nature not books. As Bacon put it, "Books must follow sciences, not sciences books." The world of my childhood taught me to build things—toys, gadgets, shacks, and eventually apparatus. I have read for pleasure but less often to learn, and I am poorly read in psychology—that is one of the ways in which I "neglect my contemporaries." My experiments came out of other experiments, not out of theories. My books were written out of nature, not out of other books.

To say, as Bacon said, that knowledge is power is simply to say that it is successful action. It is what we do to the world, not a representation of that world enshrined in our mind. Mach's *Science of Mechanics* naturally appealed to me by showing that science emerged from craftsmanship. For the field as a whole as well as for me personally, the reflex was an entering wedge because it pointed to something one could do to "make an organism behave." I moved to a different causal mode when my research, following Thorndike's, clarified the role of selection by consequences—a principle which I used not so much in understanding behavior as in changing it.

A SECOND BACONIAN PRINCIPLE has played a much more powerful role in my life, both as a person and as a behaviorist: *Nature to be commanded must be obeyed.* Knowledge is effective action, but there is no initiating actor. We control the world around us, but only because that world has taught us to do so and induces us to do so. It is easiest to accept that view when the behavior is punishable. Juvenile delinquents do not argue when bad environments are blamed for their crimes. During the Dark Year in Scranton, I began to write notes about intellectual suicide. The behavior I had acquired in college was not paying off, and I was depressed. I did not consider actual suicide; behaviorism offered me another way out: it was not I but my history that had failed. (Intellectual suicide is a bad metaphor, however. The mind commits suicide if, with its supposed help, one becomes a behaviorist, but since there has never been a mind there is no corpse. One gives up the ghost, but it is oneself, not the ghost, who then reaches that heaven which only a science of behavior can promise.)

I have continued to seek relief from the effects of punitive consequences in the same way. I have learned to accept my mistakes by referring them to a personal history which was not of my making and could not be changed. My behavior at the Royal Society dinner, for example, was, to say the least, unfortunate, but I could reflect that my early life was very different from that of Lord Adrian's or most of the other guests'. Just as one learns to live with one's physical limitations, so one can learn to live with one's behavioral deficiencies. One may add to a personal history but never take it away. One can never *not* be the person one has become. To understand is to forgive.

It is much harder to relinquish praise for one's achievements because the compensating gains are far less compelling. Frazier could point to one in *Walden Two*. He has committed a kind of intellectual suicide by suppressing his role in the founding of the community and by exerting no current power because only in that way can he be sure that he has created a community which will survive without his intervention. I have tried to do something of the sort with respect to the field called the experimental analysis of behavior.

Assigning one's achievements to one's genetic and environmental histories is an act of self-denial that would have been understood by Thomas à Kempis. I like to contrast it with the self-aggrandizement of those who claim to have been born in the image of God the Creator. Amos Wilder gave me some help with a related theme in the Gospels. The Revised Standard translation of Luke 17:13 puts it this way: "Whoever seeks to gain his life will lose it, but whoever loses his life will preserve it." (Matthew [10:39] and Mark [8:35] add that the life must be lost for Jesus' sake, and they are all, of course, talking about gaining a life in another world.) The theme turns up in mundane philosophy (e.g., Schopenhauer's annihilation of the will as the way to freedom) and literature (e.g., Conrad's Secret Sharer learning that true self-possession comes from self-abandonment). It is, of course, a strong theme in Eastern mysticism. It will no doubt strike many people as strange that it should be, as I think it is, the central theme of a behavioral science.

Certainly it would be inconsistent to blame our sins on our genetic and environmental histories while continuing to claim credit for our achievements, but the issue runs deeper than that. In my lecture "On 'Having' a Poem" I argued that a poet is only a literary tradition's way of making more of a literary tradition, and I could have said that a scientist is only science's way of making more science. Variations in genes and in the environments of person and group are the sources of novelty or, to use Darwin's word, the *origins* of things.

I have accepted the implications with respect to myself. After film-ing the BBC program in the Royal Institution, I wrote a note:

Bannister [one of the discussants] took great delight in applying my principles to me as if that somehow or other invalidated them. My theories were only what I had been conditioned to say, etc. He seemed taken aback when I readily admitted as much and made the point that the behavior of the scientist is shaped and maintained by the subject matter.

My analysis of the role of the individual in *Beyond Freedom and Dignity* was so convincing that by the time I had finished the book I actually did not feel that I had written it. I do not mean that I attributed it to some mystical "other one." There was no divine afflatus. My book was the inevitable consequence of what had happened to me and of what I had read.

I WAS NO DOUBT INCLINED to reach that conclusion because it solved an old problem—my conceit. When I was a Junior Fellow, Professor John Livingston Lowes asked if I had yet written my autobiography. "Only the first sentence," I said, "—'My grandmother was a fool.'" In the short autobiography I wrote for the *History of Psychology in Autobi-ography*, edited by Garry Boring, my first sentence was gentler but to the same point: "My Grandmother Skinner was an uneducated farmer's daughter who put on airs." *Particulars of My Life* begins with a sketch of my ridiculous grandmother. I think that her pretense of being a lady explains why her son resigned as draftsman in the Erie Shops, read law, and became a lawyer and why, though he was successful, he was never quite successful enough and constantly needed praise. As a result, he often praised himself. As a young man he was called "bumpy," and he once asked me with some embarrassment whether anyone had called me that. No one had, but in both college and graduate school I was called conceited and punished for it.

It was, I think, the same problem of the upwardly mobile. Susque-hanna High School was good, but some of my classmates at Hamilton came from much better schools. Where I, self-taught, had barely passed the Regents Examination in second-year French, several Hamilton students spoke French fluently. My English was regional. I said "tremenjous" and "stupenjous" and "yet" when I meant "still," and I pronounced "been" "ben." I joined the least prestigious fraternity. I came to Harvard as a graduate student without ever having had a course in psychology, and I was soon associating with physiologists and biologists whose contempt for psychologists did not go unspoken. Like my father I needed reassurance, and when necessary I reassured myself. I did so less often when I began to have something I could be proud of.

From the very first I believed in a science of behavior and in behaviorism as the philosophy of that science, and I valued the evidence I could offer from my own research. When I recorded my first extinction curve (by accident) and crossed streets very carefully until I could tell someone about it, it was the curve and not my accomplishment that I was carefully preserving. I have felt the same way when writing some of my books: I must stay alive until they are finished—but again because I believe in the importance of what I am saying. *The Behavior of Organisms* was written in the first person (a colleague at Minnesota once expressed his surprise), but except for a few lighter papers I now stay in the third person (and envy those who use the first person gracefully). I now see that I greatly exaggerated the extent to which the first edition of *Cumulative Record* was boastful and that I suffered unnecessarily.

CAN I TELL YOU what I really think of myself? I can at least offer some objective evidence. In many of my notes I record my failures and mistakes, and the explanations are never excuses. In 1966:

> I do not admire myself as a person. My successes do not override my shortcomings. Last night at dinner Babs Spiegel said that I was the one person she knew who had not been changed by success. This morning I thought of a quip: "Yes, I was impossible *before* I was successful."

Critics have pointed to the discrepancy between Racine the man and Racine the dramatist and between Wagner the man and Wagner the composer, and Frazier makes the same point about himself in a scene that I typed out, as I once reported, "in white heat."

In many notes I have recorded my reaction to acclaim. In 1967:

> At the Conference on *Walden Two* at Wingspread I collected kudos. The President of the Johnson Foundation began his speech of welcome by saying how honored they were that I was there, etc., etc. I suppose it is impossible to convince anyone that I am not reinforced by such things. (Never mind the bad contingencies. I have discussed those in writing about prizes.) But I am not. There is a certain embarrassment, which I try not to show or to offset by looking either humble or pleased. At times I do reflect on my achievements and their consequences with satisfaction and pleasure, but I am convinced that my effect on the world will be greatest (and there's my reinforcement!) if I minimize all personal blandishments.

Unlike Diderot, whose "fond recollection," according to Arthur M. Wilson, "began to play him tricks, so that he came to believe that [The Skeptics Walk] was one of his best works," when I go back and read something of mine it always seems much better than I remembered it.

I do not like being an eponym. I have asked my friends not to use the expression "Skinner box." I have never quarreled about priorities. I have never displayed my trophies, medals, or honorary degrees; they are all in a box in our basement. I have never been an empire builder; others have been responsible for the journals and organizations which promote the experimental analysis of behavior. I have given interviews, appeared on talk shows, made documentaries, and engaged in other kinds of publicity, but only, I think, to promote a scientific position. I have not enjoyed these things and have written dozens of notes on their possibly harmful effects on me.

I am willing to concede that I have committed a kind of intellectual suicide in writing this autobiography. When Anthony Trollope confessed that he had written his novels partly for money, his reputation suffered. By tracing what I have done to my environmental history rather than assigning it to a mysterious, creative process, I have relinquished all chance of being called a Great Thinker.

My answer to Montaigne's question has shocked many people: I would bury my children rather than my books. But I would give the same answer with respect to myself. If some Mephistopheles offered me a wholly new life on condition that all records and effects of my present life be destroyed, I should refuse.

There is another gain. Fred Keller's students once assembled a great stack of their reprints and asked me to make the presentation to Fred. I recalled something that Ernst Mach had written to Dr. Paul Carus about the educational work of his Open Court Publishers: "In this way you have attained to the only possible form of immortality." In that stack of reprints, I said, Fred could see himself a hundred years hence. In relinquishing any personal share in the immortality of my books, I, too, no longer have any reason to fear death.

Henry Aiken once told me he had visited a distinguished Harvard philosopher, a great champion of the individual, and found him, in his old age, terrified of dying. I was remembering that when, in *Beyond Freedom and Dignity*, I wrote that the individual who values nothing beyond his freedom and dignity "has refused to be concerned for the survival of his culture and is not reinforced by the fact that the culture will long survive him. In the defense of his freedom and dignity he has denied the contributions of the past and must therefore relinquish all claim upon the future." (George Homans, a great individualist, called the passage "guff.")

If I am right about human behavior, I have written the autobiography of a nonperson. I have collected alms for oblivion, but not, I think, for no reason. There are consequences.

A third Baconian theme completes the story. *The New Atlantis* was the first utopia I read. A better world was possible, but it would not come about by accident. It must be planned and built, and with the help of science. Salomon's House in *The New Atlantis* was the model of the Royal Society, and the American Philosophical Society, which Benjamin Franklin founded on the model of the Royal Society, was dedicated to "the promotion of useful knowledge." It was the theme of the Enlightenment and, very early, of my own intellectual life.

By its very nature an experimental analysis of behavior spawns a technology because it points to conditions which can be changed to change behavior. I said as much in my own *New Atlantis*, *Walden Two*.

In the last section of *Science and Human Behavior*, I dealt with more explicit steps in the design of a better culture and with the problems raised by the cult of the individual. But I had seen the issue earlier in Bacon, and, appropriately enough, in my high-school science. A year after reading Bacon, I began to study botany and in the text, by Asa Gray, I found that passage which I copied and preserved among my papers. It is about a radish:

> So the biennial root becomes large and heavy, being a storehouse of nourishing matter, which man and animals are glad to use for food. In it, in the form of starch, sugar, mucilage, and in other nourishing and savory products, the plant (expending nothing in flowers or in show) has laid up the avails of its whole summer's work. For what purpose? This plainly appears when the next season's growth begins. Then, fed by this great stock of nourishment, a stem shoots forth rapidly and strongly, divides into branches, bears flowers abundantly, and ripens seeds, almost wholly at the expense of the nourishment accumulated in the root, which is now light, empty, and dead; and so is the whole plant by the time the seeds are ripe.

A modern Asa Gray would put it this way: "A radish is the way in which radish genes make more radish genes." If I am right about human behavior, an individual is only the way in which a species and a culture produce more of species and culture.

NOTES

10   Project Pigeon: The nose of an experimental pigeon-guided missile is now in the Smithsonian Institution.

25   reinforcing the successful shot: Playing Ping-Pong was not easy to condition. Possibly pigeons are not inclined to peck at things so much like their eggs. At first the ball was fastened at one edge of the table, and pecking was immediately reinforced by operating the food dispenser beneath it. When the ball was moved to one side, the pigeon pecked at the empty air where it had been. It was not yet "using the ball as a tool." Later the ball rested behind a slight elevation on the edge of the table and was free to roll toward the middle when pecked. A bar was then put across the table and food was automatically delivered whenever the ball reached it. By gradually increasing the distance, more and more forceful pecks were shaped, and eventually the pigeon drove the ball over the center ridge and on toward the far edge. A ball was then "served" by rolling it slowly toward the pigeon, who eventually pecked quickly enough to keep it from falling off. When two birds thus prepared were put into the apparatus together, they played a respectable game, often with rallies of several returns.

37   Ben Wyckoff: Something of the character of our research at the time is suggested by a letter I wrote to Wyckoff before he came for the summer:

> I suggest a single-key setup using some other property besides position. E.g. red or green bulb behind key which can be either flashing or non-flashing—two or three times per sec—on, most of the time. Use four new recorders (you may have to help finish them). Use long experimental periods—say, four hours—to get whole change in one day. Three or five minute APR [aperiodic reinforcement, later called variable interval].
>
> Possibilities: given the four cases, red flashing (RF), green flashing (GF), red non-flashing (RN), and green non-flashing (GN), compare birds extinguishing RF and GF (IEF) with birds extinguishing RF and RN (IER) and also with birds extinguishing RF and GN—to see if any "concepts" of "red" or "flashing" aid the former cases. Also compare extinction RF and RN after previous extinction of RF and GF, etc.
>
> In other words plan a sequence to check interference, reversibility, etc., of the process.

Ben was his own man and did the work his own way.

37   a much more effective device: I described the apparatus that reinforced rapid responding in a letter to Fred:

The apparatus is a phonograph motor into which the bird feeds juice by pecking at a contact. The turntable gradually picks up speed and at a critical value an arm flies out centrifugally and bumps a fixed arm to stop the motor and reinforce. If the bird hesitates, the table slows down and he is that much farther from reinforcement. Two birds on this schedule seem clearly to be preserving all advantages by heightened activity near reinforcement.

45 **"appraisal of sales potentialities":** Another reader for Macmillan wrote, "This is a very important book, and I hope you will publish it. But it is almost unreadable. Only in its last part—about 10 percent of the whole—can it be read by *anyone.*" I found some consolation in the reader's prejudices:

This manuscript is important because it lays out a new psychology, or rather a new psychotherapy, and the one which, in all probability, will succeed psychoanalysis. It will be some years before "functional behaviorism" attains a vogue equal to that of psychoanalysis. But I am not hesitant to say that it, or something akin to it, is on the way. . . . This book can really be made into something. The campaign should be thought out, especially the tactics of combatting the psychoanalysts, who will stop at nothing to do this down, for it will mean the end of their racket. . . .

48 **his first painting!:** Nearly thirty years later, I phoned one of the two men (he had become a sculptor) and asked whether they had ever told their roommate what they had done. They had not. The man I called did not know what had become of him, but said that he had seen him recently—in the Museum of Modern Art!

51-2 **The New Yorker got an endpiece:** *New Yorker,* February 20, 1965.

54 **"ratio of non-psychotic to psychotic behavior":** Psychiatrists in general seemed to pay little or no attention to behavior, whether psychotic or non-psychotic. At a meeting on mental health, I once jotted down all direct references to the behavior of the mentally ill, and during three hours collected only five. The discussion was about *types* of symptoms or illnesses. No one raised the question of why normal behavior did not occur. Og and I could not fully answer that question, but we had shown that under carefully designed contingencies of reinforcement, it was within range.

60 **"into deterministic language":** Garry's letter continued:

At this point it suddenly occurred to me that this is what [Ralph Barton] Perry was driving at when he was talking about the egocentric predicament, of which Max Meyer's Psychology of the Other One is a special case. There must always be a Thinker when thought goes on; or a Speaker when language is in play. When the Subject becomes the Object he is changed and there must be some other subject or he could not be the object. That's another way of saying that a universe of discourse, like science, deals with constructs, not data.

I thought I had treated those issues effectively. I had defined a self as a repertoire of behavior. There could be—there must be—more than one self within one skin, among them selves that managed and controlled other selves.

62 *any other undergraduate course:* When a Spaniard working in the Department of Pharmacology at the Medical School killed himself, I heard that he had "cursed me in his ravings," but W. H. Morse, who was in the department at the time, has supplied the following account:

I have no information on whether you were singled out in his ravings. He had been reading Science and Human Behavior *and working through the Holland and Skinner program in the two or three weeks he was with us. He was immediately concerned with your writings just before he became sick, but I personally do not think that that has any particular significance. We learned later that he had been repeatedly hospitalized in Madrid. . . . I leave it to you to decide whether reading Skinner should be contraindicated for a person with a psychotic history.*

67 *Prof. S. goes back:* My teaching machine skit continued:

SCENE II

One year later Barrelbottom is seated behind a desk on which a good deal of electrical apparatus can be seen. He has the tube in his mouth and is typing furiously. A long roll of paper comes out of the machine and falls in a pile on the floor of the stage. After a moment, Professor Skinneybox enters with a Distinguished Visitor.

Prof. S.: Now here we have a second-year student already well along with the more creative aspects of graduate work. He is beyond the question and answer stage now, and we are shaping up his original ideas. (*Barrelbottom jumps only occasionally; he chews frequently. Prof. S. points to the taping machine hanging on the wall.*) We've got the whole sum and substance of psychological knowledge taped into this device. We generate original ideas by cutting and pasting the tapes into new patterns. These often cause some disruption in the behavior of the subject, but the effective novel ideas work themselves out very well. Let me show you a sample of the material we put into our graduate students at this stage. (*Prof. S. picks up part of the paper coming out of the machine. Suddenly he starts.*) Holy smoke! (*Dashes to the tape timer and turns the switch.*) Jumping Jehoshaphat! (*Runs to desk and speaks into the intercom.*) Get Professor Steamer on the inside phone right away. Holy Cow, Holy Cow! (*into phone*) Hello, Stanley?—Say, there's trouble again. . . . No, we've lost another graduate student. . . . He hasn't *left.* It's the taping again. Somebody must have got into the safe. . . . No, not the Catechism this time, it's worse than that . . . (*whispers:*) Marx. Karl Marx. . . . *The Communist Manifesto!* . . . Well, how should *I* know? But that's what it is. . . . But what can I *do?* I'm running the tape backward right now, but that won't work. We've tried it before, and besides, it's dangerous. (*long pause*) Unh-huh, unh-huh. Yes, Stanley, but that cleans out *all* the engrams. Leaves a perfect *tabula rasa.* The man we tried

4 1 7

that on last year is selling papers in Harvard Square. . . . Yes, I know it's a living, and this fellow could make a living in Russia or China. Maybe we can work out an exchange. After all, *their* training programs must go wrong sometimes. . . . (*During this conversation Barrelbottom has vanished. A small wisp of smoke rises from the chair.*) Hold it, Stanley, it's too late. Barrelbottom has exploded. (*Puts down phone, goes over and picks up Barrelbottom's smoking clothing.*) My God! It's finally happened—the Disappearance of Organisms. Charlie, Charlie, Oh, Charlie! (*Charlie enters.*)

Charlie: What's up?

Prof. S.: Look!

Charlie: (*looking at Barrelbottom's chair*) Who was it?

Prof. S.: Barrelbottom. (*Prof. S. picks up Barrelbottom's trousers, from which smoke rises.*) Alas, poor Barrelbottom. He knew it well.

Charlie: (*picking up a smoking sock*) Not a trace—how do you explain that, Professor?

Prof. S.: Explain it? It was bound to happen. Look at your equations. (*Prof. S. goes to blackboard and writes* $E = mc^2$.) That's why it happened. After all, what is conditioning? It's simply energizing human behavior. And what is extinction? De-energizing. I've been running the tape backward.

Charlie: (*horrified*) Oh! No!

Prof. S.: Yes. It was a calculated risk. We had to de-energize him, but (*pointing to the equation and striking out the* E *and the* m) no energy, no mass. You see that smoke? That's c^2. Charlie, I sometimes wonder if it's all worthwhile.

69   My machine was on the platform: The teaching machine I demonstrated at Pittsburgh is now in the Smithsonian Institution.

97   built a different kind: One of the disk machines is now in the Smithsonian Institution.

107   he once reported it: F. S. Keller. *Summers and Sabbaticals* (Champaign, Illinois: Research Press Company, 1977).

122   "All men control and are controlled": Rogers had seen a resemblance between *Walden Two* and George Orwell's *1984*, but I had written a reply to that at Putney:

Orwell purports to show the horrors of thought control versus individual freedom, but the horrors turn out to be only one mode of control (aversive) and freedom is again freedom from aversive treatment. Orwell himself attempts to control the thoughts of his readers, warning them away from control of a different sort.

The issue is not freedom versus control. It is how one man is to treat another. When Big Brother watches, he watches in order to punish defection. It is not the watching, but the consequences, we fear. God is said to watch over us; if he does so in order to care for us, we are grateful. 1984 is closer to 1384 [the Inquisition]. The only new techniques come from physiological and biological science—not behavioral. Churches and governments have been guilty of the distortion of history. Hitler took us *back* in history; the only road forward is through the use of alternatives to punishment. There is none of that kind of future in Orwell, who never understood the problem. It is easy to write for those who hate and fear murder, starvation, and torture. A better world is unbelievable.

122 *"I once saw Dr. Johnson":* John Hollander's poem was later published in his *A Crackling of Thorns* (New Haven: Yale University Press, 1958).

123 *A formal analysis . . . was worthless:* My memorandum on statistics continued:

1) When put in a given situation, an organism shows a certain probability of response (the "prior probability").

2) A response is eventually made and possibly reinforced.

3) Since the situation then contains a recent history of responding with or without reinforcement, a response of the same sort will occur again with a different probability.

4) A second response is eventually made and possibly reinforced.

5) The situation is thereupon changed in a more substantial way, not merely by doubling the effect in (3). . . . The actual "experienced contingencies" will continue to change, departing further and further from the contingencies to be discovered by analyzing the equipment. . . .

When we now complicate the space by introducing two levers or keys, we vastly increase the interactions between equipment and performance. These cannot be avoided in any study of "decision-making". . . . All the interactions already noted between scheduling equipment and performance survive, and in addition we must consider the special problems presented by "change-over." If both keys are on interval schedules, the probability of reinforcement of a second response on the same key is less than that of one on the other key (because the equipment may have set up a reinforcement there while the first response was being made). Change-over is therefore differentially reinforced. . . . Two ratio schedules may lead to a performance on one key only; one ratio and one interval schedule produce other interesting cases. . . . And if we permit the programming system as a whole to change as a function of performance, as in game theory or other arrangements involving changes in the behavior of another organism which contribute to the contingencies, even more complex possibilities arise. . . . In spite of the prestige of game theory, I think this kind of analysis is moving much more rapidly toward an understanding of the essential features of such situations *as they affect behavior.* . . .

134 *The result of the experiment:* Another unpublished experiment gave a dramatic result. When I first reported what I called periodic reconditioning, I noted a "second-order effect." The cumulative record for each interval was a scallop, but if the rat started late in one interval and hence emitted fewer responses before reinforcement, it tended to start early in the next and responded more often. The curves for each pair of intervals composed a bigger scallop. This second-order effect turned up suddenly in an experiment with pigeons in which Bill and I were comparing the effects of two amounts of food at reinforcement. Occasional responses to a red key were followed by access to grain for four seconds, responses to a green key by access for twelve seconds. We changed the color every six intervals and could see no substantial difference in the rates of responding, but when, for some reason, we began to change the color at every reinforcement, a beautiful second-order scallop immediately appeared. Responding to green *was* slightly slower, and there were therefore two reasons why the pigeon started sooner and emitted more responses in the next interval, when the key was red.

138 incorporated as publisher: Some of us thought that the Society for the Experimental Analysis of Behavior could serve other functions. I proposed a committee on standards and one on nomenclature. As I wrote to Charlie, "the Committee on Standards could set down the dimensions with plus or minus tolerances of several standard pieces of apparatus." If a piece fell within the limits of such a standard, it could be referred to by name and number only in a publication. I offered to work up standards for pigeons and rats and thought Murray could do avoidance and escape, Joe Brady the Monkey Chair, and Og and others dogs, human children, and adults. I would be willing to define *positive reinforcement* for the Committee on Nomenclature.

140 what it meant to teach . . . by machine: At the end of the term, the students filled in a questionnaire. Sixty-two percent said that working on the machine made the text (*Science and Human Behavior*) easier to understand. Thirty-three percent said they learned much more (and forty-six percent somewhat more) on the machine than studying the text for the same amount of time. Seventy-seven percent said that they would have learned less from the course if they had not used the machines, and sixty-seven percent would like to have the machines used in other courses.

Not all replies were favorable. Fifty-seven percent of the students said they felt anxious while at work and ten percent felt "generally pressed for time but could not say why." Thirty-seven percent thought they were "missing many opportunities to reflect on material and consider its implications" (but that was not true of the students who got the better grades in the rest of the course). Five percent felt that using machines infringed upon their dignity as human beings. Nevertheless, forty-four percent believed that "the instructor was trying to teach me as much as possible with a given expenditure of time and effort."

150 an axiomatic statement of principles: My memorandum on voluntary associations, dated April 28, 1958, read in part as follows:

> In order to focus attention upon observable facts I suggest that we consider certain questions about the activities of the members.

> *The member joins.*
>> What does he get by joining? (Badge, glad hand, opportunities to attend meetings, other results of "belonging.")

What does he escape from by joining? (Pressure to join, exclusion from consequences just listed, release from frustrating condition of being unable to do anything about various issues.)

What must he give up to join? (Fees, contacts and opportunities incompatible with membership.)

The member remains a member.

What does he continue to get from membership? (Continued consequences of joining, repeated gains resulting from membership, "fellowship," profits, instances of protection or support.)

What does he avoid? (Criticism for quitting, ostracism, return to disadvantages of non-membership, etc.)

What does it cost him? (Continuing dues, time of participation, other contacts which must be foregone.)

The member resigns.

What does he get by resigning? (Return to other contacts, release from duties and cost of membership.)

What does he escape from? (Demands made by membership, dues.)

What does it cost? (Criticism, ostracism.)

The member participates (votes, serves on committees).

What does he get? (Appreciation of members, more active identification in work of the association, more intimate contacts with other participants, greater congruence between his own interests and the activity of the association.)

What does he avoid? (Criticism as inactive, greater likelihood that association will act in opposition to his interests.)

What does it cost? (Time, effort, foregoing incompatible activities.)

I suggest that we could obtain from the answers to such questions a fairly convincing explanation of the origin and continuation of voluntary associations.

153 *minimize their personal involvements:* I made an additional point while reading Edward Hallett Carr's *New Society*:

Very often one who tries to analyze political control is challenged: what would you do about China, Cuba, Algiers, etc.? and it is implied that success or failure in following one's recommendation would be a test of the underlying principles. But any one case is a unique assemblage of conditions, not all of which are known or within reach. However, if we accept, not on faith but on the evidence of controlled experiments, the validity of certain behavioral processes, we may make a sustained application not easily deflected by occasional failure. Possibly we could write a guide to, say, international action which would indicate the better of two courses, other things being roughly equal. Only in the long run would this be supported by significant improvement; in the short run support would have to come from the scientific analysis.

155 *joined Merck, Sharpe, and Dohme:* Some of the people doing operant research in drug-company laboratories: Merck, Sharpe, and Dohme—John Boren,

Harley Hanson. Eli Lilly—Thom Verhave. Pfizer—Albert Weissman. Schering—Francis Mechner. Lederle—Ron Hill. Smith, Kline, and French—Roger Kelleher, Charles Catania, William Holz. Wyeth—Larry Stein, Irving Geller. Ciba—Dom Finocchio. Hoffmann La Roche—George Heise. Upjohn—Douglas Anger. Squibb—Peter Carlton.

174 *a lecture called "Men and Machines":* The Denison lecture was published in *Psychology Today* (April 1969) under the title "The Machine That Is Man." It was reprinted in *Contingencies of Reinforcement* under the title "The Inside Story."

174 *and wrote the programs:* As a graduate student I had invented a device that solved the barrier problem which Köhler called *Umweg*. A ball on the end of a thread "naturally wanted to be as near the earth as possible" and, if free to do so, hung straight down. When pulled back and released, it swung like a pendulum, overshooting in its zeal but soon coming to rest "where it wanted to be." When a barrier was placed in its path as it swung down, it tried to go through but quickly drew back and went around. Dropped a second time, it went around without "trying to go through." All of this followed from the fact that the ball was made of pith and the barrier, a strip of celluloid, was given an electrostatic charge. The ball acquired a like charge when it struck the barrier, was repelled, and swung around it, and when brought back without being discharged—"without being allowed to forget"—it immediately went around. As a field theory of *Umweg*, it was not far from a Gestalt analysis; Lewin's vectors were at work.

185 *The class completed a full year:* Programmed Learning: The Roanoke Experiment. E. W. Rushton, Ph.D. (Chicago: Encyclopaedia Britannica Press, 1965).

190–1 *Watson obituary:* Science (October 10, 1958).

201 *"Education in this country":* The passage by J. P. Guilford is quoted from "Factors That Aid and Hinder Creativity," published in *Teachers College Record* (February 1962): 392.

210 *to strengthen . . . through operant reinforcement:* Burt Wolin, as a graduate student at Indiana, had discovered a possible connection between phylogenic and ontogenic behavior. He had reinforced pecking a key with food when a pigeon was hungry and with water when it was thirsty. The hungry bird struck the key smartly with an open beak, the thirsty bird gently pushed it, with the beak only slightly open. The topography of the conditioned response resembled the behavior appropriate to the reinforcer. Bill Morse and I tried to confirm with the pigeon that responded to one key for water and another key for food during the same session. We were unable to detect any difference in the times the two break-circuit keys remained open. I was puzzled by this until I remembered that Wolin had given his pigeons water in a small ceramic cup which had a white circular top about the size of the key. I wrote to Wolin in 1963, and he agreed that similarities between the stimuli for the key and the magazine might have been important.

210 not its topography: One casualty of my frenetic life was an experiment on social behavior in which a "stooge" was conditioned to behave in ways which should affect another organism. For example, if one rat stood near a screen separating it from another but moved away and went into hiding whenever the other rat approached, would the other rat become aggressive, possibly running against the wall to "drive the stooge away"? What happens to the man who is so repulsive that people move away when he approaches?

223 ". . . long-held views about human behavior": Proceedings of the conference were offered for sale in a set of six cassettes in 1976.

225 not to be controlled by pigeons: See "The Inspector General" by Thom Verhave in *Psychology Today* (1967).

230 was at the time Director: Brady also organized a series of seminars in the Washington area. Lieutenant Richard Herrnstein, of the Walter Reed Army Institute, spoke on "Behavior and Environmental Control: Adjustive Mechanisms," Donald Blough, of the National Institutes of Mental Health, on "The Behaving Organism: Its Perception of the Environment," and Murray Sidman, in the Department of Experimental Psychology at Walter Reed, on "The Punishing Environment: Its Consequences for Adaptive Behavior." I discussed verbal behavior.

240 Rochelle J. Johnson replied: *Philosophy of Science*, 30 (1963): 274–85.

251 a lecture called "Utopia Now?": Part of my lecture "Utopia Now?" appeared in 1967 in two articles in *The Listener*, based upon the BBC talk, and then under the title "Utopia as an Experimental Culture" in my *Contingencies of Reinforcement*, reprinted from a book edited by Paul Kurtz, called *Moral Problems in Contemporary Society* (Englewood Cliffs, N.J.: Prentice-Hall, 1969).

261 "conditioning them into perfect virtue": Joseph Wood Krutch. "Danger: Utopia Ahead," *Saturday Review* (August 20, 1966).

277 two Norwegian philosophers: Kvale and Grenness. *Review of Existential Psychology and Psychiatry*, 7 (1967): 128–50.

283 "the necessary knowledge": I had given my students in Psychology 7 a paraphrase of a definition of knowledge from Mortimer Adler's *What Man Has Made of Man:*

> "Almost all human knowledge is a product of the cooperative activity of the senses and intellect, as these are involved in processes of observation and reflection."
> (Translation: *To know is mostly . . .*)

"(1) By sense, or the powers of observation, I mean all those perceptual abilities which are exercised through the activity of bodily parts called sense-organs and brain."

(. . . *to respond to the environment* . . .)

"(2) By intellect, or the powers of reflection, I mean the following abilities: abstraction (the ability to conceive, define, distinguish, generalize, make inductions and analyses);"

(. . . *as the result of certain contingencies of reinforcement* . . .)

"judgment (the ability to formulate propositions and to assert them);"

(. . . *this behavior being mainly verbal and under the control of non-verbal environmental conditions* . . .)

"reasoning (the ability to infer and demonstrate, to systemize knowledge deductively)."

(. . . *or verbal environmental conditions.*)

Rules for translation: (1) convert nouns into verbs whenever possible to get back to actual processes (e.g. *to know* rather than *knowledge*), (2) convert "powers" and "abilities" into the behavior for which they are said to be responsible (e.g. *observing* rather than *powers of observation*), (3) drop gratuitous physiologizing (*sense-organs* and *brain*), (4) then reformulate "observing," "reflecting," "judging," and "reasoning" in terms of the behavior which is said to result from them. (Neither the passage from Adler nor the translation does this in detail.)

296 *a systematic analysis:* The manuscript that I was calling *The Technology of Teaching* was not the book I eventually published. It was a much more systematic analysis. An outline of a course called the "Advanced Experimental Analysis of Behavior," which I gave during the fall term of 1961, is the best record of what it was about. An abbreviated version:

I. *What Is Teaching?* The goals of education. Techniques of teaching.

II. *Negative Reinforcement.* Aversive control in education. Its by-products: escape, counter-aggression, apathy. Attempt to abolish aversive control.

III. *Positive Reinforcement.* Shaping the topography of behavior. Stimulus control. Maintaining the probability of behavior. Natural versus artificial reinforcements and the nature of what is learned.

IV. *The Topography of Verbal Behavior.* Speaking and writing (execution only). The problem of the first instance. Priming devices: the duplicative repertoires. Priming devices: the non-duplicative repertoires.

V. *Intraverbal Behavior.* The basic intraverbal relation. Programming. The "meaningfulness" of intraverbal behavior.

VI. *Knowledge about Things.* Naming, describing, announcing. Specificity of stimulus control. Verbal knowledge in review.

VII. *Nonverbal Behavior.* Specific kinds of nonverbal "knowledge." Stimulus-producing repertoires. Identifying responses. Duplicating responses. Translational responses.

VIII. *Thinking.* 1. Setting up repertoires of covert behavior, including perceptual repertoires. Raising the probability of a response by strengthening or clarifying stimuli (e.g. attention). Raising the probability of a response by rearranging or restructuring stimuli (e.g. classification). Raising the probability of a response by constructing new stimuli for which responses are available (e.g. counting, measuring, graphing). Raising the probability of a response by generating new responses through the manipulation of formulae (e.g. reasoning).

    IX. Thinking. 2. *Self-management in the Evocation of Behavior.* The use of self-prompts and self-probes. Suppression of incompatible behavior. Strengthening weak responses. Composing and ordering responses. Translating, paraphrasing, recasting. Responding and listening with understanding. Decision-making. Techniques of thinking.

    X. Self-instruction and Research. Teaching the student to learn. Teaching the student to increase his repertoire through reading and exploration. Acquiring behavior for future use.

    XI. Other Goals of Education. Enjoyment and appreciation. Interest, enthusiasm, zeal. Confidence, determination, courage. Industry, perseverance, dedication. Aspiration. Emotional and attitudinal traits.

    XII. Discipline and Self-control. The suppression of behavior via punishment. Teaching "how to take" punishment. Avoiding the strengthening of behavior-to-be-suppressed and directly reinforcing alternative behaviors. Building good work habits, effective ways of life, etc. Ethical extensions of these principles.

    XIII. Independence, Creativity, Dignity, Freedom. How to make the student independent, creative, How to give the student dignity and a sense of freedom.

    XIV. Teaching in Review. Education as acting via the environment, not directly on the student. "Drawing out knowledge" versus implanting behavior. Genetic and other physical limitations on instructional processes. The growth and development of the student. The meaning of improvement in education.

    XV. Practical Problems. Current proposals for improving education. Problems of curriculum. Measurement of the effects of education. Educational research.

    XVI. The Design of an Educational Culture. Why do we teach what we teach? Answers: The immediate reinforcement of the teacher or those who encourage teaching. Remote effects and the survival value of education for the group. Objections to design (e.g. infringing freedom, regimentation, misuse of power, etc.). Alternatives to design (e.g. Can the student design his own education?). Making the most of the human organism through the explicit design of educational practices.

The last three chapters of the published version contain some of this material.

305 *Conference on Biopsychology:* This conference was reported in Tobach, Aronson, Shaw (eds.), *The Biopsychology of Development* (New York: Academic Press, 1971).

306 *T. H. Pear had asked:* T. H. Pear. *Bulletin of the British Psychological Society* (1967), and *The Ethical Record,* 72 (1967): 4–6.

NOTES

311 Robert L. Stillwell: Robert L. Stillwell. "Literature and Utopia: B. F. Skinner's *Walden Two*," *Western Humanities Review* (Autumn 1964).

315 BBC program: While in England for the BBC show, I was asked to speak at a symposium in Bangor, North Wales, on "Conceptual Bases of the Experimental Analysis of Behavior." It was held at an Operant Studies Unit at the University College of North Wales, for which Peter Harzem was responsible. The symposium was chaired by Professor Arthur Summerfield of the University of London. Debs drove me to Bangor in leisurely fashion.

317 Krantz reported: David L. Krantz. *Journal of Applied Behavior Analysis*, 4 (1971): 61–72.

320 Chomsky's "Case Against B. F. Skinner": Noam Chomsky. *New York Review* (December 30, 1971). Reprinted in *For Reasons of State* (New York: Pantheon, 1973).

335 "a gross heresy": "Clockwork Marmalade" by Anthony Burgess. *Listener* (February 17, 1972).

336 a respectable fifteenth place: Unfortunately, not all biologists were up to date. An article in the *New York Times* (3/28/71) described research by a physiologist at the University of Michigan in which monkeys pressed levers to inject heroin into their own bodies and became addicted. It was operant conditioning, but the physiologist called it Pavlovian. It was said "to teach a monkey how heroin feels" or "to build a 'longing.'" The numbers of times the monkey pressed the lever (from a few hundred to three thousand) were reported with no reference to schedules, but since a drug takes some time to have an effect, many "unreinforced" responses must have occurred.

359 still another edition: In the preface to the new edition of *Walden Two*, I cited a report of the Young Committee, appointed by the National Academy of Sciences and the National Research Council to advise the government on programs in behavioral research, which avoided any threat to Congress or the President by insisting "that knowledge is no substitute for wisdom or common sense." But what were the wisdom and common sense denied to the social scientist but available to the legislator if not the remnants of a prescientific conception of autonomous man, unsupported by evidence and obscuring measures which would be more likely to solve our problems?

361 The loss of reinforcing power could not be denied: When, at a meeting of the Grand Rounds at Massachusetts General Hospital, I called myself a benign anarchist (aware of the contradiction), someone said that that was not like the dictatorship of *Walden Two*. But Walden Two *was* anarchistic. No *person* was in control. The community was designed in such a way that police, clergy, entrepreneurs, teachers, and therapists were not needed. The functions delegated to them in the world at large were performed by the people themselves through face-to-face commendation and censure.

365   *Stoppard said:* Tom Stoppard. *New York Times* (April 26, 1972).

372   *Phi Beta Kappa Oration:* I gave roughly the Phi Beta Kappa Oration again in Mexico City, Stockholm, and elsewhere—and published it under the title "Can We Profit from Our Discovery of Behavioral Science?" in *Human Nature*. It is reprinted in *Cumulative Record*, third edition.

390   *Times Educational Supplement: New York Times* (March 28, 1982).

402   *Jonathan Edwards:* The relevance of the philosophy of Jonathan Edwards has been pointed out in some detail by David R. Williams. *Harvard Theological Review*, 74:4 (1981), 337–52.

PAPERS CITED IN THE TEXT

PAGE

12 "Are Theories of Learning Necessary?" *Psychological Review*, 57 (1950): 193–216.

34 "Some Contributions of an Experimental Analysis of Behavior to Psychology as a Whole," *American Psychologist*, 8 (1953): 69–78.

42 "How to Teach Animals," *Scientific American*, 185 (December 1951): 26–29.

68 "The Science of Learning and the Art of Teaching," *Harvard Educational Review*, 24 (1954): 86–97.

99 "The Control of Human Behavior," *Transactions of the New York Academy of Sciences*, 17 (1955): 547–51.

102 "A Case History in Scientific Method," *American Psychologist*, 11 (1956): 221–33.

106 "Freedom and the Control of Men," *American Scholar*, 25 (Winter 1955–56): 47–65.

114 "The Experimental Analysis of Behavior," *American Scientist*, 45 (1957): 343–71.

115 "What Is Psychotic Behavior?" In *Theory and Treatment of the Psychoses: Some Newer Aspects* (St. Louis: Committee on Publications, Washington University, 1956): 77–99.

121 "Some Issues Concerning the Control of Human Behavior: A Symposium," *Science*, 124 (1956): 1057–66 (with C. R. Rogers).

128 "A Critique of Psychoanalytic Concepts and Theories," *Scientific Monthly*, 79 (1954): 300–305.

133 "Sustained Performance During Very Long Experimental Sessions," *Journal of the Experimental Analysis of Behavior*, 1 (1958): 235–44 (with W. H. Morse).

133 "Fixed-Interval Reinforcement of Running in a Wheel," *Journal of the Experimental Analysis of Behavior*, 1 (1958): 371–79 (with W. H. Morse).

139 "The Flight from the Laboratory." In B. F. Skinner, *Cumulative Record* (New York: Appleton-Century-Crofts, 1959): 242–57.

141 "Teaching Machines," *Science*, 128 (1958): 969–77.

149 "The Programming of Verbal Knowledge." In E. Galanter (ed.), *Automatic Teaching: The State of the Art* (New York: John Wiley, 1959): 63–68.

PAPERS CITED

PAGE

157–8 "Conditioned and Unconditioned Aggression in Pigeons," *Journal of the Experimental Analysis of Behavior*, 6 (1963): 73–74 (with G. S. Reynolds and A. C. Catania).

169 "Pigeons in a Pelican," *American Psychologist*, 15 (1960): 28–37.

174 "The Machine That Is Man," *Psychology Today*, 2 (April 1969): 22–25, 60–63.

174–5 "Concept Formation in Philosophy and Psychology." In S. Hook (ed.), *Dimensions of Mind: A Symposium* (Washington Square: New York University Press, 1960): 226–30.

177 "The Design of Cultures," *Daedalus*, 90 (1961): 534–46.

190 "John Broadus Watson, Behaviorist," *Science*, 129 (1959): 197–98.

199 "Teaching Machines," *Scientific American*, 205 (November 1961): 90–102.

210 "Squirrel in the Yard: Certain Sciurine Experiences of B. F. Skinner," *Harvard Alumni Bulletin*, 64 (1962): 642–45.

213 "L'avenir des machines à enseigner," *Psychologie Française*, 8 (1963): 170–80.

237 "Behaviorism at Fifty," *Science*, 140 (1963): 951–58.

251 "Utopia Through the Control of Human Behavior," *The Listener*, 77 (January 12, 1967): 55–56.

263 "What Is the Experimental Analysis of Behavior?" *Journal of the Experimental Analysis of Behavior*, 9 (1966): 213–18.

264 "Operant Behavior," *American Psychologist*, 18 (1963): 503–15.

269 "The Technology of Teaching," *Proceedings of the Royal Society*, 162 (1965): 427–43.

274 "The Science of Human Behavior." In *Twenty-five Years at RCA Laboratories 1942–1967* (Princeton, New Jersey: RCA Laboratories, 1968): 92–102.

276 "The Problem of Consciousness—A Debate," *Philosophy and Phenomenological Research*, 27 (1967): 317–37 (with B. Blanshard).

283–4 "An Operant Analysis of Problem Solving." In B. Kleinmuntz (ed.), *Problem Solving: Research, Method, and Theory* (New York: John Wiley, 1966): 225–57.

285 "Contingencies of Reinforcement in the Design of a Culture," *Behavioral Science*, 11 (1966): 159–66.

285 "The Phylogeny and Ontogeny of Behavior," *Science*, 153 (1966): 1205–13.

287 "Some Responses to the Stimulus 'Pavlov,'" *Conditioned Reflex*, 1 (1966): 74–78.

PAGE
291 "B. F. Skinner (An Autobiography)." In E. G. Boring and G. Lindzey (eds.), A History of Psychology in Autobiography, vol. 5 (New York: Appleton-Century-Crofts, 1967): 387–13.

296 "Why Teachers Fail," Saturday Review, 48 (October 16, 1965): 80–81, 98–102.

303 "Contingency Management in the Classroom," Education, 90 (1969): 93–100.

304 "Creating the Creative Artist." In A. J. Toynbee and others, On the Future of Art (New York: Viking Press, 1970): 61–75.

305 "A Behavioral Analysis of Value Judgments." In E. Tobach, L. R. Aronson, and E. Shaw (eds.), The Biopsychology of Development (New York: Academic Press, 1971): 543–51.

322 "A Lecture on 'Having a Poem.'" In B. F. Skinner, Cumulative Record (3rd ed.) (New York: Appleton-Century-Crofts, 1972): 345–55.

325 "Compassion and Ethics in the Care of the Retardate." In B. F. Skinner, Cumulative Record (3rd ed.) (New York: Appleton-Century-Crofts, 1972): 283–91.

337 "Answers for My Critics." In H. Wheeler (ed.), Beyond the Punitive Society (San Francisco: W. H. Freeman, 1973): 256–66.

340 "Freedom and Dignity Revisited," New York Times (August 11, 1972): 29.

342 "Humanism and Behaviorism," The Humanist, 32 (July/August 1972): 18–20.

346 "The Steep and Thorny Way to a Science of Behaviour." In R. Harre (ed.), Problems of Scientific Revolution: Progress and Obstacles to Progress in the Sciences (Oxford: Clarendon Press, 1975): 58–71.

347 "Reflections on Meaning and Structure." In R. Brower, H. Vendler, and J. Hollander (eds.), I. A. Richards: Essays in His Honor (New York: Oxford University Press, 1973): 199–209.

351 "The Free and Happy Student," New York University Education Quarterly, 4 (Winter 1973): 2–6.

353 "Designing Higher Education," Daedalus, 103 (1974): 196–202.

354 "The Ethics of Helping People," Criminal Law Bulletin, 11 (1975): 623–36.

356 "The Shaping of Phylogenic Behavior," Acta Neurobiologiae Experimentalis, 35 (1975): 409–15.

358 "The Freedom to Have a Future" (The 1972 Sol Feinstone Lecture). (Syracuse, New York: Syracuse University, 1973).

358 "Are We Free to Have a Future?," Impact, 3(1) (1973): 5–12.

PAPERS CITED

PAGE

359 "Comments on Watts's 'B. F. Skinner and the Technological Control of Social Behavior,'" *The American Political Science Review*, 69 (1975): 228–29.

362 "Farewell, my LOVELY!" *Journal of the Experimental Analysis of Behavior*, 25 (1976): 218.

362 "How to Discover What You Have to Say—A Talk to Students," *The Behavior Analyst*, 4 (1981): 1–7.

367 "Why I Am Not a Cognitive Psychologist," *Behaviorism*, 5 (Fall 1977): 1–10.

368 "The Force of Coincidence." In B. C. Etzel, J. M. LeBlanc, & D. M. Baer (eds.), *New Developments in Behavioral Psychology: Theory, Method, and Application* (Hillsdale, New Jersey: Lawrence Erlbaum Associates, 1977): 3–6.

371 "Freedom, at Last, from the Burden of Taxation," *New York Times* (July 26, 1977): 29.

372 "Why Don't We Use the Behavioral Sciences?" *Human Nature*, 1 (March 1978): 86–92.

375 "Herrnstein and the Evolution of Behaviorism," *American Psychologist*, 32 (1977): 1006–12.

382 "Symbolic Communication Between Two Pigeons (*Columba livia domestica*)," *Science*, 207 (1980): 543–45 (with R. Epstein and R. P. Lanza).

383 "'Self-Awareness' in the Pigeon," *Science*, 212 (1981): 695–96 (with R. Epstein and R. P. Lanza).

383 "The Spontaneous Use of Memoranda by Pigeons," *Behaviour Analysis Letters*, 1 (1981): 241–46 (with R. Epstein).

383 "'Lying' in the Pigeon," *Journal of the Experimental Analysis of Behavior*, 38 (1982): 201–3 (with R. P. Lanza and James Star).

384 "The Species-Specific Behavior of Ethologists," *The Behavior Analyst*, 3 (1980): 51.

384 "Selection by Consequences," *Science*, 213 (1981): 501–4.

BOOKS CITED IN THE TEXT

PAGE

3 *The Behavior of Organisms: An Experimental Analysis* (New York: Appleton-Century-Crofts, 1938, 1966).

3 *Walden Two* (New York: Macmillan, 1948, 1976). Translations: Spanish, German (new preface), Portuguese, Dutch, and Italian.

44 *Science and Human Behavior* (New York: Macmillan, 1953). Translations: Yugoslav, Spanish, Italian, German, and Portuguese.

109–10 *Schedules of Reinforcement* (with C. B. Ferster) (New York: Appleton-Century-Crofts, 1957).

130 *Verbal Behavior* (New York: Appleton-Century-Crofts, 1957). Translations: Italian, Portuguese, and Spanish.

198 *a programmed text:*
The Analysis of Behavior: A Program for Self-Instruction* (New York: McGraw-Hill, 1961, with J. G. Holland). Translations: Italian, Czech, Portuguese, Spanish, and German.

296 *"Yesterday I finished":*
The Technology of Teaching (New York: Appleton-Century-Crofts, 1968). Translations: French, Swedish, Japanese, Spanish, Italian, German, Hungarian, Romanian, and Portuguese.

300 *Contingencies of Reinforcement: A Theoretical Analysis* (New York: Appleton-Century-Crofts, 1969). Translations: French, Italian, German, Japanese, Portuguese, and Spanish.

300 *Cumulative Record*, third edition (New York: Appleton-Century-Crofts, 1972). Translations: Spanish and Italian.

305 *Beyond Freedom and Dignity* (New York: Alfred A. Knopf, 1971). Translations: French, Brazilian, Norwegian, Danish, Japanese, Spanish, Dutch, German, Hebrew, Swedish, Italian, Portuguese, Finnish, Polish, and Flemish.

350 *About Behaviorism:*
About Behaviorism (New York: Alfred A. Knopf, 1974). Translations: Japanese, Danish, Spanish, Italian, Hebrew, German, French, Portuguese, and Dutch.

373 *Reflections on Behaviorism and Society* (Englewood Cliffs, New Jersey: Prentice-Hall, 1978). Translation: Spanish.

381 *Notebooks* (Englewood Cliffs, New Jersey: Prentice-Hall, 1980).

389 *Skinner for the Classroom* (Champaign, Illinois: Research Press, 1982).

INDEX

433

ACKNOWLEDGMENTS

I am greatly indebted to Dr. Margaret Vaughan, who has given invaluable help in reviewing the correspondence, notes, and publications which have accumulated during the thirty-four years covered by this volume. Jean Kirwan Fargo has been equally helpful in the preparation of the manuscript. Passages from letters by Willard Van Orman Quine, McGeorge Bundy, and Henry Kissinger are published with their kind permission.

A NOTE ON THE TYPE

The text of this book was set in Electra, a Linotype face designed by W. A. Dwiggins (1880-1956), who was responsible for so much that is good in contemporary book design. Although much of his early work was in advertising and he was the author of the standard volume *Layout in Advertising*, Mr. Dwiggins later devoted his prolific talents to book typography and type design and worked with great distinction in both fields. In addition to his designs for Electra, he created the Metro, Caledonia, and Eldorado series of type faces, as well as a number of experimental cuttings that have never been issued commercially.

Electra cannot be classified as either modern or old-style. It is not based on any historical model, nor does it echo a particular period or style. It avoids the extreme contrast between thick and thin elements that marks most modern faces and attempts to give a feeling of fluidity, power, and speed.

This book was composed by Maryland Linotype
Composition Company, Baltimore, Maryland.
It was printed and bound by The Haddon Craftsmen, Inc.,
Scranton, Pennsylvania.
Typography and binding design
by Christine Aulicino